MW01273608

Making and Breaking Settler Space

Making and Breaking Settler Space

Five Centuries of Colonization in North America

Adam J. Barker

30 29 28 27 26 25 24 23 22 21 5 4 3 2 1

Printed in Canada on FSC-certified ancient-forest-free paper (100% post-consumer recycled) that is processed chlorine- and acid-free.

Library and Archives Canada Cataloguing in Publication

Title: Making and breaking settler space : five centuries of colonization in North America / Adam J. Barker.
Names: Barker, Adam J., author.
Description: Includes bibliographical references and index.
Identifiers: Canadiana (print) 20210235624 | Canadiana (ebook) 20210235780 | ISBN 9780774865401 (hardcover) | ISBN 9780774865425 (PDF) | ISBN 9780774865432 (EPUB)
Subjects: LCSH: Indigenous peoples – North America. | LCSH: Indigenous peoples – North America – Social conditions. | LCSH: Settler colonialism – North America. | LCSH: North America – Colonization. | LCSH: Indigenous peoples – Land tenure – North America. | LCSH: Decolonization – North America. | LCSH: North America – Race relations – History. | LCSH: North America – Ethnic relations – History. | LCSH: Colonization. | LCSH: Imperialism.
Classification: LCC E77 .B37 2022 | DDC 970.04/97—dc23

Canadä

UBC Press gratefully acknowledges the financial support for our publishing program of the Government of Canada (through the Canada Book Fund), the Canada Council for the Arts, and the British Columbia Arts Council.

This book has been published with the help of a grant from the Canadian Federation for the Humanities and Social Sciences, through the Awards to Scholarly Publications Program, using funds provided by the Social Sciences and Humanities Research Council of Canada.

Printed and bound in Canada by Friesens
Set in Segoe and Warnock by Apex CoVantage, LLC
Copy editor: Robert Sean Lewis
Proofreader: Helen Godolphin
Cartographer: Eric Leinberger
Cover designer: Alexa Love
Cover image: *Home Less Ness,* by Margaret August (Coast Salish artist)

UBC Press
The University of British Columbia
2029 West Mall
Vancouver, BC V6T 1Z2
www.ubcpress.ca

This book is dedicated to the Indigenous communities fighting, surviving, and thriving in the face of settler colonialism so that we might see the day when all people are free from oppression.

To my partner, Emma; you are the best of me.

Contents

Illustrations

Acknowledgments

In this work, positionality matters: I am a settler Canadian, and my family home is in the overlapping territories of the Haudenosaunee and Anishinaabe peoples. The benefits that I and my family have experienced or accrued have come at the cost of the safety, freedom, and well-being of Indigenous peoples. I also lived in the territories of the Coast Salish people during my studies, and parts of this book were written in all of these territories as well as in the city of Leicester, England. Although I have lived in England for most of the past decade, I have continued to benefit from the setter colonization of Turtle Island in many ways. Taking the settler out of the settler colonial nation-state does not end the obligation to pursue justice and decolonization.

It is my hope that this book supports making positive change in the places on Turtle Island that I have called home. However, the real work being done by Indigenous communities is far more important. From Idle No More to NoDAPL, Shut Down Canada, and 1492 Land Back Lane, it has never been more obvious that Indigenous peoples' movements are strong, vibrant, and increasingly successful. Black Lives Matter and movements for racial justice are continuing to force change in ways that no academic ever can; as I write, the United States of America is in well-earned and heroic upheaval over the police murders of George Floyd, Breonna Taylor, and a staggeringly long list of others. More and more brave folks are putting their lives on the line to fight institutional and systemic injustices. I hope that this book contributes to understanding and action to bring about fundamental change in North America. In my analysis and ideas, but particularly by making my failures a key part of this project, the book forms the next step in my attempts to help settler people like me catch up to the incredible work being done by those directly confronting colonialism and racism while honouring our obligations to work out some aspects of our decolonial practice.

I have benefited from the support, mentorship, and constructive critique of incredible academic mentors who have guided me on my path. For this project, I particularly want to thank Professors Gavin Brown and Jenny Pickerill. Jenny and Gavin have been models of compassion, relationship building, and networking while showing me how to funnel righteous anger into both scholarship and activism. I extend my sincere thanks as well to my postdoctoral supervisor with the Carceral Archipelago project, Professor Clare Anderson, whose intellectual and practical advice opened up exciting new areas of research, and to Professors Peter Kraftl and Jason Dittmer for their strong collegial support. I remain forever indebted to the scholars and activists who shaped my thinking over the past decade, including Danielle B, Liz Carlson, Jeff Denis, Adam Gaudry, Damien Lee, Adam Lewis, Eva Mackey, "Roots" Ogilvie, Dan Rück, Claire Shamier, Audra Tallifer, Lorenzo Veracini, Sakej Ward, Vanessa Watts, Bonnie Whitlow, and so many others. I want to specifically thank Margaret August, the Coast Salish artist whose piece *Homelessness* is on the cover of this book, for their friendship and support over many years. In remembrance, I also offer special thanks to David Dennis and Trish Rosborough, two friends and leaders who played significant roles in my personal and scholarly growth. Both Dave and Trish left this world too soon, and I am among the many who will treasure the transformative teachings, experiences, and laughter that they so generously shared.

I would be remiss if I did not acknowledge the hard work, encouragement, and patience of the editors at UBC Press, especially Emily Andrew (now with Cornell University Press) who helped get the first submission off the ground, and Darcy Cullen who saw the final versions home. As well, production editor Ann Macklem has been a sharp and positive presence through the final stages of preparation. I would also sincerely like to thank the expert, engaged, and constructive anonymous reviewers who significantly improved this work.

I am deeply grateful to my parents, Joe and Kathy, and to my parents-in-law, Melanie, Robert, and Mary, whose loving support has made all the difference in my ability to pursue this work. Early in the writing of this book, my first nephew, Charlie, was born to my brother and sister-in-law, Chris and Deanne, whose family has grown alongside its emergence, and Charlie is now big brother to Weston and Harry; I'm a very lucky uncle. My heartfelt thanks go to my Leicester family – Jo, Tim, Ben, Harry, and Milly; Kevin, Jody, William, and Olivia; Lorna and Alex; Jo and Mandy; Tine; Lou and Jane; and Adam – for their unending love, dog joy and support, cooking, and adventures. The incomparable Neil Connolly, my partner in no crime whatsoever, has kept me (somewhat) sane, which is no small feat; thank you.

My dear partner, spouse, and friend, Dr. Emma Battell Lowman, inspires me every day with her brilliance, heart, meticulous strategies and flashes of creativity, and profound vision for who and what we can be. The strength of our relationship and ability to work together fuels the passion that keeps me striving to do and be better.

During the decade of work on this project, Xena, a gorgeous ginger coloured rescue mutt who came home to us in early 2010, was my closest friend and companion. Through two transatlantic moves and a half-dozen different jobs, triumphs, and successes along with bottomless depression and myriad disappointments, she was with me every step. Most of this book was written with her at my side, and my writing breaks consisted of taking her to the park or the woods for the joy of watching her run. She was the most loving, calming, encouraging presence anyone could wish for while working on such a long and difficult project. Shortly after I completed the final revisions of this book, Xena was taken by cancer, and I miss her every day. Her successor, Gabrielle, may not have yet achieved Xena's grasp of colonialism and social theory, but has otherwise taken over admirably.

Making and Breaking Settler Space

Introduction

In 1812, the United States of America declared war on the British Empire. Seeking to liberate their settler brethren from imperial control and convinced of the superiority of their republican citizenship, American forces invaded what is now Canada. One of the few major battles of this odd historical conflict was the Battle of Stoney Creek, which took place in June 1813. A ragtag group of British soldiers, their Indigenous allies, and settler militia, alerted to a much larger invading American force that was marching westward along the Niagara Peninsula, ambushed the American camp in the dead of night. In the darkness and confusion, many shot or bayoneted their own soldiers, and both sides withdrew without claiming victory, although the British did capture American artillery pieces and officers, and the American forces consequently withdrew back across to the American side of the Niagara River – perhaps an apt summary of the entire War of 1812 (1812–15).

Almost two centuries later, in 1978, my family moved into a suburban residential neighbourhood in what had since become the Town of Stoney Creek, Ontario. As children, my brother and I, along with our neighbourhood friends, often played in nearby Battlefield Park, a place dominated by a remarkably phallic faux-gothic castle built as a monument to the honoured dead of the War of 1812. We walked past Smith's Knoll, the battlefield cemetery for both British and American soldiers killed in the Battle of Stoney Creek, on our way to our elementary school, whose playground was more than once the site of archaeological digs looking for buttons, musket balls, and other battlefield scraps and remains. We went on annual school tours of the Battlefield House Museum, a farmhouse that the American forces had taken as their headquarters, which has since been converted into an educational re-creation of white British pioneer life complete with animators – frequently local history undergraduates – in early-nineteenth-century frontier dress shearing sheep with iron tools or cooking in the large stone fireplace. We were taught about the battle that had taken place in the quiet middle-class suburb where we lived and played as part of the moment when Canada became Canadian, largely by refusing to become American. For me, as for so many others raised in this densely populated part of Canada, the War of 1812 quietly became a quotidian and important part of the landscape of 'home.'

In the grand sweep of history, this relatively small and indecisive conflict is easily forgotten. As historian Alan Taylor (2010) argues, neither the Americans nor soon-to-be Canadians won the War of 1812, but Indigenous peoples very definitively lost. The history of the two hundred years that followed is well known: Canada and the United States pushed westward across the continent, with pioneers practically racing each other to occupy pastoral homesteads or to stake a mining claim while both nations competed to extend and consolidate their territorial holdings. From open war to friendly rivalry, Canada and the United States have become staunch allies, inseparable trading partners, and modern democracies offering some of the highest standards of living in the world.

Long before they were called Canada and the United States of America, these places already had other names – many of them. One common name for the continent as a whole or for the land writ large among the Haudenosaunee and Anishinaabe people is Turtle Island,[1] a reference to creation stories that explain how the land was built on the back of a giant turtle. Turtle Island is home to hundreds of Indigenous peoples with languages, cultures, and social and political traditions of incredible complexity and vitality, and it has been since time immemorial. These societies repeatedly assisted, traded with, and saved the lives of early colonists and imperial agents. It is no stretch to say that neither Canada nor the United States would exist in anything like their current forms without substantial aid from Indigenous people and communities from across Turtle Island at key moments. Yet in both nation-states, Indigenous nationhood and sovereignty are explicitly denied both by political institutions and by public discourses. Indigenous people have long faced racism and violence from average Canadians and

Americans and also from the state and its agents. Politically and economically marginalized, spatially restricted, and simultaneously culturally disregarded and exploited by American and Canadian societies, Indigenous communities are circumscribed within liminal or exceptional spaces. And in both states, Indigenous nations have built thriving traditions of resistance, repeatedly challenging colonial erasure, displacement, and persecution.

Making and Breaking Settler Space: Five Centuries of Colonization in North America makes a critical intervention in understandings of the geographies of settler colonialism by identifying patterns of spatial production that have recurred across time and in many places. In doing so, it describes the ways that settler people – those of us from cultures, nations, and states predicated on settler colonization – enable, identify with, expand upon, benefit from, and forcefully defend these spaces. This book focuses on embodied practices of making settler colonial spaces that span the continent and cross centuries and looks at the resultant spatialities that bind Canadian and American people together through common identifications with settler colonial ways of being. Under the rubric of the northern bloc of settler colonialism, I argue that both the Canadian and the American polities are primarily and particularly defined by their drives to dominate and monopolize land and to erase challenging Indigenous sovereignties; these objectives are pursued in many ways but with the same focus on eliminating Indigenous peoples and nations with functional and foundational ties to the land. Perceived differences between Canada and the United States distract us from attending to their shared processes of settlement facilitated by attempted genocide. The dominating narratives of both Canadian and American exceptionalism have common roots in settler colonial processes of land theft, racialization, and discrimination and in the attempted erasure of Indigeneity.

Making and Breaking Settler Space draws from pasts, presents, and imagined futures to demonstrate the remarkable consistency, relentless drive, and contemporary relevance of settler colonialism across the stories and geographies of the places currently known as Canada and the United States of America, while also tracing the contours of settler colonial spaces to identify – and then widen – the cracks, flaws, and failures that expose the contingency and fragility of settler colonial projects in these lands.

In this book, it is my goal to expose the ways that the settler nation-states of Canada and the United States of America, and the settler peoples who occupy them, remain bound to a "logic of elimination" (Wolfe 1999, 27) and a desire to transcend settler colonial pasts in order to secure unchallenged – that is, settled – belonging on the land claimed by settler colonial orders. Despite their wide diversity, settler communities from across these two enormous nation-states are linked in a destructive dance that reshapes space and time. But this reshaping is neither absolute nor permanent, nor are all settler colonizers united in their strategies and tactics. There are weak points and there are limitations to the power of even this dominating assemblage. Learning to identify such weaknesses is critical, as it can direct efforts to make interventions with the best chances of success. Further, the development of tools to identify points of vulnerability in the settler colonial assemblage accelerates the pace at which interventions are possible in different contexts and lowers the resource investments needed to do so.

In settler colonial contexts, the overriding focus on land, belonging, and transcendence of the settler colonial past leads to the repetition of certain spatial patterns. It is these patterns that I draw out from their broadest origins in European imperialism to their insidious and disruptive spread both through activist and social movement spaces and through interpersonal relationships and internalized identity constructs. However, these patterns of spatial production also betray the limits of settler colonization both within this continent and more widely; these spaces are not destined to be or created by accident but are intentional. Consequently, by examining what relationships and ways of living on the land are eschewed by settler colonization, we can target the incommensurable – the things that settler colonization cannot tolerate and with which it cannot coexist. We can use these patterns to identify where material transformations of both the landscape and embodied behaviours, in addition to their associated sociocultural narratives, are required. It is then possible to theorize beyond the settler colonial assemblage and beyond a world dominated by its systems, structures, and stories.

This theorizing is vitally important because social justice and rights-based movements, from the mildly progressive to the wildly challenging, have rarely succeeded in addressing ongoing settler colonialism. Radical anti-capitalist imaginings of postcapitalist futures have long been mainstays of science fiction and utopian literature, as have many imaginings of post-statist and radically liberated futures. Yet imagining a future beyond what historiographer and theorist Lorenzo Veracini (2015) has usefully termed "the settler colonial present" still seems nearly impossible. That is, in part, because most of the inhabitants of Canada and the United States take these nations' settler colonial contours so much for granted that the systems of originary dispossession and domination are made invisible to settler people or recede both figuratively and literally into the landscape. By fully exploring the patterns by which settler colonialism structures space, and therefore life, across Canada and the United States – and by doing so from the perspectives not only of systems of power linked to states and capital but also of individuals and grassroots communities entangled with settler colonial space across the continent – I expose the ways that space, power, and identity are produced in these settler colonial societies, and I contribute theoretical and practical work on how to confront and ultimately dismantle the settler colonial assemblage.

The focus of this project has changed dramatically over the course of research and writing since I began in 2009. This change has been due in no small part to the shift that has occurred over the first two decades of the twenty-first century in social and academic discourses related to colonialism on Turtle Island, with the latter very much following the former. I initially set out to use the framework of settler colonialism to explain the distribution of spaces and development of non-Indigenous identities in Canada and the United States. At the time, settler colonialism was only unevenly discussed in academic research on Turtle Island. My first academic publication was an article in *American Indian Quarterly*, in which I argued that Canada should be understood as hybrid – that is, simultaneously enacting subtle acts of settler belonging and naturalization alongside overt colonial violence against Indigenous peoples (Barker 2009). I was grappling with a now definitional feature of settler colonialism: the fact that settler colonial spaces are imbricated with other imperial and colonial spaces. But I lacked the conceptual grounding to fully make sense of what I was seeing.

The scholarly terrain has shifted quickly. Settler colonialism is now a recognized and critically debated framework for understanding Canada and the United States (e.g., see Amadahy and Lawrence 2009; Elkins and Pedersen 2005; Hoxie 2008; Veracini 2007, 2008; and Wolfe 2006). At a foundational conference at the National University of Ireland in Galway, 2007, Canada was discussed alongside the United States (and specifically Hawaii), Israel-Palestine, and Australia, as a clear core of settler colonial geographies. By 2010, I had incorporated into my published work the use of the concept and the term "settler" as an accurate description of my own and most others' positionality in the northern bloc. By 2013, "settler" had exploded as a term used both within and beyond the academy due in large part to a series of major Indigenous-led activist moments. In the winter of 2012–13, Idle No More emerged as the latest powerful expression of Indigenous dissent and quickly spread across Turtle Island and around the world (Barker 2015; Kino-nda-niimi Collective 2014). Idle No More teach-ins often featured passionate and uncomfortable conversations as would-be allies expressed their deep dislike of the term "settler," usually prompting decolonial activists to use the term more frequently. It became clear that the affective responses to the term indicated a point of intense feeling and therefore potential intervention. Whether or not one identified as a settler became, in some places, a baseline for indicating that one was ready to accept personal responsibility for ongoing colonial harms and to understand and work from the very different places of responsibility and accountability that non-Indigenous activists occupy with respect to Indigenous people and communities.[2] Subsequently, in the academy, in community work and organizations, and around kitchen tables, discussions have continued over the appropriate use of the term "settler," its relationship to whiteness and capital, and the extent to which the settler state or institutions like universities can ever be decolonized, all conducted in a way that would have been rare, if not impossible, a decade ago. A growing number of scholars from around the world are now doing exceptional research and making important interventions, some of which resonate closely with those of this project. Indicative examples include spatialities of place-based anti-colonial activism (Greensmith and Giwa 2013; Kilibarda 2012; Steinman 2012); settler colonial attachments to place and identity (Banivanua Mar and Edmonds 2010; M. Johnson 2011; A.C. Rowe and Tuck 2017; Veracini 2015); and intersectional struggles between Indigenous and non-Indigenous peoples within and beyond the settler colonial context (Crosby and Monaghan 2016; Dhamoon 2015; Leroy 2016; Walia 2013). These interventions have allowed this book to provide a spatially focused synthesis of settler colonial literature in order to identify and describe the settler colonial assemblage, the patterns generated as it spreads across and transforms the material landscape of the continent, and the internal hierarchies, recruitment, and control processes that link the bodies of settler colonizers to the political projects and embodied assertions of settler colonial power. In addition, this book delivers an extended investigation of how this assemblage also restrictively structures the spaces of social change and activism of those who would oppose it and what we can ultimately do about this obstacle in the interests of supporting Indigenous-led decolonization struggles.

Rooted in my commitment to understanding and deconstructing the settler colonial northern bloc, this book has a number of specific objectives. First, it identifies the origins of the settler colonial worldview – how it evolved from European identities and cosmologies and shifted to the creation of related but independent regional, national, and supranational settler identities in response to early contacts with Indigenous peoples of Turtle Island.[3] Second, it describes the contours of the settler colonial world – the dynamic spatialities that inform shifting but related identifications with land and territory, which in turn generate systems of law, politics, and economics in support of dominating settler claims to property and state sovereignty. Third, it develops a model for how settler colonizers across the northern bloc have transformed and produced space, including the entangled generations of narratives of conquest, the "peacemaker myth" (Regan 2010, ch. 3), and other cultural tropes that go along with the transformation of the land itself, which are evident in particular patterns of spatial division and urban development. Fourth, it investigates the persistence of settler colonialism in anti-capitalist, anti-racist, and other leftist political spaces – an important intervention into progressive narratives common in both Canada and the United States that colonize Indigenous spaces and co-opt Indigenous political agency. Lastly, this book proposes a low theory of settler decolonization – an autoethnographic reflection on solidarity activism, self-identification as a settler Canadian, personal failure, and decolonizing affinity building. These objectives are framed by three scholarly subdisciplines: Indigenous studies and settler colonial theory, geographical theories of affect and assemblage, and social movement studies related to discourses and practices of decolonization.

Settler Colonial Theory

Settler colonial theory argues that there are distinct types of colonialism and that the colonization of places such as Canada, the United States, and Australia, to name just a few, generates cultural narratives and political economies that display remarkable similarities despite varied geographies and histories. As critical Indigenous scholars had pointed out for many years, these commonalities can be traced to historical and ongoing efforts to destroy Indigenous societies and to usurp and exploit their lands to the benefit of settler peoples. The work of anthropologist Patrick Wolfe (1999, 2006) collects these ideas into a discourse centred on reading the history of Australia and North America as histories of *invasions that never ended*. Wolfe refers to invasion in the form not of marauding armies but of imposed structures, which have proven extremely durable, surprisingly flexible, and at times difficult to identify. Veracini (2010b, 33–52) discusses the settler colonial processes of building structures of invasion through a series of "transfers" of Indigenous land bases to settler colonial control, which by extension also erase Indigeneity from the land being claimed. For example, historical geographer Daniel Clayton (1999, xi–xii) describes how between the 1770s and 1840s the Nuu-chah-nulth, whose territories are located along the west coast of what is now called Vancouver Island in British Columbia, "were engaged by three sets of forces" – "the West's scientific exploration of the world in the Age of Enlightenment, capitalist practices of exchange, and the geopolitics of nation-state rivalry" – with the result that "local, intensely corporeal, geographies of interaction were gradually subsumed into an abstract imperial space of maps and plans." In my own work with historian and sociologist Emma Battell Lowman on settler colonialism in Canada, we have developed the argument that settler colonial transfer is effected through the creation of interlocking structures (e.g., racialized relationships around labour or title to land), systems (e.g., legal and political governance structures such as the Indian Act), and stories (e.g., pioneering valour or peacemaker myths) that tie settler people to the land (Battell Lowman and Barker 2015). This trio of structures, systems, and stories will remain important throughout this book.

Settler colonialism has been constructed as a method of transferring control over land – conceptualized broadly – from Indigenous to settler polities, but geographical theories of settler colonization have remained relatively underdeveloped. *Making and Breaking Settler Space* addresses this problem. More than a decade ago, historian Frederick Hoxie (2008), through a historiography of settler colonial analysis, argued that settler colonialism has been underapplied and undertheorized in studies of place and space, especially with respect to the geographies of Canada and the United States. Although more recent work has explored settler colonial geographies in relation to geographies of resource extraction (Hall 2013; Hoogeveen 2015; Preston 2013) and to geographies of radical activism (Barker and Pickerill 2012; Mott 2016), it still remains more common to see settler colonialism taken up in historical geography (e.g., see Clayton 1999; and C. Harris 2004).[4] Several excellent edited volumes speak to the richness of these studies, most notably *Making Settler Colonial Space: Perspectives on Race, Place and Identity* (2010), edited by Tracey Banivanua Mar and Penelope Edmonds, which examines how settler colonizers constructed the worlds that they inhabited around the Pacific Rim through complex means of dividing, ordering, and regularizing the spaces that they claimed. A parallel volume edited by Zoë Laidlaw and Alan Lester, *Indigenous Communities and*

Settler Colonialism: Land Holding, Loss and Survival in an Interconnected World (2015), considers the historical experience of settler colonization from Indigenous perspectives, examining how Indigenous communities have struggled to hold onto their lands and how they have been impacted by the loss of many of those lands. These are positive and important developments, but much work remains to be done.

Scale is still an especially thorny issue, as the connections between broad, abstract articulations of a general theory of settler colonialism and site-specific, localized practices of settler colonization are not always clear. In this book, I set out to articulate this middle scale with respect to Turtle Island, describing both how the dominating power of the Canadian and American settler colonial states came into being – which I collectively refer to as the "northern bloc" of settler colonialism – and how those societies continue to pursue and profit from the end goals of settler colonialism. That this articulation obscures some local dynamics and fits imperfectly within the established framework of settler colonial theory is not a problem; rather, it is proof positive that there are global patterns and trends in settler colonization that must be acknowledged and understood, while also remembering that settler colonization in practice continues to change, adapt, and evolve in response to local social, environmental, and political conditions. As a result, this book presents a snapshot of how settlers have long attempted to transform Turtle Island into this northern bloc.

Settler colonial theory predates what might now be called a "settler colonial turn" that has occurred across many disciplines – especially those like history, sociology, and geography that have engaged with earlier postcolonial and critical turns. Although contrasts have been made for years between settlement colonies – or "the colonies proper," as Friedrich Engels labelled them[5] – and "franchise colonies" (Banivanua Mar and Edmonds 2010, 19n4), the distinctions were often hazy. Researchers have repeatedly attempted to address the settler colonial distinction, describing the colonization of the Americas either with metaphors such as "swarming" (Crosby 1978), through theories of fragmentary cultural replication (Butlin 2009, 10–12), or as part of processes of capitalist modernization (Bhambra 2007a, 2007b; Flanagan 2008).[6] Some foundational classic anti-colonial texts, such as French-Tunisian Jewish author and essayist Albert Memmi's *The Colonizer and the Colonized* (1965), take up early examinations of claiming foreign land and the psychological and sociocultural contortions that involvement in this project require. Martiniquan psychiatrist and political philosopher Frantz Fanon's (1963, 1967) reflections on the Native and colonizer as locked in a dialectical relationship have proven prophetic in that they have been foundational both in establishing Indigenous studies as a field and in shaping settler colonial theory as a mode of analysis. Maoist intellectual J. Sakai's famous *Settlers: The Mythology of the White Proletariat from Mayflower to Modern* (1983), an early reading of labour and American politics through the lenses of colonialism and Marxism, undoubtedly laid the foundation for many later works. Most crucially, the rise of critical Indigenous scholarship, from Vine Deloria Jr. (1985, 1988, 2003) to Haunani-Kay Trask (1991, 1996, 1999) to Winona LaDuke (1994, 2002, 2005), fractured orthodox thought across many academic disciplines, making possible – and necessary – closer examinations of assumptions related to colonialism, whiteness, and Eurocentric and Anglocentric thought, along with examinations of many of the other underpinnings of power across Turtle Island. It is most proper to describe settler colonial studies as a subdiscipline of Indigenous studies more broadly. Settler colonial theory is a tool that has largely been developed through the analyses and critiques presented by Indigenous scholars and community leaders, which made the structures of settler colonialism impossible to ignore, even within the academic disciplines fundamentally created by those structures.

In 1999, two books were released by scholars located in settler colonial nation-states in the southwestern Pacific Ocean – New Zealand and Australia respectively – that fundamentally shifted engagement with settler colonialism as theory. The first, Maori scholar of education Linda Tuhiwai Smith's *Decolonizing Methodologies,* incontrovertibly established the long-term and normalized colonialism and dispossession embedded in academic research and relationships. It had the longer-term effect of demanding that non-Indigenous scholars find ways to decolonize their scholarship, which inherently meant deeply reconsidering and revising their practice at every stage to take account of and address ongoing colonialism. The second, Patrick Wolfe's *Settler Colonialism and the Transformation of Anthropology: The Politics and Poetics of an Ethnographic Event,* saw previously nascent analyses of the settler as a distinct phenomenon deployed in a fully realized form. Settler colonialism is, in Wolfe's book, a functioning theoretical framework that – crucially – is most useful for demonstrating resonance across histories, institutions, and regions. It is important that his text is often located as the point at which settler colonial theory entered into contemporary usage because it was at this moment that settler colonial theory was first used as a tool of self-critique, opening an important avenue for non-Indigenous researchers to begin to effectively respond to Smith's challenge.

As discussed, settler colonialism has been usefully expanded by a number of scholars working to generate broad theories, develop historical geographies, and consider effective activist practice, all of which are foundational to this book. Further research, such as historian Walter Hixson's *American Settler Colonialism: A History* (2013), political theorist Kevin Bruyneel's *The Third Space of Sovereignty: The Postcolonial Politics of U.S.-Indigenous Relations* (2007), and Chickasaw critical theorist Jodi Byrd's *The Transit of Empire: Indigenous Critiques of Colonialism* (2011), has described the United States as a historical and ongoing project of settler colonization, mirroring works making the same argument with respect to Canada (e.g., see Battell Lowman and Barker 2015; Coombes 2006; and Regan 2010). Further, settler colonialism has increasingly been adopted as a useful frame of analysis by Indigenous scholars, including Mohawk anthropologist Audra Simpson (2014), who frames violence and territorial restriction in terms of the assertion of settler control over Indigenous lands and bodies, and Yellow Knives Dene political theorist Glen Coulthard (2014), who situates settler colonialism as necessary to understanding the dangerous effects of the politics of recognition in settler nations like Canada and the United States.

The development of settler colonial theory has raised a number of important points of consideration: the always localized character of settler colonialism in practice (Banivanua Mar and Edmonds 2010, 2); the settler collective as the primary unit of settler colonization (Veracini 2010b, 59–62); the interplay between settler colonialism and other types of colonialism and sovereign power (Cavanagh 2009; Morgensen 2011; Veracini 2010b, 66–69); the intersections between settler colonialism and anti-Blackness (I. Day 2015; Leroy 2016; Patel 2016); and the production of both material cultures and cultural anxiety among settler populations as a necessary part of the colonial process (Mackey 1998, 2016). These strands of settler colonial theory can be gathered together to help flesh out existing sketches of settler colonial geographical imaginaries. My focus on the imagined geographies of settler colonialism is in the tradition of geographical theorists like Derek Gregory (1994) and historical geographers like Cole Harris (2004). Even as this book differentiates settler colonialism from other forms of colonization, which decolonial frameworks suggest we must do in order to avoid confronting one oppression while reinforcing another (Tuck and Yang 2012), it emphasizes settler colonial continuity between periods and places across two vast nation-states comprising much of the continent. The goal is to identify and expose the imagined geographies that underpin the spaces, power structures, and institutions of privilege that sustain settler colonialism throughout the northern bloc so that they can be fundamentally dismantled.

Always All about the Land, Always in Relationship

In the broadest possible sense, settler colonialism inheres in relationships between people as collectives and between people and the more-than-human world, and these relationships – whether cooperative, indifferent, exploitative, or violent – come to define broad political and social organizing, cultural narratives, and expectations of social behaviour. Relationships structured by settler colonial ideologies, narratives, and histories come to structure the spatialities of both settler colonizers and Indigenous and other non-settler populations. In our book *Settler: Identity and Colonialism in 21st Century Canada* (2015), Battell Lowman and I argue that Indigenous and settler people must always be understood through a relational analysis (48–53, 116–20). This is to say that "Indigenous" and "settler" as concepts make sense only as a "non-discrete, non-binary" dual (Waters 2004); what we consider to be colonial or Indigenous depends heavily on how we define the complementary term. Similarly, the expertise of Indigenous scholars, mentors, critics, and friends has been crucial to my efforts to understand my own subjectivity and identity in settler colonial North America. The relationships in and through which these learnings were shared are absolutely central to my work, so it is important to define clearly what I mean when I say "Indigenous" and why decolonization and resurgence are absolutely essential to my conceptual framework and powerfully inform my engagement at every stage.

My work is situated in relationship to Indigeneity as a lived quality of being Indigenous[7] both in relation to land – as a network of more-than-human life, as a traditional territory, and as a basis for material self-determination – and in relation to other Indigenous people, communities, and nations. Being Indigenous in this context means inherently being in opposition to colonial forces that would displace Indigenous peoples from their homelands, disrupt Indigenous communities and cultures to attack their sovereignty, and destroy Indigenous territories through extraction and development (Alfred and Corntassel 2005, 597). To be Indigenous in this context also implies being in relationship with particular Indigenous communities. Indigeneity is not genetic, ethnic, or racial, nor is it a nationality or other identity conferred by dint of simple residency in or recognition by a state. Identifying as Indigenous is a collective act. A person must claim and be claimed by an Indigenous community, which itself has a concept of peoplehood rooted in sacred histories, relationships to particular places, a cyclical and ceremonial social organization, and a language and other forms of expression that encapsulate the unique worldview of the Indigenous community (Holm, Pearson, and Chavis 2003).

Specific articulations of and critical engagements with the concept of Indigeneity and what it means to be Indigenous on Turtle Island today can be found in the work of an exceptional and growing group of Indigenous scholars, and critical Indigenous scholarship is central to the foundations of this project. In particular, the work of the following experts has had the largest impact on this book: Indigenous geographers Jay Johnson (Delaware), Sarah Hunt (Kwakwa̱ka̱'wakw), and Michelle Daigle (Cree); political scientists Glen Coulthard (Yellow Knives Dene) and Sheryl Lightfoot (Dakota); anthropologists Audra Simpson (Mohawk), Theresa McCarthy (Onondaga), and Zoe Todd (Métis); sociologists Vanessa Watts (Mohawk and Anishinaabe) and Chris Andersen (Métis); scholar, activist, organizer, and poet Leanne Simpson (Anishinaabe); Haudenosaunee historians Rick Monture (Mohawk) and Susan Hill (Mohawk); poet and performance artist Janet Rogers (Mohawk and Tuscarora); and eminent theologian, legal scholar, philosopher, and activist Vine Deloria Jr. (Lakota). I also draw from what I have learned through personal relationships with activists, warriors, and community leaders, particularly those in the wider Indigenous community around the University of Victoria (2004–09), including Chaw-win-is Ogilvie (Nuu-chah-nulth) and Sakej Ward (Mi'kmaq), two former members of the West Coast Warrior Society from whom I have had the privilege to learn. These scholars and community leaders have spent decades developing comprehensive and grounded critiques of colonialism and assertions of Indigenous identity and nationhood. Through their works, I position Indigenous relationships to place as essential for understanding settler colonialism on Turtle Island as not only a historical phenomenon but also an ongoing fundamental conflict over belonging on the land.

Assemblage, Affect, and Scale

Indigenous scholarship and understanding of settler colonial theory are the core of this book, and I employ a variety of important geographical concepts and tools to more fully explore the spaces and spatialities of the settler colonial northern bloc. A particularly useful geographical theory in framing this discussion is that of assemblage, which is a concept

> often used to emphasise emergence, multiplicity and indeterminacy, and [which] connects to a wider redefinition of the socio-spatial in terms of the composition of diverse elements into some form of provisional socio-spatial formation. To be more precise, assemblages are composed of heterogeneous elements that may be human and non-human, organic and inorganic, technical and natural. In broad terms, assemblage is, then, part of a more general reconstitution of the social that seeks to blur divisions of social-material, near-far and structure-agency. (B. Anderson and McFarlane 2011, 124)

That is why assemblage is so useful for engaging with settler colonialism, whose materiality, apart from being dispersed among individuals making decisions based on a wide range of values, concerns, and limitations, is not only spread through systems of governance, law, and economics that are at once diffuse and durable but is also interconnected with and supported by even wider-ranging networks of capitalism and white supremacy. Crucially, although structures of power – the key to Wolfe's development of settler colonialism as a distinct formation – remain important within a given assemblage, thinking in terms of assemblage allows for greater flexibility in considering how power shifts and how processes of domination change over time. Assemblages are defined not by a necessary internal configuration but by their interactions with their environments. As political geographer Jason Dittmer (2014, 387) outlines with the metaphor of the human body,

> these relations of exteriority mean that component parts of a whole cannot be reduced to their function within that whole, and indeed they can be parts of multiple wholes at any given moment. The parts are nevertheless shaped by their interactions within assemblages, and indeed it is the *capacities,* rather than the *properties,* of component parts that are most relevant in understanding resultant assemblages. While the properties of a material are relatively finite, its capacities are infinite because they are the result of interaction with an infinite set of other components. (Emphasis in original)

A human is more than a collection of organs and limbs, and a human remains human despite remarkable diversity among humans. Likewise, the settler colonizations in nineteenth-century New York State and twenty-first-century British Columbia – just two examples – may appear different on the surface, but they are revealed as contiguous through the consistency of settler colonial dispossession, the erasure of Indigenous peoplehood and nationhood, and the reconstruction of settler nation-states. They are varied in appearance but contiguous with the wider set of settler colonial formations. Thus made legible, settler colonial power cannot disappear behind banal or taken-for-granted social structures of race and class or narrative fictions of dying Indians and empty lands.

Both the human and nonhuman worlds are recruited into and impacted by settler colonization in a variety of ways, and unlike more traditional theories of geopolitical power and domination, assemblage thinking demands that these more-than-human relationships be foregrounded in attempts to map and analyze systems of power (Dittmer 2014, 388–89). This imperative is important because of Indigenous scholarship's emphasis that the more-than-human must be generally considered in research and especially considered in the context of settler colonial destruction of Indigenous spaces and place-based relationships. Viewing the settler societies of the northern bloc as an assemblage, I outline how multiple systems of power, interacting simultaneously yet at times seemingly without coherence, produce patterns across space and time that can be identified, described, and analyzed.

Scholarship on North America has developed extensive geographies of racism and white supremacy that detail the exploitation of enslaved, indentured, and racialized labour, the capitalist usurpation of land and environmental destruction, and imperial and colonial dispossession and displacement. Understanding settler colonization on Turtle Island through the lens of assemblage theory is intended to add important nuance by examining areas of resonance and dissonance between these entangled trajectories of power. The assemblage is multiple and shifting but also contradictory and subject to limits. I engage closely with the contours and limits of this assemblage by focusing on how settler colonizers transform the land and themselves in the process of building the systems, structures, and social narratives particular to settler colonialism and by looking at how they incorporate fragments of European and other antecedent heritage, as well as co-opted and assimilated aspects of Indigenous knowledges and cultures.

Affect is another concept from geographical theory that is particularly important throughout this book (see generally Barnett 2008; Carolan 2009; Dittmer 2010, 91–98; Pile 2010; and Seigworth and Gregg 2010, 1–3). More than just a political transfer, the embodied experience of being a settler person has positioned the claiming of lands by settler colonial regimes as an intensely affective act that settler colonizers conceptualize, rationalize, and describe in a variety of ways. Affect in this context refers to the diffuse force generated through the engagement between an individual and other people and things that can inspire action or change. My research accords with the stream of thought on affect that "focuses on relationships between people, or people and objects" (Dittmer 2010, 92). This is a "version of affect" that "is precognitive, or existing prior to active decision making," meaning that it is a way of explaining how exposure to particular places or spatially shaped relationships can inspire or motivate action – not in a mechanistic or predetermined way but "as 'a sense of push in the world'" (92, citing Thrift 2004, 64). This "experience of affect comes in the form of feelings and sensations prior to their being labelled as particular emotions by the mind" (93). This last point is key. Political theorist William Connolly (2006, 69), who has frequently worked with theories of affect in relationship to media and politics in the United States, describes an "intrinsic connection" between mind and body, although not a strict correlation. This idea is important, as I frequently shift back and forth between articulating the perceptions and internally logical arguments of settler colonizers, on the one hand, and analyzing their bodily positions in space relative to each other, to Indigenous peoples, and to the material elements of place, on the other hand. This final point on place is crucial, as Chicana scholar of communications Aimee Carrillo Rowe and critical race theorist Eve Tuck (Unangax̂ Aleut) (2017) make clear in their critique of the ways that cultural studies is at times complicit in settler colonialism because it obscures the centrality of the struggle for and transformation of material lands by settler peoples.

The degree to which settler people enact colonization as a physical usurpation of place and the attendant mental process of justifying and forgetting this usurpation through a transformative and affective situation in place are significant. Settler colonization, as a project, relies on individuals and collectives rationally identifying particular opportunities as ripe for exploitation in what is, at least in part, a conscious process. However, the ability to perceive particular kinds of opportunity in place and to recognize the drive that transforms an almost infinite set of permutations of settler collectives into a limited range of self-constituted spatial forms is related to a preconscious, affective push toward particular colonial forms. Although it is tempting to assume that settler people are nefarious or unrepentant conquerors, that is too simple a construction, even if the vast majority remain unmitigated colonizers.

At various points, I engage with Veracini's (2010a) discussion of narratives that settler collectives weave in order to justify their colonial acts and with

Eve Tuck and ethnic studies scholar K. Wayne Yang's (2012, 9–28) identification of "moves to innocence" by which settler people attempt to exempt themselves from colonial blame. I raise these considerations here to emphasize that settler people devote a great deal of personal and social energy to denying the existence of settler colonialism, the damage of colonization, and the personal implication of being part of and benefiting from a settler colonial society (Mackey 2016; Regan 2010). If settler people could be taken at their word when they express heartfelt remorse upon being confronted by colonial realities and their part in them, colonization would disappear from the social landscape. Thus affect here is explicitly deployed to counter "overly cognitivist models of action" (Barnett 2008, 188) that provide conceptual cover for settler colonization. The entanglement between conscious rationalizations and affective pushes in settler colonialism manifests as a sort of social "dysconsciousness," an "uncritical habit of mind ... that justifies inequity and exploitation by accepting the existing order of things as given" (D.M. Johnson 2011, 110).

Finally, as discussed briefly above, the scale of the areas engaged in this book is important to consider because discussions of settler colonialism simultaneously implicate a variety of scalar powers and perceptions. As discussed below, I work to develop a "low theory" (Halberstam 2011, 2) or "weak theory" (Gibson-Graham 2008, 619) that navigates a course between globalizing narratives and location-specific perceptions, exposing tensions and conflicts that help to explain how settler collectives invest their identities in spaces and societies to which they may be only tenuously connected. How settlers imagine themselves is a product of both metanarratives and personal or site-specific experiences, and the two impact each other. The dynamic tension between global-scale theories of colonialism and local-scale histories of colonization is the arena where intermediary geographies – such as the Canadian and American nations, ranches across the historically highly networked Pacific Coast region of Cascadia, temporary middle-ground spaces like the eighteenth-century Great Lakes region, and a perceived continent-wide 'land of opportunity,' to name a few – are generated.

With regard to the concept of the northern bloc of settler colonialism, scale-jumping between local, regional, national, and international levels is crucial to exposing the operation of settler colonialism. Although there are differences in Canadian and American laws and policies and diverse communities across both settler states, it is important not to allow differences at the scale of the nation-state to obscure deep entanglements of power and mutual complicity at broader scales or the ways that settler collectives and communities can remain diverse while still operating in a clearly colonial manner. For this reason, I have intentionally asserted a spatial framework that does not correspond to the settler-created boundaries of these nation-states and have sought to connect global flows both through regional structures and down to particular embodied effects. This spatial frame is roughly the territory claimed by the Canadian and American settler states, and where white Anglo-dominated settler colonial formations have become predominant. This northern bloc of settler colonialism encompasses both a unique and internally contiguous colonial history, with roots in the legal, political, and economic structures of British, French, Dutch, and Spanish imperialism,[8] and a paradoxical character that positions this territory as simultaneously metropole and colony, core and periphery. It is also important to note that the border between these two nation-states – the 49th parallel, recognized as the longest undefended border in the world – bisects Indigenous territories, serving itself as a colonial tool for controlling movements within a geography that is also very much a space that Indigenous people traverse in order to assert their sovereignty contra both settler states (A. Simpson 2014). Mindful of sociologist Raewyn Connell's (2007, 59) argument that definitions of global and local are "conceptually arbitrary," I emphasize that the settler peoples of this continent are entangled with colonial power and practices at multiple scales: as imperial architects and elites (Stewart-Harawira 2005; Tully 2000); as active, localized primary colonists (Arnett 1999; Kupperman 2000); as transient labour alienated from place by capital and dependent on colonial states and nationalisms for social cohesion (C. Harris 2004; Walia 2010); as both architects and profiteers of neocolonialism beyond the northern bloc (Blanchard 1996; French and Manzanárez 2004; McKenna 2011); and as the subjects of contemporary juridical neocolonialism in their own territories (Barker 2009; R.J.F. Day 2005).

Social Movement Theory and Decolonization

Social movement studies is a broad, multidisciplinary field that seeks to understand effective practices for creating social change, especially those undertaken through grassroots and community organizing, and is generally invested in producing scholarship that supports struggles for liberation from the violence and dispossession of colonialism, capitalism, racism, and state intervention.[9] Geographical literature on social movements can provide important context, including ways of thinking through how settler and

Indigenous people can pursue solidarity on "uncommon ground," a useful concept developed by social movement geographer Paul Chatterton (2006) in the context of anti-petroleum-industry protests in the United Kingdom. Likewise, political geographer Paul Routledge has developed the idea of "convergence space" (2003), which I directly discuss later in this book, and the idea of the "third space" of academic activism (1996), which has influenced my own understandings of ethical positionalities and responsibilities and which also finds resonance with Kevin Bruyneel's (2007) "third space" of Indigenous sovereignty. Similarly, geographies of activism are some of the areas where geographers have explicitly grappled with the demands of Indigenous peoples while seriously attempting to trace the influences and impacts of settler colonialism in motivating different grievances (Barker and Pickerill 2012; Counter Cartographies Collective, Dalton, and Mason-Deese 2012; Mott 2016; Nash 2003; Pickerill 2009; Tucker and Rose-Redwood 2015).

More specifically, however, this book is aligned with an overlapping area of scholarship related to broader social movement research: studies of decolonization and Indigenous resurgence. Perhaps the best articulation of what "decolonization" means in the context of settler colonial states is Tuck and Yang's landmark "Decolonization Is Not a Metaphor" (2012). The authors contest overly broad interpretations of decolonization, which have been generated in part by the historicization of colonialism through some postcolonial discourses (Lewis 2012, 231) and in part by the "moves to innocence" through which settler people try to exempt themselves from implication in and complicity with – and thus guilt or responsibility for – colonization (Tuck and Yang 2012, 9–28; see also Veracini 2010b, 14). By contrast, Indigenous articulations have been remarkably clear that decolonization means the return of Indigenous peoples' land bases and the relinquishment of settlers' sovereign claims to those places (Corntassel and Bryce 2012; Coulthard 2014, 171); the establishment of nation-to-nation political relationships, including the right of Indigenous nations to "refuse relations" (A. Simpson 2014); and a fundamental deconstruction and rebuilding of economic systems across the continent (Tuck and Yang 2012, 23–26).

Given the massive shifts required to decolonize the northern bloc and restore Indigenous nationhood and territories across Turtle Island, decolonization is frequently articulated as a process rather than a state of being; although settler colonial power is unevenly distributed and there are places where Indigenous and decolonial spaces are being asserted, nowhere is colonial imposition absent. For settler people who hope to support decolonization, there is no ideal or fully realized decolonized state because we remain vectors for colonial power regardless of our intents, understandings, or spatial positions. Instead, the process of pushing back against these powers and working to disentangle ourselves from them must by necessity entail ongoing and uncertain processes without clear end. It involves a constant grappling with internalized colonial mentalities and external pressures that are both material and cultural (or narrative), and it is fundamentally a social and collective process about transforming interpersonal relationships at both intimate and larger social scales (Holmes, Hunt, and Piedalue 2015). This process, for Indigenous communities, has been discussed under the rubric of resurgence.[10] Resurgence is an approach to decolonization centred on revitalizing relationships to land and place through the regeneration of Indigenous languages, governance practices, and land-based economies and international trading routes, and it is conducted within the self-conscious frame of the need for flexibility and cooperation in both personal and political relationships. Key here is the decentring of imposed colonial systems and approaches in favour of a focus on applying traditional knowledge in a contemporary context and on embodying specific Indigenous legal, political, and spiritual relationships to land. Resurgence, as a social movement practice, has often taken the form of direct action to assert Indigenous presence, persistence, sovereignty, and identity in places of importance, from Idle No More round dances in shopping malls and urban intersections (Barker 2015; Dhillon 2017, 243–48; Kino-nda-niimi Collective 2014) to pulling invasive species and planting traditional food plants in public parks, as Cheryl Bryce of the Songhees First Nation does in Victoria, British Columbia (Corntassel and Bryce 2012), to building houses and settlements in traditional territories that are under threat of development and exerting the authority to remove surveyors and other colonial agents, as the Unist'ot'en have done for over a decade (Barker and Ross 2017). None of these acts in and of themselves dispel settler colonialism or restore Indigenous nationhood, but as Bryce articulates, they are each individually insufficient yet collectively necessary (Corntassel and Bryce 2012, 159–61). They must be understood as "overlapping and simultaneous processes of reclamation, restoration, and regeneration" through which "one begins to better understand how to implement meaningful and substantive community decolonization practices. Future generations will map their own pathways to community regeneration, ideally on their own terms" (161).

My hope is that this book will help to further a growing discourse on how settler people can and should support Indigenous resurgence and develop their own decolonizing processes and that it will help to embed these imperatives in geographical approaches to understanding North America. Academic discourses on settler decolonization and support for Indigenous resurgence often lag well behind efforts and experiments in grassroots activist communities, but there have been important developments in this area over the past few years. Special journal issues (e.g., see L. Davis, Denis, and Sinclair 2017) and edited volumes (e.g., see Maddison, Clark, and de Costa 2016) that focus on the potentialities and limits of settler ability and willingness to confront settler colonialism, while remaining inextricably bound up with it, have made significant inroads into unpacking the complex baggage that even the most educated, practised, and critical settler people bring into their anti-colonial activism. By synthesizing much of this literature through a theoretical lens created by framing this study within settler colonial theory and critical geographies of power and belonging, this book brings diverse examples into productive proximity through a regional theoretical model of settler colonial spatial production.

The conceptual frameworks introduced above, in particular Indigenous thought and settler colonial theory, assemblage thinking and the issue of scale, and social movement theory in the context of decolonization, serve as the high theory of this work. They shape and limit the extent of this research, providing a broad framework but one in need of detail and sustained critique. To that end, I have also framed my methods and approaches through low theory. In taking into account the personal and particular, low theory allows for the perception and articulation of possibilities obscured under larger narratives and helps to maintain a focus on what people – individuals and communities – can actually do about structures of power that may seem invulnerable and monolithic. Here, low theory helps to maintain a focus on the spatialities of colonial relationships that people – Indigenous, settler, and otherwise – form with the land and with each other. The resulting intellectual-experiential conversation between the two approaches is effective in meeting the challenge of pinning down the notoriously slippery and shifting settler colonial assemblage.

A Low Theory of Failure

The academic world is meant to deal in truth, facts, proof, and evidence. As scholars, we are meant to make claims that, despite pushing boundaries and creating new knowledge, are also 'made safe' by adherence to disciplinary protocols and by accepted and valorized forms of knowledge production. However, for many years I have referred to myself as a theorist when asked what type of scholarship I pursue, identifying not with a particular tradition of thought but with the contingency and possibility of theory. Theory is risky, as theorists often make claims that are unprovable in some fundamental sense, and the more interesting and groundbreaking the theory, the more it stands out on a ledge, at risk of proving to be unsupported by the material evidence of conventional scholarly practice. This inherent risk, or perhaps necessity, of pushing a theory to the point of rupture is why I came to identify so strongly with gender theorist Jack Halberstam's description of "low theory" in *The Queer Art of Failure* (2011, 2).

Halberstam's (2011, 15–16) "low theory" is an attempt to break free of the rigid dialectics of "high theory" by attending to the messy, the interpersonal and private, the unexpected, queer, and unsuccessful. Low theory, in Halberstam's use, is intended to reveal "subjugated knowledges," those that are either officially or popularly denied, submerged, or suppressed (11). For Halberstam, these knowledges encompass the many possible queer alterities that do not correspond to the aesthetics and modes of being deemed acceptable to the dominating status quo, which seeks to recapture queerness in heterosexual, patriarchal, and cisnormative practices and symbols. Halberstam investigates what 'failures' to live up to these standards of acceptable queerness can say about how invisible and unspoken standards are enforced, the consequences faced by 'unacceptable' queer people in society, and the creative ways that artists, activists, and other everyday folks are defying or rewriting these normative standards. In so doing, Halberstam marshals a broad range of queer art and expression, from erotic art to a "silly archive" of animated television shows (20).

Halberstam (2011, 2) engages with eminent Jamaican-British cultural theorist Stuart Hall's work to develop an approach to thinking about queerness in contemporary society in a way that avoids the "usual traps and impasses of binary formulations." This approach is particularly relevant given that so much work invoking settler colonialism fails to avoid the pernicious "Manichean binaries" of Indigenous and settler (Byrd 2011, xxix). Low theory works through diverse representations in fields ranging from popular culture to avant-garde performance art in order to interrogate what success means in the context of living a contemporary life. Rejecting the narrative of success as economic stability and social integration, Halberstam attempts to envision the paradoxical possibility that success is actually found in failing. Failing need not be terrible even if it is painful, and as Halberstam

(2011, 5) discusses in reference to pop culture portrayals of failures to meet the American middle-class norm of success in films such as Jonathan Dayton and Valerie Faris's *Little Miss Sunshine* (2006), failing has the potential to reveal a great deal about the obscure processes, hidden meanings, and assumed realities of contemporary life.

In this book, I take a similar approach. However, my low theory is directed at exposing subjugated knowledges regarding how to be a non-Indigenous person on Turtle Island in an ethical way, whether or not settler colonialism has structured one's identities and perceptions of power, class, race, gender, and so on. Following Halberstam, I too must investigate 'failures' to do what settler colonizers are supposed to do, and to this end, I assemble my own archive of motley memories and pop culture moments. For this archive, I have chosen places where I unexpectedly encountered settler colonialism through the formative years of my life – including childhood stories told about family migration and history, encounters with the landscape of the overlapping Haudenosaunee and Anishinaabe territories near my home and with the Coast Salish territories in and around Victoria, British Columbia, and television shows situated around Turtle Island that I watched while homesick in England. Reflecting on this archive is partly an autoethnographic process, as I examine my own experiences as a settler Canadian in association with media representations, stories from activist events and conflicts, and the reactions of Indigenous individuals to my own actions in and through settler colonial spaces. I thus fail to normalize settler colonialism in my own experiences, making it possible to map the ways that settler colonial societies like Canada and the United States discipline settler colonial subjects by disappearing them into the emergent spaces of the settler colony.

This engagement with low theory looks at two types of failure at once: my failures to ignore settler colonial norms and instead to actively seek out settler colonization happening in the spaces around me *and* my failures to effectively challenge settler colonial spatialities, identities, and power structures. Throughout this book, I move from memories of my grandmother to discussions of contemporary television to the knowledge generated when activists fail in their aims, all in an attempt both to show the extent of settler colonization in structuring social, political, cultural, and economic life across a continent and to demonstrate the myriad ways that this vast settler colonial assemblage can be and is being confronted, countered, and dismantled. My practice of low theory takes the idea of failure as inevitable – in this case, the individual failure to fully decolonize as a settler person and the collective failure to bring about the decolonization of settler society. But as I hope to demonstrate in this book, the fact that failure is inevitable does not mean that all types of failure are undesirable; it depends on how a settler fails and at what.

Autoethnography and the Settler Self

Given that low theory dwells on the messy and odd in the otherwise banal and quotidian, autoethnographic exploration is a fruitful method for investigation. Phenomenological and autoethnographic approaches have increasingly informed my work (e.g., see Barker 2013, 2018; and Barker and Battell Lowman 2016) because the intellectual, the personal, and the political are very deeply intertwined. This book is fundamentally the culmination of an intellectual project begun in 2002, when I committed to Indigenous studies during my undergraduate course work at McMaster University under Mohawk professor of anthropology Dawn Martin Hill. Since then, numerous personal and professional experiences have given rise to profound transformations in my thinking about myself, where and how I belong, and my responsibilities and lines of accountability. Emma Battell Lowman and I similarly positioned our co-authored book as resulting from ten years of discussion, learning, and experimentation (Battell Lowman and Barker 2015), and *Making and Breaking Settler Space* is likewise a result of years of intellectual and scholarly attempts to theorize how colonization works and to identify its connections to the processes of my own life. Developing a habit of self-critical reflection is vital to this work, so each chapter opens with a story that connects to how the concepts developed in the chapter have played out in my life. These stories are intended either to establish touchstones of personal experience that readers may find familiar or relatable or to illuminate choices in research development and production that might otherwise remain obscured.

The analysis that I derive from this combination of high and low theories, conducted through an autoethnographic effort to unpack the entanglements of my agency and sense of self as part of a larger decolonizing effort, is – predictably – messy. 'Unsettling' experiences have been key moments of disruption and spurs to critical self-reflection as I have failed my way toward understanding what it means to be a settler Canadian and a part of the settler colonial assemblage. Sociologist Eva Mackey, in *Unsettled Expectations* (2016), describes the way that Indigenous land claims unsettle many Canadians and Americans whose lived experiences are premised on Indigenous absence from the land. Mackey discusses the way that these unsettled expectations are often expressed through feelings of discomfort and the assertion of narrative turns that evidence affective panic and fear as well as the denial of facts and logical argument. For example, in her examination of attitudes toward the Caldwell First Nation claim for land in southern Ontario, Mackey points out that many rural landowners' opposition to the creation of a reserve in the area was rooted in imagined rather than expressed intentions for the land on the part of the Indigenous community (79–83, 92–95). The emotional responses of these landowners were evidence of pre-existing fears of Indigenous peoples and taken-for-granted understandings of terra nullius and similar concepts explored throughout this book that made Indigenous claims to land unimaginable. Confronted with the unimaginable, many of these settler people became unsettled – destabilized, uncertain, and conflicted – and thus sought to rapidly re-establish comfort at the expense of actually engaging with Indigenous people and their voices.

This book is intended to contribute to scholarship on the geographies of settler colonialism and decolonial social movement studies, while also raising deeply personal questions about belonging, relationship, identity, and responsibility. In finding myself to be a settler person, and therefore an everyday, 'normal' embodiment of the settler colonialism that I was seeking to understand and analyze, I ended up becoming my own "strategic exemplar" (Stevenson 2012, 602). By self-consciously reflecting on my own emotional, affective responses to failing in my intent to be a 'good settler,' I expose the unavoidability of these moments and the necessity of moving on from them as part of the process of limiting the control that the settler colonial assemblage exerts over individuals and society writ large. My experiences are not universal or even representative, as my whiteness, cisgendered male identity, lower-middle-class suburban upbringing, and experiences in education and work all draw stark dividing lines between my lived experience and those of many others across the northern bloc of settler colonialism. That is partly why my analyses and arguments for particular kinds of decolonizing action are not prescriptive and why I reflect openly on my own experiences, following the example set by historian Paulette Regan in her own work (2010). The intention is to create accessible moments that may help readers to make their own personal connections with this work, whether because we share elements of identity, positionality, or experience or because I share key characteristics with settler people with whom they are connected or in conflict. By joining the intellectual and the affective, the high and the low, *Making and Breaking Settler Space* demonstrates that this approach is a necessary part of efforts to achieve fundamental changes in settler colonial relations and to expose and dismantle settler colonialism on Turtle Island.

Chapter Overview

This book looks first at broad studies of historical imperialism and settler colonial encounters on Turtle Island, then at regional examinations that consider both the production of the northern bloc of settler colonialism as a space and the functioning of the settler colonial assemblage in producing that space, and finally at the failures and successes of work undertaken by settler activist groups and individuals in solidarity with Indigenous people in the here and now. This progression through scale and time is intended to establish a framework for understanding how complex and broad systems of power operate in hidden or taken-for-granted ways in the lives of everyday settler colonizers. Ultimately, in identifying these connections, I hope to provide tools for scholars to further intervene in and disrupt the (re)production of space and power in the northern bloc.

I begin in Chapter 1 by investigating the large-scale historical legacy of European imperialism and colonization that instigated settler colonization in the northern settler bloc. I frame the spatialities of colonization through the perception of a core-periphery binary and terra nullius thinking, both of which not only set the material foundation of private property and state sovereignty in the northern settler bloc but also persist in the ways that settler people perceive the lands that they call home. This investigation connects with historical constructions of early colonial contact, with articulations of sovereignty through the creation of a legal-political regime by means of concepts such as homo sacer and designations such as spaces of exception and terra nullius, and with settler colonial theories of isopolitical shift and transfer. The analysis of these elements of colonialism is coupled with low theory autoethnographic engagements regarding family history and narratives of becoming settler Canadian and, more broadly, with discussions of settler origin stories and "mythistories" (Battell Lowman 2014, 143).

Chapter 2 moves from the scale of international and intercontinental imperialism to the scale of settler collectives engaged in transforming the lands of Turtle Island in order to generate power and privilege, produce social hierarchies of belonging, and seek the elimination of Indigenous peoples, nations, and histories. I examine the settler colonial assemblage through its spatial products, which comprise a series of spaces that generate settler colonial aspirations, movements of populations, and perceptions of social belonging and exclusion. These spaces form the basis of institutionalized power and the experiences of increasing privilege that structure many aspects of the settler nation-state. These spaces are also analyzed here as dynamic, for they are always in the process of being constructed in concert with the deconstruction of Indigenous spaces. I analyze entwined acts of occupation, erasure, and bricolage as essential to the creation of both material and imagined spaces that weave settler national, regional, and personal identities into the land itself at the expense of Indigenous relationships to place and practices of self-determination.

In Chapter 3, I show how the settler colonial assemblage recruits materials and bodies and spatially configures them by examining how issues of difference and diversity are subsumed into a homogenizing settler colonial landscape. I consider the interlocking processes of racialized dispossession, class-based oppression and dehumanization, and the settler colonial remaking of land and place, while interrogating the extent to which these processes mutually reinforce each other. Crucially, however, I also identify the limits of the imbrication of state and capital with the settler colonial assemblage. I then describe the ways that the resonances and dissonances between these large-scale processes inform imagined geographies of urban, rural, frontier, and wilderness spaces. Finally, I consider the suburban form of North American settlement as an ultimately failed attempt to transcend the settler colonial legacy of Canada and the United States.

Chapter 4 shifts the discussion from higher-level theories of state formation and capital production to the experiences of those who try to moderate, modify, resist, or revolt against state and capital. I examine the broad spectrum of the North American left – from liberals to radicals, including anti-state anarchists and anti-capitalist socialists. I work through social movement theory, critiques of the "limits of liberalism" (Grande 2013), and intersections of racial and class politics to two primary ends. First, I disentangle settler colonialism from capitalism and state power, demonstrating not only the ways that the settler colonial assemblage overlaps and is interconnected with assemblages of capital accumulation and nation-state sovereignty but also the ways that it can function apart from these assemblages through a very different set of political-economic structures and imagined geographies. Second, I examine the ways that many actions by settler political activists are not actually anti-colonial but reinforce settler colonialism through assumptions about Indigenous nations and colonial formations. Here, I sketch out the limits of contemporary anti-colonial activism in order to turn attention to the possibilities of an authentically decolonial activism for non-Indigenous people on these lands.

The narrative of settler becoming and of my own understanding of myself as a settler comes full circle in Chapter 5, where I return to the considerations in Chapter 1 through the frame of low theory, asking how did we get here, what are we doing, and how could we be otherwise? This time, the investigation is not historical but urgently present as I examine the role of scholar activists and work to generate a relational, ethical framework with which people like myself can engage in grounded, relational, decolonial projects. I work through understandings of affect, relationality, and place-based struggle. The low theory approach in this chapter draws inspiration from the work of Indigenous poets, moments in which pop culture brushes against settler colonial analysis, and my own messy recollections of proximity to Indigenous-led activism. Ultimately, I advocate an attempt to be a 'bad settler' as a way of refusing both the siren song of settler futurity and the arrogant assumptions of postcolonial responsibility.

In Chapter 6, *Making and Breaking Settler Space* concludes with a persistent question: how can we scale up individual experiences of being unsettled so that they form the basis for decolonial alliances that are transformative at both the individual and societal levels? Driven by the concept of "co-becoming" (Bawaka Country et al. 2016), I work through the necessities of settler-to-settler engagement, the imperative of turning toward and centring Indigenous systems of governance, and the possibility of supporting Indigenous resurgence by generating complementary movements and engagements on "uncommon ground" (Chatterton 2006). Inspired by mentors who have helped me to grapple with my own settler colonial affective responses, I situate critical compassion as necessary to reformulating relationships – to each other, across difference, and with land and place – in pursuit of decolonizing social movements.

1

Cores and Peripheries: From Imperial Contact to Settler Colonial Claims

My grandmother Nancy was a teenager in England following the Second World War when she departed for Canada with her family – her mother, stepfather, and siblings – eventually settling in Hamilton, Ontario, where both my parents and I would be born. Grandma's family came for a new and better life, looking to escape a nation that was struggling economically, dealing with the damage of the war, and still subject to rationing. My great-grandparents did what many thousands of others did, what many people seeking a better quality of life for themselves and their children had done before their time and would continue to do in the future: they moved to a new life in the settlement colonies. When my grandmother boarded a steamer at age fourteen and sailed from the port at Liverpool to Canada in 1948, she probably did not really understand that she would not see the place that she had called home again for more than four decades.

My grandmother crossed a threshold that I never will: she was at home in the heart of the British Empire and then became a citizen of a settler society. By the time I knew her, she had an accent that was not really English but still noticeably – even if only slightly – different from the southern Ontario English of me and my parents, which shares similarities with the 'neutral' accent known as general American. She did not travel back to England until her sixtieth birthday and definitely considered herself Canadian, but she rarely missed an episode of the television show *Coronation Street* (1960–present) and had a deep fondness for beautifully garish English ceramic figures, which adorned nearly every surface in her house. I wonder now how her view of the world differed from mine. I think about her life and the way that it represents a strand connecting me in a deeply personal way to the history of settler colonialism. I wonder what she saw when she arrived here and what knowing that might tell me about how my own sense of identity and belonging was shaped. I wish I had asked her these things.

The Imperial Gaze and the Colonial Experience

In this chapter, I take up the challenge of mapping some of the key ways that European invasions of Turtle Island cascaded across the landscape, transforming Euro-American understandings of here and there and ultimately setting the stage for a settler colonial revolution that continues to unfold today. My goal is to synthesize understandings of imperialism, colonialism, and settler colonization in the early stages of the invasion of Turtle Island in order to develop a basic spatial model of the expansion of settler colonial space that will frame further detailed investigations. I describe the worldview of European imperialism that informed the development of settler colonialism in Canada and the United States of America and that continues to underpin these nations' political institutions, legal systems, and norms of individual rights to land and property. Settler people do not arrive in new lands free of biases but rather import "fragments" (Butlin 2009, 10–12) of their cultural, national, religious, and subjective frameworks. The settler colonial gaze sweeps across the landscapes of Turtle Island in particular ways, imposing upon them logical structures such as grids, networks, and borders, which are ordered according to the expectations, fears, and logical and narrative forms of the settler colonial population. These expectations originate partly in Euro-Christian cosmology, institutional traditions, and ontologies imported along with early settler populations. However, they are also uniquely of the lands that settler collectives claim and transform, for they were built when embodied practice met ontological frameworks in particular places. Some settler colonial imagined geographies are inherited, but many others originate with the embodied experience of settling.[1]

And so I return to considering my grandmother's experience of immigrating to Canada and my own experience of relocating to England, where I have now lived for a decade. There is a strange symmetry to my writing about settler colonialism through the experiences of my grandmother's move from England to Canada given that I myself have now done the reverse – although the xenophobic nationalism of the British government means that citizenship is still years and thousands of dollars away. I research and write most days in the city of Leicester, whose industrial heritage, culturally and ethnically diverse population, and scrappy outsider status all remind me of my hometown of Hamilton, Ontario, and this perspective has been instrumental in my understanding of settler colonialism from both the inside and outside. What follows deploys this duality to grapple with longer trajectories of settler colonial cultural and political heritage.

Seeing the Periphery from the Core

When Europeans began to settle on Turtle Island, they did so by undertaking long – often arduous, uncertain, and potentially deadly – trips away from their homelands. The places that they encountered and the people who inhabited those places were drastically different from what they knew. So began the construction of complex imagined geographies to help early colonists make sense of the very different world they came to inhabit. This difference has changed form, to be sure, but has remained a defining feature distinguishing the imperial homeland from the colonies. These two spaces share important similarities but differ in ways that can at times be jarring. The fault line between the heart of the originary empire and the colonial space is something through which many early settlers "transited," to use Jodi Byrd's (2011) term describing imperial movements enacted via the perception and imposition of racial difference, which was then projected across places, cultures, and worldviews, with cacophonous results. However, in the early days of sustained European settlement, many of the key decisions that affected the lives of settlers and relations with Indigenous nations were made by European rulers and officials for whom actual contact with Indigenous people was limited to encountering the comparatively small, but not insignificant, number of Indigenous people who travelled overseas as willing or unwilling visitors (Thrush 2016)[2] or was made possible only by later constructs like the travelling shows and human zoos that toured Europe, such as the Nuxalk singers and dancers from the Pacific Northwest Coast of North America who toured Germany in the late nineteenth century (Hager 2006). Such contact did not include direct exposure to Indigenous peoples' place relationships or to the construction of colonial spaces. Much metropolitan writing on Indigenous peoples during the early colonial period was based on second-hand or wholly fanciful accounts, leading to the mixing of fact and fiction in the minds of Europeans. However, as historian of early American colonization Karen Ordahl Kupperman (2000, 20) points out, "the more direct experience a colonist had, the more complex became the description" of Indigenous peoples. So the situated knowledge of on-the-ground informants such as priests and missionaries, traders, plantation workers and managers, and military officers, for example, whose work necessitated close contact with Indigenous people, became vital to the ties of trade and diplomacy in pursuit of imperial ambitions. Thus informed, these European agents of empire perceived and, in many material ways, imposed a set of spatial structures that continue to shape the spatialities of settler colonies.

Early colonists – those who arrived under the European regimes that dominated colonial life prior to the American Revolution (1765–83) – in what became New England treated many of the various "Indian" peoples as kingdoms or political entities equivalent to what they knew from Europe, acknowledging their authority and integrating them into existing political and economic practices when necessary. Kupperman (2000, 96–97) discusses how chiefs or other local leaders were regarded as "kings" and "emperors," relating that this view was partly rooted in a perception among English colonists that England was "degenerating into a cockpit of competing particular interests marked by disrespect for authority." Early colonists were often impressed by the deportment of Indigenous leadership, in part because they were looking for marks of authority to contrast with critiques of the metropolitan core that they had left behind. The allegiance and friendship of Indigenous leaders were pursued by imperial agents and early colonial elites both because of their perceived rank – as the friendship of powerful 'kings,' 'chiefs,' and other leaders was seen to add to the prestige of colonial leaders and explorers, whose station in Europe therefore benefited – and for their practical utility. However, despite the attempts of early imperial agents and settler colonizers to filter their perceptions of Indigenous peoples through their European lenses of social dynamics and Christian historical worldviews and cosmology, they struggled to understand the meanings of the new places that they encountered (Cruikshank 2005; V. Deloria Jr. 2003; Kupperman 2000). This confusion is an example of "colonial difference" in action (Mignolo 2000).

Argentinian semiotician Walter Mignolo (2000, 3) describes "colonial difference" as the ways that colonizers conceived of themselves and their spaces as fundamentally different from Indigenous people and spaces, measured in everything from relationships to history as a concept and the use of writing to the occupation of particular kinds of environments. However, I deploy this term in a slightly different sense, regarding colonial difference as a distinction between the colonizer's expectations of colonization and the reality of doing colonization in place.[3] Crucially, this colonial difference is enacted physically *and* socially. Among many early European settlers in what became the northern settler bloc, it is particularly evident in their strong tendency to perceive that they were leaving behind a society that had somehow gone "profoundly" wrong (Kupperman 1980, 141). This view was evident not only among those seeking the freedom to pursue stricter versions of Christianity, such as the Puritans and other early Protestant settlers in New England (Kupperman 1980, 141; 2000, 18), but also among the many poor and destitute for whom undertaking the risky and dangerous task of participating in the founding of a colony was preferable to the deprivations of poverty or the violence of punishment, both of which were near certainties in the metropole. The vast majority of early settlers – and this is a trend that continues to this day – were attempting to escape an 'old world' that, although maybe not actually collapsing, was falling apart *for them*. This perception did not always align with the actual shifts in geopolitics; as the British Empire grew in power, it ground poor and disenfranchised people to pieces both within the imperial core and even more so throughout its reach. But the key here is that many settler colonizers who transit willingly from an imperial metropole to its settler colony encounter the colonial difference in an unavoidably immediate way when their expectations based on life in the metropole meet the reality of dispossession and violence that underpins the new place that they will call home.

But the violence that enables material accumulation and social mobility in the colonies is directed outward rather than inward, in contrast to the familiar hierarchies of the former homeland. This inversion causes outsiders to perceive the colonies and dominions as places of inherent opportunity, thus informing a wide range of affective impulses that bridge the colonial difference. Support for these impulses includes emotion-laden narratives that posit the settler society as a "special locale" (Veracini 2010b, 55) to explain away violence and to disappear Indigenous histories and narratives that question the facts of colonization. Once the move to the settlement has been made, the expectation of improvement with respect to the corrupt and fallen metropole left behind informs a whole range of aspirations and expectations crucial to recruiting new people into the process of colonization.

A colony is, importantly, a spatial process rather than a simple physical location. According to Lorenzo Veracini (2010b, 2–3), a colony can be a reference to either of two different but related things: "a political body that is dominated by an exogenous agency, and an exogenous entity that reproduces itself in a given environment (in both cases, even if they refer to very different situations, 'colony' implies the localized ascendancy of an external element – this is what brings the two meanings together)." Here, "domination" and "ascendancy" are references to a process of dominat*ing*, defined by the active creation of an imbalance of power. The effect is the creation of a geographical imperial core and colonial periphery. Through colonization, an invading society hopes to draw the periphery into the orbit of the core and to reorient patterns of resource use, trade, migration, and development in the newly created periphery in order to serve the wants of the self-declared (and power-backed) centre. This core-periphery dynamic underpinned early encounters between Europeans and Indigenous people of Turtle Island. Political theorist Nevzat Soguk (2011, 38) has argued that these encounters between the 'old' and 'new' worlds gave rise to a new "matrix of positionality" among Europeans that reconfigured the pre-existing Eurocentric belief in Europe as the centre of the universe. Whereas Europe, particularly western Europe, was actively and tacitly constructed as the heart of the 'civilized' world, the Americas entered the European imperial imagination as a bountiful periphery ripe for exploitation. That this periphery was also constructed as available – spatially and morally – meant that "from the beginning, European programs and projects were set to conflict with Indigenous civilizational practices" (38).

The biggest dividing factor between this core and this periphery in the early colonial period was distance: the oceanic crossings were fraught, uncertain, and long. The vast and varied continents that we know as the Americas defied the ability of many Europeans to traverse them as they wished. European empires created and sustained their far-flung imperial peripheries through the projection of "lines of force" (C. Harris 2004, 167, citing Fanon 1963, 38) across distance and also across difference. At times, the distance across which power was projected constituted a real place, a physical barrier or divide, or wilderness areas that evaded capture and control by colonizing forces (Bell 2005): the Atlantic Ocean, the Rocky Mountains, dense northern boreal forests, or the arid plains and deserts of the Southwest. At other times, the spatial divide was a result of wider geopolitics in the form of competing imperial lines of force, such as the way that violence precipitated by conflicts between the British and French, spilling over into warfare between their Indigenous allies, created contested spaces where no particular political power could predominate (R. White 2011). Early on, however, no lines of force were more important to the project of European imperialism than those being projected directly across the

Atlantic Ocean – with the networks of power creating an Atlantic (and later Pacific) imperial periphery. The colonial lines of force can be traced through many material spaces and routes but most often took the form of ships that crisscrossed the Atlantic, transporting or supplying colonists and soldiers, raiding each other, and always returning extracted resources, or their profits, to the metropole, along with valuable knowledge about these Indigenous places and spaces (Clayton 1999; Featherstone 2005; C. Harris 2004). Spatially stretched, resource intensive, and requiring large numbers of metropole citizens to participate in highly specialized roles, the complex contact and exchange processes required to connect metropole and Indigenous spatial networks of power ensured the material visibility and reinforcement of colonial power flows.

European empires sought to overcome the complicating factor of the core-periphery divide by generating wider, stronger networks of power and influence, which required building (often using unfree labour)[4] forts, settlement colonies, transportation infrastructure, administrative structures, and other nodes that connected places and people. Historically, metropole colonialism has relied upon a developing suite of technologies to shrink space and cross barriers, including transportation and navigation technologies such as sail or steam engines and advanced cartographic techniques that made it easier to traverse oceans and continents, as well as later telegraph, telephone, and other communication technologies and systems for coordinating action and sharing information over distances. All of these conduits require infrastructure of various kinds, and this infrastructure indicates the shape of the imperial network at any given time. For example, much work has been done on the spaces of ships, especially those of the British Navy during their imperial height (e.g., see Clayton 1999; and Featherstone 2008). These ships, with their complex systems of surveillance and discipline and their intense spatially shaped cultures, were one kind of conduit-in-action, and the routes that they travelled, the people they moved and relied upon, and the conflicts in which they engaged gave early transatlantic European colonization a particular form.

The nodes connected by such conduits are spaces where imperial power is focused and projected into distant places. They assert imperial sovereign authority over local lands and people by transforming the landscape through the construction of imperial infrastructure, including defensive works, ports, barracks or elite homes, and roads, thus providing the groundwork for the low-level instigation of surveillance and discipline as tactics of sovereign authority. Fur trade forts are a common example of this infrastructure (C. Harris 2004, 168–69), and the monopolization of the legitimate use of violence by Hudson's Bay Company officials can be seen as an extension of sovereignty from the metropole into the colonial periphery (Cavanagh 2009), but missions, plantations, mines, military outposts, and other configurations served as nodal points as well. These nodes, as much as they are considered to be imperial spaces, are not to be confused with the spaces of the metropole itself. Forts often existed outside of the juridical reach of empire, colonies were seen as dangerous places, and plantations or mines were primarily peopled by the indentured, the enslaved, and others constructed as nonhumans or as existing without rights for the purpose of rendering their bodies suitable for labour. As we draw out the differences between settler and metropole colonialisms, distinctions between metropole, core, conduits, and peripheral nodal spaces are crucial to understanding the shifts that occurred and how these impacted Indigenous place-based practice.

Figure 1 illustrates the spatial functioning of an imperial assemblage. The placement of trading posts, military forts, and missions was not random or accidental but followed the contours of both the physical and human landscape. As historian Jon Parmenter (2010) discusses in his history of Iroquoia, 1534–1701, the geographical situation of a colonial fort or trading post often had a great deal to do with forces working at different scales. The geopolitics informing the Dutch colony of Fort Orange, founded in 1624 and later the site of the city of Albany on the Hudson River in New York State (250 kilometres upriver from New York City), included competition for territory with other European empires, as both the English and French were also active in this area; alliance building with the Mahicans who established a trading settlement across the river from Fort Orange as well as conflict with the Haudenosaunee and many other Indigenous nations in the area; and the ability to access particular resources, including material profit in the form of furs as well as local knowledge of terrain and transportation routes (32). However, this same history also demonstrates the contingency of many of these spatial creations of the imperial assemblage. Fort Orange initially lasted little more than a year, as Mohawks moved to claim territory and control the trade route between the Dutch and Mahicans. After a French embassy that was dispatched to the Mohawks with the intention of securing free trade through the area ended in disaster, the Dutch were so fearful of potential Mohawk attacks on the settlement that they evacuated and abandoned it for five years (32–34).

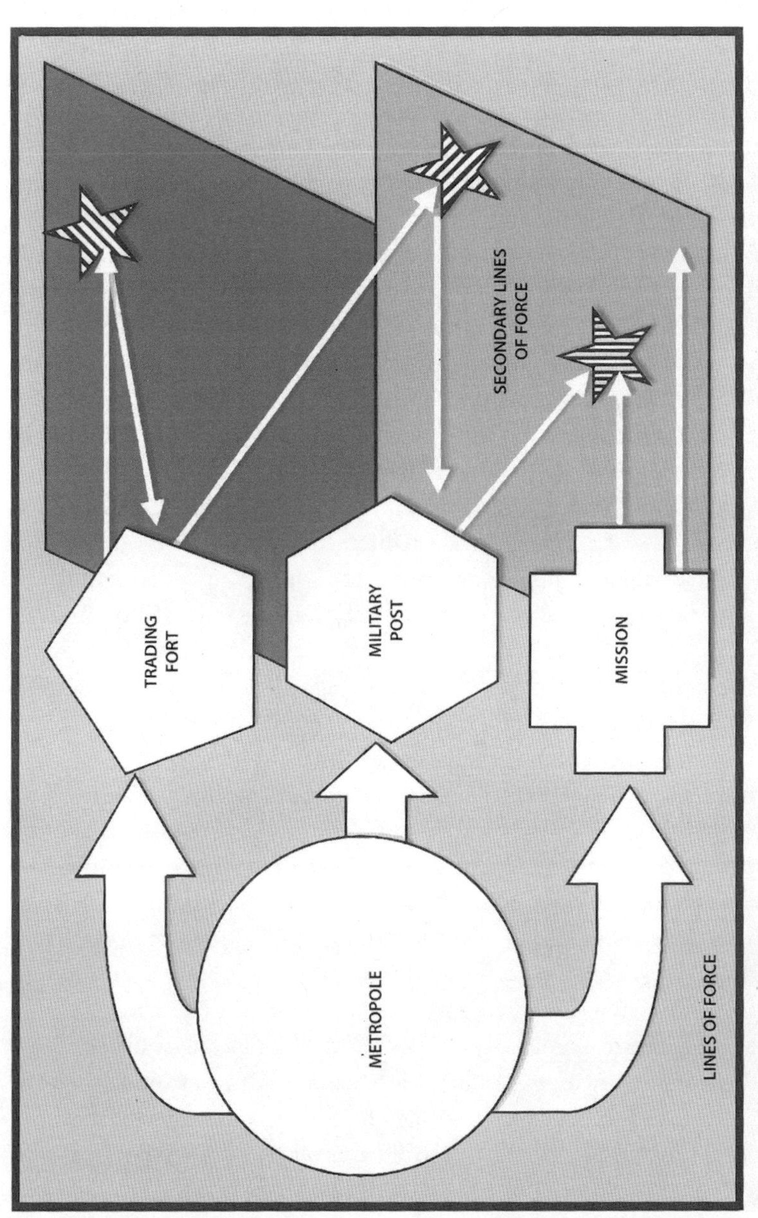

FIGURE 1 Spatial configuration of classic or metropole colonization

Crucially for this study, settler colonial assemblages germinate within and then spread out through and beyond imperial assemblages. The spatial knowledge acquired by imperial agents is therefore transmitted to settlers in a variety of forms, including travel writings, government reports, and folk stories. In some cases, the material bases of imperial infrastructure become the literal basis of settlements. In the same geographic region, the city of Fort Erie, on the Canadian side of the border between the province of Ontario and New York State where the Niagara River meets Lake Erie, would not likely exist where or as it does if not for the establishment of a British fort to guard the mouth of the Niagara River in 1764 following the Seven Years' War (1756–63). Various settlers, including discharged soldiers and their families, traders and merchants setting up shop, and immigrants from Europe tempted by the promise of farmland, gravitated to, filtered through, and settled near the fort, which acted as a supply depot and shelter, especially during the frequently harsh winters in the area. Not far to the south, in New York State, the capital city of Albany was incarnated as Fort Nassau and Fort Orange (under Dutch control) and as Fort Frederick (under British control) before dropping "fort" from the name around the same time that the literal masonry fort was being dismantled in order to help the city expand. Ironically, the protection afforded by the fort caused the settlement to grow so large that the original infrastructure was surpassed. However, in both cases, imperial geopolitics set the stage for – while not overdetermining – settlement.

Figure 1 also visually represents the tension between the presence – and European awareness – of complex Indigenous societies and the assertion of 'empty' land. In this colonial formation, lines of force crossed differently occupied spaces and were often contingent upon cooperation and assistance from Indigenous people. Many of those making important decisions that shaped early colonial contact, who had little first-hand experience of these lands or people, accepted embodied occupation while also assuming that the lands they claimed across the Atlantic Ocean were empty in a legal sense. Res nullius, or empty space, is a legal concept drawn from Roman law under which lands that are not occupied by any recognized civilization can be claimed freely. Under the Doctrine of Discovery, a legal and political concept derived from a papal bull issued by Pope Alexander VI in 1493, shortly after the European 'discovery' of the Americas, the colonies were declared terra nullius – land unclaimed by any recognized or civilized nation. Later, as reflected in the works of Enlightenment philosopher John Locke, English law drew from these traditions to codify terra nullius, arguing that 'improvements,' including the construction of homesteads, farms, mills, and other industry buildings, were the litmus test for terra nullius (Tully 2000). In other words, because Indigenous peoples in what became the northern settler bloc did not build the kinds of structures associated with European political economies – and, notably, did not engage in Christian and European religious and cultural practices – their lands were free for the taking by anyone who would 'improve' the land in accordance with Euro-American perceptions (MacMillan 2011). As more and more lands in the Americas were claimed in this way, systems of private property and the regularized division of space into discrete units were developed and implemented to systematize the process. This undertaking created what legal scholar Brenna Bhandar (2016, 119–21) has described as a dual system of property. The first system is based on "title," or recognition of ownership by law, and the second on "possession," which is rooted in the same systems of antiquated and deeply biased laws and customs that inform terra nullius.[5]

However, terra nullius is more than a legal concept; it has become a key part of how later settler societies that developed out of the early claims of European expansion understand their own histories and relationships to land. Eva Mackey (2016) has established terra nullius not only as a key part of historical articulations of colonial sovereignty but also as a major part of present-day settler colonial national myths and legal systems. Her studies of opposition to Indigenous land claims among settler communities in Ontario and New York State have shown that the terra nullius myth has changed form and been redeployed by settlers, based on a backward logic, to assert that because the settler states of Canada and the United States today hold title and exercise sovereignty over the territories that they claim, Indigenous people must never have done so or must have surrendered their claims. The undeniable presence of Indigenous peoples must therefore be effaced in a number of ways to maintain this colonial fiction and the benefits that it confers upon settlers and settler society. But early settler colonists could not simply conceptually erase Indigenous presence, and their encounters with assertions of Indigenous sovereignty, trade with Indigenous communities, and intercultural exchange also continue to mark settler societies in ways that make Canada and the United States different from the European kingdoms and metropoles that spawned them.[6] The transatlantic world that was created by the export of imperial power and populations to the Americas necessitated a reorientation of Christian, European cosmology and, in fact, of foundational ideas and assumptions about geography.

Invasion, Disruption, and Settlement

For the English, contact between permanent colonies and Indigenous people on the Atlantic Coast helped to defray the more fanciful notions of early travel writing – even if, as Kupperman (2000) points out, colonists perceived Indigenous peoples through European lenses. Chiefs occupying positions of respect and wealth but not coercive power were construed as monarchs reigning over hierarchical kingdoms, and "graded status markers in badges, body painting, and tattooing were reassuring, because they indicated impressively sophisticated social and communal distinctions and an orderly society" (64). However, as imperial ambitions grew and changed, with the network of colonies, forts, and other imperial infrastructure shifting the balance of power as it spread, empires began to take more assertive steps to claim land, bringing them further into conflict with Indigenous nations, disrupting political and economic networks, and extending conflicts between European kingdoms into Indigenous homelands. The English originally differentiated their own colonization from that of the Spanish by seeking to render it legitimate through a 'benign' policy with respect to Indigenous peoples. The English did not necessarily seek open warfare and conquest on Turtle Island – at least not initially or when other relations were more expedient and cost-effective – but instead set up plantations and trading outposts and frequently limited the ability of colonists to expand into the territories of recognized Indigenous nations without title first being secured through treaty or purchase by the Crown. However, as British interests became more settled, as permanent colonial populations grew, and as shifts occurred in geopolitical rivalries with the Spanish and French, among others, these seemingly benign policies were abandoned in favour of a more belligerent ideology (MacMillan 2011).

Colonizers, including early settlers, were not always looking for conflict with Indigenous people, and some explicitly avoided it. However, settler colonization as a whole has traditionally remained premised on founding violence (Veracini 2008, 2010b, 78). Indigenous peoples, initially through legal discourses of terra nullius and later through racist discourses of white supremacy, Indigenous degeneracy, and Manifest Destiny, were reconstructed not as sovereigns but as problems to be managed by Euro-American colonies and representatives. Indigenous people were increasingly racialized through pseudoscientific claims and were portrayed as inherent and existential threats to the survival of the colonies because of their "treacherous" natures (MacMillan 2011, 41). In some places, especially in what would become the southern United States, the dehumanization of Indigenous people intersected with the process of enslavement, including the enslavement and transportation of both Black Africans and Indigenous people. Contrasting South Carolina with the Puritan North, historian Alan Gallay (2003, 3) argues, "from first settlement, South Carolina elites ruthlessly pursued the exploitation of fellow humans in ways that differed from other mainland colonies, and they created a narcissistic culture that reacted passionately and violently to attempts to limit their individual sovereignty over their perceived social inferiors." To the extent that enslavement might seem a continuation of Indigenous labour as 'useful,' Gallay also contrasts the reliance of early colonists on Indigenous knowledge, protection, and production, and Indigenous perceptions that they gained more by trading with than destroying the colonies (4–5) with the shift towards enslaved labour through the metaphor of a devastating disease (6, emphasis in original):

> This [slave] trade *infected* the South: it set in motion a gruesome series of wars that engulfed the region. For close to five decades, virtually *every* group of people in the South lay threatened by destruction in these wars. Huge areas were depopulated, thousands of Indians died, and thousands more were forcibly relocated to new areas in the South or exported from the region.

And it should be no surprise what phenomena accompanies this devastating shift: the arrivals of settlers primarily interested in land in the 1750s, prior to which "the colony mostly attracted people preoccupied by the search for exportable commodities" (5) produced by others.[7]

In its broadest strokes, the shift from the perception of Indigenous peoples as potentially useful to inherently threatening Others was part of the shift from a metropole colonial logic to a settler colonial logic. The creation and maintenance of a perception of threat help to justify violent acts of settler colonial conquest and erasure. This shift in colonial logics corresponds with increasing ambitions for control of Indigenous land and is indicative of a shift in how colonization is conceived by the colonizers, for "underlying this common frame of reference is the unspoken assumption" that settler states are "an inevitable by-product of modern history – the global move toward industrialization, the consolidation of diverse peoples into nations, and the expansion of political democracy" (Hoxie 2008, 1154). Nonetheless, both the development of settler states, whether out of the white settlement colonies of the former British Empire or in the many other contexts where they arose, and the attendant colonial displacement were not and are not inevitable or accidental. Rather, they are connected to the political processes through which settler people try to differentiate themselves as a distinct people from their metropole progenitors and develop their own institutions and structures to confer power and privilege upon themselves.

The penetration of lines of force into and through Indigenous networks of place-based relationships disrupted and reoriented local, Indigenous social, political, economic, and cultural life. Often, metropole colonialism did not destroy Indigenous peoples' place relationships, but it certainly had an impact. For example, Indigenous peoples' access to and processing of natural resources, such as furs, attracted traders, whose own supply of exotic resources encouraged changes in Indigenous relationships around resource maintenance and acquisition. Historian James Daschuk (2013) has outlined how the fur trade on the Plains during the eighteenth century induced some communities to uproot and pursue increasingly distant trapping grounds as local sources were exhausted, especially where disease had created labour shortages among the local Indigenous populations. This was the case, for example, when Anishinaabe communities from the Great Lakes regions moved west into the territories of the Assiniboine in the 1740s (21–22). Historical geographer Daniel Clayton (1999, 70–71) describes a related but later case where trade with British and American ships in the Pacific Northwest changed traditional patterns of hunting sea otters in the late eighteenth and early nineteenth centuries. As trade goods became more desired by the Nuu-chah-nulth and other coastal peoples, the hunting of sea otters changed from being something integrated into traditional patterns of sustainable economic practice to an extractive process, and sea otter populations were almost wiped out. This outcome had subsequent effects on the environment, as species normally preyed upon by sea otters spread out of control, disrupting entire marine ecosystems.

Of course, disruptions to Indigenous lifeways and ecosystems did not bring about their end, although this theory was popular among, and made powerful by, non-Indigenous experts and laymen starting in the eighteenth century. This is the "fatal impacts" thesis, which posits that Indigenous communities were irretrievably polluted by contact with European cultures (Veracini 2010b, 41). This idea is now dismissed as overly simplistic and lacking attention to Indigenous agency and resistance (Fisher 1977), although versions still persist. Further, such an explanation of Indigenous decline in the northern settler bloc is ultimately predicated on Indigenous peoples lacking the capacity to change, adapt, or evolve to new and shifting conditions. Regardless of the terminology in which it is couched, this is fundamentally a racial argument, as it maintains that Indigenous people are incapable of something that is natural to the members of every other society and therefore – in a remarkable demonstration of circular logic – must be inherently doomed to fade into the past as the world changes around them. This argument is an extension of the racialization of Indigenous peoples as weak and therefore unable to survive in a modern – that is, a colonized – world. This racialization has had an enduring impact on the way that settler colonial societies regard Indigenous peoples and construct narratives about colonialism. The powerful, yet never hegemonic, construct of Indigenous peoples as simple beings who could be easily exploited by savvy Europeans became a key narrative in metropole interactions with Indigenous societies, reinforcing paternalistic narratives through fundamental, and often deliberate, misunderstandings of Indigenous peoples' spiritual practices, rituals, and family and other basic social structures (Kupperman 1980, 2000). Clayton (1999) has also described how colonial agents and traders in Nootka Sound on the Pacific Northwest Coast were frequently, by their own admission, so dismissive and dehumanizing toward the Nuu-chah-nulth people whom they encountered that they misunderstood various acts of Indigenous agency during trading. Because the Nuu-chah-nulth engaged in practices of gifting and in political manoeuvring involving exchanges, often putting very different value on items than their European counterparts did, they were frequently able to gain trade advantages over the European traders (90–91, 142–43), who were too entrenched in their own Eurocentric superiority to see Indigenous people as credible merchants and shrewd trading partners. This duality of the colonial construction of Indigenous peoples as simultaneously terrifying and threatening *and* weak and powerless continues to inform settler colonial constructions and perceptions of Indigenous peoples.

Settler Colonial Sovereign Claims and Spatial Reproductions

In the differences between the embodied and perceived realities of the colonial experience, we can point to the origins of the split between metropole and settler colonial logics that would eventually drive the American Revolution and the slow devolution of British power to the Canadian state. This isopolitical shift of sovereignty from an imperial core to a former periphery that had turned into a metropole typifies the settler colonial form (Veracini 2011). This process drastically changed the locus of colonial power on Turtle Island. In this section, I outline key points of settler colonial theory and show how the burgeoning European settlements in North America began to coalesce into a new coherency.

Rather than thinking of settler colonialism as being done by empires and through a smooth outgrowth of the lines of force that project imperial power across space, I align with Veracini and others who have argued that settler colonialism is carried out primarily by settler collectives, which operate either within or beyond the reach of imperial networks of power. Carrying sovereign capacity with itself through space (Veracini 2010b, 59–74), settler collectives can take on many forms and can construct states and other forms of governance as they go, linking into existing systems of property, law, and government as well as creating new ones. But all of these systems are predicated on enacting the total and enduring transfer of land from Indigenous to settler control. Settler colonialism produces particular spaces based on assertions of sovereignty over Indigenous peoples and on the production of "a pervasive colonial mentality" (Barker 2009, 326) that justifies and shapes those spaces and that is shaped by them in return. This is not a process that happened only once and in one place; it is iterative. Caroline Elkins and Susan Pedersen (2005, 3) assert that "settler colonialism cannot be seen as an essentially fleeting stage but must be understood as the persistent defining characteristic, even the condition of possibility, of this new world settler society." Thus settler colonialism is not over, nor is it elsewhere (Veracini 2015).

Settler Sovereignty and Spaces of Exception

Settler colonizers carry their sovereignty with them, and as they transit from core to periphery or between different colonial spaces, they do not see themselves as entering or traversing the sovereign space of Indigenous nations. Rather, settler colonizers derive from the concept of terra nullius the idea and belief that in order to legitimately claim space, they must use their sovereign capacity to 'improve' it and must signal this 'improvement' by transforming it. Settler colonial sovereignty is asserted in a variety of ways, the most important being the application of violence to Indigenous communities. As ethnographer and historian Scott Morgensen (2011) argues, foundational and enduring sovereign assertions by settler states are located in the enactment of violence upon Indigenous communities. This enactment certainly includes state-driven violent practices but also violence by self-organized settler paramilitaries and mobs. Cattle ranchers pushing westward in the United States caused some of the most violent conflicts between Indigenous and settler people (Barta 2014).

Morgensen (2011, 53–54, 60) articulates the link between sovereignty and this trend of violence in terms of philosopher Giorgio Agamben's (1998) concept of homo sacer, derived from Roman law and an underlying component of later European and American assertions of sovereignty. When a person of power or status declares that another person does not have value and places this person outside of natural law – meaning that the person can be killed without penalty – this person is described as homo sacer. The key point here is the exercise of power to suspend natural law and substitute a particular order in its place; this is the enactment of sovereignty. If one has the power to suspend natural law with respect to another person, one can claim to be sovereign. This logic is deeply rooted in the understanding of sovereignty imported with the earliest European settlers, and so Indigenous people – regarded as part of the natural order from the times of earliest sustained contact, an idea that gave rise to the myth of the "ecological Indian" (Kim 2015, 206–7; see also P.J. Deloria 1999) – become the Other who is to be abrogated. Indigenous peoples are collectively rendered homo sacer, and their claims to place are delegitimized along with their humanity.

Transfer of land from Indigenous to settler control is the primary goal of settler assertions of sovereignty. Even insofar as some 'Indian Country' has always been recognized by Euro-American settler societies, this designation has largely served to bolster colonial claims and to identify potential frontiers of future expansion. As historian Allan Greer (2018, 10) argues, "dispossession is really the essence of colonization ... Colonial property formation therefore had a dual thrust: in creating property for colonists and property for [Indigenous people] it effectively defined the boundaries, social and political as well as territorial, dividing colonists from 'Indians.'" Because securing an unquestioned and uncontested land base for an emergent settler polity is central to settler colonization, we can understand settler colonialism as constantly active so long as settler people continue to live and assert sovereignty over Indigenous peoples and lands. However, this sovereignty is not only directed against Indigeneity but also constructed in opposition to metropole imperial sovereignty, distinguishing settler colonial spaces from metropole colonial spaces.

Biological metaphors have proven useful in the literature on settlement for expressing this double differentiation. Recalling the movements of insects founding a new colony, historians and anthropologists have described the settlement of Turtle Island as a "swarming" (Crosby 1978), where huge numbers of settlers, motivated by some sort of collapse or disruption in the imperial core, rush into an area and drastically alter its political ecology to meet their own needs. This metaphor perhaps inspired Veracini (2015) to liken the difference between metropole and settler colonialism to the difference between viruses and bacteria. He argues that either may invade a host organism – or lands, in the colonial case – but whereas a virus seeks to take control of local organisms to its own benefit, bacteria displace local organisms and take their resources. Although a virus may be carried inside a bacterium, the two have distinctly different goals (16–31).

The merits of relative biological metaphors aside, there are two points here that warrant clarification. First, the initial application of settler sovereign capacity is directed toward the erasure of Indigenous presence and the anchoring of settler people in occupied places (see Chapter 2). Settler colonial sovereignty is always violent because it requires the destruction of Indigeneity. This destruction is part of the process of differentiating the emerging settler polity from the metropole. Settler collectives asserted their right to control without interference from 'violent' indigenous Others – a conceptual pre-existing population constructed as threatening, but not often having anything to do with real Indigenous communities – or from paternalistic metropolitan Others (Veracini 2011, 172). All further applications of settler sovereignty are built on this foundation of violent differentiation and displacement: the "structure" of invasion identified by Patrick Wolfe (1999, 163).

The erasure of Indigenous presence by settlers is pervasive and necessary within settler colonialism but is invisible to settlers despite its importance. As discussed below, settler colonialism follows a logic of collapsing difference. This is what Wolfe (1999, 27) calls a "logic of elimination" with respect to Indigenous people, which eventually disciplines Others perceived as competing for sovereign control. As Morgensen (2011, 53) identifies,

> Wolfe has observed in histories of the Americas that a settler colonial "logic of elimination" located Indigenous Americans relationally, yet distinctly from Africans in the transatlantic slave trade or colonised indentured labour, thereby illuminating (as Mark Rifkin [2009] notes) the "peculiar" status of Indigenous peoples within the biopolitics of settler colonialism. Western law is troubled once European subjects are redefined as settlers in relation to the Indigenous peoples, histories, and lands incorporated by white settler nations ... Western law incorporates Indigenous peoples into the settler nation by simultaneously pursuing their elimination.

Attached to the production of people as homo sacer is the production of spaces of exception, which comprise places where people can be put if they are exceptions to the rule of law – that is, exceptions to the rule that life is sacred – or, more sinisterly, places where people can be 'produced' as exceptional. Slave camps are an early and common form of these spaces, the extermination camps of the Second World War are posited by Agamben (1998) as the key exemplar, and Morgensen (2011) argues that Indian reserves and reservations are also definitively spaces of exception. Through deprivation, reserves and reservations are deliberately and structurally made into places of "bare life"[8] by Canadian and American societies, whose material wealth contrasts so sharply with the carefully maintained poverty of reserves and reservations. But this "bare life" applies even more so to the denial of political sovereignty and individual rights by settler colonial nation-states, as it maintains the perceived fundamental division between core and periphery, and thus between 'advanced' Euro-American peoples and Indigenous peoples, despite the change in the actual location of the core from a European kingdom to an emergent settler polity. Soren Larsen (2003, 92–93) notes that the "frontier myth," central to multiple types and methods of colonization, is premised on implied segregation. 'Civilized' spaces – recognizable by the presence of colonial populations and social institutions – are defined in part by the absence or lack of Indigenous presence. Meanwhile, frontier spaces are areas where Indigenous presence is still registered but where it is also confined and spatially restricted as well as politically limited as it is registered.[9] And as literary scholar Mark Rifkin (2014) articulates, to the settler, the frontier becomes a "movable space of exception" that can be projected according to the desires of the settler colonial polity.

Paradoxically, settler societies can and do recognize Indigenous people into invisibility. This is to say that by creating specific places that are seen as part of "Indian Country," settler societies deem the rest of the content to be open – terra nullius – by contrast. For example, the Royal Proclamation of 1763 recognized some Indigenous territories and ostensibly set the terms of respect for Indigenous sovereignty vis-à-vis land purchases west of the Thirteen American Colonies, but it also erased enduring Indigenous claims to the territories claimed by the Thirteen Colonies (Hill 2017, 122–26). The colonial sovereign capacity to erase Indigenous sovereignty conceptually and the willingness to use violence in order to remove people not just *from* particular places but also *to* spaces of exception combine to bridge the understanding and fact of settler sovereignty as rooted in an ever-present founding violence (Veracini 2008).

Affect and Attachment to Place

It is important to remember, as Goenpul Quandamooka feminist scholar Aileen Moreton-Robinson (2015) argues, that colonization is not a strictly rational process and that the rationalization of this process by means of legal and political regimes often followed from on-the-ground decisions that departed from established law and policy for engaging with Indigenous peoples and lands. The processes of asserting sovereignty and creating dehumanizing spaces and narratives are not produced from above but are the articulation of ongoing, messy processes of claiming and asserting belonging, a combination of multiple legal and property claims – what Greer (2018, 95) refers to as "tenure pluralism" – and more intimate and affective senses of ownership. Belonging is something beyond the realm of simple legal status. In this context, it has far more to do with a sense of fundamental rights to particular places and with close personal and social identifications with them. However, although settler people in the northern settler bloc have certainly come to form a wide variety of distinct relationships with the land, many are deeply rooted in distinctly Eurocentric goals and desires. Settler people often remain convinced that the land should – must – be able to yield up more, if only it were properly reconstructed, a holdover from the imagined geographies of the core and periphery that is in accordance with the drive to 'improve' terra nullius in order to claim it for one's own. This conviction generates the perception that settler spaces legitimately *should* replace Indigenous spaces. Both this drive and later affective impulses such as fear and aspiration comprise what Mackey (2016, 7–8) describes as a "structure of feeling" that is fundamental to how settlers locate themselves both in relation to the land and differently from metropolitan forerunners and from dehumanized indigenous Others.

One of the affective drives of settler colonialism is the quest for a sense of worth, value, or specialness. In the settler colonial context, settler people see themselves as special and distinct from their metropole forebears by right of "residency in a special locale" (Veracini 2010b, 55). Intent is important. Indeed, Veracini locates the difference between settlers and sojourners or migrants in the *animus manendi,* or intent to stay, and the *animus revertendi,* or intent to return, which motivate their respective colonial mobilities. A sojourner is not 'at home' in the colonies but intends to return home at some future time or after the accomplishment of certain goals. However, we must be clear that "it is not the intention to return that precludes a colonial predicament; *it is the lack of an intention to stay that rules out a settler colonial one*" (149–50n15, emphasis added).[10] Consequently, belonging – with the intention to stay that it draws from and projects into the future – is a necessary part of the settler colonial structure of feeling.

Whether undertaken by Europeans engaging in early transatlantic migration or by later American-born people moving west as the Plains and Pacific Coast were brought into the sphere of settler colonialism, settlement was often motivated by a desire to escape decline or decay (Veracini 2010b, 101–2). Kupperman (1980, 141) reminds us that many early transatlantic colonizers were surrounded by interlocking discourses of American opportunity and European decadence and decline, with "early English commentators on America" displaying attitudes that showed they "were profoundly unhappy about their own society. They believed that they lived in a country which was undergoing rapid change and that the change was almost always for the worse" (141). One humorous passage from a nineteenth-century travel journal kept by Thomas Fowler (1832, 188) as he toured the Great Lakes region picked up on this sense of metropole malaise in an assessment of gendered labour presented under the heading "Female Industry": "It has often been reported in Britain that the females in America are lazy and actionless, and indeed, I have seen some of them very much so; but, as I observed, these were from Britain or Ireland. The females who have been brought up in this country, are the most active, cleanly, and industrious, that ever I have seen." Here, we see both a clear example of the expectation that the women born in the settlement colonies and labouring in the frontier would be 'better' than their European counterparts – rendered special by dint of "residency in a special locale" (Veracini 2010b, 55) – and a drastic departure from the early fear that 'unhealthful' environments in the colonies would cause dire consequence for those who lived there (Merrens and Terry 1986).

To say that settler colonization on Turtle Island has been an affective process is to point out that it did not develop from a centralized agenda or power; rather, structures like the state and systems of capital represent refined advancements on spaces often originally claimed and created by small groups of settlers in chaotic and, at times, irrational and conflicting ways. Likewise, national myths have grown up out of the stories told by localized settler colonizers to justify their own claims to land and simultaneously disappear, erase, or eliminate Indigenous people from the land and from history. Colonial logics – the internal axioms that underpin settler colonial "common sense" (Rifkin 2013, 2014), which are frequently profoundly illogical – must be understood as emerging from this affective frame and as clearly articulating the contours of affect-driven settler culture and practice. Settler peoples internalize, justify, and articulate colonial logics in a multitude of ways, commensurate with their relative privilege and position within the multiple socioeconomic hierarchies of settler societies.[11] Settler identities are inextricably linked to the production and occupation of settler spaces but also coexist with or cut across many other discourses of identity and belonging, which are, of course, multiple and layered. Nationalism, racism, classism, Eurocentrism, Christianity, and other allegiances and positionalities factor into settler identity constructions. None fully defines or encloses the settler identity, and in fact, each also extends beyond the settler identity in ways that connect settler people with various other societies and classes – including the founding metropole society – and that challenge the coherence of the settler self (Battell Lowman and Barker 2015, 13–19).

The key point here is that affective attachments are often channelled into the production and maintenance of durable mythistories, as Battell Lowman (2014, 143) calls them, around which the diverse settler polity coalesces. Over many generations, settler colonial spaces have become normalized such that, even if the colonial past of Canada or the United States is acknowledged, settler Canadians and Americans are conceptually distanced and insulated from their histories of violent oppression and dispossession. This is an example of the affective phenomena of social "dysconsciousness" (D.M. Johnson 2011, 110), which is not produced simply through a lack of critical awareness but involves a corresponding assertion of what colonizers expect to encounter or see in place. The term "settlement," whether intended to reference colonization and dispossession or heroic tropes of frontier conquest, conjures up images of pastoral landscapes and homesteading families – the romantic ideal of the frontier.

This archetype, the settler nuclear family "in which white woman and white man advance hand-in-hand with white, native-born family in tow, contributing at the same time to a settler society that denies Indigenous presences and a settler economy that has freed itself from its reliance on Indigenous labour" (Cavanagh 2011, 159), has of course rarely, if ever, represented the reality of settlement in practice. Likewise, neither does my use of the term "settlement" identify the simultaneously heroic and banal myth of familial settlement. Rather "settlement" inherently refers to the process of settler colonization via the claiming of land by settler polities or collectives and the direct or indirect removal and exclusion of Indigenous peoples through whatever means are considered acceptable to those settler groups. Consider that Turtle Island has been colonized at various times by large extended family units and communities coming from places like Iceland (Eyford 2016) or by religious sects such as early Mormons (Bonds and Inwood 2016, 725–26) moving into new territories en masse. Whether escaping poverty or looking for a new holy land, these communities of displacement and replacement worked to generate colonial power far greater than a pastoral homesteader could and to apply it in enduring ways even in the absence of a sovereign state. The eventual subsuming of these spaces into the state did not abrogate this settler colonial power, which was instead enhanced by networking it with established settler colonial spaces across the continent. For a contrasting example, consider settlers of Japanese origin in Hawaii, from early plantation workers of the nineteenth century to twentieth-century "picture brides," who have moved as individuals or in small groups, often contributing to oppressive contexts. Despite these fragmented, individualized migrations, several studies have shown that contemporary Japanese settlers – both those descended from earlier arrivals and those more recent arrivals who have joined an established community – do work largely in concert to thwart the sovereign claims of the Kanaka Maoli (Native Hawaiian) population (Fujikane and Okamura 2008; Kauanui 2008; Saranillio 2013).

Chapter 2 examines the dynamics of spatial perception and attachment that help to account for settlement booms related to these large-scale migrations. Here, it is important to understand that there is no pure settler identity or settler colonial polity. The stereotype of the (white) man, woman, and children on a pastoral farmstead is a relative rarity compared to highly masculine and homosocial collectives building railways and other infrastructure, mining and logging, and otherwise setting the stage for mass settlement, with families and larger collectives coalescing around the spaces created by these transformations of the land. These collectives were united around settler colonial usurpation of land, but it must be noted that such settler collectives are never internally homogeneous and often differ greatly in their visions for the settler colonial world. I now turn to an examination of the ways that settler collectives manage their internal differences through familiar projects of dehumanization and settler supremacy.

Population Management and Triangular Relations

Settler colonialism can be characterized by assertions of settler sovereignty in part through the control of "population economy" (Veracini 2010b, 12). Central to this discussion is one of the structures imposed by settler colonialism: a racialized set of triangular relationships that conceptually separates settlers from indigenous Others and exogenous Others (20–28).[12] In this triangle of relationships, settlers are not clearly defined so much as they are differentiated by a perception of 'us' in the settler social imagination and by markers of 'not us' that are assumed to apply to the other two groups. As Veracini notes, settler colonization "produces a tension between sameness and difference" (23), and the dynamics of how people are brought into or excluded from this subjectivity are the concern of Chapters 2 and 3. Indigenous Others, by contrast, are identified as one particular group of concern, a 'problem' to be solved through removal or destruction as peoples, as described above and as so awfully and neatly encapsulated in the twentieth-century settler phrase "the Indian problem." Exogenous Others are 'the rest,' everyone not Indigenous but not officially or socially accepted into the settler society. Historically, "the exogenous Others category" has been defined "primarily by its not belonging to the settler and indigenous collective," and it can include "enslaved peoples," migrant workers who do not intend to stay and have little sovereign capacity, and imperial or metropolitan sojourners who carry some degree of social, class, and race privilege but may still be marked out as different and do not intend to belong in the colony (123n13).[13] The goal of settler colonialism is to empty the relationship of the Others, collapsing all populations into settler racial and class hierarchies (28). With respect to exogenous Others, this undertaking is pursued through a variety of means, including selectively extending official citizenship and visa status, changing or altering ideas of multiculturalism or nationalism to selectively admit some while excluding others, and legally reducing people to things, as has been done repeatedly in Canadian and American societies, such as through the institution of chattel enslavement of transported Africans and their descendants and the internment of Canadians and Americans of Japanese descent or origin during the Second World War. For indigenous Others, this emptying is tantamount to permanently extinguishing Indigenous peoples' cultures of place, claims to sovereignty, and ability to articulate or defend both. It is the elimination of Indigenous people as *peoples* – as integral nations and cultures with claims to belonging in particular places.[14] This elimination accompanies a total transfer of land, both legally and narratively, to settler polities in order to foreclose the land question by eradicating the Indigenous sovereignties. Today, as has been the case since the advent of the European colonization of Turtle Island, the continued existence, the "survivance" (Vizenor 2008), of Indigenous peoples forces the land question, to the ongoing consternation and ire of settler nation-states and their citizens.

Total elimination and transfer are commensurate with a process understood as settler indigenization: the attempt to resolve the ownership of land in favour of the settler polity and to claim its members' unquestioned legal right and legitimate belonging on the land as virtual – if not actual – 'natives' of the territory. This claim to nativism goes hand in hand with the assertion of settler sovereignty in the foundation of a new society. Exogenous Others, to the extent that they help to define the limits of settler colonial space, are crucial to the settler colonial transfer of lands. For example, under "transfer by settler indigenisation" (Veracini 2010b, 46), settler people assume the mantle of the true native population of an area. This manoeuvre, of course, requires an exogenous population that is demonstrably – or perceived to be – antecedent to the settler population in question. An instance in popular culture is the portrayal of conflicts between 'native Americans' – white, American-born New Yorkers – and Irish immigrants in Martin Scorsese's film *Gangs of New York* (2002). Without the influx of exogenous populations against whom settler indigenization was defined, this type of transfer would be untenable. Canadian settlers enacted the exact same nativist pushbacks against perceived exogenous Others, simultaneously barring newcomers from claiming benefits of membership in the settler colonial nation and, due to the hyper-marginalization of these populations, forcing them into exploitative and dangerous labour. This externalization of foreignness was directed at many different populations over time, including the perhaps most well-known example: Chinese immigrants who were severely exploited in building the national railways (E. Lee 2002).

The narratives and political discourses of settler colonialism are always bound up with this drive to permanently displace Indigenous peoples and finalize settler claims. Consider, for example, Quebecois national identity, which is rooted in many of the same processes as Anglo-Canadian and American settlement but recalls a very different history of and connection to Europe through the French Empire rather than the British. Just as early English statesmen were heavily invested in discursively distinguishing their 'benign' approach to colonization from Spanish aggression, much contemporary scholarship is preoccupied with explaining away French colonial impacts as an inevitable clash of cultures in contrast to the more dastardly and vicious British approach (e.g., see Delâge and Warren 2017). Consider also that, as part of claiming an inherent difference from Anglo settlers, there is a longstanding practice in Quebecois communities of claiming a belonging on the land through a 'métis' identity. As scholars such as sociologist Darryl Leroux have examined in detail, Quebec and the wider maritime region of Canada are experiencing a massive upsurge in a particularly pernicious form of settler indigenization, or race shifting, that is a cynical attempt not only to cash in on the limited rights and fiduciary obligations owed to Indigenous people by the Canadian government but also to stake a claim to authenticity that is a direct challenge to the legal coherence of the term "Aboriginal" in the context of the Canadian state (Gaudry and Leroux 2017; Leroux 2018; Vowel and Leroux 2016). It is a deeply affective move to claim a material link to the land via remote or fictitious Indigenous ancestors so that one may solidify belonging and displace Indigenous challenges by *becoming indigenous* and therefore permanently beyond critique. That this indigeneity is claimed largely based on a genealogical fantasy rather than through relationships of belonging and kinship with Indigenous communities and people should not limit our understandings of settler indigenization only to expressions of genealogical legitimacy. The nativist sentiments expressed by Bill the Butcher in *Gangs of New York* would likely resonate well with Cliven Bundy, the Nevada rancher whose rugged individualist family claimed sovereignty over Federal Bureau of Land Management territory in Oregon in 2016 during a dispute over the right of the government to tax private individuals (Bonds and Inwood 2016, 723–28). Without recourse to genealogical fantasies, Bundy still presented a (white) settler assertion of unquestioned naturalization and therefore belonging – which, in Bundy's mind, even trumped the claims of the state itself, much as Indigenous sovereignty does (or should).

It is natural to wonder how settlers can be hyper-aware of Indigenous peoples, constructed in their cultural narratives simultaneously as treacherous threats and "noble savages," and also pursue trajectories of self-indigenization. Here, again, affective responses inform inventive and circuitous colonial logics. Settler colonialism, particularly in Canada and the United States, is premised on a fundamental "non-encounter" (Veracini 2010b, 76–85). This is to say that even as Indigenous people and histories are acknowledged, they are dismissed. Indigenous people may be dismissed as not Native enough because of blood quantum, band or tribal enrolment status, or even the perception that they are too white. Indigenous people who drive vehicles, use cellphones or global positioning systems, or work in technical and professional jobs are portrayed as not authentically Indigenous because they do not meet the rigidly applied expectations of the settler. This can include benign practices such as eating pizza, which has literally been used by Canadian Crown lawyers to attempt to legally disprove the Indigeneity of entire peoples – in the *Delgamuukw* case in 1997, the dietary habits as well as methods of living and earning of ordinary members of the Gitxsan and We'tsuwet'en people were offered as evidence that they were assimilated and thus not Indigenous (Roth 2002, 154–55). The result is that only a small and dwindling number of fragmented and dispossessed individuals (not peoples or collectives) can ever meet settler standards regarding what it means to be Indigenous enough to be respected. Whether Indigenous people are constructed as less civilized, doomed, racially inferior, or otherwise not in need of consideration, the result is the same. This framing of Indigenous people shapes powerful narratives claiming that history started with initial colonial settlement. Historian Victoria Freeman (2010) details this view with respect to the city of Toronto and not only documents a strong tendency across many demographics to proudly construct the city as historyless and therefore full of possibility based on assertions of a break with corrupt or limited past regimes, a ploy typical of settler narratives, but also uncovers a pronounced hostility to suggestions that pre-colonial Indigenous histories have been displaced by settler colonization. This erasure of an Indigenous past is more than historical revisionism and must be understood as contributing to the denial of Indigenous humanity at the root of settler claims to land and belonging, a denial that has facilitated the racialized violence that has driven settler colonial expansion for over five centuries on this continent.

The (Re)production of Settler Societies

Although settler colonization as a practice had already existed for centuries,[15] the settler colonization of Turtle Island, which began as an attempt by competing imperial powers to claim resources, land, and territory, became a runaway genocidal land grab well beyond the control of Europe. That occurred in part because settler colonization, once firmly established, is self-perpetuating, unlike metropole colonization, which relies on the constant assertion of power from the imperial core to the periphery. As the cover illustration for *Settler Colonialism: A Theoretical Overview* (2010), Veracini chose the painting *Wives for the Settlers at Jamestown* (1876) by William Ludwell Sheppard. This painting, representing the moment that Veracini locates as the inception of settler colonialism on this continent, depicts the arrival of white European anglophone women and families, which opened up (sexual) reproductive possibilities for the settler collective. Historian Adele Perry (1995, 33) has similarly argued that the Colony of Vancouver Island on the Pacific Northwest Coast moved from simply a node in networks of imperial power populated disproportionately by single men engaged in trade and resource extraction to a self-perpetuating settlement with the arrival of 'bride ships' in 1862–63. Women – specifically white English-speaking women in the majority of colonial settlements – were "civilizing agents who could quell the disorderly masculine behaviour associated with the frontier" (32–33) both through their ability to produce new ideal settlers and through their assumed responsibility for the domestic realm, where they produced settler colonial spaces.

In constructing a model of settler colonial space, there is the need to deal with the complexity of an assemblage – a series of trends united by practices of state sovereignty and by affective social responses to challenges confronting the imagined geographies of settler domination and control, which are positioned as intersecting "sovereigntyscapes" (Sidaway 2003) and as structures of feeling but which evolve, diversify, and spread rapidly in ways difficult to predict. In Figure 2, I develop a model of how the settler societies that would become Canada and the United States spread from their origins in metropolitan colonial ventures.

Figure 2 is a simplified version of Figure 1 (discussed above), and here two types of imperial nodes – a trading fort and a settlement – have been established, the first overlapping with two Indigenous-controlled territories and the second adjacent to them. Stars represent Indigenous centres of governance. Lines of force connect the settlement to the imperial core. Further, secondary lines of force are projected through the nodes. In this case, something like a trading, military, or diplomatic expedition has ventured forth from a trading post, resulting in the movement of goods to the nearby settlement. A historical example of this configuration would be the relationship between what is currently southern Ontario and upper New York State just prior to the American Revolution. Despite British territorial claims, outside of the scattered forts and settlements, most territory was still practically controlled by Indigenous groups, with the Haudenosaunee playing a key role in the politics and economics of the area, as demonstrated by a famous map created by Guy Johnson for New York governor William Tryon in 1771 (see Figure 3).

In Figure 4, two important developments have occurred. First, new settler colonial infrastructure has been built – in this case, railways and similar transportation infrastructure, which at this stage were still at least partially produced by the imperial core, with lines of force continuing to connect the metropole to the settlement and other nodes. Because such transportation infrastructure allows for the more efficient and reliable movement of people and goods, and for potential effective connections to more distant nodes in the imperial network, the capacity of the nodes to exert force increases and the number of lines of force grow. In the case of the areas of upper New York State and the Niagara region of Ontario, the development of networks of

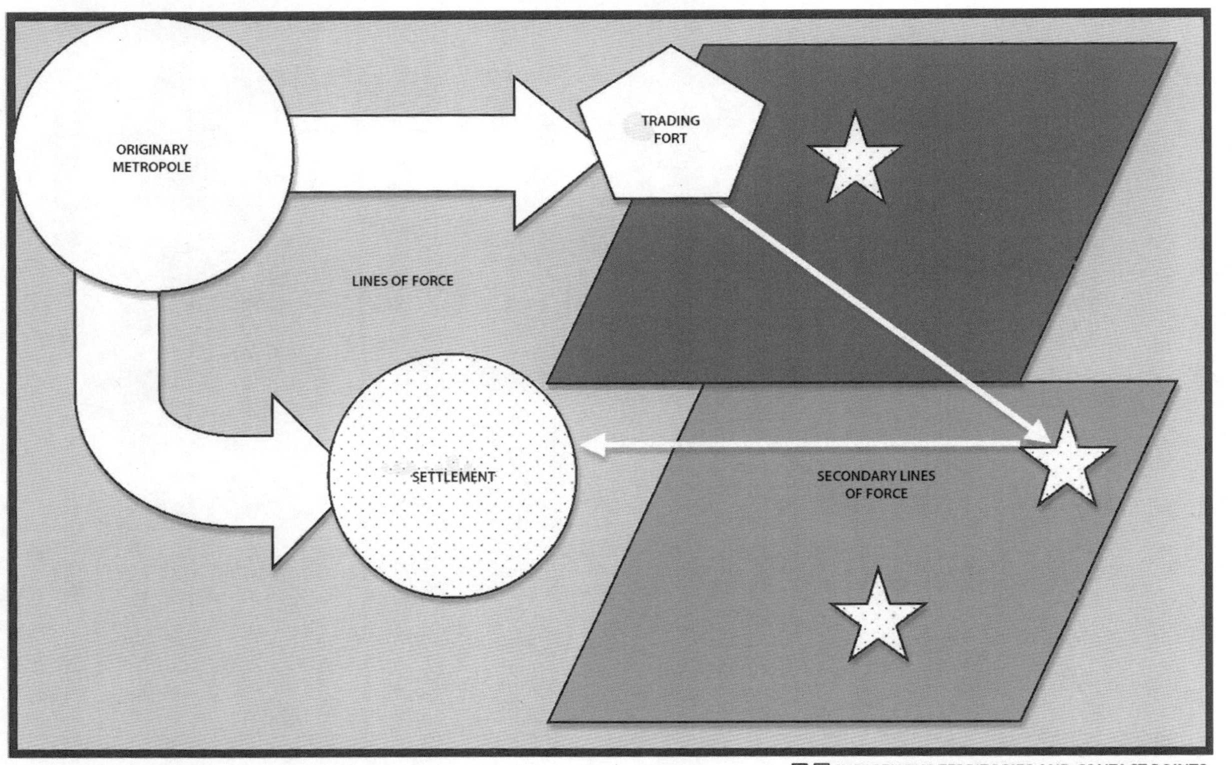

FIGURE 2 Early settlements sustained by imperial networks

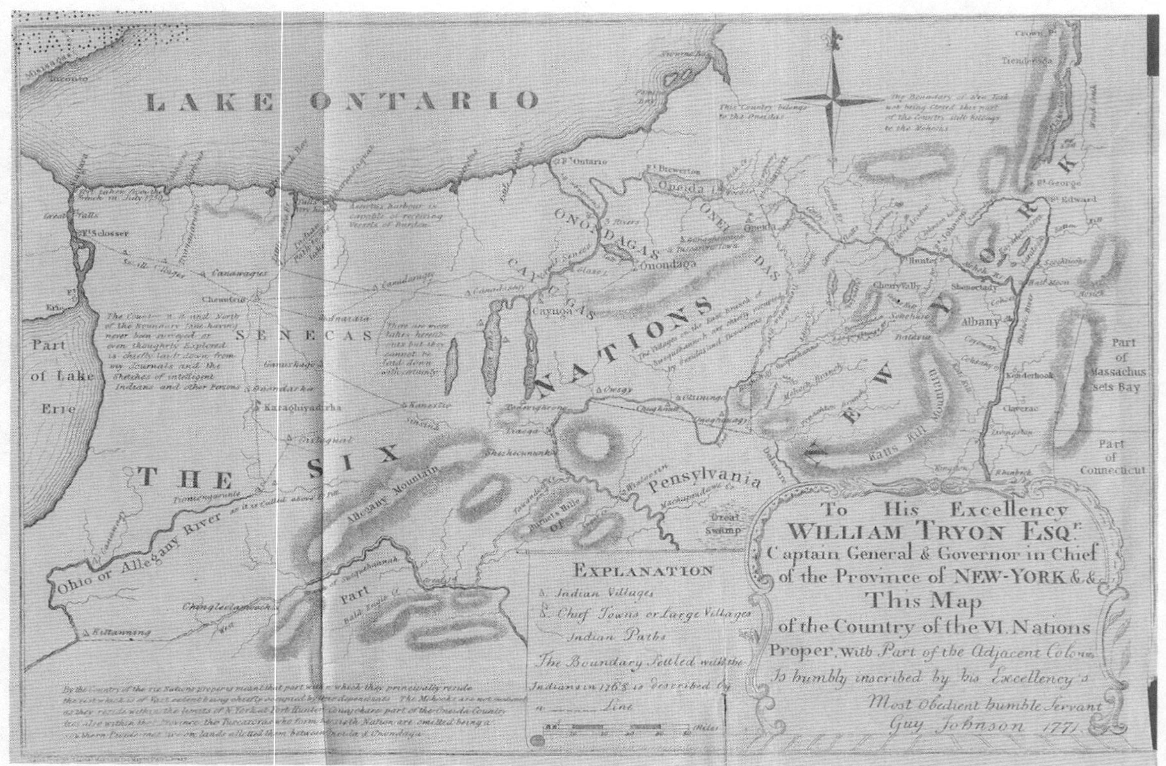

FIGURE 3 Territories of the Haudenosaunee (Six Nations) Confederacy, 1771 | *Source:* Digital version downloaded from Schenectady Digital History Archive (www.schenectadyhistory.org)

roads fundamentally reoriented space. Prior to this change, transportation in this area was largely maritime – both along the shores of the Great Lakes and through the extensive river system of the region. The Haudenosaunee and other Iroquoian people of the area found this mode of transport to be no barrier to mobility; rather, "European observers noted a particular flair for travel among the Iroquois" (Parmenter 2010, ix). The Haudenosaunee and other Indigenous nations frequently shared the technologies that enabled travel around the region, including maps, canoes, trails, and other methods for transporting large amounts of material over the water and woodland terrain, and mobility was both a common feature and a powerful ability of Indigenous people in the area well into the settler colonial period (ix–xi).

However, settler colonizers reshape landscapes away from Indigenous knowledges and technologies and toward their own, promoting colonial mobility while hindering that of Indigenous people. In 1892, there was a centenary celebration for the Province of Upper Canada (now Ontario) at Niagara-on-the-Lake, which is near Niagara Falls and was the first capital of Upper Canada from 1792–97. At that centenary, Lieutenant Governor George Kirkpatrick read a speech purporting to sketch the history of the area and to glorify the first lieutenant governor of Upper Canada, Colonel John Graves Simcoe.[16] In this version of history, the transformation of transportation in the region is recognized as being of key importance:

> Governor Simcoe found this country at that time [1792] covered by a dense and almost impenetrable forest, and he made his journeys from Kingston by water. When he went to Detroit, he had to go through an almost trackless wilderness ...
>
> Let us all endeavour to learn something of the early history of our country and see what our forefathers have done for their posterity. When we think of the progress of Ontario we ought to feel proud. What a change has come over this country. How differently we travel, coming here on those magnificent steamboats or railways. How different means of transit had Simcoe and the members of Parliament whom he invited to give him the benefit of their advice at Niagara in 1792. (*Centennial of the Province of Upper Canada* 1893, 14)

Clearly, the ability to move in ways that corresponded to the contours of imperial and colonial space and time would have been advantages to settlers, but this benefit required a new landscape marked by railways, ports,

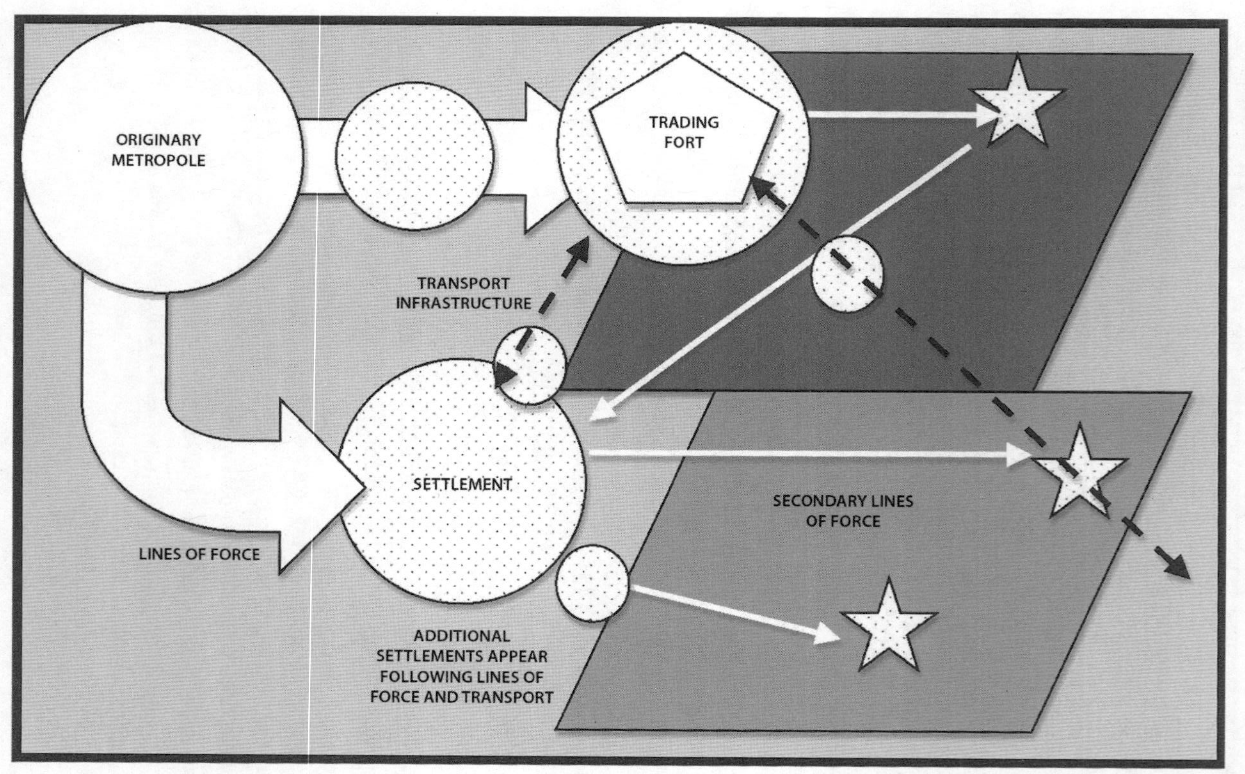

FIGURE 4 Spreading settlement and the development of infrastructure

machinery, and heavy industry, in addition to the appropriation of the existing Indigenous system of trails, roads, and navigable waterways; it is likely, after all, that even Simcoe travelled over land on Indigenous-made routes, regardless of the 1893 myth.

The second important development shown in Figure 4 is the material spread of settlements, which require and tend to cluster around infrastructure built either for the use of settlers or for other purposes that still permit settler access. In Figure 4, settlements have formed irregularly around places that are accessible and that provide an opportunity for private or corporate gain (see Chapter 2). Not only has the metropole-controlled fort become part of a larger settlement – recall Fort Erie in Ontario or Albany in New York as the examples mentioned earlier – but another settlement has also appeared along the transport infrastructure, and a third has developed somewhere along the line of force projected by the core, which was perhaps originally a resupply station or similar infrastructure that has since acquired a permanent population. The major settlement has also expanded into the surrounding territory, as indicated by the smaller circle to the lower right of the larger one. Like the settlement around the fort and the new settlement on the railway line, this expanded settlement now overlaps with Indigenous sovereign territories, putting pressure on local resources and likely prompting outbreaks of frontier violence on Indigenous lands. Continuing in the same region, this process would have corresponded roughly with the first two years of the War of 1812 (1812–15) with respect to the territories that were still British-controlled, and the expansion of American territories would have accelerated, as per the configuration depicted in Figure 5. At this point in the development of settler colonies, something like a settler colonial assemblage emerges. Figure 4 indicates increasingly complex and networked movements of bodies both in support of existing extractive processes such as trading and mining, and in the interests of burgeoning settlements, alongside the beginning of large-scale transformations of landscape in pursuit of settler colonial strategies and goals. It is also important to note that although Indigenous territories are still coherent, there are increasing incursions into these territories corresponding to changing settler understandings of *where* the frontier is located. As a greater number of settlers acquire more local knowledge and extend their tenure in a landscape shaped increasingly to meet the goals and expectations of settler colonizers, the more the consensus grows that land and territory should properly belong to 'us' and indeed already does.

In Figure 5, the settlement colony has now broken away politically from the metropole and has become a settler state. The settler society has taken

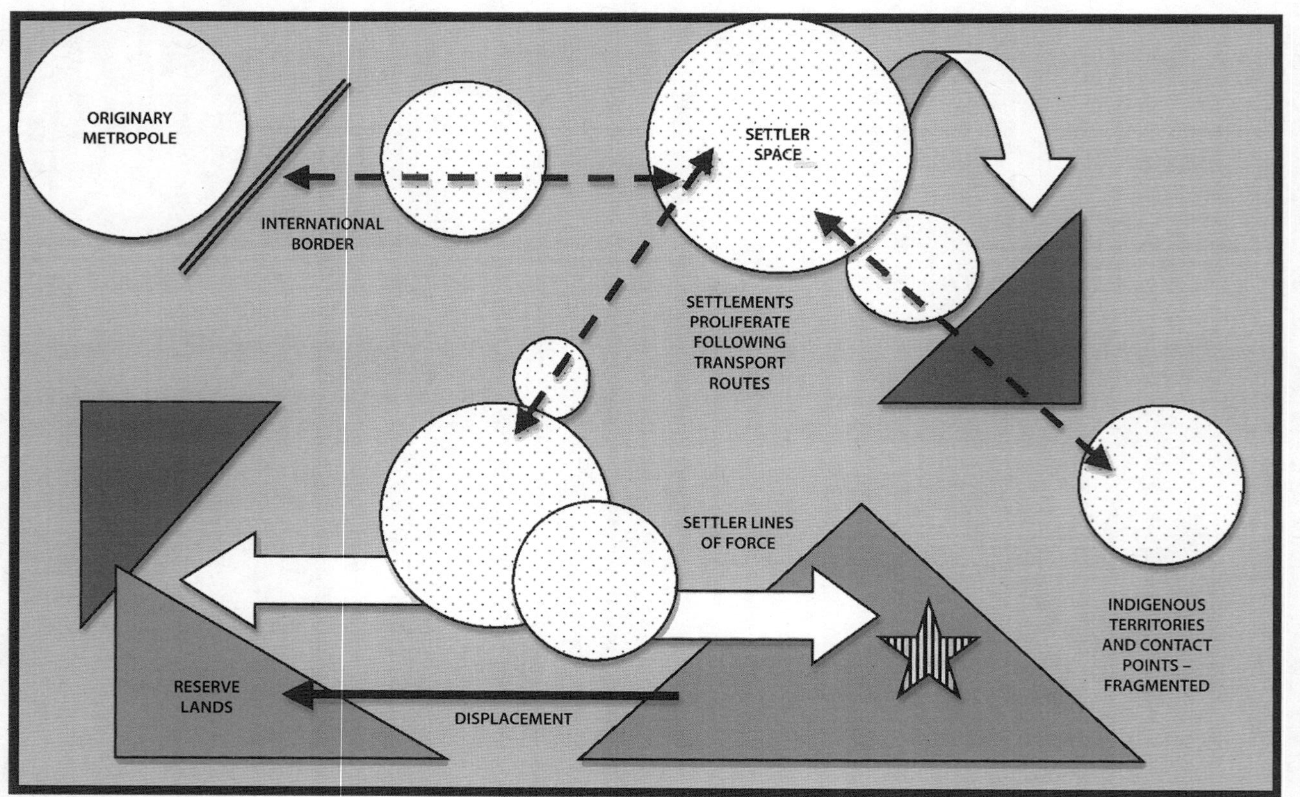

FIGURE 5 Displacement of Indigenous people by settlement and the imposition of new boundaries and barriers

on the mantle of civilized core with respect to an Indigenous periphery. However, the process of settler colonization continues and intensifies, with the state lending increasing weight to efforts to displace Indigenous peoples. This is the situation that faced the Haudenosaunee living along the Grand River in Ontario in the late nineteenth and early twentieth centuries. Mohawk historian Susan Hill (2017, 213) explains that from the 1880s onward, "when the Department of Indian Affairs (formally established as a separate department in 1880) started to interfere in council decisions the department had previously deemed to be the domain of the Confederacy," the Six Nations of the Grand River community faced increasing encroachment from squatters, fraud and legal swindling by the Crown, and divisions imposed on the Haudenosaunee Confederacy by the institution of the Canada-US border. In this example, the erosion of the original Haldimand Grant – the 950,000 acres of territory promised to the Haudenosaunee by the British Crown in 1784, which had been forcibly reduced to 46,000 acres, or 5 percent of its original size, by the mid-twentieth century – is an instance of the fragmentation of Indigenous space. The imposition of private property and thus the technologies of surveying and mapping are both crucial here. Transportation routes included road and rail routes around Lake Ontario but also, perhaps more importantly, the construction of multiple canal systems that allowed for the extension of resource extraction and the industrial movement of materials in the nineteenth and twentieth centuries. The larger and more sustained lines of force in Figure 5 were embodied in the form of police and other government officials who had been empowered to dispense particularly racialized justice, whether against Indigenous people criminalized by legislation or against racialized exogenous Others, consistent with the roots of policing in the capture of people escaping enslavement. Indigenous territories are broken up and sometimes moved; whereas members of the Six Nations community willingly relocated from their homelands in what is currently upper New York State, many of their Cayuga and Oneida relatives were forcibly removed to Wisconsin following the American Revolution. This relocation was undertaken in part because George Washington had burned any Haudenosaunee villages that he could and in part because land in New York State had suddenly become much more valuable, providing impetus for settler Americans to seize territory at an accelerating rate.

Such entangled acts of occupation and settlement, construction and extraction, and imposition of 'law and order' work together to subsume Indigenous spaces and governance structures and to apply assimilatory pressures in an attempt to break up the cultural and political life of Indigenous communities. This process can be seen in the imposition of Indian Act band councils in Canada on Indigenous communities without consultation or consent, as was done notably in the Six Nations community when the Royal Canadian Mounted Police carried out orders to forcibly close the traditional council longhouse in 1924. In the United States, such forced assimilation occurred on a mass scale through a policy of termination from the 1940s–60s, as the federal government summarily decided to delegitimize and dispossess over one hundred Indigenous communities all across the country. This was not always done in one fell swoop; in New York State, for example, Indigenous sovereignty was eroded by multiple pieces of legislation between 1948 and 1950 that extended the jurisdiction of state governments over various aspects of tribal affairs. This approach did not immediately submerge Indigenous sovereignty within the American state, but it raised the waterline significantly.

In the first instance, the Canadian state abrogated traditional governments with the aid of the military and police in favour of limited, disciplined extensions of state bureaucracy. This approach maintained a small fiduciary obligation on the part of the government and allowed some exercise of local autonomy in governance, but it also enabled colonial economic pressure through denial of access to resources – including water (Matsui 2005) – the withholding of rations, and similar types of enforced dependency (Barker and Battell Lowman 2019). In the second instance, the state sought to abrogate fiduciary obligations entirely and to enforce assimilation into the settler society, and thus to pursue both the elimination of indigenous Others and the naturalization of the settler society through claims to 'Indian heritage,' by refusing to extend recognition or resources of any kind to Indigenous communities. Many of these communities had previously established tribal councils during the allotment era of the late 1800s and early 1900s, which were then fatally undermined by this withdrawal of state support (Fixico 1986). Both methods, in conjunction with previous, overlapping, and later policies across the northern settler bloc, from allotment in the United States to the 1969 White Paper in Canada, helped to frustrate opposition to the expansion of settlement into Indigenous territories.

This account, of course, is a simplified description of an undertaking that has varied widely in form and process across space and time. The colonization of the Pacific Northwest in the nineteenth century differed in terms of timeline, on-the-ground politics (especially among Indigenous nations), and the industrialized power and military strength possessed by colonizer empires compared to the colonization not only of the Great Lakes region from the seventeenth to the twentieth centuries but also of many other regions during various periods, and the legacies in terms of how these places have transformed under settler colonial domination consequently differ as well. However, some version of this spatial change, variously weighted depending on availability of resources, presence of particular nodes of power, and wider geopolitics, including warfare, trade deals, and population movements, can be observed across much of Turtle Island. This continuity should not obscure our understanding of the place-based specificity of colonization, but it does allow us to delve more deeply into the logics and spatial perceptions that underpin settler colonialism in the northern bloc, which is my pursuit in the next two chapters.

Ongoing Agonism

In the early seventeenth century, when the famously self-aggrandizing explorer and settler colonizer "Captain John Smith asked Amoroleck, a Manahoac captive ... why his people were hostile to the English ... 'He answered, they heard we were a people come from under the world, to take their world from them'" (Kupperman 2000, 177). This assessment turned out to be remarkably accurate and could just as well be applied to the conduct of generations of later colonizers who equally sought to take and distort the worlds of Indigenous peoples for their own gain. However, although both settlers and metropole colonizers wanted to profit from the new lands, they did so in remarkably different ways.

Metropole colonial contact did not result in either the simple creation of colonial spaces or the replacement of Indigenous spaces. Rather, the networks of power that created and sustained colonial spaces interfaced with place-based Indigenous networks of power, such that each power's networks were changed and affected in both overt and subtle ways. Indigenous peoples were formidable and active adversaries, allies, and "agonistic" Others (Featherstone 2008, 48–49) who both contended and cooperated with early colonists. In some senses, European empires incorporated Indigenous peoples of many political, social, and cultural arrangements into their pre-existing systems of contention and understandings of political space. If chiefs and leaders were seen as kings, so too were the rest of Indigenous societies positioned as subjects or even serfs. Insidiously, the patriarchal societies of Europe refused to perceive or recognize women as leaders (Martin-Hill 2004a, 2004b), a misogynistic stance that continues to impact Indigenous peoples, as is evident in the ongoing genocide of missing and murdered Indigenous women and girls in Canada (National Inquiry into Missing and Murdered Indigenous Women and Girls 2019; Starblanket 2017).[17]

Regardless of European technology, population advantage, and rapidly shrinking and increasingly interconnected global spaces, Indigenous nations largely held the balance of power on Turtle Island throughout the early colonial period. Indigenous nations possessed many advantages over European colonizers, including their place knowledge and access to wider networks of place-based relationships with the more-than-human world (e.g., see Robertson 2016). Indigenous nations knew and understood the terrain of encounters. They practised military strategies and fighting techniques developed to engage such terrains to their best advantage (Benn 1998, 78–80) and intelligently integrated European technologies like rifles (74–75) and horses (Cronon and White 1985, 32–33) into their social and martial systems. In some areas, they grouped together into large political coalitions, confederacies, and collectives – such as Shawnee leader Tecumseh's confederacy of Indigenous peoples opposed to American expansion in the early nineteenth century (Sugden 1999) – all of which made them formidable allies and antagonists. European colonizers ignored Indigenous political power, economic resources, and military advantages at their peril.

The projection of lines of force across space left metropole-dependent colonies vulnerable to both natural and human disruption. Indigenous peoples frequently disrupted colonizing projects, as did storms, fires, and violent interference from competing imperial powers. Colonizers, despite the Euro-American arrogance that pervaded many encounters, were not flawless and could often undermine their own imperial interests, such as in the case of Lieutenant Commander Horace Lascelles, an officer in the British Navy. His violent treatment of Coast Salish peoples around the Salish Sea as the commander of the gunboat *Forward* (c. 1860) turned the press in the nearby colony of Victoria against the colonial governor, James Douglas, and precipitated conflicts that damaged the reputation of the British Navy as an invincible force, ultimately strengthening calls for independence from the Crown (Arnett 1999).[18] Both colonial agents and indigenous Others could at times be unruly and unpredictable, exerting massive influence on fragile networks of power in imperial peripheries. As Cole Harris (1997, 46–47) points out, metropole colonial powers often desired greater control but lacked sufficient disciplined populations and disciplinary structures, as well as sufficient funding – imperial expansion is expensive – to achieve it, or they insisted that colonies be funded by their own labours, limiting how much imperial power could be called upon. Settlement was often encouraged for this reason, regardless of whether or not settlement – which is to say the deployment of settler colonial logics in imperial applications of power – ultimately undermined metropole control.

Veracini (2015) argues that we now live in an age of global settler colonialism where settler colonial logics are relevant almost everywhere and across all societies. If this is the case, that is in no small part because of the promise of liberty, freedom, and equality of economic opportunity that defines the triumphal narratives of both Canadian and American nationalisms. However, even as this narrative is spread around the world, driving North American economic and cultural hegemony, the settler colonial invasion of Turtle Island clearly remains unfinished. Indigenous resistances remain vibrant and multiple, and settler people have not been able to transcend their colonial past, largely because persistent Indigeneity continues to insist upon attention to histories and present-day realities that settlers would prefer forgotten. It is because this struggle continues – a struggle for survival and a struggle to define the basis of social relationships to the land across much of a continent – that it is important to examine and understand the way that settler colonial space is produced, materially and narratively, in landscapes and in identities.

2

Spatialities of Settlement: Remaking Landscapes and Identities

I love my hometown and am unashamedly nostalgic for it. A borough at the eastern end of the city of Hamilton, Stoney Creek, was a place I was happy to grow up in. I had a peaceful and stable childhood in this southern Ontario suburban setting and nearby woodlands, and I enjoyed a great deal of freedom as a youth. My early memories are of my brother and I, and some combination of neighbourhood friends and cousins, chasing each other through the forest behind our house and then spending the afternoon in the old town centre, usually at the comic book store.

Things have changed over the past few decades in Stoney Creek, although slowly and perhaps, most would think, not too drastically. Near the comic book store, in what used to be an oddly shaped parking lot, a small urban park has been built. This park has had a slow evolution. It first sprang up in relatively bare form – just concrete slabs and some benches – when I was a teenager. By the time I was working for the City of Stoney Creek during my summers in my early twenties, large metal trellises around the perimeter and a rocky water feature in the middle had been added. During my years at McMaster University in the early 2000s, some friends and I filmed a scene for a student film that resulted in all of us falling into that small pool in the dead of night. Most recently, sometime after I moved away from Stoney Creek, a bronze statue of a man and a bird were added atop the water feature.

I saw the statue for the first time when I came home for a family visit after I had moved several thousand kilometres away to pursue graduate studies on the West Coast. I was vaguely aware of who the statue represented: a United Empire Loyalist by the name of Augustus Jones, complete with compass. But far more vivid is my memory of sitting in that park in early 2014, having returned home from even farther away – England – under less happy circumstances and with fresh eyes. Suddenly, it felt important to read the historical plaque giving details about Jones's life. It stated that he was a friend of the Six Nations, the Haudenosaunee community on the Grand River whose reserve is the closest one to Stoney Creek, and I recall reading that a Mohawk woman named Sarah Tekarihogen had married him in 1798. Jones also surveyed the grids that would become the property lines of many of the nearby towns and cities, Stoney Creek included. The Six Nations Reserve sits on a fraction of the land promised under the original Haldimand Grant, and I have learned over the years how it was eroded and taken by settler individuals and groups, bit by bit or in larger chunks, and turned into some of the most valuable property in the region. Now, whenever I am back and pass the statue, I am struck with a profound sense of disquiet.

Too Much Geography?

William Lyon Mackenzie King (1874–1950), former prime minister of Canada, is said to have quipped that the country had too much geography and not enough history. In a way – although likely not in the sense intended by King – that is true: Canada, like the United States of America, has too much geography insofar as settler and Indigenous perceptions of space compete for the same places, which cannot coexist because the settler space, premised on the complete displacement of Indigeneity, is totalizing. These efforts at displacement and dismantling are not uncontested, nor are they simple and straightforward. The process has been ongoing for centuries in some places and is still not complete. As a result, a huge amount of history accompanies the transformations of land and productions of space, but these are histories that are premised on erasing Indigenous peoples and nations, along with the violence of settlement. As settler people, we cannot tell our histories wholly and honestly and still avoid the violence and illegitimacy of our societies, so we paper over the gaps that we do not want to see or do not want seen by others. That means that narratives of Canadian and American national cultures and identities are carefully tended mythistories (Battell Lowman 2014, 143) marked more by absence than by presence: the absence of Indigenous sovereignties, the absence of broken treaties, and the absence of genocidal policies and acts of violence. The erasure of these histories is the fulcrum on which space is opened: space for the expansion of settlement and for the movement of settler colonizers through and into imposed terra nullius. Against this falsely blank backdrop, settler people go through a process of identifying opportune spaces and leveraging personal and collective sovereign capacity, along with any privileges granted by existing institutions, in order to transform the world to advantage themselves and their communities.

The amnesiac histories of nation building rely heavily on images of the lone pioneering (white, cisgendered, heterosexual, able, northern European) family clearing a forest or plowing a prairie into farmland – promoted so effectively in my youth by the popular and long-running television series *Little House on the Prairie* (1974–83), based on the also very popular set of nine novels by Laura Ingalls Wilder[1] about her settler childhood and adolescence in the Midwest during the late 1800s. However, settler colonial spatial production is far from a lone endeavour. Because settler colonial spaces are entangled with networks of capital and other quasi-competing hierarchies, it can be difficult to understand the relationship between the messy, embodied realities of life in settler nations and generalized theories of settler colonization. One way of understanding the relationships between embodied settler actions and spatial theories that describe structural and systemic processes of invasion over long periods of time is by critically examining the spatialities that are generated along with these processes.

This chapter outlines the spatial construction of settler colonial regimes in the northern settler bloc, first through the lens of spatiality and then via the processes by which these spaces are produced. The structures, systems, and stories modelled here are the material and narrative manifestations of the settler colonial assemblage in which settler people move and live. This assemblage is discussed here as it is experienced by settler colonizers – that is, as an anticipatory and competitive topography of power.

Anticipatory Geographies and Settler Sovereign Claims

In 1832 Robert Mudie, a Scottish-born journalist and newspaper editor, authored *The Emigrant's Pocket Companion,* a book that gives an exceptional glimpse into the world that newcomer settlers expected to find in British North America and the United States of America in the years following the end of imperial hostilities with the War of 1812 (1812–15). In a time of rapid change, the Americas were seen to be not only a place of potential and opportunity for individual advancement but also a rowdy and undeveloped place, as evidenced by recent American affronts to the British world order. In the preface, Mudie bemoans that the builders of the British Empire are not doing enough to transform the Americas in order to make them more like Europe:

> It would not be amiss that we should, in those regions from which we drive the savages of America, imitate the example of the Romans, when they drove the demi-savages of Europe before them: – they made a road across the country, and when they came to the river, they builded a bridge. We make a map, and write a book; but leave the country as we found it. (vii)

Mudie here is identifying the settler's desire to make the world anew as an 'improved' version of Europe, and the form this improvement would take. Settlers imagined that the land would become different and that they knew best how it should be changed.

The creation and transformation of settler landscapes are partly rooted in what historian Darby Cameron (2010, 9) calls an "anticipatory geography" of colonization: the idea that people, values and norms, and cultural symbols would spread and diffuse through the empire as the metropole established imperial influence on the new continent. Anticipation in this sense should be thought of as affective: the longing for a land that is modelled in part on the metropole yet never quite exists except in the imagination of the settler. These anticipatory geographies are based simultaneously on settler desires and fears, and they reference spaces to come as inevitable. Anticipating a space implies anticipating the actions required to make that space, which can be used to either motivate or discourage action. As geographer Ben Anderson (2010, 793) explains, "anticipatory action functions by (re) making life tensed on the verge of catastrophe in ways that protect, save and care for certain valued lives, and damage, destroy and abandon other lives."

The need to reconcile colonial difference, by which I mean to reshape reality to match the anticipated settler colonial narrative and material landscape, manifests also in a sense of inevitability with respect to settler sovereignty. The inevitable reconstruction of the landscape must accompany an inevitable reconstruction of governance over the land. This imperative can be seen clearly in action in the proceedings of a "special commission to investigate Indian Affairs in the Canadas at the end of the colonial era (1856)," as described by historian Bill Parenteau (2012, 264). The commission's main recommendation was that Indigenous nations, described as bands and tribes, "should at once cede at a fair valuation to the Province, such lands as shall be previously decided not to be necessary for their own use" (quoted,

264). The argument used to justify the recommendation "was that the Native lands should be sold because the state did not have the capacity to control squatting and land speculation, and that the Crown itself could not be trusted to deal equitably with First Nations" (265). Here, the state, having entered into agreements and treaties that – at least from the perspective of Indigenous nations – were partially intended to protect Indigenous lands from appropriation, essentially threw up its hands and said, "But our people want the land, so what can we do?" The problem for those charged with enforcing treaties was that squatters would have to be removed at a cost to the state, that Indigenous communities would have to be compensated at a cost to the state, and that elected officials, who pocketed large amounts of money, would not likely last long in their positions if they took land from settlers while 'giving' land and money to Indigenous communities, as male, white settler Canadians were the only people who could vote.[2]

However, the logic used here was hardly exclusive to the 1856 commission. A common trope held that Indigenous nations must surrender land to the settler state because the state was unable to prevent settlers from illegally occupying Indigenous lands and from then using this occupation to justify their theft. Many histories, such as Mohawk historian Susan Hill's (2017, 168–69, 176–77) account of Haudenosaunee land tenure on the Grand River in what is currently southern Ontario, record settlers squatting on the Haldimand Tract and clearing huge amounts of land, which necessitated both removal and compensation with respect to a territory that the British had deeded to the Six Nations of the Grand River as recompense for their losses and allyship during the American Revolution (1765–83). From the colonial perspective, it would be far easier, and in fact potentially necessary, for the state to follow the demands of the settlers. By the time settler states were established on Turtle Island, masses of settler colonizers were already anticipating their own piece of land – the source of a new, special life – whether within or beyond the boundaries of the state.

Similar examples of this extraterritorial assertion of sovereignty in the form of claims to land can be found across the northern settler bloc. For example, the Mormon settlements in what is currently Utah, taking advantage of a lack of state governance capacity to enforce treaties, engaged in violent attacks on and dispossession of the Utes in the 1850s (Hixson 2013, 128). However, what we see with the recommendation from the 1856 commission in the Province of Upper Canada (now Ontario) is the state using the simple presence of settlers – even unauthorized settlers (or squatters), whom it should have removed in accordance with its own agreements and laws – to justify its claim that the state must exist in settled territories. And neither the state's purported powerlessness against squatter agitation nor the supposed benefits that Indigenous communities would derive from the land sales were "sufficient to warrant the proposed, unprecedented capital expenditure [on compensation for land] by Indian Affairs" (Parenteau 2012, 265). It is clear, on the contrary, that the costs of the land alienation were never seriously considered. The alienation itself was the point, both for the squatters and the commissioners.

Essentially, the state *and* independent settler collectives desired to alienate Indigenous peoples from the land. The only question was how, and this question was answered by the implementation of a government program "designed to replace the piecemeal dispossession of Native lands and its accompanying conflicts with a centralized state dispossession program that would proceed in an orderly fashion. It was simply a rationalization and legalization of a process that had been ongoing for generations" (Parenteau 2012, 265–66). Importantly, efforts like this one, intended to formalize land appropriation and consolidate the territory of the settler state, often appear after the seizure or occupation of lands by settler collectives working beyond the bounds or effective reach of the state. This conduct was often supported both by social narratives and by policy decisions based on the assumption that Indigenous peoples needed the land less than settlers did.[3] Consider another parallel in the allotment process in the United States, whereby the state parcelled out lands according to a census of the Indigenous population in those communities. In most cases, allotment not only resulted in the shrinking of reservations and treaty spaces but also meant that Indigenous communities were assigned lands that were less desirable, less productive, and harder to work than those allocated to incoming settler individuals and groups. This process was wrapped up in the production and promotion of narratives stating that the US government was helping to preserve a 'dying culture' by maintaining reserves and that, by shrinking reserve lands, a desirable outcome could be reached, as Indigenous peoples would be 'encouraged' to assimilate and self-terminate. Settlers saw this outcome as coterminous with social or cultural evolution – the idea that the assumed superiority and inevitability of settler ascendance implied the necessary and natural diminution and disappearance of Indigeneity.

Government commissions and bureaucracies essentially formalized what was already occurring but were required to do so through legal orders and moral frameworks that were flexible, although not endlessly so. In order to reconcile the competing ideas involved in land appropriation – from the honour of the Crown and the rule of law to narratives of terra nullius and improvement as proof of sovereignty – these transfers had to be pursued carefully. Any expenditure by the Crown on land deals, no matter how unfair, was predicated on the need to give the impression that colonial officials were concerned with securing and improving the welfare of Indigenous peoples – although in practice securing territory always trumped humanitarianism. The1856 commission contributed a particular legal and moral justification to the larger "great land rush" (Parenteau 2012) and opening of the Canadian West to settlement, but it was one that clearly hinged on the fallacy that Indigenous people were ultimately served or bettered by colonization. The commission claimed that "the proposed transfer [of title to land] is coincident with the interests of the Indians" (quoted, 264), and it must have been, for how else could the honour of the Crown and the legal basis of the property transfer have been upheld? The fact that transfer is never enacted for the colonized is obvious; however, the imagining of particular kinds of settler colonial geography is important. The social and political narrative of benevolent colonization and its counterpoint in the narrative of Indigenous savagery and deficit, through which value was attached more to some lives and more to some spaces and properties than to others, informed the mass legalization and systematization of the already ongoing dispossession of Indigenous land and destruction of Indigenous peoplehood.

Spaces of the Settler Colonial Assemblage

As the settler colonial assemblage can be understood to produce particular kinds of space, the patterns discussed in this chapter can help to identify relationships between different aspects of the assemblage, between different actors and subjectivities, and between the human and more-than-human worlds. Too often settler colonialism is articulated even by critical scholars as either a monolithic force, especially with reference to the state and its application of violence and power, or as a diffuse cultural tendency without an opposable centre. My goal here is to reveal the dynamic interplay of forces that flow both down from the state to society and up from society to the state and that span beyond the borders of states while also remaining particular and dynamic when viewed at smaller, local scales. Understanding this interplay is absolutely crucial if we are to identify contradictions and places of intervention that have the potential to weaken the broad dependency on colonial violence and dispossession that continues to define the lifeways of most settler people in the northern bloc. We already know the aims of settler colonialism writ large: to displace Indigeneity, destroy Indigenous peoplehood, and bring land under the structuring and dividing gaze of settlement in order to reconstruct it in ways advantageous to settlers while positioning them on the land as legitimate inhabitants and thus legitimately advantaged. Here, I propose a pattern of spatial development by which settler colonial space is produced and asserted against or over Indigenous spaces in a series of 'common-sense' actions taken by settler colonizers to create and occupy particular spaces, a model that I argue is necessary in order to denormalize these banal acts of colonization. These movements and claimings are individually defensible, especially in contexts where settler colonizers are recruited into their roles while attempting to escape other forms of oppression, but in sequence they are revealed to assert both materially and socially the very bases of settler colonization. These spatial constructions may be expressed differently across the continent and across time, based on local conditions, cultural values, and specific entanglements of power, but as with the patterns established in the previous chapter, they remain broadly consistent over large spaces and time spans as they shape settler colonial perceptions of opportunity and possibility at the individual and communal levels. There are many versions of this story of settler success, but the core narrative often holds true. The remarkably consistent dynamics of spatial production and consumption occur roughly in the order shown in Figure 6.

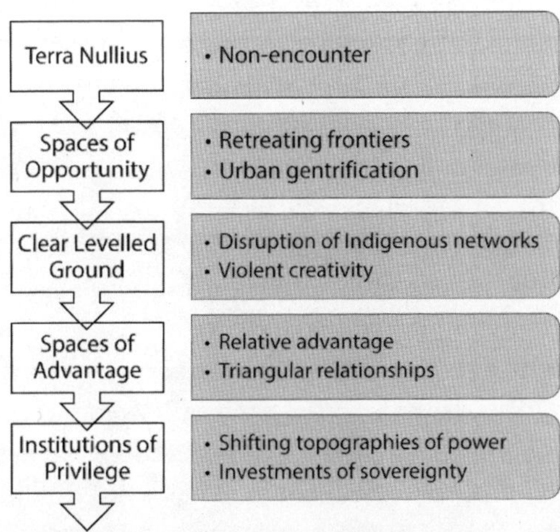

FIGURE 6 Development of settler colonial spatialities

Spaces of Opportunity and the Retreating Frontier

As an immigrant in England, I occasionally become wistful for familiar scenes, voices, and stories from home, and this longing can have a surprisingly strong influence on my choices of entertainment. That was how I found myself struck by something in the pilot episode of the Netflix series *Frontier* (2016–18), a deeply fictionalized story of the struggle over the fur trade in the Canadian Northwest co-created by Rob Blackie and Peter Blackie. In the show, Grace Emberly (Zoe Boyle) is a quick-witted 1700s tavern owner at an isolated fur trading post in Rupert's Land, a vast territory granted to the Hudson's Bay Company (HBC) under a royal charter from King Charles II in 1670, and the area served by the post is portrayed as inherently violent and beyond the law. For example, the pilot opens with the murder of British soldiers by Declan Harp (Jason Momoa), a half-Irish, half-Cree independent fur trader who formerly worked for the HBC. When Harp's actions threaten the profits of the company, Lord Benton (Alun Armstrong) sets sail on behalf of the HBC leadership with a large contingent of soldiers to bring Harp to heel. Upon hearing a rumour about the arrival of this force, Grace Emberly has but one word to describe what it means: "opportunity." For me, a staggering amount of settler colonial baggage landed heavily with that one word.

The frontier is a space that is inextricable from histories of settler colonialism in North America, and as American historian Fredrick Jackson Turner's "frontier thesis" famously asserted, American democracy was shaped by the effort to tame the frontier. Frontiers, although violent and lawless, are also portrayed as spaces where settlers can become what they are destined to be – or die trying. The television series *Frontier* powerfully encapsulates this duality of threat and promise that underpins so many spaces of settlement. Frontier spaces are beyond the clear control of a colonial authority but are revealed to colonial desire by virtue of being in contact with imperial networks or being visible/legible to colonizing authorities. They are perceived both as threatening spaces and as raw spaces that can be reconfigured to great profit and benefit by enterprising settlers – especially those backed by large state or corporate powers that have an interest in restructuring a given territory by networking with larger, existing systems of power. Mark Rifkin (2014) calls the frontier a movable space of exception that is not only considered to be within the grasp of settler sovereignty – that is to say, anticipated as properly belonging to settlers and destined for eventual settlement – but is also regarded as free from the structuring forces of the state. However, frontiers themselves are liminal spaces between 'civilization' and 'wilderness,' and the movements of these frontier spaces correspond to settler perceptions of opportunity in particular frontier spaces given the presence (or absence) of other material elements. These spaces of opportunity become the beginning point of settler colonial imagined geographies that contain settlers, meaning people deemed to belong in those spaces according to the biases of the originating polity. The spaces of opportunity perceived in the 'empty'/'emptied' landscapes that settler collectives move through or hear about in literature, news reports, and travel journals draw people to settle in particular places not for their actual content but for what settler colonizers expect to find, including wealth, privilege, utopia, or some other purported benefit.

Spaces of opportunity must be considered in the context of burgeoning settler populations that often emphasize narratives of their own impoverished or stagnant social opportunities. Hearkening back to the sense of a corrupt or fallen metropolitan core that motivated settler colonizers to leave their homelands for an imagined periphery, large numbers of 'rejects' – those individuals and communities occupying marginalized spaces and lower levels of hierarchy – undertook settler colonization. Examples from European backgrounds include Puritans, who renounced their own society as corrupt (Meuwese 2011); oppressed Christian minorities, such as Quakers and both Catholic and Protestant Irish (Ireland 2012); Doukhobors and other European ethnic communities marginalized within nation-states; Irish, Ukrainian, and other already colonized or oppressed European populations pressured by induced famine and poverty; and class-based economic migrants, the poor and destitute. Later, some of these persecuted groups in turn persecuted others and expelled them from settler colonial spaces, as happened with the expulsion of arriving Quakers from Boston by Congregationalist New Englanders (Pestana 1983); this is an early example of how settler colonial opportunity adheres to a retreating frontier as opportunities are seized and occupied by settler collectives. Spaces of opportunity later reappear in abandoned or impoverished urban areas, such as the "new urban frontier" of the "revanchist" gentrifying city (N. Smith 1996).

The value placed on particular opportunities or resources might be structurally dependent on local conditions, including not just the availability of a resource but also the ability to extract, transport, and trade it. Such was the case, for instance, with cattle ranching, one of the common occupations that brought settlers westward across the centre of the continent throughout the nineteenth century and into the twentieth. John Thistle (2011, 420) discusses how settler colonizers who relocated to the West with the intention of cattle ranching, despite not knowing much about the actual physical environment, quickly identified particular places as opportune based on their physical characteristics: lowlands with light, infrequent snowfall and warm winter winds that allowed for year-round grazing. However, Indigenous communities from many nations were already using these same places as winter herding grounds for horses, a key component of the Indigenous economies of the area, and they had long tended these places through complex systems of environmental maintenance, including seasonal burns. As Thistle discusses, settler ranchers demonized these horse herds, blaming them for all sorts of environmental disruptions, and denigrated their owners, who were, predictably, portrayed as savages without rights to the lands desired by settler newcomers. That these spaces of perceived opportunity conflicted with ongoing and evolving Indigenous uses was not allowed to frustrate opportunistic settler plans.

In the present, settler Canadians in Vancouver have recognized opportunity for material gain through gentrification of the city's Downtown Eastside neighbourhood, a place long perceived as wild, uncontrolled, and filled with violence, drug use, and – of course – dangerous Indigenous people (Dean 2010, 2015). Settler colonial recognition of opportunity for profitable gentrification of the Downtown Eastside was made possible in part by the massive flows of capital into Vancouver prior to the 2010 Winter Olympics (O'Bonsawin 2010), but the narrative construction of this neighbourhood as a space of opportunity links to much broader settler colonial narratives: "The Downtown Eastside is frequently cast ... as a 'mythical frontier' that is 'wild, dangerous, and, ultimately, [an] empty space, ripe for (re)settlement' ... The repetition or recycling of language and metaphor evident here indicates that colonization is not a finished, settled, or past project, but instead is ongoing and continually remade in the present" (Dean 2010, 118, citing Sommers and Blomley 2002, 45). The consistent pattern, from the early English settlers on the Atlantic Coast to the multiethnic contemporary gentrifiers of the Pacific Northwest, is that settler peoples recognize in particular places the potential for the exploitation, extraction, or generation of wealth. This recognition includes the implicit assumption that Indigenous peoples cannot legitimately benefit from these spaces of opportunity; it is settlers who 'improve' the land, thereby justifying their ownership and exploitation. Of course, any similar improvement by Indigenous peoples, whether by building houses or farms in a European-inspired fashion or by using tools imported from colonial societies, is taken as evidence of Indigenous inauthenticity because, in the minds of the settlers, indigenous Others are synonymous with landscape and incapable of learning, developing, or adapting.

Clear Levelled Ground

Opportunity is not an end point but an opening – a perception that a particular place, if made profitable and useful, could become a "special locale" (Veracini 2010b, 55). The amount of effort required, however, is contextual. Would an early settler prefer an ideally situated but heavily forested plot of land for farming or a plot more distant from roads and markets but clear of cover and easy to work? Would a contemporary settler speculating on real estate prefer a property with an existing structure that might be demolished to build a newer, bigger structure or an empty lot ready for development? Insofar as settler colonization "destroys to replace" (Wolfe 2006, 388), I posit here that the goal of destruction is to create clear levelled ground: a flexible conceptualization of the ideal environment in which to settle and seize place-based opportunities. As a metaphor, this idea derives from the archetype of the ideal site for a frontier homestead: ground that is clear of barriers such as trees, stumps, and rocks or obstacles such as hills, making for the easy construction of houses and the rapid establishment of commercial agriculture.

A short 1833 emigré's guide to choosing between Canada and the United States makes assertions about the climate of the northern part of Turtle Island and offers curious speculations about how clearing the land might affect it:

> The latitude of Canada corresponds with that of the most fruitful regions of Europe and Asia. At present it is subject to a degree of cold not felt in those regions; but we know by experience that the climate is becoming milder as the country is cleared and the forests disappear; and it would be difficult to give any solid reason why the climate of Canada should not gradually assume something like the mildness of the old parts under the same parallel of latitude. (*United States or Canada?* 1833, 7)

The author goes on to make many unfavourable comparisons of Canada in relation to the United States, but the interesting point is the direct connection between the idea of the land being cleared of obstacles and the generation of a wider providential environment. It bears noting here that obstacles are more than material, as Indigenous sovereignties must also be cleared. Further, as a metaphor, the idea of clear levelled ground applies to any situation where settler individuals and collectives perceive an especial right or providential benefit in a place that motivates the decision to invest their sovereign capacity in a place and settle, thereby initiating a process that transforms the land to meet the expectations and aspirations of a settler polity to come. Clear levelled ground is a transitional, affective space created in the moments when settler collectives, in pursuit of perceived opportunity, begin to assert belonging by transforming the land.

Clear levelled ground is frequently perceived in spaces disrupted by colonial impact on and interface and interference with Indigenous networks. Historical examples speak to this dynamic, including historian Richard White's (2011) "middle ground" of the Pays d'en Haut, which began to disappear following the American Revolution when American settlers, freed of the restrictions of the Royal Proclamation of 1763, began to flock to the southern Great Lakes and Mississippi regions[4] – or, if wealthy enough, to speculate wildly on land sales, a tradition that includes luminaries of American mythistory no less than George Washington, as well as other land-hungry Founding Fathers of the United States. Historian Rob Harper (2018) has argued that individual and small groups of settlers in the Ohio Valley during this period actually found ways to cooperate and coexist with Indigenous communities, but aggressive settlers, either backed by government policy and power or accessing resources of the state indirectly, were able to violently fracture Indigenous political power in the region in ways that the previous century of mass disruption had not. Although this area had been characterized by social and cultural hybridity and shifting political alliances, once settlers could "swarm" (Crosby 1978) into the territory unchecked by any European or American authority and once colonial sovereignty could displace Indigenous claims based on occupation and possession, the ongoing disruptions to Indigenous nationhood due to war and disease were perversely read as an absence of Indigenous claims.[5] In essence, the clearing began before the perception of spaces of opportunity, which required the removal or abatement of the Royal Proclamation.

Similar dynamics can be observed all across the northern settler bloc. For example, during the British fur trade monopoly of the eighteenth century (Daschuk 2013), the Northwest was disrupted by increasing numbers of settler fur traders who preceded military intervention and settlement. As a result, the Métis and Cree communities in what is currently southern Manitoba and Saskatchewan became heavily reliant on the fur trade economy in the nineteenth century. This reliance meant that Indigenous communities needed to exert their own governance over territory for the purposes of maintaining and regulating the fur trade, a necessity that led to their involvement in resistance struggles like the Red River Rebellion (1869–70) and the North-West Rebellion (1885), the latter of which drew Cree chief Poundmaker (Pîhtokahanapiwiyin) into armed conflict with the Canadian military (McCoy 2009, 182; Stanley 1949). The influx of traders and alcohol was accompanied by increases in violent competition for dwindling furs. Given that this conflict both challenged Canadian sovereignty and frustrated plans to 'open' the West to settlement, the nascent government under Canada's first prime minister, John A. Macdonald, formed the North-West Mounted Police to capture or kill the Métis leaders and assert Canadian sovereignty in place of Indigenous sovereignties. Another example of the dynamics of clearing can be seen in the Grand River area of Ontario with the relocation of the Haudenosaunee Confederacy, which functioned as a regional government parallel to the settler government until the forced displacement of the confederacy chiefs in the early 1920s by the Royal Canadian Mounted Police – the successors to the North-West Mounted Police – who have maintained their track record of violence and racism toward Indigenous communities (Hill 2017, 234–36; Monture 2014, 114–32). Consider also the hybrid Seminole culture that was created prior to the American Civil War (1861–65) from the combination of Indigenous and Black communities and individuals in what would become Florida, only to be displaced following the Seminole Wars (1816–58) and the clearing of the Everglades that accompanied and followed them (Mulroy 2007).

Of course, the seizing of the opportunities presented by the disruption of Indigenous societies is always chalked up to settler colonial ingenuity and efforts to transform 'waste land' – literally land deemed to be wasted since it is not put to productive use, as per terra nullius – into productive property. Settlers consistently associate the production of clear levelled ground with virtuous pioneering ethics rather than with illegitimate seizure and occupation of Indigenous lands. The violence of the pastoral frontier is often forgotten or romanticized away, as are the later displacements of Indigenous peoples that occurred as more and more settlers perceived opportunities on the edges of settlements, leading colonial settlements to devour more and more land. Seizing these opportunities has often involved destroying ecosystems that sustained Indigenous economies, such as the draining of swamps and wetlands in places like Florida, the Carolinas, and Louisiana, undertakings that are among the many examples of how enforced environmental change displaces Indigeneity as a side effect of development.

The destruction or restriction of access to Indigenous peoples' sacred sites is also a common tactic, especially through intentional flooding, such as in the creation of hydroelectric dams, from those on the Colorado River that have interrupted Hopi rituals to those across Canada that hide settler environmental violence behind the discourse of green power.[6] These same dams draw populations into frontier areas to construct and maintain them, while empowering engines of industrial modernity that in turn contribute to the consumption and disruption of Indigenous place-based networks across the continent (and world). Almost forty years ago, geographer Hugh Brody (1981) predicted exactly this sort of thing in relation to the complex of potential sites for hydroelectric dams and for the extraction of oil, gas, and similar resources in northern British Columbia and Alberta. Given the development of tar sands, fracking operations, and pipeline construction throughout northern Alberta and British Columbia (Preston 2017) and the existence of projects like the highly controversial and contested Site C Dam development in the Peace River region of northeastern British Columbia (Cox 2018), Brody's (1981) perception of a new energy frontier has proven especially prescient.

The assertion of spaces of clear levelled ground by settler colonial collectives serves as a strong claim to place: the declaration that a place is not, in fact, filled with meaning but is instead property waiting to be improved through transformation so that it may be used for habitation or repurposed for sale. This claim generates property out of nothingness and is the first real 'profit' of settler colonization; it is primitive accumulation in some senses (Coulthard 2014) but also a "violent creativity" (Walker 2011, 398–401) that produces a new, hegemonic space where before there were many overlapping, networked Indigenous spaces.

Spaces of (Relative) Advantage

Once settler collectives identify an opportunity in a given place and transform space to clear the way for its occupation and exploitation, spaces of (relative) advantage are created. I say "relative" because the opportunities for personal and collective advancement are almost always premised on gaining and asserting power over someone else – including Indigenous peoples, exogenous Others, and even other competing settler people and collectives. These advantages often appear in the context of a social "pyramid of petty tyrants," a hierarchy based on complex calculations of class and race, where authority over Others takes the place of immediate material advantage (Barker 2009, 327, 346–47; see also Memmi 1965). Moreover, these spaces are predicated upon the imposition of the triangular relationships of settler colonialism, which both differentiate settlers from indigenous Others and exogenous Others and lead to Indigenous erasure. After advantage is claimed in place, Indigenous peoples are increasingly constructed as stuck in the past and unwilling to 'progress' and are thus deemed to be intolerable challenges to the transfer of land, which is where the material advantages of wealth and property and the immaterial advantages of political sovereignty and collective identity rooted in place are founded. Advantage is conceptualized as resulting from individual labour and hard work, cultural superiority, religious piety, and/or technological innovation and sophistication. Fundamentally, however, settler colonial advantage is dependent on dispossession, especially of Indigenous peoples, and on the redirection of the resources and land base of those peoples. Everything else, from cultural expression to industrial development, follows from and remains rooted in this dispossession and invested in expanding it.

Spaces of advantage are clearly linked to the concept of living in a "special locale" (Veracini 2010b, 55), which in turn is connected to territorialized identities at several scales, including the local, regional, and national. These collective identities, reliant on common tropes and invested in similar or interconnected spaces and material places, obscure the hierarchical relationships between settler individuals or collectives beneath a common commitment to upholding tropes of settler belonging and Indigenous absence or disappearance. This commitment can be seen to create a kind of "resonance machine" (Connolly 2005) that encourages the construction of the kinds of spaces most acceptable to understandings of the particular roles and positions of the elite and the populace, as well as the roles and positions of problematic "agonistic" Others (Featherstone 2008, 48–49), especially Indigenous people, who by and large are collectively excluded from the settler colonial assemblage or individually assimilated by it.

Spaces of advantage are places where collective identities that cut across all kinds of differences in settler colonial societies are initially developed, including national identities. But these spaces should not be conflated with spaces of the nation (much less the nation-state). As discussed, settler colonizers often begin seizing and building settler colonial spaces in advance of state institutions or effective control, and smaller, regional identities are most often grafted onto larger-scale identities rather than consumed by them as nation and state coalesce. How this process plays out can be seen with gold rushes, such as in the Black Hills area of present-day South Dakota and Wyoming in 1876–77 and along the Fraser and Thompson Rivers in the interior of British Columbia in 1857–60. Both areas were strongholds of Indigenous sovereignty. The Black Hills fell inside the territory of the second Fort Laramie Treaty, signed in 1868, in which the victorious Lakota and their allies were recognized as sovereign, and the South Central Interior of what is currently British Columbia remained relatively inaccessible to settlement before the gold rush due to complexities of terrain and distance that reduced the profitability and security (or perceived advantage) of settler labour or industry. At that time, these regions were in fact officially unceded territory claimed by neither the United States nor Britain, licensed to fur trading corporations such as the HBC and the North West Company (NWC).[7] However, both areas saw sudden, huge influxes of sojourner miners and traders, settlers, and officials when gold was discovered and newspapers with vast distribution spread the news around the world (Storey 2017). Populations exploded in nearby official colonies, like the Colony of Vancouver Island and the squatter settlement of Deadwood (discussed below), and settlement camps and mining boomtowns multiplied throughout both regions.

Alongside these massive population movements came assertions of sovereignty – with miners often organizing militias and local governance – and the hardening of identities. Miners rushing north from the exhausted California goldfields brought their regional identities and practices with them, including virulent and extremely violent anti-Indigenousness, and when present in overwhelming numbers, as with the Fraser Canyon gold rush, they posed a particular problem for the British Crown. American miners' self-organization suggested a move to assert and extend American independence in a territory that the British viewed as very much within their sphere of influence (Marshall 2018). In 1858, Britain created the mainland Colony of British Columbia, which covered about half the territory of the present-day province, both to normalize its jurisdiction of this increasingly desirable region contra American claims and to ensure that the Hudson's Bay Company did not successfully lay its own claim to the gold deposits. It did so without signing treaties with Indigenous peoples and annexed huge swaths of Indigenous lands contrary to British law. The American state did something similar in 1864 when it broke its own laws by allowing Army commander George Armstrong Custer and his troops to enter Lakota territory without permission, violating the first Fort Laramie Treaty, signed in 1851. It is not often mentioned that when Custer and the 7th Cavalry were wiped out at the Little Big Horn during the Great Sioux War (1876–77), their expedition was in violation of both Lakota sovereignty and American law, as the treaty with the Lakota had been ratified by the Senate, putting it on a standing equivalent to that of a constitutional amendment. This expedition also brought the first reports of gold in the Black Hills to the American public, setting the stage for overwhelming invasion and consequent dissolution of the sovereign Lakota territory (Dunbar-Ortiz 2014, 188–92). Here we see yet another example of independent squatters preceding the sovereign state, being used to create a justification for state expansion, and then retroactively absorbed into it. British Columbia, South Dakota, Wyoming, and several other official territories were created as state jurisdictions only because settler colonial sovereignty beyond the state had previously been asserted in order to turn a potential opportunity on the frontier into a settler collective advantage by converting labour and local knowledge into wealth.

In some ways, contemporary fracking and pipeline construction in Alberta, Nebraska, and surrounding areas connected to the Athabaska Basin (the centre of northwestern oil extraction) follow the same pattern. Labour-intensive but high-paying jobs attract thousands of tradespeople from across the continent to an area that is partly governed by corporate fiat (Preston 2013), recalling the sovereignty frequently exercised in these areas by corporations such as the Hudson's Bay Company two centuries earlier (Cavanagh 2009). These are but a few examples of settler people carving out spaces of advantage that are quickly networked into the larger settler colonial assemblage. Finally, and very crucially, these territorializations also inform the implied, embodied, performed norms of settler society. In time, these norms become the institutions of power and privilege that dominate the social landscape of the continent.

Institutions of Privilege

Once settlers perceive a particularly useful patch of clear levelled ground – a space where Indigenous sovereignties have been fractured or displaced, often by targeting and bodily harming Indigenous people – settlers join or begin expanding collectives that transform the physical and social landscapes around and across these spaces in ways that generate particular personal and communal advantages. These claimed advantages often resonate with the advantages being generated by other settler collectives, both nearby and distant, which are linked through imperial and colonial networks and, increasingly, through state structures and flows of capital. As these resonant structures of advantage become aggregated, they normalize and stratify the spoils of settler colonial invasion in the form of powerful social institutions and national structures with which various settler individuals and groups come to identify. These institutions, then, make up the superstructure of settler colonial privilege.

Such institutions vary widely in form and function, depending on local histories and environments and on the desires of settler collectives to guarantee, perpetuate, and justify privilege. These institutions also change over time as sovereign capacity shifts between institutions and as settler colonial polities change in character. Institutions of privilege may therefore be paradoxically seen both as an impediment to settler colonial freedom and as a guarantee of established advantage, depending on the configuration of a specific settler polity.

There are innumerable examples of this settler colonial production of space and power, but one popular dramatization of historical settlement is particularly demonstrative: the HBO television series *Deadwood* (2004–06).[8] Created by David Milch, it focuses on the unincorporated town of Deadwood, founded in the Black Hills as part of the gold rush. Although a fictionalized portrayal, it is based on real events surrounding the founding of the town sometime in the early 1870s following the American violation of the second Fort Laramie Treaty with the Lakota. As the town of Deadwood, located outside the borders of the United States, pursues annexation by the state through absorption into its legal system of property and rights, the characters repeatedly and ironically note that soon the town will have "law and every other damn thing." The residents of the town have invested their own personal sovereignty both in the institutions of the town, including deeds to properties that are not in any way backed by a state, and in its authorities, like saloon owner Ellis Alfred ("Al") Swearengen (Ian McShane), a notoriously devious and well-connected pimp, criminal, and businessman who controls the economic life of the town. Law, in this case, is seen as a threat to the liberty of the town's residents, not all of whom identify as American in an explicitly multiethnic settler collective that has created a clear levelled ground outside of the boundaries of the American state. When a massive mining conglomerate encroaches upon the town, seeking to replace independent miners and businesspeople with the exploited labour of Cornish migrants, the town pursues incorporation into the legal and political landscape of the United States in order to guarantee at least some of the privileges that its residents have generated through their collective investment of sovereignty in Deadwood. The settlers make the choice to collectively invest their sovereignty in the institutions of the nation and the state at the expense of the institutions of the town and the community because the former are able to defend some privileges against the encroachment of other (often newcomer) settlers and capitalists, whereas the latter are not.

Institutions of privilege grow up at the intersections of the structures of governance, systems of social production, and stories about settler superiority, which are the primary building blocks of settler colonization. As products of the settler colonial assemblage, these institutions interlock, interact, and change over time, occasionally even standing in opposition to each other as crosscutting trajectories within the assemblage itself inform the production of very different types of institutions. The interpenetration of these institutions forms a dynamic and shifting vertical topography of power (Ferguson 2004; Ferguson and Gupta 2002, 983–84). We must understand the settler civil society that mediates between individual and state as a constantly negotiated collectivity, wherein various institutions rise and fall depending on their ability to organize people and produce space. As an example, the Catholic Church was much more powerful in organizing the lives of settler people in the early twentieth century than it is today, but the decline of power and influence held by this church in the northern bloc of settler colonialism can hardly be read as a sign of decolonization. Rather, competing currents of dominance within settler colonial hierarchies can coexist since the competition as a whole is premised on Indigenous dispossession.

Colonizing Acts

All of the different kinds of settler colonial spaces described thus far are diverse and mutable. They also exist simultaneously, as different stages of settlement can coexist alongside one another. New spaces of opportunity can be identified in urban frontiers, and institutions of privilege can stretch across space, granting power and position to some settlers striking out in search of new opportunities. Crucially, all are produced by the same combination of forces exerted and shaped by the settler colonial assemblage. Here, I present settler colonial spatial production as three entangled, interdependent types of colonizing acts: erasure, occupation, and bricolage. Each of these acts is informed by the spatial logics of settler colonialism and accords with settler colonial spatialities, but the specific arrangements of power in place produced through these colonizing acts can vary significantly. There are nonetheless consistent features of settler colonialism that are asserted through these dynamics, not the least of which is the way that colonizing acts are normalized, taken for granted, and perceived as "banal" (Berg 2011).

It is useful for this discussion to take the Pacific Northwest as a "strategic exemplar" (Stevenson 2012, 602) of settler colonial spatial dynamics. Also called "Cascadia," this is an imagined region with no single agreed upon boundary but is roughly commensurate with the bioregion presented in Figure 7, or roughly with parts of the province of British Columbia and the states of Washington, Oregon, and California. Prior to the establishment of east-west international borders and rail routes, this area saw a great deal of transport and trade but largely in a north-south direction that followed either the mountain valleys of the interior or the coastline of the Pacific Ocean. However, settlement and networking with continent-wide colonial systems soon reoriented mobility in the region. As a consequence, this region has long been of interest to scholars focused on Indigeneity and colonialism, from anthropologists and historians to political scientists and geographers, because the colonial settlement of this region occurred much later than on the rest of Turtle Island, largely after the mid-nineteenth century. As a result, the Pacific Northwest was subjected to techniques of settler colonization already tried and tested in easterly and southern regions, from treaty making to violent invasion. Further, the records from this time are far more complete and accessible than those of a century or more prior, making this a prime area for historical and political analysis.

For me, it was a place that I barely knew until it became my home from 2004–09, first as a graduate student in the Indigenous Governance Program at the University of Victoria in Lekwungen (Songhees) and W̱SÁNEĆ (Saanich) territories and later both as an instructor at the Saanich Adult Education Centre in Tsartlip First Nation territory and as an education analyst for the Aboriginal Education Branch of the British Columbia government. I was fortunate to travel extensively all across British Columbia and all three states, mostly for work but also for pleasure. I fell in love with the area's landscapes, people, and places, but I remain disturbed by much of what I saw and learned as well. My travels were often at the side of Indigenous people from isolated or impoverished communities who were fighting for any chance to make things better for their people, or I was accompanied by activists and warriors who had been the direct targets of state violence for decades. Everywhere we went, these teachers and mentors showed me signs of settler colonization in what I thought was simply a beautiful, natural place.[9] It was in this area that I truly came to understand the depth and complexity of settler colonialism. The signs were everywhere, and once my Indigenous instructors, fellow students, colleagues, and friends taught me how to see them, I could not stop.

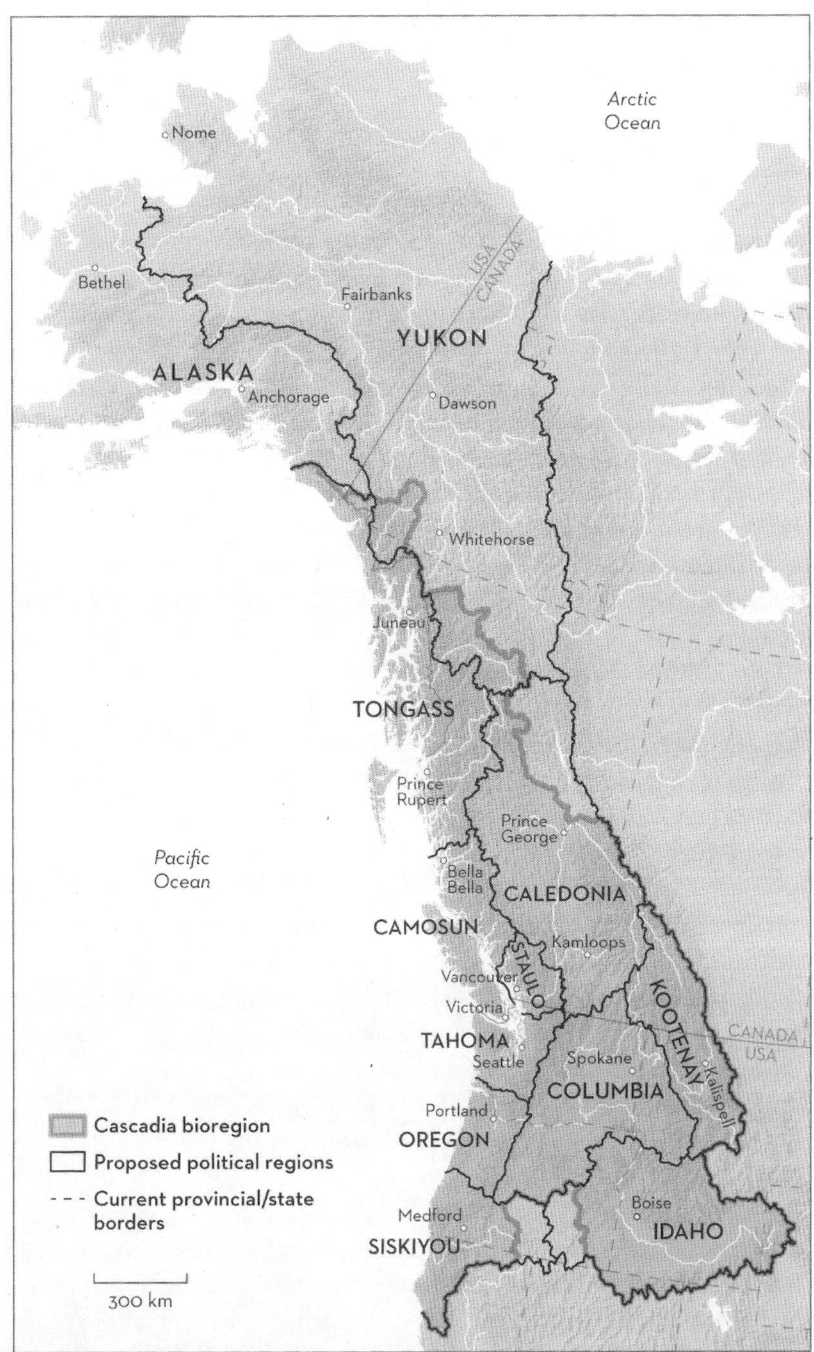

FIGURE 7 Cascadia, showing its bioregion and provincial and state boundaries

The Pacific Northwest was divided between the emerging transcontinental states of Canada[10] and the United States and was incorporated into the settler colonial assemblage in earnest beginning in the mid to late nineteenth century after a population boom in the area caused by a series of gold rushes – including the Fraser Canyon gold rush, discussed above (Alper 1996; Lindquist 2012). Wrested from Mexico by the United States in 1848, just ahead of the first major gold rush in the region, northern (Alta) California today overlaps with the southern extent of the area roughly called the Pacific Northwest – understood here to be more or less interchangeable with Cascadia, meaning the Pacific watershed west of the Cascade Mountains. Following extended negotiations with Britain over the placement of the international boundary line and prompted by the American need to secure peace in the northern part of the country as the Mexican-American War (1846–48) loomed, Oregon became a territory in 1846 and would join the Union in 1859 (Commager 1927). The province of British Columbia, encompassing the former Crown colonies in the region, which had amalgamated in 1866, joined Canadian Confederation in 1871 following another gold rush, and Washington was admitted to the United States in 1889, completing the state divisions that we recognize today. Historian Gray Whaley (2010) argues that Oregon is best understood as the spatial product of a clash between British and American settlers, notably a number of Methodist missionaries, with a variety of Indigenous groups caught in the crossfire. A similar argument could be made about British Columbia. In fact, the entire region emerged out of entangled histories of contact, conflict, exchange, and most importantly, colonial settlement and Indigenous resistance. Correspondingly, a detailed and growing body of literature, both historical and contemporary, has been developed regarding this region that speaks not only to the vibrancy of the cultures and peoples in the area but also to the pervasive racial violence and exclusion of settlement and to the radical transformation of space that they enact (e.g., see Alper 1996; Ault Jr. 2014; and Shobe and Gibson 2017).

Erasure: Direct Attacks on Indigeneity

In the late 1990s, historical geographer Cole Harris (1997, xvi) chose to reprint his essay "The Good Life around Idaho Peak," originally researched and written almost twenty years prior, "partly because it contains an egregious error that reflects the mind-set of colonialism." In the first version of this essay, Harris asserted that Idaho Peak, north of Nelson, British

Columbia, had never been a site of Indigenous settlement. In the later version, he recanted: "My proposition that no Native people had ever lived near Idaho Peak is absurd, and grows out of the common assumption, with which I grew up, that a mining rush had been superimposed on wilderness" (194). Harris, one of the most important and influential scholars of Native-newcomer histories in the Pacific Northwest, bases this striking reversal on a 1930 report by ethnographer James Teit, released by the Smithsonian Bureau of American Ethnology after his death, of which Harris had previously been unaware.[11] Drawing on interviews conducted between 1904 and 1909 with elders of the Sinixt (Lake) people whose ancestors lived in the region, Teit's report details Indigenous village sites and the devastating impacts of imported disease (194–95). In this case, not only were the physical bodies and communities of Indigenous peoples destroyed and reduced by pathogens introduced by European and American newcomers, but even knowledge and awareness of Indigeneity were discarded or ignored. In Harris's own analysis, this disregard for history "is another example, from one who should have known better, of the substitution of wilderness for an erased Native world" (xvi). Such disregard indeed constitutes erasure – the total removal of Indigenous presence on the land, even from history, memory, and culture – through simultaneous moves to destroy Indigenous peoples as peoples by means of violence, disease, and starvation, to implant a substituted memory so that, in this case, miners and homesteaders encountered 'empty' wilderness, and to buttress popular terra nullius perceptions of the region in the works of a major scholar who did not (and was not expected to) check to see whether his assessment was in fact true. Whether it be a stated goal or an unintended result, the outcome is the same: the transfer of those lands to settler control and imaginaries. This outcome can even be accomplished without the removal of Indigenous bodies because it is *Indigeneity* – embodied practices of Indigenous relationships to land and place that coproduce Indigenous sovereignty, identity, knowledge, and culture – rather than *Indigenous people as such* that settler colonialism seeks to erase.

The goal of erasure is the materialization of terra nullius, which can be thought of as the creation of a vast, conceptual space of exception. This space of exception – whether internal or external to officially claimed settler spaces – is applied anywhere that settler colonial ambitions identify opportunity on a frontier beyond direct structuring and effective control of a central government (Rifkin 2014). When this space of exception is applied, there are a variety of ways that settlers can consume or dispose of

Indigenous people, reduced to bodies stripped of humanity in the eyes of settlers, without individual consequences or social sanction. As more and more land is claimed by settler societies and incorporated into settler states, more and more space is perceived as antithetical to Indigeneity. Indigenous presence is to be disposed of or 'civilized' away along with the frontier itself.

What lands officially remain in the hands of Indigenous people in the northern settler bloc – today, primarily reserve and reservation spaces – can still be understood as spaces of exception, and Indigenous lives and bodies within them remain subject to both physical and existential disintegration (Belcourt 2018). Similar to the way that concentration camps reduced the humanity of prisoners to spatially managed numbers and figures by restricting bodies to particular, bounded places – the key example in Giorgio Agamben's (1998) construction of spaces of exception – both Canada and the United States impose band lists on Indigenous communities as part of their governance structures. These lists of names of official members, later identified by numbered personal identification cards issued by the government, were frequently used to control the movement of Indigenous people on and off of reserves and to prevent the entry of Indigenous individuals into colonial spaces, like cities and towns, throughout the first half of the twentieth century (Frideres, Kalbach, and Kalbach 2004, 95–102). As geographer Madeline Jacobs (2012, 6–7) observes, in Canada the Indian Act (like similar legislation in the United States) does not just impose status on Indigenous people but also creates specific crimes that can be committed only by those designated "Indian." The "non-Indian" by contrast does not have the status of individuals recognized as "Indian" by the government and is not subject to the same laws. Similarly, reserve spaces are intended as specific spaces for "Indians," with the concomitant understanding that all other spaces are not for them. In this way, the imposed visibility of Indigenous people actually undermines Indigenous sovereignty, as spaces constructed for settler people are predicated on clearing them of Indigeneity.

Again, population management and settler colonizers' assertions of the sovereign right to identify and manage population in 'their own' territories are key parts of the erasure process. Band lists correspond to rules of eligibility, which are often drawn up by settler governments or operate within restrictive legislation ensuring that sovereignty and citizenship cannot be commensurate with membership in an officially recognized band or community. This selecting and sorting allows state governments to turn the extermination of Indigenous peoples into a demographic issue. By claiming the sole responsibility to determine who is "Indian," as per the Constitution and the Indian Act in Canada and a whole host of statutes at the federal and state levels in the United States, states were able to legislate rules of heritage. Such status laws are often based on varying levels of blood quantum in the United States (Garroutte 2003, 38–60) and on an intentionally collapsing system of parentage in Canada (Lawrence 2003, 6). They ensure that even as Indigenous populations increase, the number of Indigenous people who are recognized by the government as having official status and who are therefore due some limited rights or benefits diminishes steadily.

As settler colonization spreads, erasure is projected ahead of settlement in several ways. First, settlement is often accompanied by state violence under the excuse of "self-defence," which historian Chris Arnett (1999, 146) has drawn out in detail in his history of the violent origins of what is now Victoria, the capital city of British Columbia. Colonial officials propelled settlers into conflicts with the Cowichan by encouraging them to illegally claim farmsteads in the Cowichan Valley on Vancouver Island. This was no accidental blunder: the Cowichan Valley is reachable from Victoria only by traversing the Malahat Mountain or by crossing the Saanich Inlet from the Saanich Peninsula. Neither area was controlled by the colonial government at the time and lacked roads or other infrastructure that homesteaders might require. Rather, colonial officials viewed the Cowichan Valley as inevitably theirs, and thus by definition unoccupied or empty, despite the fact that Cowichan people were actively farming in that very spot. The same colonial officials claimed the right to exercise justice through violence committed on the bodies of Indigenous people while refusing to recognize Indigenous legal or political orders. These two acts – the destruction of life and the erasure of sovereignty – are clearly related, but the doctrine of "just war" (Hardt and Negri 2000, 10–12) that motivates them is also used by contemporary settler people to deflect responsibility for either physical or sovereign erasures.

The second way that settler people deflect responsibility for the 'disappearance' of Indigenous peoples in this region is to attribute the majority of Indigenous deaths to nonhuman factors such as uncontrollable diseases like smallpox or influenza, with the effect of washing settlers' hands of responsibility. In reference to Idaho Peak, Cole Harris (1997) is correct in noting that diseases had huge impacts on populations throughout the Pacific Northwest (and, of course, across the continent) but recognizes his error in equating impacts with disappearance. This error is of the same kind made by Jared Diamond in his much critiqued *Guns, Germs, and Steel: The Fates of Human Societies* (1997), which seeks to distance colonizers from the complex consequences of settlement and to "explain away plunder as the work of nature" (Correia 2013, 3). This equivalency accords with the settler rationale that Indigenous peoples "cease being indigenous" if their lifestyles change, even if that change is induced by an "ethnic transfer" such as "forced removal" (Veracini 2010b, 35). It is one of the reasons that court cases, like *Delgamuukw v. British Columbia* (1997), and other decisions, especially around the legally contested Pacific Northwest, often stipulate that Aboriginal title to land will be recognized only if an Indigenous community can prove continuous occupation and use of a territory. As Harris (1997) goes on to describe in his reflection, the impacts of disease in the Pacific Northwest caused great migrations and movements of people, with villages combining, sometimes along kinship or linguistic lines, as people adapted to major social upheaval. However, change and adaptation are not equivalent to disappearance, no matter what settler people might wish.

Deflecting responsibility for physical erasure to pathogens also ignores the degree to which many diseases affecting Indigenous populations were bound up with settler colonization – not to mention diseases spread intentionally and early bioweapons.[12] I am referring here to diseases like tuberculosis that have afflicted Indigenous communities for centuries, which historian James Daschuk (2013) has shown are diseases of poverty, the rates of transmission, morbidity, and mortality all being greatly increased by the physical impacts of economic deprivation and exclusion from settler standards of medical care. In the late nineteenth and early twentieth centuries in the Pacific Northwest, rations allocated to First Nations communities in British Columbia – which had already been denied access to the trade networks by which they had once obtained traditional food sources – were repeatedly cut, the age at which a child was moved from half to full rations was increased from ten to twelve years, and Indian Agents were empowered to treat ration allotments as an upper limit. Access to fresh water was often prevented when water was diverted for settler infrastructure, including railways (Matsui 2005). Housing was inadequate. Although the catastrophic rates of disease, starvation, and ill-health that followed in these communities were nothing but predictable, they were understood as inevitable by most settler people rather than attributed to imposed conditions (Barker and Battell Lowman 2019, 352; Kelm 2012, xv–xvi).

Taken together, these two factors create a narrative structure that mirrors the historical terra nullius narrative and also inform laws and politics in the present. In claiming that colonization once existed as a violent act that cleared the land – an act that can be historicized as having a clear beginning and end – and in asserting that it was done by other people or was just due to bad luck or fate or the way of the world, individual settler people deny their collective colonial responsibilities through a form of limited liability that allows them to selectively choose whether or not to identify with the actions of other, prior settler colonizers. For example, there was widespread consternation following historian Ian Mosby's (2013) revelations that the government-run and church-operated Indian residential schools in Canada, including one in Port Alberni, British Columbia, were sites of starvation experiments on children in the 1940s and 1950s. The public outcry, of course, failed to connect to existing calls from Indigenous people to address malnutrition and the underfunding of both reserve and urban Indigenous communities literally across the continent. In a sort of temporal deferral of outrage, past malpractice is held up as barbaric, even as current policies and practices that underpin ongoing malnutrition and deprivation are ignored. It is more acceptable to suggest that the British Empire and the American state used to be colonizers than to suggest that the settler populations of the northern bloc continue to colonize and dispossess right here and right now. This attitude is part of a complex dynamic whereby settler people, even when they become aware of the existence of settler colonial atrocities, are able to deny their own complicity (Regan 2010) or even the complicities and atrocities of their forebears.[13]

Physical Erasure

Settler colonization is an inherently violent process in many ways. That is particularly evident in the actual physical violence inflicted on Indigenous bodies and material connections to place, including the militarized and pathogenic violences discussed above. However, in addition to those examples, settler collectives also participate in direct physical attacks on Indigeneity beyond the reach of the state or without state sanction. For example, during the California and Fraser Canyon gold rushes, huge numbers of miners and fortune seekers entered into contact with Indigenous peoples in the Pacific Northwest. Miner collectives set up their own de facto corporate governance structures and attacked local Indigenous peoples whom they pre-judged as a threat (Marshall 2018). These attacks were among the acts that prompted the knee-jerk creation of the Colony of British Columbia when American miners, self-organizing to claim land and resources, represented a potential assertion of sovereignty and attempt to 'improve' the land per John Locke's theory of property. However, this was not merely a paranoid fear. The United States was more than ready to use self-organizing migrants of American origin as a Trojan horse to claim new territories, as it had previously done in the Mexican province of Texas when the Old Three Hundred, comprising Anglo-Americans who had purchased land titles there between 1824 and 1828, made use of liberalized Mexican immigration policies in the territory to establish a colony that immediately flouted Mexican law and eventually formed the basis of American claims to annexation (Menchaca 2001, 198–99), a tactic that would be used again in the seizure of the Dakota Territory in the 1870s. Manifest Destiny drove American acquisitiveness, and the Pacific Northwest of the nineteenth century was a stage on which empires competed. This competition left many casualties and displaced Indigenous societies and cultures as a matter of course.

In addition to exacerbating disease through deprivation, settler collectives also play direct roles in spreading disease and in capitalizing on the disruption that diseases cause to Indigenous societies. Many of the outbreaks that would devastate nations across the Pacific Northwest were spread by trappers, traders, homesteaders, and miners, who were again operating beyond the reach of the state but were also well aware by this time that Indigenous communities were particularly susceptible to certain European diseases. Settler colonizers exerted control over people's movements in ways that worsened the spread of these diseases. The settler instinct was on full display during smallpox outbreaks in the Pacific Northwest in the 1860s, as all Indigenous people were ordered out of the settlement of Victoria – even those who had always lived there or nearby – and when they returned to the outlying or distant Indigenous villages, they brought the seeds of new epidemics with them (Van Rijn 2006).

As Indigenous populations dispersed, disappeared, moved, consolidated, or retreated from contact in the wake of epidemic diseases and associated settler violence, they often appeared to leave behind lands ideal for grazing and raising cattle, which 'providentially' became available to settlers, from the American West to the interior of British Columbia. Contact between stock farmers and ranchers and Indigenous communities led almost inevitably to some of the most strikingly violent moments of the colonial project (Barta 2014), but even in historical cases of ranching settlement that did not involve overt conflicts, physical erasure often preceded the arrival of ranchers and settlers. Ranchers did not necessarily intend to physically erase Indigenous populations, but their monopolization of both grazing lands and food markets deprived Indigenous communities of networks of resources that had been mutually sustaining since time immemorial (C. Harris and Demeritt 1997, 234–40; Thistle 2011). Erasure through deprivation continues to this day. Despite the fact that settler societies on Turtle Island are among the most affluent in history, Indigenous communities continue to endure food insecurity and deprivation, long-term lack of access to clean drinking water, deficits of medical and other health and social services (including education), enforced isolation, and denial of a sufficient land base for social health, cultural reproduction, and material sustainability.

A key example of contemporary erasure being confronted by Indigenous activists, community leaders, scholars, and journalists is the epidemic of missing and murdered Indigenous women and girls. As will become a common refrain throughout this book, the hierarchies of settler colonial society are both racialized and gendered, and Indigenous women are specific targets of settler violence (Eberts 2017; Kuokkanen 2017; Maracle 1996, 14–19). In the northwestern areas of the continent, gendered violence came early, as the Indigenous women who married fur traders – whether in Christian unions recognized by settler society or according to local customs and traditions (Van Kirk 1980) – were frequently mistreated and taken advantage of once installed inside the boundaries of the colonial fort or trading post (C. Harris 2004). Over the years, this racialized misogyny became entangled with cultural narratives and with the effects of violence, poverty, and disease to create the idea of Indigenous women as particularly disposable. Indigenous women and their allies are fighting this devastating construction to this day (Blaney and Grey 2017). The selective dehumanization of Indigenous women by settler colonizers contributes to very real physical erasures. Consider the contemporary case of the hundreds of missing and murdered Indigenous women in and around the Downtown Eastside neighbourhood of Vancouver (Dean 2010, 114), which has become renowned both for the pervasive racialized and gendered violence against Indigenous women and for the powerful grassroots responses to this violence. The annual February 14th Women's Memorial March in Vancouver has a strong element of Indigenous leadership, a fact that speaks to the particular level of violence that Indigenous women face. Elsewhere in British Columbia, the so-called Highway of Tears, a 725-kilometre stretch of Highway 16 between Prince George and Prince Rupert, has seen so many women – mostly Indigenous – abducted and attacked that there are plans to install billboards warning women not to travel it alone. Of course, although I am using examples from the Pacific Northwest in this section, I could make the same arguments just as easily regarding locales across the continent. For example, consider the Great Lakes region, where a thriving international trade in trafficked Indigenous women between Ontario and both Minnesota and Wisconsin has been linked to an appalling range of disappearances and acts of sexualized violence (Farley et al. 2011). Violent erasure particularly targeting Indigenous women is fundamental to Canadian and American societies (Green 2017, 9–11).

Conceptual Erasure

As well as the removal of the physical presence of Indigenous people from the land, settler colonialism is also premised on the removal of Indigenous people – as autonomous, intelligent actors – from the understood history of places (Freeman 2010; Veracini 2007). Both Canadian and American societies are rife with pervasive interpretations of history that confidently project a conceptual erasure backward in time. This is to say that when settler people write and tell the histories of Canada or the United States, they tend to do so absent Indigenous peoples who exist as present agents rather than historical artifacts. On this point, historian Kelly Black (2015) argues that in many places settler colonialism has "shallow roots" – which the glorifications of local history attempt to portray as deep and profound. Black's study of rural British Columbia, where the markers of settlement are still easily traced in the names of the roads and towns imposed fairly recently on Coast Salish lands, articulates settler colonialism's tenuous grip on place, which is easily discomforted by assertions of prior occupation. So when settler people repeat nationalist narratives absent Indigenous peoples – like convicted fraudster Conrad Black's (2014) much critiqued great man history of Canada, which positions Indigenous people as essentially primitive non-actors in the prehistory of Canada (Scowen 2014), and twice-impeached former president Donald Trump's jubilant reiteration of the violent conquest of the land that became the United States to score political points with his white settler base (Cultural Survival 2019) – this effacement of Indigenous peoples' historical presence has to be understood as an aggressive act of colonization.

Settler histories create and perpetuate powerful fictitious colonial narratives such as the "peacemaker myth" (Regan 2010, ch. 3), the heroic trope of the frontier pioneer (Nettleback and Foster 2012), and the myth of the self-made settler (Ramirez 2012). Across the continent, these mythistories (Battell Lowman 2014, 143) are asserted in place of and against the histories of Indigenous peoples. Insofar as settler people often define themselves in relation to perceived others (Veracini 2015, 40–44), Canadian and American mythistories are codependent. Arnett (1999, 14), situating his study of British warfare and judicial terrorism in the Pacific Northwest prior to the clear demarcation of territory along the present border, observes that "there remains the colonial myth that, contrary to what happened south of the 49th parallel, the British resettlement of British Columbia was benign, bloodless and law-abiding." He further reflects that, although it is impossible to deny that the "'Indian Wars' of British Columbia came nowhere near the wholesale slaughter of aboriginal people that too often characterized the inter-racial conflict in the western United States," the difference is in scale, not in kind (14).

This observation underscores the importance of seeing erasure and other settler colonial dynamics as spanning the 49th parallel: the false binary of British and Canadian versus American colonization is often used to justify, obscure, or finalize settler colonialism on both sides of the border. American glorification of the opening of the West serves the same purpose as self-congratulatory Canadian narratives of benevolence and treaty making. Both erase competing Indigenous claims to land with the broad brushstrokes of settler nationalist master narratives, whether rooted in military or diplomatic forms of conquest and control. As Canadians think of and promote themselves as peaceful in comparison to Americans and therefore able to legitimately claim a level of 'métis' belonging through tenuous cultural connections to Indigeneity,[14] so do Americans think of their nation-building project as finished because the Indian Wars (1609–1924) settled the 'Indian problem' (Byrd 2011; Dunbar-Ortiz 2014). Both contrast themselves with the other. Of course, these narratives are red herrings. American and Canadian settler colonization are built with the same toolbox, which includes a spectrum of combinations of treaty making and breaking, violent military and paramilitary force, and concerted attempts at coercive cultural assimilation or extermination.

As an example of the pervasive systemic erasure of Indigeneity at work in 'peaceful' Canada, Regan (2010, ch. 3) juxtaposes the "peacemaker myth" not with violent American conquest but with the violent reality of the Indian residential school system, comparable to (and indeed, influenced by) American Indian boarding and industrial schools, which operated throughout the latter half of the nineteenth century and much of the twentieth. These schools, which were designed to isolate Indigenous children from their families and to use education, labour, and punishment to form them into 'civilized,' Christianized subjects, played a key part in a system of overall forced assimilation that has been authoritatively and decisively identified as "cultural genocide" (Truth and Reconciliation Commission of Canada 2015, 1). As Regan (2010, 5–6) points out, the narrative of peaceful nation building in Canada is so powerful and insidious that even the evidence of historical violence in the form of the physical residential school buildings – many of which still exist – is often (almost literally) invisible to settler Canadians.

Occupation: Coming to Stay

The second settler colonial act that produces sovereign settler spaces is occupation. Occupation is a nuanced concept involving flexible and changeable modes and standards for perceiving a place as occupied, which means that it must be understood as more than simply taking space. The methods by which occupation is pursued may vary, but the fundamental reasons why it is done – to claim places from Indigenous peoples and integrate them into settler colonial spaces – remain the same.

For example, it is often overlooked that much of the Pacific Northwest, from Oregon north through British Columbia, was appropriated into the sovereign territories of settler states despite vast swaths of terrain continuing to be occupied and used almost exclusively by Indigenous peoples. The first official census of the province of British Columbia in 1881 shows no data for the entire northeastern part of the province (C. Harris and Galois 1997). This omission occurred not only due to a lack of settler collectives to be enumerated and surveyed in that region but also because the power of the state in that place was largely theoretical. Importantly, the absence of such data is not an indication of terra nullius, as Indigenous people lived in that area in large numbers, with Indigenous political and trade networks remaining vibrant in this period, even as Indigenous communities developed new strategies for communicating and trading with newcomer and increasingly mobile Indigenous populations, such as the development of complex trade languages, both oral and written (Battell Lowman 2017). Similarly, south of the border, the abrupt assertion of American sovereignty over the Oregon Territory did not mean that Indigenous peoples had suddenly been exiled and could be found only "behind bushes, roaming the woods, consigned to the wilderness" (Barr 2012, 521). A state or empire's claim to territory does not equate to the displacement of Indigenous peoples, who are often not even aware that such claims have been made until years after the fact. Rather, occupation and erasure go hand in hand in producing displacement. Regardless of Indigeneity in place, settler occupation is always predicated on the projection of terra nullius.

Occupation as Praxis

As settler colonists across the continent began to think of themselves as distinct from the metropole, a related concept of 'homeland' developed in parallel. Settler peoples became invested in the lands that they claimed because their ideas of freedom and personal opportunity for advancement were tied up with the availability of new frontiers, with new spaces of opportunity and advantage that could be occupied by pioneers, and with measures of success usually involving ownership of property and advancement in settler institutions. Because of these investments, settler people began to see Indigenous peoples' very existence as a fundamental threat to their freedom and prosperity, which in part explains the vast security and disciplinary apparatus that has been erected around Indigenous peoples since the nineteenth century (Barker 2009; Crosby and Monaghan 2016, 2018; K.D. Smith 2009).

Occupation is based, in the barest sense, on acquiring knowledge of place. The ability to scientifically break place into separate elements and reposition (and constrain) these elements in settler systems of knowledge is critical to settler colonial claims to ownership, habitation, and belonging (Bhandar 2016; Soguk 2011, 41). Indeed, occupation can happen even in the absence of urbanization, homesteading, or the construction of forts or other common physical manifestations. Premised on the construction of frontier areas as destined for settlement, settler people exert claims to places that are not occupied by settlers and where the embodied acts of settling have not happened. For example, "wilderness" may be "protected" as a national park (Banivanua Mar 2010, 83–85), such as Banff in Canada and Yellowstone in the United States, and incorporated into settler topographies of power not because they are occupied but to serve as a reminder that they could be in the future and thus need protection from the seeming "inevitability" of settlement (Wolfe 2006, 392). The places are occupied by settler colonial power in order to control how the lands are used. The embodied presence of park rangers, naturalists, campers, and other recreation seekers in these spaces simply draws attention to the fact that settler colonizers exert claims over and expect rights to access places even from a distance or at a remove from significant population centres. By asserting all-encompassing systems of title through legal frameworks, by adding conceptual value to places deemed naturally special and granting them status as national parks or conservation areas, or by exercising the ability to remotely view and thus affectively connect to distant, isolated landscapes, settler society occupies places even without the embodied markers of settlement.

'Improvement' of Land

As discussed in relation to terra nullius, occupation in Euro-American legal traditions is justified by embodied acts of 'improving' empty land. If habitation can be conceptual – comprising knowledge of, the intent to use, and the assertion of a juridical claim over space – then so can improvement. The complex interplay of being in place and the transformation of space by settler colonizers is often couched in positivist terms like "improvement," but studies of these dynamics in action reveal a far messier production and consumption of space (Thistle 2011; Veracini 2015, 62–67). Consider again the complex dynamics of the mid-nineteenth-century Pacific Northwest. By the period of state consolidation, settler colonizers had developed the array of aforementioned juridical, militant, and sociocultural methods of colonizing. However, from the initial moments of colonization, a fundamental premise remained that land could be claimed only if it was occupied *and* improved (MacMillan 2011; Tully 1995). In the East, such improvement had already come to include plantation farms, town squares, and other recognizable aspects of transplanted English culture (MacMillan 2011, 51).

By the time settlement of the Pacific Northwest gained momentum, the idea of improvement had been reinterpreted through centuries of experience of settler colonization and advancements in technologies to connect spaces across distance, taking on what historian Ken MacMillan (2011, 33) categorizes as a more "belligerent" form. The islands and coastlines of the Strait of Georgia, an arm of the Salish Sea, were considered 'improved' by the presence of British naval and military power (Arnett 1999, 317). This presence in turn drew new and more occupants to the area, namely settlers who took the improved security from the threat of Indigenous violence and the connectedness with existing networks of colonial power and privilege to mean that these lands were open for business. The presence of the military helped to create a space of opportunity that would otherwise have been frustrated by Indigenous resistance to settlement.

The way that military presence enabled occupation and how this enabling was seen as justification for occupation demonstrate an important point: improvement is conceptually construed as that which facilitates occupation by increasing the mobility of settler people. Settler mobility is not simply "movement through space" since this mobility "involves paying close attention to how the displacement of people entails meaning, power, practice and embodiment" (Leitner, Sheppard, and Sziarto 2008, 165). Examining the ties between mobility and improvement reveals that imposed settler colonial technologies that facilitate material movements transform the meanings of places. It seems obvious that the development of transcontinental rail routes in both Canada and the United States was intended to bring their Pacific Coast settlements and claims fully into the ambit of the settler colonial nations founded in the East. But key to this undertaking is that the rail routes allowed for the places that they connected, not just the places that they physically occupied, to be seen as 'improved' through technological proximity to centres of 'civilization.'

Conceptual Occupation

The stereotype of the white settler pastoral homestead represents only one kind of settlement, but it is one that accords smoothly with settler colonial tropes (Cavanagh 2011). In practice, ideas of and distinctions between settlements, pastoral homesteads, and Indigenous spaces were never as clear as settler people might have liked (Edmonds 2010). Indigenous spaces in Vancouver and Victoria were approached differently by settlers based on the perceived proximity to whiteness – in behaviour, language, dress, and so on – of the Indigenous peoples occupying them, a perception that many Indigenous communities understood well enough to turn to their own benefit. Performances of whiteness could be a boon in business negotiations, whereas performances of Indigeneity were required to demarcate Indigenous spaces from encroaching settlement (Barman 2010). The nuances of these exchanges in spaces of shared occupation, however, are often obscured both by time and by the flattening, erasing narratives of settler colonial nationalism.

After the claiming of the Pacific Northwest by the Canadian and American states, and the international recognition of such, state power increasingly played a vital role in settler colonization of the region, as it allowed the state to claim occupation on behalf of settlers to come in any place where force could be brought to bear against Indigenous peoples and spaces. Although, as mentioned previously, there were not enough settlers in much of the new province of British Columbia in 1881 to necessitate a census of their numbers, the Crown had already begun in 1861 to allot reserve lands to Indigenous peoples. This measure was partly anticipatory and partly instrumental, as the restriction of Indigenous people to small plots of land opened up the remainder of the territory for sale and, in this way, became a self-fulfilling prophecy: by treating the land as always already desirable for settlement, the colonizers created the conditions that made the land desirable. The annexation of the Washington and Oregon Territories was similar: vast state claims were made over lightly settled territories on the assumption that settler occupation was inevitable. Whereas some settler collectives asserted sovereignty beyond the state, which were then absorbed during territorial expansion of the state or used as narrative justification for this expansion, in some cases a settler 'nation' came into being and filled this pre-made spatial container. The idea of a settler nation can arise irrespective of actual physical settlement; what matters is whether or not a place is occupied in the settler colonial imagination.

Occupation and Dividing Space

It could be seen as a paradox that this opening-up of land to occupation followed the assertion of borders designed to restrict and control the movement of people, including the miners who flooded into British Columbia from California, Oregon, and Washington. However, borders play a particularly important role in settler colonial territorialization. Borders should not be confused with frontiers: whereas frontier spaces are open to possibility but also to risk, borders are securitized spaces that channel mobility, encouraging some bodily movements while restricting others (R. Jones 2016). Borders are noteworthy for the specific ways that they play into transfers of land. One of the most obvious is the role of borders in "administrative transfer," whereby a settler state abrogates Indigenous sovereignty, along with any pre-existing treaties and agreements between Indigenous nations and the colonial polity, by claiming or annexing Indigenous territories (Veracini 2010b, 44). Administrative transfer allows Indigenous rights to be transferred away while Indigenous bodies remain, although it can then be used as an excuse for actual physical removal. When territories like British Columbia and Oregon were claimed by larger settler states, borders were essentially drawn around or past existing Indigenous communities – borders that were seen, as if by magic, to subsume Indigenous sovereignty into the state.

This assertion of sovereignty enables a further set of transfers, including using legislation to drain rights and entitlements guaranteed through treaty or constitutional recognition. For example, imposing "a definition of indigeneity that is patrilineally transmitted" – as Canada did through the Indian Act, under which official Indian status could be lost if a child had a non-status father – "can allow the possibility of transferring indigenous women and their children away from their tribal memberships and entitlements," including the right to live on a reserve (Veracini 2010b, 44). In this way, the drawing of state borders contributes to Indigenous dispossession more generally, as these borders are not only linked to an occupation of territory justified by an underlying settler colonial sovereignty but also support the actual occupation of land by settlers. The generation of states and borders must be seen as a social arrangement – a spatial geometry of power imposed by settler people and structures – that amplifies the settler colonial claims to land made through occupation.

Bricolage: Settler World-Making

So far, I have discussed dynamics of settler colonization that pursue the destruction and erasure of Indigeneity and its replacement with settler spaces and population economies. However, in this discussion of erasure, the selective preservation of elements or representations of Indigeneity in settler society must also be examined. Settler people do not intend to completely destroy either the material or cultural manifestations of Indigeneity that they encounter in place. Rather, settler colonizers seek to preserve particular elements as a form of primitive accumulation particular to settler colonialism.[15] These elements, disconnected from their relational contexts and repurposed through repositioning, form both the physical and conceptual basis of settler colonial "world-making" (Karagiannis and Wagner 2007). Indigeneity would seem to pervade settler colonial societies; it is (intentionally) impossible to miss it in Seattle and Vancouver, where Indigenous iconography is used in the symbols for sports teams like the Seahawks and in large public art installations like renowned Haida artist Bill Reid's massive installations that greet newcomers at Vancouver International Airport. All around the region, Pacific Northwest art and style, whether authentically Indigenous or copied and reproduced, is pervasive in popular culture, fashion, and style. The presence of Indigenous people and cultures would seem to be undeniable; however, what settlers actually perceive is not true Indigeneity but a collection of colonial signifiers denuded of meaning that copy Indigenous expression without the stories to make sense of these expressions, thereby rendering the power and connectivity of Indigenous nationhood circumscribed and controlled by settler colonial institutions.[16] This is the settler colonial "*bricolage*" (Selbin 2010, 40–41, emphasis in original) – a synthetic collection of elements of Indigeneity and metropole cultural "fragments" (Butlin 2009, 10–11) organized and contextualized to give meaning and the appearance of deep tradition to settler spaces, despite "shallow roots" being the norm (K. Black 2015). This bricolage changes over time, comprising a constantly evolving legend of the present (Stevenson 2012, 593).

Linked to narrative and cultural products that inform identity and subjectivity in powerful ways, it marks the material production of the settler colonial assemblage on the landscape and on bodies.

Settler Bricoleurs: *Story and Reality*

The process of erasure can be totalizing without being total. Selective Indigenous erasure casts settler colonizers as "*bricoleurs*" (Selbin 2010, 41, emphasis in original) with the power to select, preserve, and recontextualize elements of Indigenous cultures and histories in settler colonial spaces – including bodies, stories, artwork, names, and terms – and of course this power also extends to the creation of implicit meaning. Much of settler colonial bricolage consists of telling different stories, to ourselves and others, about elements of place, their meanings, and how settler people come to know and be in relationship to them. These narratives then inform particular settler colonial embodied performances on the land. In broad strokes, these performances can be thought of as "cultural appropriation" (Haig-Brown 2010, 928–32) with specific purpose. All sorts of imperial projects have relied on cultural appropriation, and on attendant notions of exoticization, commoditization, and cultural superiority, in the exercise of colonizing power, as seen, for example, in the nineteenth-century exploitation of Africa by Europeans (Driver 2000). What makes settler colonialism different is primarily that objects are decontextualized and moved around but not necessarily dislocated. Rather, objects are at times claimed and re-storied in situ to provide conduits through which settler colonial structures of feeling are rooted in particular places. This process can be contrasted with European metropole colonization, which involved people, artwork, and even buildings being relocated from places such as Egypt and India – and also totem poles and other 'cultural artifacts' from the Pacific Northwest – to reside in London museums. This undertaking, too, served to generate particular stories about and meanings for places but with different effects.

For settler people, Indigenous artifacts preserved in place become settler colonial objects through the stories told about them, as much as through their material situation. Consider Nuu-chah-nulth scholar Gloria Jean Frank's "'That's My Dinner on Display': A First Nations Reflection on Museum Culture" (2000), which suggests that the Royal British Columbia Museum maintains artifacts from the Indigenous peoples of the province, largely gathered around or before the settler colonial consolidation of the Pacific Northwest, as part of the popular, positivist, regional story rather than for the sake of the Indigenous peoples who produced and used them.

This same critique can be made of the vast majority of museums in Canada and the United States. Museums, especially those associated with universities, have a long history of refusing to return Indigenous artifacts and bodies under the narrative that contributions to science – meaning white, settler, elite, academic knowledge – far outweigh any benefits that could be made by returning them to the communities (L.T. Smith 1999; Thomas 2001). Even when these artifacts are not moved out of their lands of origin, by dint of being contextualized by settler colonial institutions, they are used to support colonial stories about these lands.

Land itself is an interesting case, especially in the Pacific Northwest. The consolidation of this area involved closely connected physical and conceptual bricolage as part of processes of making settler colonial space. The early settlers of Victoria recognized the physical benefits of Indigenous farmlands in the Cowichan Valley because Cowichan farming and use of the area made it clear that the place was suited to agricultural production. Moreover, Cowichan labour, along with care of and interactions with the land, contributed significantly to its desirability as a potential space of settler agriculture. However, this Cowichan knowledge of the land was not simply instrumental but was part of longstanding ontological relationships to place. The settlers who occupied the area through pre-emption – essentially by squatting beyond the boundaries of the colony, 'improving' the land, and then submitting a claim to the property (Arnett 1999, 102–10) – preserved the physicality of the land as an agricultural base while appropriating and transferring the idea or knowledge of the space from Indigenous spatial imaginaries into the colonial political and legal framework. Settler people and collectives narratively constructed Indigenous people as too primitive to practise agriculture so that their agricultural expertise and techniques, and prime, well-tended agricultural spots could be claimed by settler colonizers much as they would claim a usefully shaped rock without ever considering that it might have been made so rather than having simply occurred that way. This same pattern of recognizing the value of land through Indigenous knowledges and economic practices and then laying claim to it – or to be frank, stealing it – was repeated across the Pacific Northwest, whether what was recognized were good areas for fish and game or ways of traversing the myriad rivers, islands, mountains, plateaus, and valleys. It was also repeated in many ways across the continent, and so wider settler colonial ambitions with respect to the frontier must be understood as ambitions to invade Indigenous spaces and to displace and/or destroy Indigenous peoples while selectively keeping many of their practices, cultural symbols, and products. Settler space can exist only because much of it was first produced by Indigenous peoples and then appropriated and repurposed by settlers, who erased Indigenous labour and stewardship by crediting these fortuitous spaces to the bounty of nature in their new homelands.

Reconciling Appropriation and Non-Encounter

Settler bricolage is made of both physical and conceptual elements. The appropriated works of art and cultural display that fill museums and private galleries are obvious, as is their use in reminding settler people of their cultural superiority and victorious condition with respect to Indigeneity. As alluded to above, the settler appropriation of stereotypical West Coast Indigenous imagery in the Pacific Northwest, whether by artists (Braun 2002) or by sports teams like the Vancouver Canucks and Seattle Seahawks (Mandelker 2000, 371–72), helps to remind settler people of their residency in a "special locale" (Veracini 2010b, 55), contributing to the settler's mimetic character. Settler people also directly appropriate Indigenous cultural traditions, technologies, knowledge, and words. Essentially, there is nothing in Indigenous lifeworlds that settler people have not at some point turned into a consumable product. As historical archaeologist Barbara Voss (2005) notes, early buildings in San Francisco used common local building practices, mostly developed by Indigenous people of the northern Mexican and central Pacific regions, until changes in concentrations of wealth led to more individuated design. In Oregon, early settlers took lands illegally from Shasta communities and then promptly accused the Shasta of stealing from them (Whaley 2010, 193–95). Words from Indigenous languages and trade pidgins have been incorporated as markers of regional settler identities (Battell Lowman 2017, 81–82). How, then, can this pervasive appropriation be reconciled with the "non-encounter" (Veracini 2010b, 76–85) at the core of settler colonialism? How can settler people use Indigenous technologies, concepts, and words every day yet not register Indigenous presence and relationships?

Consistent with the Eurocentric worldviews that informed narratives of terra nullius, settlers across Turtle Island have tended to proceed in their settlement as though unreconstructed land is by definition 'wasted land' that must be transformed through 'honest' (meaning white-settler-controlled) labour.[17] Consequently, anything that settler people produce is claimed entirely as their own by right of labouring for it, regardless of the reliance upon or positive impacts of unfree labour, the assistance of imperialist military forces, or the reliance upon Indigenous knowledge and land-based practices. Indigenous peoples are likewise devalued and construed as being part of the wilderness and at one with nature. As a result, for many settler people, the selective assimilation of Indigenous peoples' knowledges, cultures, histories, and names into settler colonial society is no different from the use of timber and stone from the landscape to construct buildings as part of a settlement created through settlers' organized labour. As ethnographer Celia Haig-Brown (2010, 931–32) points out, even well-intentioned and educated settlers appropriate Indigenous knowledge and concepts through a form of "post-modern quotation," where Indigenous knowledge and ingenuity are acknowledged but the products of these knowledges in the form of ceremonies or land-based practices are still seen as essentially open for settler use; the acknowledgment of historical production does not equate to an acknowledgment of contemporary Indigenous rights to or ownership of these knowledges.

Further, Canadians and Americans are often culturally illiterate with respect to Indigenous peoples and quite literally cannot perceive or understand the symbols and signifiers expressed in performative acts of Indigeneity. As a result, assumptions are often made about shared feelings of national belonging or economic and political positivism that drastically miss the mark. Political recognition, on Yellow Knives Dene political theorist Glen Coulthard's (2014) terms, is limited to aspects or products of Indigeneity that settler people are willing and able to acknowledge and accept, such that assertions of Indigenous nationhood and identity often become entangled with settler colonial displays of nationalism (Battell Lowman and Barker 2015). One example of this occurrence can be found in the Four Host First Nations (FHFN) associated with the Vancouver Winter Olympics in 2010. According to International Olympic Committee regulations, all bids to host the Olympic Games must seek cooperation from Indigenous communities in the proposed area. In the case of Vancouver, the FHFN comprised the Tsleil-Waututh, Musqueam, Lil'wat, and Squamish, four local First Nations bands whose members agreed to work with the Vancouver Winter Olympics committee in exchange for various community benefits, such as enhanced tourism funding and programming for their communities. However, this campaign ran up against a powerful anti-Olympics movement organized under the banner No Olympics on Stolen Land, which exposed the degree to which the FHFN protocol papered over wider denials of Indigenous sovereignty in the Pacific Northwest (O'Bonsawin 2010, 2012, 2015). Despite recognizing First Nations, their incorporation into the Vancouver Winter Olympics was not a celebration of Indigenous sovereignty so much as a celebration of the incorporation of the trappings of Indigeneity into the multicultural Canadian mosaic. Thus the recognition of Indigenous presence on the land became an act that actually further subsumed Indigenous sovereignty into the settler state.

Settler Collectives Today

A central theme of this chapter has been the ways that settler colonizers, in a variety of self-directed forms, claim and transform land, displace and erase Indigenous presence, and build structures of feeling that attach and root settler senses of self and belonging in particular places. These actions precede the state but also continue long after the imposition of such systems and structures of power. These claims to ownership and perceptions of belonging became the baseline – the temporal origin point – for settler colonial national myths and for the consolidation of wealth and power by the institutions of privilege that eventually developed into the landscape of Canada and the United States as we know and experience it today. Even as the next chapter turns to an examination of the larger structures and patterns of spatiality that result from the aggregate efforts of many settler collectives over time, it is important to remember that these corporate forms can be reassumed and reasserted, even against powerful structures like the state itself. Settler collectives invested in institutions such as white supremacy have frequently resisted state efforts to enforce liberalist notions of inclusion that discipline the most egregious acts of racial violence and segregation. The Bundy Ranch occupation of 2016 is one such example of highly privileged settler Americans referencing a particular version of the national narrative – freedom and liberty expressed through rugged individualism and Second Amendment rights – while also asserting a particular settler colonial corporate identity that makes specific claims to land and place (Inwood and Bonds 2016). States and corporations wield enormous power, but we must never forget that our settler colonial impulses pre-exist and can survive beyond these structures and systems.

3

Remaking People and Places: States, Suburbs, and Forms of Settlement

I can remember the moment when I became aware that living outside of a settler colonial society did nothing to make me less of a settler. In 2009, my partner and I moved to England to begin work on our doctoral degrees. We lived in Leicester, an unpretentious city in the unfashionable East Midlands region, which has been a market town since the time of Roman occupation and whose vibrant multicultural community I regard as the best of what England can be. In a small terraced (row) house built for nineteenth-century factory workers, while ensconced in a kitchen small enough that I could touch all four walls from the middle of the room, I was listening as a BBC news update on the radio gave way to the perennially popular rural-farming soap opera *The Archers* (1951–present) when a thought struck me: *I will never belong here*. The years that have since elapsed have confirmed this impression to be true.

More interesting, however, was that as I researched the northern bloc of settler colonialism from across the pond, I saw more and more of the behaviours and thoughts ascribed to settler colonizers in my own ongoing reactions toward living in England. The narrative of the rugged frontier came to me easily as I mocked the English for complaining of the cold and shuttering businesses when the temperature dropped below freezing or for wilting like insufficiently watered houseplants as soon as it became warm enough to wear shorts. I laughed at how they thought that a ninety-minute drive was a long way. I sneered at their idea of camping, just some tents in a field, and giddily told stories of my few sightings of moose and bears in Canada.

At the same time, there were aspects of English society that exasperated me because they seemed like relics of a bygone past, such as the class consciousness tied to a complete inability to define class in a way that made sense to an outsider – never mind the cultural imperative to judge people based on accents that I could not even distinguish. Moreover, the road signage was ghastly, as it required that drivers already knew exactly where they were going – a holdover, my partner and I (sort of) joked, from the Second World War and plans to thwart a German invasion. One also had to be able to see through trees, around corners, and under ivy to perceive and discern tiny, rusted plates bearing street names. Maybe most disorienting was my constant battle with the infamous "computer says no" attitude toward service, popularized by the sketch comedy show *Little Britain* (2003–06), where even the most basic requests made to a character who is alternately a bank teller, travel agent, and hospital receptionist (all portrayed by David Walliams) are denied because the computer system refuses to cooperate after a single, half-hearted attempt by its operator. Even though all Brits knows that this is not merely a stereotype but a deeply ingrained approach to service, one that contrasts sharply with the over-the-top friendliness and "customer is always right" culture of North America, they laugh all the same, just as they laugh at the unimaginative and officious Vogons in Douglas Adams's 1978 radio and 1981 television shows *The Hitchhiker's Guide to the Galaxy* or at the portrayals of the inward-looking and dysfunctional BBC in the sketch comedy show *Monty Python's Flying Circus* (1969–74). They laugh partly at the absurd reality of this approach to service yet also temper their glee with a bitter acceptance that it will never change, leading a settler like me to complete vexation.

I frequently fell into a malaise rooted in the feeling that "something was profoundly wrong about this place," to paraphrase historian Karen Kupperman (1980, 141). My sense of Canadianness – of being from a "special locale," a settler colonial narrative that I learned about in Lorenzo Veracini's (2010b, 55) work – was reinforced as something that made me special when people wanted to ask about the West Coast or talk about their cousin in Toronto or their friend in Calgary. The more I read about settler colonialism and the more I observed myself in my everyday interactions in England, the more I saw my own self in words meant to apply to settler colonizers in general, even though I was far from home.

Managing Difference through State and Capital

In this chapter, I attend to some of the durable, aggregate, and high-level spatial constructs of settler colonization in Canada and the United States of

America, while seeking to articulate the way that settler colonialism shapes international and global concepts in modes particular to the settler project. I first examine entanglements of state and capital as evidenced through migration and forced mobility, which together materialize a shifting topography of power that is the product of widespread settler colonial spatial production driven by a state-capital political economy and by a white masculine patriarchal ethic. I then describe how settler colonial logics of elimination writ large – that is, the attempt to eliminate problematic indigenous Others and exogenous Others by erecting a set of triangular subjectivities that separates them from settlers – manifest in politics of recognition and complicity. These politics unevenly extend settler colonial benefits in an anticipatory way to convince newcomer people, people of colour, and others marginalized by the settler colonial project to seek benefits inside rather than outside of it, while revealing the point at which liberalism as an ideology, the state and capital as a political economy, and settler colonialism as a defining ideology intersect as a kind of "resonance machine" (Connolly 2005).

Next, I re-examine four familiar spatial concepts: urban, rural, frontier, and wilderness. Although the use of these concepts often assumes some level of common understanding, it is well understood in geography that each one has multiple meanings and no single, fixed definition. However, these concepts, relating as they do to dividing land and territory, to zoning and building, and to generating place-based identities, are all exceptionally germane to understanding the settler colonization of Turtle Island. Positioning these four spaces in relationship through the use of a semiotic square, I examine the importance attached to each one and how it is defined both by proximity to and by difference from the other types of space. This investigation further shows how social characteristics associated with different variants of settler colonial spatiality are ascribed to or claimed by the residents of these spaces. I then consider suburban space as a deeply conservative and ultimately failed attempt to transcend the tensions between these spaces by creating a new space for occupation by settlers that has the benefits of all the other spaces and the drawbacks of none of them.

Given the shifting topographies of power produced by the settler colonial assemblage, two of the most widely critiqued social constructs – the state and capitalism – must be considered differently when they are positioned not just as global processes but also as entangled with Indigenous displacement and dispossession across Turtle Island and with the bricolage of settler colonial spaces that transforms the material and social landscape.

In Canada and the United States, state and capital are inflected with the violences and desires of the settler collectives that embody their spatial forms and dynamics (see broadly Adams 1989; Bruyneel 2007; Coulthard 2014; Morgensen 2011; and A. Simpson 2014). Settler colonial spatialities may not overdetermine the function of the state and capital in creating hierarchies of opportunity and advantage, but they certainly shape these hierarchies in specific ways. This influence is extremely important to understand because there are ultimately contradictions between, on the one hand, what settler people demand of the states of the northern bloc and what opportunities they expect under "whitestream" (Grande 2003) capital and, on the other hand, the actual lived experiences of racially and class-divided hierarchical systems, which on balance benefit wealthy white elites at the expense of poor settlers, Indigenous peoples, and dehumanized and exploited migrant or racialized labour.

Migrations of People and Circuits of Capital

How people move is fundamentally tied to how economies are built and operated. Insofar as states and corporations intersect in controlling the ebb and flow of labour, and given that many settler colonizers may be regarded as economically motivated, we can begin examining settler colonial population movements through attention to borders. One of the ways that hierarchies are shaped can be identified through the example of the Canada-US border. Canada and the United States are separate nations; there are crucial differences in their laws and policies, in their population distributions and social makeup, and so on. However, as argued throughout this book, even as we acknowledge the importance of these differences, we must be wary of the "narcissism" of these settler colonial governments, which traditionally emphasize their "petty differences" to cover up a great deal of similarity (Hatter 2012). In this regard, the function of the Canada-US border in controlling population movements benefits both states, channelling migrant labour along the circuits of capital in ways advantageous to both settler polities. But settlers move too. The international borders between these settler states have always been selectively porous. For much of the period following the American Revolutionary War (1775–83), migrations of people across the Atlantic Ocean and across the British-US border underscored and furthered the similarities of varied settlers to each other and, through these similarities, tied British, Irish, American, and other white anglophone nationalist subjectivities to one another (A. Taylor 2010, 8–9). The result was a multiplicity of settler positionalities with ambiguous relationships to each other but with common bonds forged in narratives of frontier struggle and the isopolitical rejection of imperial authority.

The commonality of this underlying settler colonial territoriality is often obscured by the nationalistic discourses that in part adhere around these state borders. Canada and the United States increasingly form an integrated economic area, share major cultural practices and references, often coordinate policy, and have relied on the common tropes of pioneering spirit and Indigenous decline to build their collective identities.[1] At times, it can be argued that the two nations have functioned as variants of a core imperialism, divided largely by leaders who have narcissistically focused on minor differences (Hatter 2012). Regardless of how Canadian and American national identities might be positioned contra each other – as are regional identities in both countries (discussed below) – the border serves less as a dividing line than as a melding point. The border is fundamental to regulating flows of labour, migrant and otherwise, through a variety of administrative pathways and in a way that benefits corporate interests – a process that enlarges the security state while integrating surveillance and enforcement systems across the two nations (R. Jones 2016, 29–47; Walia 2010, 2013). The settler colonial state thus serves to maintain the circuits of capital built along with it.

As Albert Memmi (1965, 3) famously noted, "the economic motives of colonial undertakings are revealed by every historian of colonialism." That said, the relationship between capitalism and settler colonialism is complex, with neither being absolutely subordinate to the other. As much as settler colonization relies on capitalism to help move commodities and labouring bodies through space, capitalism relies on the settler colonial structures of invasion to provide sites where capital may take root in a material sense. Across Turtle Island, Indigenous leaders like Métis scholar and activist Howard Adams (1989) and Secwépemc (Shushwap) political organizer and leader George Manuel (G. Manuel and Posluns 1974) have long made the connection between material dispossession under conditions of colonialism and the spread of capitalism to and through Indigenous communities. Nascent British mercantile capitalism helped to fund many of the earliest efforts at settlement in the Americas through franchises granted by the Crown, and the British Empire eventually came to dominate trade throughout North (and South) America by virtue of its oceanic monopoly, industrial capitalist economy, and outmanoeuvring of competitive European empires (Galeano 1997, 173–204; A. Taylor 2010, 115–19). Metropole colonial contact through traders began creating the conditions for the spread of circuits of capital across the continent and throughout Indigenous territories. This colonization by capital, a "relentless" and "omnipresent" commodification of Indigenous lifeworlds accompanied by an invasive, pervasive "economy of desire" (Mooers 2001, 69; see also Holloway 2010), is one of the many ways that settler colonization and other forms of colonization imbricate in the settler colonial assemblage. Shifting modalities of capital accumulation, often dependent on global currents and commodity demands, became materialized in particular ways that served as vectors for the spread of settler colonization. For example, fur trade colonialism, a colonial logic that has historically involved the direct assertion of sovereignty by capitalist corporate entities like the Hudson's Bay Company, the North West Company, and the American Fur Company (Cavanagh 2009), helped to spread capitalist circuits throughout the interior of Turtle Island, and settlements tended to follow these circuits. By the time settler colonization came to dominate the continent, capitalism was a familiar economic form, and capitalist elites wielded enormous power.

Drawing on political economists Jonathan Nitzan and Shimshon Bichler's (2009) theoretical construct of the dynamic interactions of capitalist entities under neoliberalism, capitalism and settler colonialism can be similarly articulated as methods of transforming organized human efforts into vast reservoirs of power. Nitzan and Bichler describe capitalism not as a linear accumulation through investment and profit but as a vast leveraging of advantage with striking similarities to settler colonial advantage. They present the capitalization of power as dependent on a greater ability than one's competitors to organize and deploy more power through multiple systems – financial or otherwise – rather than on the maximization of profits and production, as in classical capitalist economics. This deployment of power can include sabotage and other types of forced disadvantage that, despite imposing a cost on the assertive capitalist entity's resources without direct returns, undermine competitors in a way that changes market share and relative leverage, resulting in a net gain in power, if not liquid capital.

Through the capitalization of power, the pace of settler colonial accumulation increases. For example, in the nineteenth and early twentieth centuries, a few wealthy ranchers were able to very quickly monopolize the majority of grazing land in the British Columbia interior, displacing both Indigenous and settler ranchers alike (Thistle 2011). However, such a process opens up settler colonial dynamics to influence from flows of capital connected to globalizing sources of power not beholden to settler collectives. Following the establishment of ranches and farms in the fertile lands of

British Columbia's Okanagan Basin (Wagner 2008), the first wave of settlers saw their original dispossession of Indigenous lands overtaken by the nouveau riche, who have turned much of the area into pocket wineries or vineyards. A similar situation can be seen in California, where Anglo-American settlers displaced early California farmers (meaning settlers under Spanish jurisdiction) only to be displaced themselves by wealthy newcomers, who have built houses, bed-and-breakfasts, and hobby wineries on the same farm and ranch lands (Soto 2008). Likewise, just east of my childhood home, in the Niagara region of Ontario, orchards once gave way to grapes and wineries that are now giving way to stylish and manicured middle-class subdivisions and gated suburban communities. Although each stage in such processes accumulates wealth and advantage for some, it is undertaken in part at the expense of fellow and future settlers – driving up property values, permanently changing the land, and imposing a class hierarchy on such spaces that forecloses opportunities for some in order to guarantee advantages for others. This is one of the ways that capital helps to shape the topographies of power across the continent.

Model Minorities and Exogenous Others

Of course, even though settler Canadians and Americans must be understood as distinct in some important respects, our societies are not disconnected from wider global trends, including urbanization and suburbanization, industrialization and deindustrialization, and other spatial dynamics of globalizing capital (Pollard et al. 2009; Wood and Rossiter 2011). These capitalist influences and state policies have not dispersed settler colonialism. Rather, they have combined or resonated in particular ways, such as through the racialization of labour in accordance with the set of triangular relationships that separates the settler self from indigenous Others and exogenous Others. Settler people, themselves exogenous to Indigenous populations, differentiate between the other two groups based not only on the ideologies of race and cultural superiority but also on their susceptibility to incorporation or assimilation. As mentioned previously, exogenous Others are often practically divided into two populations: sojourners, who comprise visitors, tourists, diplomats, and similarly privileged international Others; and migrants – or "chattel" labour (Tuck and Yang 2012, 6) – who are permitted to enter settler territory for the purpose of labour but lack or are actively precluded from claiming basic civil protections or officially recognized attachments to land, citizenship, or other institutions that might support them. As Canadian and American societies have developed, they have demonstrated particular and distinct patterns for dealing with and accounting for each of the three groups.

Indigenous labour was crucial to earlier colonial regimes and to the development of settler colonies whose economic ambitions outstripped their labour capacity, whether in the primary production of commodities, as in the fur trade (Daschuk 2013), or in secondary roles, such as the labour of Indigenous women in salmon canneries (Mawani 2009, 35–76). However, the settler colonization of Turtle Island has tended toward the elimination of Indigenous labour and its replacement by (in theory) white settler efforts and by (in reality) white ownership of the means of production and domination of racialized and exploited labour. Numerous historians and sociologists argue that the clearing of land in order for white pioneers to take over is actually a relatively rare circumstance. More frequently, lands seized from Indigenous nations were linked into circuits of resource extraction under the direction of wealthy white European landowners but worked by enslaved and coerced labour (Veracini 2013, 322–23; Vimalassery 2013). Mass systems of incarceration, surveillance, and gruesome punishment were developed alongside legal and political systems of racial superiority (K.D. Smith 2009). The outputs of this system were measured in valuable commodities, such as the precious metals, coal, or minerals produced from mines and the cotton, sugar, or tobacco produced from plantations. The costs frequently entailed the exploitation and destruction of Black people and their communities as well as other peoples situationally deemed not white. Later, in other eras and in other places, rail barons used Chinese workers as another racialized workforce without the official sanction of state slavery but certainly in a vacuum of rights that would be all too familiar to racialized migrant workers from Mexico or the Philippines today, who continue to labour in agricultural resource extraction and domestic service work that amount to contemporary forms of indentured servitude (Walia 2010, 2013).

The shifting systems of institutions of privilege, which are unevenly open to membership, create a process of increasingly complex settler belonging. Entrance into the legal institution of the "franchise colonies" (Banivanua Mar and Edmonds 2010, 19n4) did not, for example, permit either Indigenous people or Black Canadians and Americans to access privileges associated with the institutions of whiteness. However, given that these institutions are not fixed but rather ongoing reproductions of the settler colonial assemblage that exist in tension with global politics and economics, the topography of power does provide entry points, or routes, by which contemporary settler collectives can join already existing settler societies and institutions. Veracini (2010b, 4) observes that migrants from the originary metropole are often extended immediate membership and benefits in settler society. Yet, in the present, there is no single originary metropole for the settler societies claiming and transforming Turtle Island. Both Canada and the United States have been colonized by multiple European empires and collectives from around the world, including the English, French, Dutch, Spanish, and Russian, and the isopolitical shifts of earlier settlers have fully matured into a complex system of state documentation and control. A migrant from England, the historical metropole with the most influence on these lands, is likely to be extended membership in some institutions of privilege but not others. White English migrants will immediately be accepted into many spaces of white settler privilege but will not necessarily receive the state's immediate jurisdictional recognition in the form of citizenship and the protection of rights. They are, however, certain to face fewer barriers to gaining such recognition than people of colour or those with non-Western or non-Anglo European backgrounds. Meanwhile, wealthy newcomers with nonwhite backgrounds may be able to access fast-track visas and citizenship options, even as they experience social racism and discrimination. Both cases, as instances of partial or conditional acceptance into settler society, illustrate that belonging is something that cannot be exclusively granted by any one social group or institution. Nonetheless, for racialized people, much performative work remains to be done to achieve further belonging, and it is certainly possible that they will never be accepted as full and equal members since both white supremacy and the capitalist drive to exploit underclasses work to prevent this method of collapsing the triangular relations of settler colonialism.

This struggle to belong is further explored below, but before turning to how these systems for incorporating (or producing) new settlers function, let us consider how the anticipatory geographies of settler colonialism shape the aspirations of newcomer peoples. As historian and social organizer David Austin (2010, 21) discusses, various nonwhite settlers have participated in imperial projects and have both benefited from and been marginalized through the production of colonial spaces to varying degrees (see also I. Day 2016). Difference matters: complex dynamics of race and class that cut across scales and connect settler colonial spaces to global networks and transnational discourses mean that there is no 'pure' settler form. This situation demands that we consider not *who* is part of the project of settler colonization but *how* they become involved and *to what end.* Subaltern populations are always more than the simple economic value of their labour, and many communities have struggled and won concessions and rights from "whitestream" (Grande 2003) settler colonial societies. However, what they have frequently achieved, as mentioned above, is a form of limited membership in settler institutions that raises questions about how racial hierarchies are entangled with the process of settlement and about how oppression for the purposes of exploitation can support dispossession for the purposes of erasure in multiple ways (on anti-racist politics, see Chapter 4).

Scholar of gender and sexuality Beenash Jafri (2012) suggests that the concept of *privilege* in settler colonial contexts, a concept drawn largely from engagements with the systemic experience of whiteness, is less useful than the concept of *complicity*, where racialized or oppressed populations can contribute to the displacement or dispossession of Indigenous peoples. In this understanding, people whose labour sustains them by means of stolen resources while displacing Indigenous economies are complicit in settler colonialism, regardless of racial identity or whether full, partial, or marginal acceptance into settler society has been achieved. Complicity, as a concept, helps to take the focus away from strident and intractable debates over who counts as a settler and puts it on how people are incorporated into the spaces, systems, and stories of settler colonial society across multiple lines of cultural, racial, linguistic, and other differences. Similarly, Emma Battell Lowman and I have developed the idea of "settler benefits," the purported "good things" that come to folks who are complicit with settler colonization, not least of which is full membership in some of the greatest institutions of power in settler society (Battell Lowman and Barker 2015, 84–89). Most widely understood through the trope of the American Dream, these benefits often do not – or are never intended to – materialize, yet this outcome rarely blunts their anticipatory affect.

For non-Indigenous, nonwhite people – who are most frequently construed by settler society as exogenous Others by dint of being denied membership in the institutions of whiteness, which are certainly among the most powerful settler colonial institutions – complicity with and assimilation into settler society is encouraged through narratives of the model minority. The concept of the model minority was originally described by professor of education and Asian American studies Stacey Lee (1994) with respect to racialized Asian communities in the United States and was later picked up by author and community organizer Harsha Walia (2010, 2013) as a means of understanding how settler colonial society pits migrants and people of colour against Indigenous peoples. The model minority is the mythical 'successful' postracial subject, who is able to become a contributing member of society through employment, taxation, and conspicuous acts of public service while maintaining some cultural and religious freedoms. The model minority discourse serves settler colonial interests in a number of ways, including obscuring the white ethno-nationalism that characterizes much of Canadian and American national discourses while supporting a liberal and progressive multicultural and postracial narrative that is still fundamentally assimilative and invested in existing settler colonial inequalities (Coulthard 2014; R.J.F. Day 2000).

The differences between these narratives of model minority acceptance and the reality of racialized exclusion are stark. Insofar as some minority populations or migrants seeking to settle in Canada and the United States can occupy settler colonial spaces, they contribute to the biopower capacity of the settler state, encouraging the further disciplining of indigenous Others and racialized exogenous Others. For example, settlers in Hawaii of Japanese background have been fundamental to the development of settler colonial political economics across the islands (Fujikane and Okamura 2008). Japanese settlers' property purchases, economic success stories, and increasing presence in government and civil service all combine to provide a supposed pathway to inclusion for other exogenous alterities, yet many other racialized communities have to struggle against white supremacy in state institutions and only ever occupy liminal settler colonial spaces, with opportunity always sought but never fully achieved. There is a reason why poor and racialized neighbourhoods like Vancouver's Downtown Eastside (Culhane 2003; Dean 2010) and the housing projects and abandoned industrial sites of Baltimore (Merrifield 1993, 2003; N. Smith 1996) are often described as frontiers or as a Wild West: they are seen as places whose potential for civilizing (or gentrification) is thwarted by the presence of too many problematic Others. Often, communities endure both racial and class abuses in these spaces in the hope of being able to enter spaces of clear levelled ground as they pursue the mythic equal opportunity that they are promised will manifest in the ability to purchase property, develop an economic base, and become 'successful' low-level capitalists, and begin transmitting their wealth intergenerationally. Of course, the game is rigged: settler colonial institutions are not meritocratic despite the pioneer narrative implying just that, and comparatively few individuals – much less whole communities – can be said to have 'succeeded' in this way.

Despite the reality that settler colonial inclusion rarely lives up to the myth, the model minority narrative is a key part of the discourse that brings more and more newcomer people into complicity with settler colonial systems of usurpation and transformation. Perhaps most insidious is that these communities of marginalized people are encouraged to identify with and support the very institutions that exclude and minimize them so that they will one day be fully admitted into settler colonial society and spaces. This support in no way guarantees minority rights, legal protections, or political recognition from institutions of privilege. Even citizenship and official recognition by the state as a rights-bearing member of settler society are often more about disciplining potentially "agonistic" Others (Featherstone 2008, 48–49) through integration into systems of state control and processes of capitalist accumulation. Performing the social identity of a labouring property owner aligns with ideals of settler good conduct inside systems of "law and every other damn thing" (as discussed in Chapter 2), even though it does not necessarily imply the actual granting of privileges associated with settler colonial narratives of success and belonging.[2]

Not all racialized subjectivities experience the same kinds of assimilatory pressures or are represented equally in the model minority myth. Specifically, the racial discourses around Blackness and Black identity in the United States turn on an association between the performance of Black identity and incommensurability, thus signalling both the impossibility of assimilating Black communities into white supremacist settler societies and the ultimate unwillingness of white and white-adjacent settler colonizers, regardless of their perceived racial or cultural differences, to share space, power, or identity with Black people, who remain perpetually Othered. Because this association with incommensurability leaves Black communities forcefully displaced from both the social spaces and cultural narratives of settler colonizers, "that which 'structures' a black sense of place are the knotted diasporic tenets of coloniality, dehumanization, and resistance" (McKittrick 2011, 949). This abjection can be seen as parallel to the erasure of Indigeneity, what English scholar Iyko Day (2015, 105) calls "the two states of settler colonialism," since what is denied is the possibility of a counter-sovereignty being asserted by communities cast as explicitly Other on racial grounds.

The abjection of Blackness has led to heated and trenchant debates, both within and beyond the academy, over the extent to which Black folks in Canada and the United States can or should be considered settlers – that is, self-identifying and collectively claimed members of the larger settler colonial society.[3] Again, the question of *who* counts as a settler is less productive than the question of *how* people are incorporated into settler society. Certainly, many Black Canadians and Americans identify strongly with their respective national and regional identities, social discourses, and economic and political processes, and it would be extremely arrogant and academically indefensible to say that these individuals and communities are either duped into acting against their own interests or are willingly complicit with settler colonialism against Indigeneity. At the same time, given the ongoing state and social violence against Black individuals and communities, the continuing need for grassroots organizing like Black Lives Matter (2013–present), and the clear continuity of plantations, prisons, and the projects as the expected spaces of Black belonging across North America (McKittrick 2011), it is equally disingenuous to suggest that more than the barest of purported benefits of settler colonization have ever been extended to the vast majority of Black communities. My point echoes Iyko Day's (2015, 113, 117–18) argument that we need to explore the complex interplays between racialized labour, Indigenous displacement, and discourses of inhumanity that inform contemporary racism and exploitation. These hierarchies of racialized labour and belonging in the northern settler bloc are pernicious because they can and do produce narratives of struggle and success that themselves presume and normalize settler colonial spatialities.

As Day (2015, 103) argues, the white-Black racial dialectic at times dominates American discourses to the exclusion of considerations of Indigeneity, even though American ideology is marked by the endless invasion of both internal (or Indigenous) and external lands.[4] Day's larger point is that "settler colonial racial capitalism is a zero-sum game" (117) in which racial discourses for recognition and success within the American state often come at the expense – both conceptual and in terms of actual political power and access – of other minority groups. This point accords with literary scholar Daniel Coleman's (2016) observation that members of communities forced into diaspora or made landless in the past may with some justification regard Indigenous claims to land with suspicion. Although the systems of settler colonial state sovereignty and capitalist accumulation that usually lead to dispossession of racialized minority communities and to displacements of Indigenous nations are linked, there is a strong narrative that pits them as competing for the same set of limited rights and recognitions under the present settler-dominated social order. However, the simple adoption of Indigenous practices is problematic as well, even for nonwhite populations. Professor of English and gender studies Jodi Byrd (2011, 117–22) examines the dynamics of how Indigeneity is co-opted by some racialized communities struggling against the oppression of white supremacy and capitalism in the United States, specifically through the example of local

Indigenous influences on early Black American musicians in late-nineteenth and early-twentieth-century Mississippi, a moment of cross-cultural exchange caught up in the "cacophony" of settler colonialism, resulting in a tangled legacy of commodification of culture. In this way, claiming elements of Indigeneity can become a powerful performative act of belonging in the context of a settler colonial society that constantly seeks to leverage appropriated Indigeneity (or settler bricolage) toward transcendence of the settler colonial past, particularly the racialized contract of the exogenous Other attached to settler society.

In this context, what does it mean to be described as an exogenous Other who is beyond potential assimilation into the process of settler naturalization? Clearly, "exogenous Other" is a generalized term, a strategic catch-all. It is generally used to refer to populations and individuals who are constructed as subjectivities that settler societies see as 'not us.' These subjectivities include both racialized and dispossessed migrants – viewed as less than human or, at least, less than settler – and other imperial agents and colonizers, such as metropole sojourners, who do not intend to stay despite having interests and investments in the settlement. Migrants here are actively excluded from collective identification, perhaps pending the performance of model minority politics and material attempts to acquire permanent dwellings, whereas the positioning of foreign imperial agents is ambiguous, as they are extended some rights and privileges in the absence of identification as a settler but are also viewed with suspicion. Given the multiple and dynamic makeups of the settler polities occupying Turtle Island, it makes sense that who is considered exogenous changes from place to place and over time. Exogenous Others are targeted either for assimilation and absorption into the settler body politic or for dehumanization and removal from civil society in the context of racial capital and ethnonationalism, thus foregoing the need for assimilation.

However, the discourses around exogenous Others have shifted; "in a postmodern predicament, strangers are here to stay ... Exogenous alterities are now predominantly construed as enduring" (Veracini 2010b, 51). So exogenous Others, although still targeted for eventual elimination (as a category, not as people), are now in some senses eliminated by nonassimilation, as in the case of the Canadian practice of assimilative multiculturalism (R.J.F. Day 2000), the 'kinder, gentler' parallel to the rugged individualism of the American Dream writ large. In these processes, exogenous alterity is selectively allowed to remain visible as long as the underlying expression of this alterity is acceptable to the most powerful and privileged – wealthy, white – settler communities. This is a direct parallel to the bricolage of Indigeneity that builds the foundations of settler colonial societies on Turtle Island. This kind of multicultural assimilation may provide the state with stability and channel potential minoritarian dissent into institutions like courts and human rights commissions, but equality is forever beyond its purview. This minoritarian thinking is a powerful act of colonial forgetting and erasure that threatens to subsume all difference – including a variety of exogenous forms of social organization and the place-based relationships of Indigeneity – into settler discourses of belonging on the land.

Aboriginalism and Assimilation

Just as settler colonialism seeks to empty the subjective category of exogenous Others, so too does it seek to empty the subjective category of indigenous Others. The most obvious ways that this aim is achieved – the violent erasure of histories and cultures, the murder of community members or their forced removal from the land, and the "slow industrial genocide" (Huseman and Short 2012) associated with resource extraction and capitalist development – have all been discussed. However, another insidious method, one that is informed by Canadian multiculturalism yet operates in a variety of ways on both sides of the border, is the assimilative discourse of Aboriginalism.

It is by now common knowledge that both Canada and the United States go out of their way to encourage Indigenous people to identify with state-centric, nonsovereign constructions of Indigeneity. Indigenous people are encouraged to abandon autonomous Indigenous identities and attendant ideas of nationhood and self-determination in exchange for a circumscribed version of Aboriginal identity. Political theorist Glen Coulthard (Yellow Knives Dene), in his landmark *Red Skin, White Masks* (2014), exposes the colonial politics of recognition at work across Canada and the United States, whereby immaterial acknowledgment and 'honouring' by the settler society are offered up as fair exchange for land and sovereignty taken or dispersed by means of colonization. Through this process, Indigenous people are pressured to reject a place-based, oppositional identity in exchange for a subjective (legal and cultural) identification within settler society, one by which they accept the fact of settlement and are positioned as members of an Aboriginal ethnic minority within, rather than against, the Canadian or American national identity. This shift is marked by their subordinate relationship to settler colonial states and institutions of privilege in exchange for protection of their cultural practices – but only to the extent that these practices do not contravene or disrupt settler law or social standards – the extension of limited rights, and their recognition in official histories (although not legal processes) as founding members of Canada and the United States.

In this context, the term "Aboriginalism" is derived from how the language of the Canadian Constitution recognizes and positions Indigeneity within the confines of the state. "Aboriginal" is the term used in Section 35, which concerns the rights of Indigenous peoples within the state and the responsibilities of the state in relation to recognized Indigenous groups. This term, and its presence in the Constitution, were originally demanded by Indigenous political leaders and activists, including the renowned Shuswap labour leader and political organizer, George Manuel, who as president of the Union of British Columbia Indian Chiefs led the Constitution Express movement in 1980–81. This movement sought to pressure Canadian political leaders to officially include Indigenous people in the Constitution, in part to ensure that the main thrust of the 1969 White Paper, that proposed to eliminate any separate recognition of Indigenous people by the state, could not be revisited in the future (A. Manuel and Derrickson 2015, 65–75). Insofar as the legal recognition of "Aboriginal" individuals and communities forecloses the simple dismissal of treaty obligations and other legal and political entanglements, the Constitution Express was a major victory for Indigenous people in Canada. However, over the ensuing decades, the Canadian state has slowly advanced a denuded and limited concept of what it means to be "Aboriginal" in both legal and social discourses.

Section 35 defines "Aboriginal" as comprising "First Nations, Inuit and Métis" people, and it affirms the validity of the treaties between these peoples and the Crown. This division is itself artificial given that it is not derived from differences between Indigenous peoples but is based on the legal frameworks through which the Canadian state owes obligations to these three groups via limited systems of recognition and benefits: Indian status, Inuit disc numbers, and Métis scrip. "First Nations" is a further misnomer since, at the governmental level, the term does not refer to actual Indigenous nations – such as the Mohawk Nation, which spans from Quebec to southern Ontario and into New York State, and the Wet'suwet'en Nation, whose huge territory lies in the interior of British Columbia – but designates reserve-based, state-recognized bands, including Wahta First Nation as separate from the Mohawk Nation and Wet'suwet'en First Nation as an isolated community allocated a small reserve outside of Burns Lake. The limited recognition of Aboriginal rights under the Constitution flows through these legal constructs, which seek to minimize collective connections to land and replace them with limited financial support and partial recognition of Aboriginal and treaty rights bestowed upon selected, officially sanctioned individuals and communities.

Similar dynamics are observable in the relationships between settler Americans and Native Americans, although operating under different terminologies. Consider the Hopi, whose territory is defined by embodied travels and sacred spiritual shrines across a vast landscape but is conceptually reduced to the Hopi Reservation as a small territory embedded in both the Navajo Reservation and the state of Arizona. In both situations, the conceptual and political shrinking of territory undermines the ability of these Indigenous nations to exercise self-determination, as they cannot function economically without dependency on the state – which is, of course, intentional. Bruyneel (2007, 184–85) identifies how Americans are all for the "economic development" of Indigenous communities as long as it does not adversely impact settler Americans. Indigenous communities are encouraged to adopt capitalist political economies and to become increasingly dependent on funding from the federal government to prop up the economies of often isolated, underresourced Indigenous communities, many of which have been (forcibly) relocated away from traditional lands and resources or restricted from accessing them. However, when communities are able to develop more functional economies, whether through gaming, industry, resource development, tourism, or other initiatives, settler people push back against "invasive" Indigenous economies. An example of this is Arnold Schwarzenegger's use of anti-Indigenous rhetoric in his 2003 election campaign for the governorship of California (188–91), which demonstrated how settler Americans tolerate Indigenous economic development only when it maintains Indigenous communities in positions of "economic dependency" (Alfred 2009, 9). Schwarzenegger ran on an explicitly anti-Indian platform that positioned "casino tribes" (Bruyneel 2007, 172) as alien invaders bent on taking capital out of the California economy, and he saw his ploy rewarded with election to the governorship. Schwarzenegger played upon Californians' economic fears, insecurities rooted in the destabilizing effects of neoliberalism, by portraying "Indian casinos" (190) as essentially illegal encroachments on the rights guaranteed and protected by the state of California.

This justification for wielding state power against Indigenous peoples is similar to that made in the eighteenth and nineteenth centuries by both the British and Americans, who argued that the existence of the Five Civilized Tribes – Cherokee, Chickasaw, Choctaw, Muscogee, and Seminole – who adopted some legible (to colonists) cultural and material practices from Euro-Americans was used to rhetorically defend and justify acts of aggression against groups like the Shawnee, who resisted assimilation into a burgeoning settler society (Sugden 1999).[5] This carrot-and-stick approach, which provides recognition and elevation in status for those who conform and antipathy and erasure for those who do not, draws a direct line from these historical dynamics to contemporary politics. Indigenous people were welcome to participate in the economic life of the United States, Schwarzenegger seemed to say, but only so long as this participation did not materially or conceptually infringe on the ability of settler Americans to seek out new opportunities and did not challenge the established institutions of privilege that defined the topography of power in the region.

As in the case of model minorities, the actual exercise of counter-sovereignty is denied by the settler colonial state and replaced with packages of rights guaranteed by the state. This approach allows many settler people to regard colonial grievances as already settled through state recognition and limited fiduciary responsibility, while exempting the mass of settler colonial society from responsibility for Indigenous marginalization and displacement, both historical and ongoing. In effect, Aboriginalism has been generally well received by settler people, many of whom agree that Indigenous peoples should have the rights and respect accorded to most minority cultures but also assert in tandem that Indigenous peoples' rights should be constructed in the same way as other minority rights. An example of this thinking in political theory is the move toward "liberal culturalism" (Kymlicka 2001, 22). Many further acknowledge that the economic and social disparities between Indigenous and settler communities resulting from the legacies of colonialism should be ameliorated through limited aid funnelled to First Nations and tribal governments (meaning federally recognized administrative institutions) in the form of economic development. However, funding is not sovereignty, and these processes largely serve to reinforce the authority of settler governments and thus settler people more broadly as the arbiters of what is fair treatment of Indigenous peoples, relying on notions of culture and recognition detached from land and sovereignty and thus from self-determination on Indigenous lands. Through Aboriginalism, Aboriginal people in Canada and Native Americans in the United States are given some popular visibility via pride of place within the 'noble history' of the colonial system in exchange for ending their competing relationships to land. This is effectively an ending of Indigenous ways of life and the triumph of settler colonialism through transfer by means of a coerced lifestyle change

(Veracini 2010b, 44). Severed from the land and subsumed into the state, Indigeneity can be slowly assimilated and disappeared, a form of cultural genocide through governmental recognition that, as Coulthard (2014) has established, denies and starves the most vital parts of Indigenous lifeways.

Beyond simply describing how racialized communities, whether Indigenous or not, become attached to settler colonial structures, systems, and stories, it is important to understand how these processes are rooted in common conceptions of liberalism and equality that trouble the association of racism with conservative racial ideologies, segregation, and conspicuous violence. To do so, it is first necessary to understand how ideas of freedom associated with the frontier and ideas of civilization associated with urban space lead to enduring, subtle, and powerful ideas of land and place.

Carving Up the Land

The production of settler colonial space is like knitting with wool thread. Strands wrap around each other in ways that are difficult to disentangle, and threads of different lengths stick together in a common shape that, if necessary and with effort, can be pulled apart and reworked. The ways that strands of settler colonialism interact and intersect in different times and places produce a huge variety of spatial forms, even if they rely on the same materials and processes. Here, I turn my attention to a set of spatial divisions common to Canada and the United States: the urban-rural dyad, which makes a fine distinction between frontier and wilderness in the settler colonial imagination; and suburban spaces, which demonstrate one manifestation of attempts to spatially transcend the settler colonial form. These spaces are all produced, occupied, and animated in different ways but are mutually reinforced even as they are partly constructed through oppositional discourses.

Settler colonial spaces can be roughly divided along two axes. The first is related to control, or the extent to which political institutions define personal lives, and is intimately linked to attempts to erase Indigeneity from place. As Scott Morgensen (2011) describes, the biopolitical power of settler colonialism is in part directed against the perceived threat posed by Indigenous presence, which is always already assumed to be violent toward settler people. It is associated with the fear of the "war machine" that sweeps in off of the steppe to drive away civilization, positioned as a deeply rooted paranoia that is pervasive throughout Euro-American societies (R.J.F. Day 2005, 138–40). Thus, police forces, legally guaranteed property rights, and courts empowered to make binding decisions on land use, settlement patterns, and appropriate kinds of economic activity are all to some extent manifestations of settler colonial control structures (Barker 2009; Crosby and Monaghan 2018; Coulthard 2014). However, collectives of settler people also frequently engage in settler colonialism to seek freedom or liberation *from* oppressive regimes, whether founding metropolitan empires or rigid centralized states (see Chapter 1). The rugged individualism that has defined much of the pioneering ethic of the settler colonization of Turtle Island is premised on a rejection of the authority of settler colonial political institutions as much as foreign ones. Thus, in settler colonial space, there is a tension between whether or not a place is seen as safe for occupation and whether or not a place stifles freedom to create new colonial lifeways through bricolage.

The second axis corresponds to the relative value that a place is perceived as having, which can be exploited. Settler colonial spaces are frequently founded on the desire to enclose and extract surplus value from a given place. Fracking provides an illustrative example here, as the process for extracting bitumen-heavy crude from shale oil deposits has existed for decades but has become more cost-effective in recent years due to technological advances, loosened environmental regulations, and government backing.[6] Fracking is extremely polluting and has been very controversial. However, it has also been increasingly expanded into new areas, with homeowners in places like New York State being heavily divided between opponents and those who perceive new ways to (literally) extract profit from property that they already own (Dokshin 2016; Simonelli 2014). It is clear why large industries and governments perceive value in resource-rich lands even though these lands will be destroyed by the process of extracting their value, but it is much more interesting to observe individual settlers debating the relative changes in value of their own private property in relation to projects that require the construction and maintenance of thousands of kilometres of pipelines, along with large oil-drilling pads and wells, yet have unclear economic impacts. Clearly, seeing a place as already imbued with value available for access and seeing a place as having potential value if a transformative process is applied are two different things. In spaces where a complex settler colonial bricolage has been developed, some people – depending on their ability to conform to particular place-based standards of race, class, and gender that settlers perceive as necessary for differentiating between 'us' and Others, as well as their possession of social and cultural capital in the form of networked contacts and particular skills – can tap into this existing value. However, many settler people reject the institutions built in and around these spaces as either inappropriate for their goals or as generating the wrong kind of value and instead seek their fortune in areas where the bricolage is less developed and may be tailored more easily to their own desires.

By plotting these two axes as a semiotic square,[7] shown in Figure 8, we can visualize the relationships between the four spaces mentioned above.

To fill in these quadrants, we need to think about what sorts of spaces settler people perceive as valued or not and thus as controlled or not. In my construction, the corresponding spatial division is shown in Figure 9.

This framework requires unpacking. First, in this construct, both rural and frontier spaces are considered more proximate to wilderness spaces than are cities and built environments. As a result, narrative understandings of these spaces are also more strongly structured by a rugged, masculine

FIGURE 8 Settler colonial attitudes to land

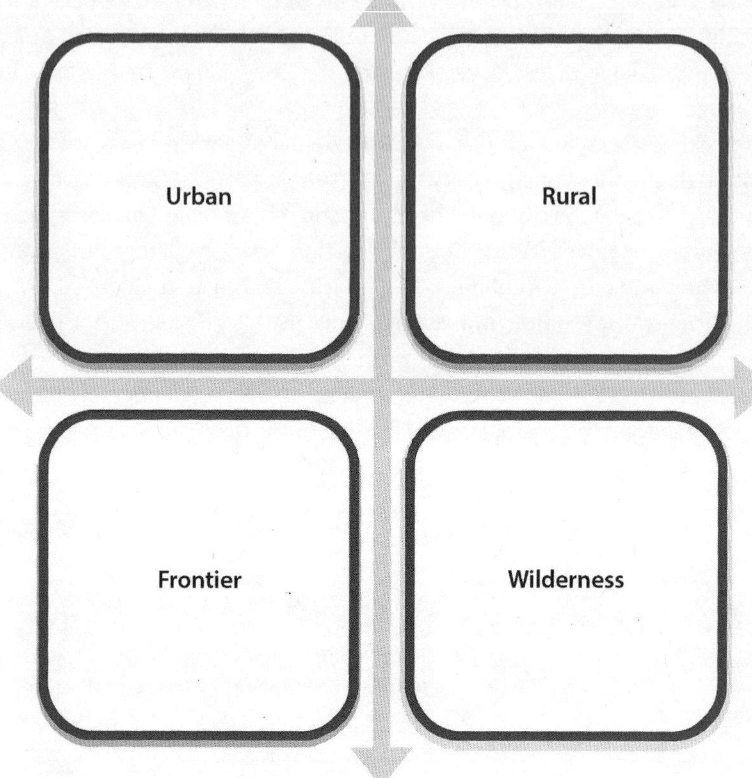

FIGURE 9 Settler colonial categories of spatial value and division

violence that is closely associated with hardy pioneer efforts to carve 'civilization' out of 'the wild' and to defend homesteads from claims made either by (Indigenous or exogenous) Others deemed to be threatening or regarded as competitors by settlers. Urban environments, by contrast, are often perceived as suspiciously far from the wilderness areas that provide the backdrop for the formation of settler identities through transformation of the land. The storied struggles to 'open' the West, 'tame' the land, and settle in a way and in a place that differentiate settler people from their metropolitan forerunners are not associated with urban spaces to nearly the same degree. However, for some would-be settlers, urban spaces may provide a respite from existential threats, especially those associated with a narrative of decline that impels outward migration from an existing metropole, whereas rural struggle for many must be seen as a foreclosure of opportunity rather than the opening of it. These relational proximities link all four types of space even as they are increasingly inscribed both in place and in the settler imagination through settler colonial acts upon the land that build ever more complex settler colonial worlds. This process is important, but first let us discuss the urban-rural binary construction that so frequently defines the settler colonial geographical imagination.

The Urban-Rural Dyad

Urban space is something that most settler Canadians and Americans encounter frequently, and the cities of North America, being composed of hyper-planned, highly valuable properties, are similar in many ways to the cities of Europe.[8] They are spaces where everything, inch by inch, is mapped, subdivided, and in the context of neoliberal capital, increasingly owned and turned toward profit or loss and toward power or disempowerment. These dynamics and perspectives are global in nature, but they resonate with longstanding attempts by settler colonial societies to displace Indigeneity through urbanization. In part, that is because all spaces, including urban spaces, are subject to the geographical imagination of their inhabitants. As geographer Derek Gregory (1994) has famously argued in his articulation of the power of the geographical imaginary, colonizing powers rework even existing urban spaces to match their ideas of how these spaces should work, regardless of whether they actually do work in that way. Gregory draws from, among other examples, the British imperial reorganization of Cairo, where the geographical imaginary of Egypt as a periphery of empire, formed in Britain and imported with British governors, was imposed in messy and disruptive ways across the city. This same effect is just as prevalent in settler colonial contexts, especially in the way that the built environment is positioned as contra the natural world, represented by national parks and similar spaces.

The existence of an urban landscape is often taken by settler people to mean that there is no history worth knowing prior to that of the built landscape. Intersecting with myths of terra nullius, urban spaces in the Americas are also portrayed as original and lacking history, as in historian Victoria Freeman's (2010) study of the city of Toronto, where residents perceive history to inhere in the material, built environment, meaning that the city quite literally helps to displace Indigenous histories. In this way, Indigenous peoples are conceptually displaced by cities regardless of their physical location, allowing cities themselves to essentially become indigenized (in the sense of the settler colonial end goal). Local histories often start with the founding and development of a particular settlement, thereby centring the city as the carrier of (legitimate) history and its occupants as carriers of this legacy – a kind of collective urban indigenization. The geographical imaginary of a city space deemed to be always already empty of prior Indigeneity has real effects on the way that services are delivered, social spaces are structured, and Indigenous lives are politicized in urban centres (DeVerteuil and Wilson 2010; Greensmith 2016). The erasure of Indigenous presence from the landscape due to urban transformations and literal ejections – from forced moves through gentrification to police and other settlers literally transporting Indigenous people out of cities and abandoning them – contributes to a sense of space that has no history and no other forms of human relationship to the land beyond the relatively recent urban formation.

Cities are also traditionally the places where many migrants become settled – from the new Americans arriving at Ellis Island and seeking their fortunes in New York City to my own family arriving in Hamilton, Ontario, following the Second World War. Despite the popularity of narratives of pastoral, frontier settlement, most newcomer people join established settler collectives in urban spaces. This may be by choice or not, as some collectives and individuals perceive particular opportunities in urban space, whereas others may be resettled in these places by government programs or connect with extended family or cultural communities that have coalesced in urban environments. Regardless, urban spaces are spaces of diversity,[9] which is threatening to some but comforting to others who do not neatly fit established perceptions of what the prototypical settler looks, acts, or sounds like.

For settlers informed by an ethic of rugged individualism, urban spaces can also be seen as spaces that stifle the individual identities of settlers behind the faceless masses, especially when these masses are increasingly neither heterosexual and cisgendered nor white, taken by many to be the definitive markers of authentic settler society.[10] In conservative, white suburban or rural communities in the United States, there is great suspicion of urban spaces and the diverse Others who inhabit them (O'Connell 2010, 541–44). This suspicion is commonly shared among the people whom former Canadian prime minister Stephen Harper attempted to distinguish from those involved in urban rioting in France – heavily motivated by resistance to racism and policies of exclusion – by labelling them "old stock Canadians" (Tieleman 2015), thereby mobilizing normative Anglo-Saxon whiteness, which strongly intersects with the pioneer mythos that underpins Canadian identity. "Nativism" is a familiar term in the United States stemming from the mid-nineteenth-century anti-immigration movements, when it was coined to preferentially distinguish the descendants of those who had been subjects of the Thirteen Colonies from Roman Catholic backgrounds – especially Irish – and other newcomers and then from later nonwhite or non-Anglo immigrant groups, whose members faced waves of white nationalist opposition. This distinction points to a contradiction inherent to urbanization and capitalism in settler colonial contexts: for those whose claim to belonging on the land precedes development, subsequent urbanization and diversification ultimately lead to a sense that something is "profoundly" wrong (Kupperman 1980, 141), which in turn motivates many to leave the originary metropole. Just as the sixteenth-century Puritans fled an England not radically Protestant enough for their beliefs, the contemporary flight of wealthy Torontonians to the Muskokas, Vancouverites to the Okanagan, or Los Angelinos to Napa Valley follows the narrative logic of settlers relocating from a degenerate metropolis to seek their own opportunities in a landscape less occupied by competing institutions of privilege. This logic imbricates with perceptions of undesirable exogenous Others populating cities and with rural spaces constructed as more conducive to authentic settler society. The result is the creation of what sociologist Anne O'Connell (2010, 553–56) has called a form of "redneck whiteness" that simultaneously contributes to the violent exclusion of indigenous Others and exogenous Others from settler space more generally and differentially privileges white, employed, property-owning settlers. In this context, self-identification as a "redneck" is an attempt to reclaim, as a point of pride, a denigrating epithet originally intended to differentiate outdoor or agricultural workers, identified by a sunburned neck, from wealthy and refined elites. O'Connell (2010) describes the complex interplay between urban and rural in settler consciousness through an examination of the Canadian Redneck Games in rural Ontario, where the idea of the redneck is turned from something shameful into something both worthy of public celebration and inextricably linked to the foundational settler colonial story. Having first emerged in Ontario and Georgia, such public spectacles are now practised across both Canada and the United States. In displays of "redneck whiteness," rural life is valorized through performances such as mudhole belly flops, tractor races, and farm animal displays. Further, the false dichotomy between liberal, diverse, 'polluted' urban spaces and conservative, monocultural, 'pure' rural spaces obscures the fact that both spaces are built on acts of erasure, occupation, and bricolage, if differently undertaken and to different extents.

Rural areas are prized by some settlers as spaces where a rugged and formative individualism can still be pursued but where, at a larger scale, the supremacy of settler colonialism remains predominant. In these spaces, there is latitude to pursue profit by working the land or by extracting resources from it, but there is also the safety of recognized and protected private property and a clear sense of white, masculine community. There is a class element here, as the economic imperatives that impel the migration of racialized or economically disadvantaged newcomers to cities where they can sell their labour also allows wealthy, white settler people to move out to pristine, pastoral environments where they can take over agricultural land and transform it into vanity or hobby properties, like the wineries that have succeeded fruit and vegetable farms in the Okanagan and the Napa Valley. Rural areas are also seen as being closer to wilderness or the natural world, and this perception sustains the contemporary relevance of historical stories of rugged masculinity, domesticated femininity, and violent struggle, which have long been markers of the asserted differences between settler and metropolitan citizens. The experience of frontier struggle is used to differentiate settlers from effete metropolitan citizens, a discourse expressed in the present through references to a 'real America' or a sort of redneck authenticity, often associated with rural spaces that still evidence recognized aspects of frontier spaces.

From Wilderness to Frontier

Frontier areas are perceived as spaces that are undeveloped or underdeveloped but that sit adjacent to or are penetrated by colonial power. They are areas that are not valuable to settlers in and of themselves but that can be made so by the presence and effort of settler people. The importance of the perception of frontier spaces for the development of American (and Canadian) identities has been much discussed since Fredrick Jackson Turner's frontier thesis famously articulated the concept, and it remains central to understanding settler colonialism. Frontier spaces, unlike urban and rural areas, are filled with the possibility of settler colonization but not with its structures. The frontier is not, to paraphrase popular science fiction, the "final frontier"; rather, it exists anywhere not yet structured by a recognized settler sovereignty. The frontier is most commonly understood to designate a liminal space between the settled spaces of city and country and the frightening, uncontrolled wilderness or natural areas beyond. However, frontier spaces can also be identified in spaces of urban decay, where the withdrawal of social relations and political and economic power leaves an exploitable, clear levelled ground ripe for opportunistic restructuring – in other words, gentrification processes. Frontier spaces are defined by their proximity to both 'settled' and 'wild' spaces. They are liminal spaces that are always already in the process of being transformed, areas that are not valuable in and of themselves but that can be made so by the occupation and bricolage of settler colonization.

American literary scholar Alex Young (2013) has interrogated enduring frontier narratives and argued that there is a strong tendency to solve problems in the United States by drawing from the example of the "rhizomatic West." In this example, frontiers are places that allow for the never-ending possibility of lines of flight away from capture by the hegemonic powers of state and capital. Young's argument is explicitly situated as a critique of settler colonial tendencies in the works of critical theorist Gilles Deleuze. That is important because although this narrative of escape from corrupt power and of rekindling individual liberty by moving westward is so often associated with a particularly conservative tendency within the United States, it is only one version of a narrative shared almost universally among settler people. The frontier exists as a place where settler people imagine that they can go to escape oppression and to pursue prosperity through ingenuity and labour. Indigenous bodies are cleared from the land in no small part to allow settler people to assert a labouring capacity, and many tenuous or aspiring settlers – whether recent migrants or diasporic populations whose members seek to settle in Canada or the United States but lack permanent status and cultural or familial connections or who maintain some level of *animus revertendi* (intent to return) – are channelled toward frontier spaces to assert this labour capacity as a way of gaining entry to settler society. That is what occurred in the nineteenth century when huge populations moved westward to build rail routes and found towns made up of members of various racialized populations – Chinese, Irish, Black, Hawaiian, and others – building social, cultural, economic, and political capital in the process. These movements are mirrored in the way that labour follows fracking expansion and pipeline construction into new frontiers, including the new energy frontier of northern British Columbia (Brody 1981).

Young (2013, 127–29) draws his construction of this "rhizomatic" frontier in part from anthropologist Patrick Wolfe, who has argued that the frontier represents the "annihilation of time." The frontier, as a "line in time" rather than a space – a distinction between the "undeveloped, natural past" and the "developed, civilized present" – serves to exclude Indigenous peoples from contemporary narratives. As Indigenous people are equated with the frontier and the frontier with anachronism, Indigenous people are rendered of the past, or in Bruyneel's (2007, 2) words, "out of time."[11] In another article on frontier violence, Young (2015, 7) goes on to point out how this narrative of liberty and freedom in the frontier is based on the assertion of a "pseudohistory" – which discusses real people and events but presents them in a way that fits an ahistorical narrative – through which the erasure of Indigenous histories contributes to the displacement of Indigenous spaces or middle-ground spaces by hegemonic settler colonial spaces. These histories may acknowledge Indigenous presence but only as elements of the frontier, and it is the Jeffersonian narrative of frontier conquest as essential to liberty that is really discussed; Indigenous people appear only as relics of the past in the bricolage of settler belonging and are deemed important not because of their existence but because they are no longer seen to exist (3–4). This is an act that requires material and conceptual violence, and so it is unsurprising that frontier spaces are so closely associated with the exercise of a violent white masculinity (12). It is this racial patriarchy that is often celebrated in rural spaces through events like the Redneck Games, which assert an equivalency between dominating the land as a farmer and dominating the land as a pioneering frontiersman. So it is that white men have frequently been induced to demonstrate direct, personal complicity with settler colonialism by seeking fortunes in the violent spaces of the fur trade, the oil rig, the mine, or the lumber camp. In fact, "man camps," defined as "temporary housing facilities constructed for predominantly male workers on resource development projects in the oil, pipeline, mining, hydroelectric, and forestry industries," have now been specifically identified by Indigenous communities as spaces of extreme, ongoing, and epidemic violence toward Indigenous women (Secwepemcul'ecw Assembly 2017). Thus they should be considered an example of how spaces of exception move through frontier spaces while following the bodily movements of settler people who are chasing resources and profits.

Given that colonial logics structure spaces of exception and segregation, informing widespread frontier and wilderness myths, a frontier can be located in a variety of places, can be produced by the separating, sorting, segregating logics of colonization, and can even emerge in areas already regarded as settled in the absence of violent impositions of settlement. A frontier is a place considered to be outside of settler colonial space but where the effects of erasure, having taken hold, are dispersing or controlling Indigeneity to the extent that settler people can perceive it as a potential place for productive occupation and bricolage – a space of opportunity that can be leveraged to a personal advantage with the correct application of colonizing power. The earlier discussion of the development of British Columbia and Vancouver revealed frontier spaces to be dependent not only on the erasure of rightful Indigenous belonging through disease, warfare, and the rewriting of history but also on the assertion of sovereignty through the occupation of territories either by direct settlement or by claims of political ownership on the part of burgeoning settler states. The configuration of frontier spaces as the targets of land acquisition for new settler colonial ventures drives the expansion of settler colonial space. Consequently, although a frontier may be outside of settler colonial space, it is incorporated into settler colonial imagined geographies. These anticipatory geographies of colonization need to reference frontiers becoming settler spaces in accordance with the myths of progress that underpin settler colonial claims to place.

Wilderness areas, by contrast, are seen as uncontrolled, uncivilized, and intimidating. Wilderness spaces are valued only to the extent that they can be tamed, meaning the extent to which elements of legible wilderness can be incorporated into the settler colonial bricolage. As mentioned, one way that this incorporation happens is through regimes of conservation and preservation, imported Euro-American concepts (Banivanua Mar 2010; Cronon 1996) that create spaces such as wilderness parks where people can visit, experience a state of nature, and then depart, temporarily affecting these spaces but leaving them fundamentally unchanged. Insofar as settler colonizers often perceive Indigenous people as elements of place and construct them as being at one with nature, the threat of violent Indigeneity that settlers fear is directly linked to the threatening nature of wilderness: there are things in the trees that seek to devour or corrupt the civilized. But the idea of settler people as aware and hardy and thus able to overcome such threats is part of what sets them apart from metropolitan contemporaries in their own legends. In this way, settler colonialism actually needs to produce and maintain wilderness, or spaces beyond the direct control of settler society, in order to maintain a key spatiality of settler identities. Simultaneously, wilderness areas must also be brought into regimes of regulation and control if settler societies are to transcend their settler colonial past; once the idea that wilderness is something of the past takes hold, the settler colonial struggle with wilderness must, by implication, also be in the past, and settler colonization must now be finished. The spatial regime of urban, rural, and frontier spaces becomes the taken-for-granted background to social life, with the natural world consigned to museum-like special preservation, along with fragments of Indigenous material culture, as a reminder of the world that both welcomed and sustained but also gave way to and was absorbed by the settler. Thus wilderness is an ambiguous space in the northern settler bloc, one that it is subject to a careful balancing act between embracing and eliminating wilderness by maintaining environments often celebrated for the healthful, rugged experience of traversing them while promoting the improvement and development that the settler geographical imaginary maps onto any terra nullius as necessary signs of settler ambition and industry.

But as much as this narrative construction exiles Indigenous spaces beyond the frontier and imagines them to be annihilated anywhere that settler colonial space predominates, it is confounded by reassertions of Indigeneity, especially in areas not associated with wilderness. Indigenous peoples contest settler colonial spatial hegemony and reassert their place relationships and sovereignties in a variety of ways: through direct-action protests against housing developments on traditional lands (McCarthy 2016); through the use of broadcast technologies to spread their messages and communicate with potential allies both within and beyond the settler state (Monture 2014); by subverting parks and similar urban green spaces to promote Indigenous food production (Corntassel and Bryce 2011); by disrupting settler "mythistories" (Battell Lowman 2014, 143) through the re-enactment of traditional movements across the land and water (especially in the form of canoe journeys: B. Johansen 2012; Hallenbeck 2015); and by many other means that involve complex interactions in and across spaces considered urban and rural.

Indigenous communities have coalesced in urban spaces and asserted Indigenous claims in many ways, including some of the most iconic protest moments of the twentieth century, such as when the urban, multination Indigenous community of San Francisco occupied Alcatraz Island from 1969–71. And as is well documented, the American Indian Movement, ongoing since 1968, and the Red Power Movement of the 1960s and 1970s were strongly rooted in the urban communities of cities like Minneapolis (D'Arcus 2010). In the present, few cities have seen as much of a resurgence of Indigenous claims to place as Vancouver, whose Downtown Eastside neighbourhood has seen a number of Indigenous-led grassroots social justice movements to reclaim space for marginalized peoples (Dean 2010). These spaces can be and frequently are targeted for recolonization, resulting in acts of erasure and intensified settler occupation that effectively create urban settler frontiers. Likewise, many urban frontiers are already occupied by racial or economic underclasses whose members are positioned as exogenous Others in the triangular relations of settler colonialism. Because these exogenous populations are not considered 'us' by settler society, their dispossession is not seen as an unjust act but as simply a by-product of securitization and the extraction of value. It is no surprise that urban geographer Neil Smith (1996) refers to the "new urban frontier" of gentrification or that, in cities such as Vancouver, gentrification has been analyzed increasingly in terms of a capitalist project of settler colonialism (Baloy 2016; Dean 2015; Edmonds 2010).[12]

Suburbia: Transcendence Frustrated

If the urban-rural and frontier-wilderness tensions define two dimensions of settler colonial space, a third dimension can be seen in suburban space. Suburbs, although not exclusively a North American formation, are certainly ubiquitous across the northern bloc of settler colonialism. Urban historians Richard Harris and Robert Lewis (2001, 262–63) show that the development of urban and suburban space has followed similar trajectories in Canada and the United States and that, although suburbs have not been exclusively white, middle-class, or spatially overdetermined by nearby cities, there remains a persistent image of the suburb as a space of white, heteronormative, patriarchal affluence. Masculinity – like patriarchal violence – inheres in the replication of suburban domestic spaces premised on feminine subservience and labour (Marsh 1988), as satirized in movies ranging from Tim Burton's *Edward Scissorhands* (1990) to Gary Ross's *Pleasantville* (1998) as part of the cynical 1990s cultural turn against the staid sameness of these spaces. Suburbs have also been shaped by the racialized dynamics of the urban development that followed the Second World War, resulting in the dominance of "sprawl, concentrated poverty and segregation (if not hypersegregation)" (Squires and Kubrin 2005, 48). The intended product of this racial and gender hierarchy is a utopian order, at times located literally behind walls, that is unassailable by changes to society or by encroaching wilderness. This is a fantasy, of course, but a powerful fantasy. It is this imagined suburb, which has never existed, that I argue gives a glimpse of the ideal form of settler colonial space in the worldview of the most privileged Canadians and Americans, a high plateau in the topography of power defined by race, class, and "something more."[13]

Suburbs are seen by many settlers to occupy the best of both worlds, one in which settlers can remain adjacent to the services and culture located in urban spaces while preserving the individual freedom and outdoor lifestyle valorized in rural settings. Settler men in the suburbs can enact what historian Margaret Marsh (1988, 165–66) describes as the two aspects of Theodore Roosevelt: the responsible "corporate drone" during the week and the "flamboyant Rough Rider" atop a ride-on mower who maintains the "homestead" on the weekends, thereby experiencing a metaphoric re-enactment of the frontier struggle of labouring to maintain a large, private garden without actually coming too close to any dangerous wilderness while ensuring that suburbs remain safe for settlers.[14] As a result, suburbs represent a utopian vision of settler colonialism because they are hybrids deemed to be free of the potential drawbacks of the danger in rural and frontier areas, the decline and decay perceived in urban spaces, and the unlivability and incommensurability (or lack of value) to be found in wilderness.

For several decades after the Second World War, suburbia held a powerful and important place in the imagined geographies of Canada and the United States. Veracini (2012) positions the suburb as an extension of common settler colonial forms, noting the similarities between the dynamics of the frontier homestead and the dynamics of settler migrations to suburbs. Although I agree with Veracini's analysis, I assert that the settler suburb also occupies a fundamentally different position given that, unlike the homestead or the city, the suburb's position is *legible through* but not inherently *located in* the settler colonial geographical imaginary. Rather, it is another aspirational space. Insofar as settler colonialism has never succeeded – either in purging places of Indigeneity or in providing promised wealth and freedom to all settlers (Veracini 2015, 96) – suburbs have arisen as an attempt to spatially overcome the contradictions and shortcomings of settler colonization as experienced by powerful, but not quite elite, settler Canadians and Americans.

The suburb has come to represent an interior frontier: a space ripe with opportunity and otherwise unoccupied by Indigenous sovereignties. Like urban spaces, suburbs are seen as historyless – except to the extent that they are often named after now-removed landscape features, just as the streets of my home neighbourhood are named after types of apples that once grew there – and therefore they are beyond the temporal reach of Indigenous peoples. Suburbs always already conform to the spatialities of settler colonialism, which are premised on the control of various populations in shared spaces because, in many ways, they materially shape the flows of these populations.

> They have a distinct materiality, a material environment that is historically constructed – networks of roads and railroads, the layout and design

> of residences, offices, factories, public parks and recreation areas, fences, walls, etc. This materiality regulates and mediates social relations and daily routines within a place, and is thus imbued with power ... The walls and fences of gated communities, a distinct feature of US suburbia, work to restrict access and exclude non-residents. In this case the walls and fences facilitate the ability of its residents to control access to "their" space, creating socio-spatial boundaries that define who belongs[,] and often become the object of contention. (Leitner, Sheppard, and Sziarto 2008, 161)

Suburbs therefore bridge the urban-rural dyad, with the interconnections of capital and technology – such as the automobile and systems of highways – serving to shrink the wide-open spaces of the rural even as lawns and horizontally stretched properties prevent the crowding seen in cities and the perceived threat of exogenous Others.

Although a number of settler colonial transfers are operative in settler suburbs, one of the most important to recognize is the type of narrative transfer that Veracini (2010b, 41–42) defines as occurring

> when a "tide of history" rationale is invoked to deny legitimacy to ongoing indigenous presences and grievances. This transfer focuses on "fatal impacts," on indigenous discontinuity with the past, and typically expresses regret for the inevitable "vanishing" of indigenous peoples. If they have had their last stand, if their defeat is irretrievably located in the past, their activism in the present is perceived as illegitimate ... Indigenous survival is thus transferred away, foreclosed.

Suburban spaces are narratively constructed as existing within their own reality bubble, one that is disconnected from preceding struggles since suburbs are disconnected from ongoing struggles through gates, distance, and surveillance. The absolute denial of contemporary Indigeneity subsumed beneath the transformed geography of the suburb frees the settler imagination from fear of settler colonial reversal or failure due to the destruction of the settlement or one's expulsion from it (see the example of Algeria in Barclay, Chopin, and Evans 2018; and Veracini 2010b, 102–4). Suburban spatialities are in part an expression of settler peoples' desires to permanently empty the Indigenous sector of the triangular relations of settler colonialism so that they may free themselves from the threat of Indigeneity forever. This goal has also been pursued through metropolitan urbanization, but suburbs also help to spatially separate privileged settlers – who are often, but not exclusively, white – from exogenous Others, including migrants and sojourners, whose increasing arrival seems to signal instability for many settler people.

Settler people almost stumble upon the suburban form as they try to reconcile their competing motives to identify frontiers with potential opportunities but to avoid dangerous Indigenous people and the loss of contact with civilization that characterizes wilderness, to occupy the particularly privileged social positions aggregated in urban spaces, and to gate-keep and discipline "agonistic" Others (Featherstone 2008, 48–49) through the frontier justice of rural spaces. To this end, suburban areas are often seen as spaces of escape, especially vis-à-vis areas of poverty or the concentration of racialized Others in urban centres. Consistent with settler collectives colonizing outward from an ostensibly degenerate imperial core, settler people flee from other settler colonial spaces to suburbs. This migration has historically been highly racialized (but not racially homogeneous), with suburbs akin to settler collectives being organized around whiteness and class privilege:

> Whiteness as economic value is, of course, one of the main reasons behind the American phenomenon of "white flight." Alongside industrial relocation to the suburbs and the Cold War fear of urban nuclear annihilation ... white homeowners relocated to the suburbs in order to protect their real-estate investments ... The fear was that as more and more black people moved into what were ostensibly white neighbourhoods property values would decline. As such, we might reinterpret white flight as a form of anticipation, a speculative hedge against devaluation both of the real-estate asset price and its underlying value: whiteness. (Baldwin 2011, 177)

This anticipation is resonant with the anticipatory geographies of settler colonialism, but in this case, it informs an anticipatory move to head off any loss of settler privilege "by turning the world inside out rather than upside down" (Veracini 2012, 345). This move is pursued by means of the reenactment of settler migrations and homesteading through automotive commutes and private property, preferably at the end of a cul-de-sac – where there are fewer adjacent neighbours, meaning more space to enact personal sovereignty. The absolute securing of space is co-constitutive with settlers' waning need to search out new spaces that are distant from imperial cores but not threatened by the encroachment of frontier elements. It is not simply security that is being guaranteed but, in fact, privilege and advantage. In this sense, suburbs represent a space of endless (but not infinite) opportunity, which contributes to the characterization of suburban space as utopian.

Suburbs can be seen as a spatial form asserted in order to manage difference across North American societies that have seen rapid change in their racial, ethnic, cultural, and linguistic makeup. Urban spaces are often portrayed as environmentally or racially polluted (e.g., see the case study of Los Angeles in Frost 2001, 364–65), and although rural spaces are portrayed as healthful (O'Connell 2010), they are also subject to intrusions by indigenous Others and exogenous Others. As a result, the lawns and green spaces of settler suburbs recall the benefits of rural homesteads in different forms that imply cosmopolitan sensibilities. Lawns and green spaces are portrayed as essential to the raising of children (Veracini 2012, 341–42). They are seen to allow for youth to "carve out" their own social spaces (Dunkley 2004, 562, citing Matthews, Limb, and Percy-Smith 1998, 196) while keeping them close to home, reflective of increasing parental fears of dangerous individuals lurking in public spaces to prey upon children (Valentine and McKendrick 1997, 223). Lawns and green spaces also represent a continuation, and perhaps a pinnacle, of preserved spaces such as wilderness parks, which denote the ultimate triumph of settler society over untamed nature. The core-periphery dynamic replayed in the suburbs is played out in individual property arrangements. Literary scholar Keith Wilhite (2012) argues that suburbs should be understood as intensifications of North American regionalism that are simultaneously secure as part of the triumphal nation-state and also engaged in internal competition with other suburban regions for desirable populations, transportation networks connecting to urban centres, economic influence, and place-based identity. In the suburbs, the distance from the metropole no longer implies a loss of privilege, and so, by definition, the proximity to spaces of nature or wilderness no longer implies an increase in perceived threat. The settler colonial frontier is effectively displaced, and rural spaces become the new periphery to the urban settler core, with the suburbs sitting apart from both. Individual lawns and parks become display places for everything from carefully manicured gardens to new and more expensive automobiles and other signs of settler identity and affluence.

Suburbs and the desirability of suburbs must be understood in part through the kinds of space that they are seen to negate. To the extent that colonial violence is normalized through its assertion in frontier spaces, suburbs normalize policing and associated violence by the absence of frontier space. Suburban spaces are not fundamentally safer than urban centres in terms of measurable statistics like crime, and both are less safe than rural areas (Squires and Kubrin 2005, 54). However, this fact is dispelled from the consciousness of (especially white, well-off) settler suburbanites, as they are distanced from the violence associated with poverty and racial marginalization and can afford to disregard their own historical or contemporary complicity in these violences. This is part of what has been called "a culture of amnesia,"[15] where the very acts that create settler colonial space are forgotten and disavowed as settlers solidify their future claims by erasing their past crimes of usurpation.

This culture of amnesia is built on social "dysconsciousness" (D.M. Johnson 2011, 110), but in addition to assumptions about how things are, settler people increasingly accept new assumptions that justify changes to space as if these changes were natural and inevitable, or they in fact portray spaces as rightly returning to normal after some period of disruption. In connection with the security of property, security against violence is assumed in the suburbs. Marxist geographer David Harvey (2000, 168) refers to the gated "securitopias" of the neoliberal United States as an aspirational space "designed to induce nirvana rather than critical awareness." There is no need for police to walk a beat because indigenous Others and exogenous Others are barred at the gates. The display of violence associated with colonial exclusion and dispossession is discarded by settlers along with the racialized violence of the rural and urban – and, not coincidentally, along with the physical presence of racialized bodies. Similarly, the classless space of a uniform middle-class polity submerges the ways that wealth and privilege accrue unevenly in settler colonial spaces, stabilizing these spaces and securing them against class unrest. Replaced by suburban lawns and green spaces, the frontier can safely be possessed and forgotten because the suburb sits as a utopian example of how to discipline space.

Richard Harris and Robert Lewis (2001) point out that the perceived suburban ideal of ethnically homogeneous and class-privileged radial communities organized around an urban core has never actually existed in reality. Suburban spaces have always involved a mixture of affluent communities seeking urban escape and aspirational communities seeking settlement opportunities in 'open' spaces on the periphery of developed cities (Squires and Kubrin 2005). Further, due to neoliberal globalization, the reification of white, affluent suburban space in the northern bloc of settler colonialism that followed the Second World War[16] has given way to a recession of the white settler middle class in the northern settler bloc. The existential horror and disconnect of exurbs, suburban sprawl, and widespread urban decay have disillusioned many settler people (e.g., see M. Davis 2007). The satisfaction of material desire through property, monocultural remove, and 'classless' capitalism has proven to many settler peoples to be a fantasy. The suburbs today in many ways actually represent the ultimate failure of the settler colonial dream, especially in places like Detroit, Cleveland, and Buffalo (Sugrue 2014; H.L. Taylor 2011), where economic shifts at the global scale have undermined the settler colonial anticipatory geography of benefits accruing due to occupation of a "special locale" (Veracini 2010b, 55), leading to whole neighbourhoods trapped by negative property values. Here, a suburb is a place where row after row of houses sit empty, an untamed urban wilderness denoted by overgrown lawns and boarded-up windows, which is an unsettling prospect for settler colonizers looking to plant themselves permanently in place.

As I conclude this chapter, there are several key points that bear restating. First, settler colonizers can and do form profound relationships to land, which is configured as individual property, as landscape, and as part of a material process of development and exchange. However, all of these attachments inhere in what land can be made to do for settlers and, most especially, in whether land can be made to be 'home.' The affective attachments that settler colonizers form to the places where they live may be strong, emotional, and meaningful, but they differ in kind from the intimate relationships that Indigenous peoples have with their lands. Settlers value land for what it can be made into, for how it can be shaped, and for the extent that these shapes support settler colonial imaginaries and ambitions. As shown in the next chapter, the complex ways that settler colonizers have shaped the lands of the northern bloc have created a shifting, dynamic topography of power that has massive impacts on who participates in settler colonization and how.

4

Revolutionary Aspirations? Social Movements and Settler Colonial Complicity

After a brief stint in my late teens during which I supported the Liberal Party – Canada's centrist political party, which held power at the federal level through much of my teenage and early adult life – I shifted my support to the New Democratic Party (NDP). At the time of writing, the NDP has never formed the government, but it is backed by trade unions and generally regarded as the standard bearer for the Canadian left. I was an unmitigated fan of their late leader, Jack Layton, and truly believed that if they could just dislodge the traditional ruling Liberal and Conservative parties, the NDP would benefit both Indigenous people and non-Indigenous Canadians. I remember during one of my early days in graduate school passionately advocating for a political movement to support Indigenous rights via the NDP. My classmates, mainly Indigenous, were not impressed. Someone, I cannot recall who, sarcastically remarked to a friend, "Future prime minister over there."

It was not long afterward that my enthusiasm for the NDP and mainstream progressive politics began to wither. I learned from my classmates again and again how they had been let down, betrayed, and actively targeted and attacked by so-called progressive activists. Some had been part of the protests to stop mass logging of old-growth forests in the Nuu-chah-nulth territory of Tla-o-qui-aht (Clayquot Sound) in British Columbia. They spoke with anger at the way that, even while fighting on the same side, white activists treated Indigenous elders, knowledge keepers, speakers, and activists as curiosities. White settler activists were always given the final say at community meetings. Indigenous people would be asked to perform welcome ceremonies and then pushed to one side so that the 'real work' could begin. Most damning, when the actions were ultimately successful and commercial logging was barred, white settler activists immediately turned on Nuu-chah-nulth community members who attempted to fell trees on their own lands in order to house members of their own community, levelling accusations of betrayal and barbarism at them. These white settler 'allies' showed what they really cared about – the stagnant preservation of a mythical, imaginary, pristine woodland that they might sometimes visit. The actual material deprivation and slow genocide of Indigenous nations was not enough to rally support; rather, any number of Indigenous deaths could apparently be accepted, whereas no amount of logging could be justified.

After several months of valuable instruction and examples from my classmates, I took a much harder look at the actual track record of the leftist parties and organizations that I supported. I realized that not a single one, no matter how much they proclaimed support for Indigenous rights, could bring themselves to discuss Indigenous sovereignty. I noted that they all referred to "our" (meaning Canada's) First Nations – an expression that I came to see as insidious and paternalistic, an extension of the Crown claiming Indigenous people as wards of the state in previous times. I noticed that their platforms almost always stumped for Indigenous rights based on the need to relieve the economic burden on the Canadian state that came with the impoverishment of Indigenous communities. Even leftist parties saw Indigenous people as problems to be solved, usually through economic development and self-sufficiency or self-government. I finally saw that I had been supporting a well-meaning but ultimately settler colonial political discourse. I was ashamed and I was angry.

Indigenous Social Movements and Settler Activists

Social movement activism constantly evolves, and the successes and failures of various social movements, as well as the responses to them, tell us a great deal about the unstated or hidden implications of their activism. Indigenous people who push for social change and an amelioration of the conditions of "bare life" (Agamben 1998) that the settler colonial society imposes face fierce opposition, as do anti-capitalist, abolitionist, and other social justice movements. Much of this opposition overlaps, although not completely, and so the successes, failures, and shifts in makeup or orientation among wider social movements can reveal shared strategic priorities, as well as areas of dissonance. In this chapter, I critique the fact that the established discourses of anti-capitalist social movements, as exemplified by the Occupy movements, leave settler colonization unaddressed, and I demonstrate how leftist calls for racial and minority inclusion or multiculturalism are used to subvert Indigenous demands for the return of land. I then discuss how contemporary 'anti-colonial' activists pre-empt Indigenous sovereignty in their constructions of mass movements, and I examine a left-utopian vision for the near future that posits a socialist, radically egalitarian society that remains deeply rooted in settler colonialism.

In considering social movements writ large on Turtle Island, it is necessary to centre the works and critiques of Indigenous people and communities partly to demonstrate that there are significant differences between Indigenous movements for decolonization and settler dominated anti-capitalist and anti-racist movements even though the two are often assumed, especially by white settler activists, to be coterminous. Indigenous peoples' social movements are movements of resistance and survival in the face of overwhelming settler colonial violence, which has been sustained across centuries and perpetrated by agents of the state, corporate representatives, and private individuals in nearly equal measure (L. Simpson 2017). The survivance (Vizenor 2008) and resurgence of Indigenous peoples in the present is a testament to the incredible success of Indigenous social movements of many kinds. In recent years, many Indigenous scholars – including Glen Coulthard (2014), Sarah Hunt (2014; Hunt and Holmes 2015), Audra Simpson (2014), Leanne Simpson (2011, 2017), and Eve Tuck (Tuck, McKenzie, and McCoy 2014; Tuck and Yang 2012) – have articulated a powerful, land-centred, embodied, and active process of resurgence that has revitalized Indigenous governance structures, materially enacted relationships to land in ways that work toward economic self-determination (Corntassel 2008), and fundamentally rejected notions of Indigenous inclusion (meaning assimilation) in settler colonial societies. This vision is drawn from lived experiences and years of working to build and understand the kinds of social change that are necessary for the survival of Indigenous individuals and nations. Indigenous political movements have long been influential in global leftist activism – perhaps most famously giving life to the philosophy and action of Zapatismo in the Mexican state of Chiapas and beyond (Khasnabish 2011, 2013) – and have succeeded in exerting pressure on colonial states through international bodies like the United Nations (Lightfoot 2016). And like leftist social movements, Indigenous struggles for survival have also evolved and changed tactics and approaches. The examples and analysis in this chapter focus on Occupy and similar progressive or leftist social movements from roughly 2008–12 and engage closely with critiques made at the time by Indigenous scholars and activists.

The development and expression of Indigenous social movements in the twenty first century are particularly important to consider for what they reveal about the differences between social movement organizing that explicitly centres Indigenous claims to land and many protest movements (even radical ones) that are organized against the power of state and capital but lack a core decolonial ethic. A key moment occurred in 2012 when Idle No More – a decentralized but coordinated series of round-dance flash mobs, protest marches, teach-ins, and site occupations and land reclamations – captured headlines across the northern settler bloc. Originally organized in response to the move by the Canadian government under Conservative prime minister Stephen Harper to remove environmental protections from waterways without consultation with First Nations recognized by the government, let alone Indigenous experts or communities, whose lifeways depend on these waters, Idle No More became a flashpoint for a number of ongoing issues: environmental racism (especially in relation to access to clean water and sanitation), industrial development, pollution of traditional territories, poverty, government underfunding of social services on reserves, failed treaty and land claim negotiations, ongoing violence by police, racism within healthcare and education, and the national epidemic of missing and murdered Indigenous women and girls. Rather than a movement in and of itself, Idle No More was more of a rallying cry, or what I have elsewhere described as a "movement moment" (Barker 2015, 44), and its importance in terms of signalling the creative resurgence of Indigenous communities must not be understated.

Since then, a large number of local movements have made many bold and powerful assertions of Indigenous resurgence, including the Coast Salish reclamation and restorative naming of the mountain PKOLS (Mount Douglas) on Vancouver Island, along with other features of the land and sea (Murphyao and Black 2015; Rose-Redwood 2016; Tucker and Rose-Redwood 2015), and the efforts of Anishinaabe artist Susan Blight and Anishinaabe political scientist Hayden King through the Ogimaa Mikana Project to reclaim Indigenous place names in Toronto (CBC Radio 2016; Henceforward 2016). Meanwhile, Indigenous protest camps have continued to provide ongoing material resistance to colonial displacement and environmental change, while creating spaces for Indigenous lifeways to be practised partially outside of pervasive spaces of settler colonialism (Barker and Ross 2017). The Unist'ot'en Camp established in 2010 is located amid mountains and valleys adjacent to the Midzin Kwa (Morris River) in the traditional homelands of the Wet'suwet'en people in northern British Columbia and is oriented in opposition to the proposed Enbridge Northern Gateway and Coastal Gas Link pipelines, among several other pipeline projects along a route through the territory of the Wet'suwet'en Nation. It became a flashpoint in the winters of both 2019 and 2020 when the Royal Canadian Mounted Police invaded and attempted to disperse the camp. These invasions led memorably to weeks of unrest across Canada in January 2020 as Indigenous communities quickly took up solidarity protests, blocking railways and highways, occupying government buildings, including the Victoria Legislature in British Columbia, and using social and traditional media to organize quickly and effectively. Presently, a pipeline expansion in southern British Columbia is being opposed using similar but modified tactics. The Secwépemc Nation's Tiny House Warriors, rather than building a single camp, are building multiple small dwellings throughout their territory to directly challenge efforts to thrust the Kinder Morgan Trans Mountain pipeline through unceded Secwépemc territory. Even more nationally and internationally visible, thanks to the strategic efforts of the Water Protectors, was the enormous protest at Standing Rock in 2016–17, where first the Lakota and later a wider movement of Indigenous and non-Indigenous activists opposed the construction of a pipeline adjacent to the Standing Rock Reservation in South Dakota, which will cross under the Missouri River, threatening the source of most fresh water in the area. Capturing both enormous media attention as well as the imagination of many progressive and leftist activists, the Standing Rock protest demonstrated that the confluence of Indigenous self-determination, environmental stewardship, and anti-corporate (if not anti-capitalist) narratives could galvanize a large number of people into action in a relatively short time despite sustained violent opposition by state and private security forces (Estes 2019).

However, Standing Rock was not an unqualified success. In addition to the camp eventually being forced to disperse after continuous and overwhelming violence by police and private security officers, mass arrests, and similar persecution, there were also significant problems within the camp itself. Primarily, many settler and non-Indigenous activists repeated the kinds of colonial behaviours that I describe in this chapter, including the failure to listen, acts of both subtle and overt racism, the appropriation of cultural practices, and the displacement of Indigenous people from leadership positions (Deerinwater 2016; Kazdin and Tu 2016; M. Robinson 2018). These settler activists, while legitimately committed to putting their own bodies on the line for a cause that they believed in, enacted relationships of colonial erasure and occupation over and over again. This is not, of course, simply a problem that occurred at Standing Rock but is endemic to almost every instance when settler 'allies' show up to support Indigenous resurgence movements. Here, I seek to articulate why this is the case and why it is important not to conflate contemporary progressive or leftist politics – even the most challenging or radical – with Indigenous resurgence struggles if broader decolonial activist networks are to emerge as an effective force for social change in the northern settler bloc.

Anti-Capitalist Movements and the Limits of Settler Solidarity

It is obvious why would-be settlers participate in and promote systems of capitalism given that primitive accumulation, the engine that drives the development of capitalist systems, is made easier in the context of terra nullius. However, capitalism and the processes of gentrification and globalization, although linked to the deprivation of Indigenous communities, are not the sole or even direct cause of this dispossession (Choudry 2010, 98–99). It is often easy – too easy – to locate settler colonial constructs in familiar spaces of conservative, nationalist, or aspirational capitalist privilege. The following explanation of the way that postcolonial geographies of capitalism have had an impact on traditional Marxist and other socialist spatial analyses closely parallels my own reasons for asserting the need for a settler colonial analysis of anti-capitalist social movements: "A postcolonial perspective pushes us to go further than traditional geographies of the Left which, though often sympathetic to the needs and experiences of the subaltern, tend to focus on systemic critiques of capitalism and analyses of the formal spaces of labour, to the detriment of vivid, complex and embodied accounts of lives and livelihoods" (Pollard et al. 2009, 138). Although geographer Jane Pollard and colleagues discuss the ways that "concentrations of poverty in the [global] North and wealth in the [global] South" (137) have been obscured under metanarratives of geography and capital, the point holds in our context. Capitalism plays a key role in the settler colonial assemblage of the northern bloc, but the experiences of settler people, of contemporary migrants and refugees, and of the diverse and dynamic racialized communities of Canada and the United States of America are not wholly defined by capitalism. It is with this understanding in mind that I turn to an examination of anti-capitalist movements in the northern bloc.

The current era of mass movements against neoliberalism and capitalism and for social justice need to be viewed as part of a continuum that runs back through much of the twentieth century. However, a major shift occurred just before the start of the twenty-first century that has marked the emergence of the "newest social movements" (R.J.F. Day 2004, 2005), which have broken with the liberal-dominated social change strategies of the 1980s and 1990s. During the Battle of Seattle – a series of protests against the World Trade Organization that threw the city into chaos from November 30 to December 3, 1999, setting a model for the next several years of summit protests – protesters used mass direct action, a diversity of tactics, and affinity group organizing to take advantage of predictable and lackadaisical preparations on the part of the police and security forces, disrupting and causing the cancellations of key meetings. However, it was not long before states responded with deadly force (Zajko and Béland 2008), costing the lives of civilians such as Carlo Giuliani, a protester who was shot by riot police in Genoa in 2001, and Ian Tomlinson, a member of the public who was struck by police while trying to make his way through a protest to his home in London in 2009. Further, such meetings were moved to locations farther from major population centres such as Gleneagles, Scotland, in 2005 and Huntsville, Ontario, in 2010. Both sites were chosen for their location in rural areas where there was little transport or accommodation access and where nonresidents could be easily identified and isolated. For activists, this change in venues increased the financial costs, time commitments, and risks of attending summits. Many important moments of protest and resistance took place in between these headliner events, but there was a fundamental reorientation away from summit protests within leftist social movement organization around the late 2000s, when the "movement of the squares" erupted. Occupying strategic sites is, of course, a long-established protest tactic, but the reinvigoration of this mode of protest in places such as Egypt during the Arab Spring of 2011, which was subsequently adopted by anti-austerity protesters in New York City during Occupy Wall Street in the same year, was a marked and important change. Rather than responding to roving high-level and high-profile political and economic meetings, protesters took places of symbolic, financial, or literal importance to the function of governance and held them.

This inspiring and innovative shift energized a generation of activists, created enduring relationships in and beyond the protest camps, and seems to have marked a fracturing of the neoliberal consensus following the financial crisis of 2007–08, but despite the widely inclusive rhetoric deployed by these movements, I argue that this change in activist tactics never fundamentally sought to address the settler colonial foundation of Canadian and American societies. This argument is not intended to attack the Occupy movements or any particular protesters; rather, Occupy is an example from recent social movement history that can be used to clearly illustrate the much broader ways that the geographical imaginaries and embodied occupations of settler colonizers can evolve, change, and adapt to differing political conditions and social narratives, even in contexts where the majority political opinion is anti-establishment, if not fully anti-capitalist. Colonialism's imaginaries of frontier and periphery, its spaces of opportunity, and its embodied acts of occupation, erasure, and bricolage can be easily read as historical or conservative dynamics of settler society and culture. Here, I argue that they remain particularly relevant in reading how progressive, leftist, and even radical social movements in the northern settler bloc have approached Indigenous people and issues of colonialism and decolonization.

"Already Occupied": Settler Colonialism in the Occupy Movements

The Occupy movements, which began with the occupation of Zuccotti Park in Manhattan in the winter of 2011 and eventually spread to cities around the world, were a radical challenge to the forces of neoliberal capitalism and austerity, the security state, and the sense of fear and hopelessness that dominated much social and political discourse in the United States and elsewhere at the time. When protesters took over Zuccotti Park – a publicly-accessible but privately-owned square in the heart of the Wall Street financial district – and established the first Occupy Wall Street camp in September 2011, it is unlikely that they believed they would be the precursor of a movement. As Occupy Wall Street gave rise to Occupy Oakland, Occupy LSX, and dozens of other protests in major cities across the United States and Canada, it became increasingly apparent both to the protest campers and to mainstream media and political elites that there was something important happening. To be sure, Occupy Wall Street is not the beginning of the story, as Occupy would not have happened without the Arab Spring and the dozens of other movements that preceded it and to which it was connected.[1] But by the same token, it is now impossible to talk about contemporary protest in the northern settler bloc without considering the impact of the Occupy movements. Regardless of where and when Occupy originated, the desire to stand bodily in the way of austerity, neoliberal globalization, and the inequalities of wealth and rights spread like a contagion – as affective impulses so often do. From hard-core, anarchistic activists and those mobilized by the personal impacts of poverty and dispossession to people who never considered themselves activists but felt that something needed to be done, folks from all walks of life and identities took to the plazas, the bridges, and the streets of cities across Turtle Island and around the world.

Occupy has now received significant attention in scholarly works and popular and alternative media. Despite the relatively brief rise and fall of this political movement, there are already many books, scholarly papers, and popular articles lauding the goals of the movement and its radical practices, from direct democracy through general assemblies to the creative uses of human and electronic communication technology (e.g., see Bray 2013; Feigenbaum, McCurdy, and Frenzel 2013; Graeber 2013; J. Jones 2014; Milkman et al. 2012; and J.K. Rowe and Carrol 2014). These works reveal that Occupy has had an impact beyond its active life, inspiring tactics among activists and transforming discourses around public versus private space. Many of these works, while recognizing that supporters of Occupy came from many walks of life and from across the political spectrum, note that the movement as a whole was deeply inspired by anarchist theory and praxis. However, despite the inclusive, anti-authoritarian, and radically democratic character of Occupy writ large, the Occupy movements have not escaped critique from social movement scholars and activists. In that vein, I turn to a particular critique of Occupy: the argument that no matter how challenging to financial institutions and the elite, Occupy's tactics and demands reinforced settler colonialism, actively erasing Indigeneity and raising the spectre of a postcapitalist settler colonial polity as a new threat to Indigenous sovereignty.

These critiques arise not because the Occupy movements were so different from other leftist non-Indigenous-led movements. Rather, like many other anti-capitalist movements throughout the history and across the territory of the northern bloc of settler colonialism, they were unable to escape settler hegemony no matter how otherwise liberatory the rhetoric or radical the praxis. One observation of this critique is that Occupy encampments in Canada and the United States were frequently dominated by educated, economically secure, white students and activists who had the time to commit to occupation tactics, whereas impoverished, racialized, and otherwise marginalized communities were less welcome or able to participate (Campbell 2011; Pickerill and Krinsky 2012, 282–83).[2] Further, the Occupy movements failed to ally with Indigenous communities in particular, despite several concerted attempts by Occupy members and groups to seek solidarity with Indigenous peoples and communities and despite frequent references to Indigenous land and invocations of settler colonial critiques, such as arguing for migrant justice in part because all non-Indigenous peoples in the United States are immigrants. These attempts were not well received, for reasons that I draw out below, and a divide began to grow between protesters who identified with the Occupy movements and those who identified with Indigenous peoples' movements. This schism between Occupy and Indigenous communities ultimately led to some of the most contentious acts and embarrassing failures of the Occupy movements.

One example of these failures revolves around a tone-deaf attempt to conjoin the goals of Occupy Wall Street and the struggles of Indigenous peoples that badly missed the mark. Early in the Occupy Wall Street campaign, posters began circulating (without an artist credit attached) that featured a call for the protesters to "Decolonize Wall Street." Tsalagi scholar Adrienne Keene (2011), author of the popular and influential blog *Native Appropriations,* quickly pointed out that the poster was more wrong than right and strongly reflected settler colonial imaginaries of Indigeneity. The errors that Keene noted were multiple. The poster was presented with the colours red, black, yellow, and white, which are frequently and at times stereotypically used to refer to Indigeneity through imagery such as the medicine wheel, and it featured a large, centrally positioned image of Sitting Bull, a Lakota leader from the nineteenth century with little relationship to Occupy or Manhattan Island. Further, the text on the poster declared Wall Street to be on Algonquin land, when in fact it is on Lenape land, Algonquin territory being much farther north. By employing all of these generalized and incorrect portrayals of Indigeneity, and doing so ostensibly in the service of an anti-colonial ethic, this poster doubled down on the imagined geographies of settler colonialism, which at best crudely swap Indigenous nations interchangeably with each other and at worst erase connections between particular Indigenous peoples and places crucial to understanding decolonizing struggles and Indigenous identities.[3] The poster created a great deal of controversy but few concrete actions to deal with accusations of ongoing settler colonialism in the Occupy movement, although some camps in places like Boston responded to the controversy by adopting resolutions in support of Indigenous peoples.

As various groups attempted to revitalize the Occupy movements with new initiatives in the summer of 2013, it became clear that many messages had not truly sunk in, evidenced by the proposal put forth in several online forums to "colonize Wall Street" (meaning to found a permanent camp there) in September of that year.[4] If settler activists in Occupy had been paying attention to Indigenous activists, they would have heard demands to reject the logics of settler colonialism. In that context, settler recommitments to the logic and language of colonialism must have been infuriating to Indigenous people. When activists – not exclusively Indigenous but also including many of those who had critiqued Occupy – spoke out about problematic language and dynamics, prominent Occupy members dismissed their concerns. In a post on the Occupy Forum (2013), editorial staff wrote that the critiques of their use of language only made them "proud to have contributed to raising awareness of the persecution of native and indigenous peoples." That, of course, was never the intent; rather, the language of colonization was used because it was seen as a legitimate tactic to turn back against the Wall Street elites. But it was deployed with no consideration of either its impact on Indigenous peoples or the fact that claiming this place for a radical settler community had implications for Indigenous peoples struggling to reassert Indigenous nationhood and place-based identities. The action never took place, but the proposal certainly contributed to ongoing frustrations among Indigenous activists.

Although many observers were both sympathetic to and critical of Occupy tactics and approaches from the start – a process ostensibly encouraged by the open-forum governance style of many encampments – the critiques of persistent settler colonialism in Occupy eventually became impossible to ignore, especially as they were increasingly backed by research from socially engaged scholars. Sociologist Konstantin Kilibarda's (2012) influential analysis focuses on Canadian-based Occupy camps, specifically those in Toronto, Montreal, and Vancouver, and reveals persistent racism and nationalism in the service of settler colonialism throughout. Most damning, Kilibarda points out that Indigenous people repeatedly brought their concerns to Occupy assemblies but were rebuffed and that, in at least one case involving the Occupy Toronto camp, they separated themselves from the main decision-making processes in order to protect themselves from further colonial imposition. Indigenous theorist Sandy Grande (Quechua) (2013), meanwhile, has taken on the supposed radicalism of Occupy Wall Street, arguing that its collapse of colonialism into capitalism represented not a radical break, as many non-Indigenous commentators had suggested, but instead continuity with liberalism, in which attempts to collectivize ownership of Wall Street (and other places) further obscured the originary violence and displacement of settler colonization. Further, Eve Tuck and K. Wayne Yang's highly influential "Decolonization Is Not a Metaphor" (2012, 9–28) positions the Occupy movements and similar attempts at urban homesteading as settler "moves to innocence," where the struggles for particular kinds of equality displace the struggles of Indigenous peoples for decolonization and resurgence. Taken together, these interventions make a compelling case that the Occupy movements were never truly able to bridge the gap between the reactionary anti-austerity agenda that drove initial engagement and the proactive and much longer-term struggles of Indigenous peoples and communities.[5]

The Occupy movements must be recognized for creating significant shifts in political-economic discourse at the start of the twenty-first century. But they also demonstrated that it is possible for movements and individuals to be politically radical and progressive with respect to economic and political systems and at the same time actively settler colonial, particularly in terms of relations to space, place, and land. Evident here are the enduring patterns of settler colonial spatiality and territoriality that I have discussed thus far, with the components of the settler colonial assemblage changing positions and internal relationships while the external relationships between the assemblage and Indigenous lands and lives remained the same. In this regard, art historian W.J.T. Mitchell's (2012, 10) meditation on the meaning of Occupy through its root word is particularly revealing:

> In the context of the rhetoric of public space, *occupatio* is, as the original meaning of the word reveals, the seizure of an empty place, one that is supposed to be *res nullius,* not owned by anyone, not private property ... But the demand of *occupatio* is made in the full knowledge that public space is, in fact, pre-occupied by the state and the police, that its *pacified* and democratic character, apparently open to all, is sustained by the ever-present possibility of violent eviction. *Occupatio* thus aims, not just at taking possession of an empty space in an argument, but [also at] provoking a response and framing it in advance. (Emphasis in original)

The Occupy movement relied on tropes of settler colonialism like this one, making the assumption that space illegitimately claimed by corporate entities is equivalent to "empty space" and free for the taking. This narrative, echoing the perception of terra nullius on the part of earlier settler collectives and the reliance on similar concepts in colonial law and political philosophy, traces a direct line from the open violence of the Indian Wars (1609–1924) to the tacit violence of contemporary Indigenous invisibility. Occupy protesters generally recognized that the public spaces that they sought to reclaim were "pre-occupied," but this occupation was ascribed to the structures of state and capital, which in turn were attacked as illegitimate. Thus they rhetorically emptied the land. As a result, corporations and the state organs that serve them were positioned as homogenizing and hegemonic, the enemy that must be provoked and attacked for the good of "the 99%."

Despite the occasional adoption of the term "decolonization," the actions and goals of Occupy were never actually about decolonizing. "For social justice movements, like Occupy, to truly aspire to decolonization non-metaphorically, they would impoverish, not enrich, the 99%+ settler population of United States. Decolonization eliminates settler property rights and settler sovereignty. It requires the abolition of land as property and upholds the sovereignty of Native land and people" (Tuck and Yang 2012, 26). The Occupy movements were not able to "reject the language and ideology of colonialism, conquest and exploitation" in order to situate "decolonization at the centre of [the] movement and abandon the language of occupation," as Leanne Simpson (2012) asserts they must. Consequently, if it can be said that protest camps like Occupy "create life by example" (Feigenbaum, Frenzel, and McCurdy 2014, 212), the life created by Occupy was that of an anarchic, anti-capitalist, but still trenchantly settler colonial society. These critiques of settler colonialism in the Occupy movements raise a fundamental question: are such situations unique? Far from it. Rather, Occupy was simultaneously a legitimate radical challenge to the neoliberal order and a clear expression of the settler colonialism that persists in leftist movements across Canada and the United States.

Settler people can be critical about capitalism without being critical of settler colonialism even though the two are so often imbricated. One reason that it is important to draw a distinction between the functioning of capitalism and of settler colonialism is that many leftist positions assert that opposing one implies a priori opposing both. However, as Tuck and Yang (2012, 4) note, "colonialism is not just a symptom of capitalism ... Capitalism and the state are technologies of colonialism, developed over time to further colonial projects." Settler people can reject spatialities like the neocolonial "society of control" (Barker 2009, 332) without rejecting settler colonial privilege. Professor of comparative literature Kirstin Ross (1988, 33), writing on the emergence of social space in the Paris Commune in 1871, observes that revolutionary struggles are not only directed toward specific goals and struggles but are also "diffuse ... expressed throughout the various cultural spheres and institutional contexts, in specific conflicts and in the manifold transformations of individuals rather than in some rigid and polar opposition of capital and labour." Similarly, revolutionary struggles in the contemporary northern bloc must be interrogated specifically because there is no rigid or polar opposition of forces that encompasses settler colonialism. Settler people may contest a specific concentration of power or privilege in settler colonial space without struggling against settler colonialism. Solidarities that are strong in one context may disintegrate when entering "centres of corporate and political power," as happened with the Immigrant Workers Freedom Ride in the United States in 2003 (Leitner, Sheppard, and Sziarto 2008, 169). While sharing buses and highways together, the various actors in the Freedom Ride were united. However, when the Freedom Ride reached New York, differences that were obscured on the buses became crucially important. Some activists were sought out for high-profile meetings or media engagements because of their personal fame or association with labour unions. Other activists were forced to disappear into the background because of their undocumented, racialized, or otherwise precarious status. This movement, which had experienced many moments of extended unity and relationship building, shattered when the power relationships around it shifted. This outcome indicates the degree to which "any social movement ... has to negotiate power relations within the movement, and the power geometry of the socio-spatial relations it is embedded in" (168). The important point here is not to vilify the Occupy movements. These social mobilizations made immediate and enduring changes to the radical political landscape of austerity-ridden Canadian and American societies. Moreover, regardless of the degree to which the movements' goals were achieved, they gave many people the opportunity to participate in radical alternative politics, to take direct action and gain experience, and to form bonds with other activists and communities, part of the ongoing evolution of any social movement. Rather, in the hope that the settler colonial pitfall might be addressed by activists, my aim is to show how even contemporary, challenging, leftist movements can and do reinforce settler colonialism. While it is quite clear how the conservative right in Canada and the United States support settler colonialism, the assumption that left/socialism is equivalent to anti-colonialism needs much more attention.

Managing Difference and the Limits of Anti-Racism

The frequent efforts by leftist social movements to ally with Indigenous peoples may be laudable in intent, but they cannot be accepted as sufficient in impact. Settler colonialism has at times "conditioned not only Indigenous peoples and their lands and the settler societies that occupy them, but all political, economic and cultural processes that those societies touch" (Morgensen 2011, 53). These processes include not just the obvious ones of capitalist accumulation but also the aspirational ones of anti-capitalist and anti-racist political movements, from the reformist to the radical. The settler colonial assemblage is after all enlivened by aspirational struggle, and these aspirations can be crafted through a wide variety of narratives beyond just those of mainstream success.

Sociologist Richard Day (2005, 6) notes that neoliberal societies, like Canada and the United States, are divided by many lines of difference and inequality that sort populations into "apparently 'natural' hierarchies" in order to justify the inability of a capitalist political economy to provide equal opportunities for all, as they are dogmatically purported to do. Reading this situation through a settler colonial analysis, it becomes clear that despite myths of freedom and opportunity, the "limits of liberalism" (Grande 2013) mean that the liberal democratic, capitalist settler nations of Canada and the United States will never be able to respond to Indigenous concerns, just as they are unable to reconcile the contradictions of capitalism (Harvey 2014), which promises wealth but delivers poverty. As Lorenzo Veracini (2015, 91–94) points out, the promises of settler colonialism have generally failed to materialize, even for proud, nationalistic settler people. It is on the grounds of these inequalities and frustrated aspirations, often in the context of demanding structural reform, that many movements and currents within what might be called the "generic Left"[6] of the North American political landscape seek engagement with Indigenous peoples through social justice or anti-racism movements, usually at the national or international level.

The goals of the generic or mainstream left, although varied, come down to a drive for increased minority rights – often framed in terms of economic support or access – through democratic state mechanisms and for a strengthening of the welfare state in general, such as through universal healthcare. To put pressure on governments and corporations, a number of tried and tested protest tactics are used, especially public rallies, solidarity strikes by organized labour, and activities and events that are intended to raise awareness. Many on the generic left identify as socialists in principle but are suspicious of post-Soviet communism or revolutionary socialism. More recently, the identifier "democratic socialist" has come back into popularity among some circles in the United States, most notably with the success of political candidates like Senator Bernie Sanders and Representative Alexandria Ocasio-Cortez. The problem, of course, is that many individuals and organizations on the generic left believe themselves to be exempt from colonial criticism by virtue of their association with the underdog politics of the left. As social movement scholar Aziz Choudry (2010, 99) observes,

> Many supposedly progressive political organisations – while proclaiming that there are alternatives to free markets, free trade and transnational corporate power and that "another world is possible" – reproduce dominant colonial worldviews and resist challenges by Indigenous peoples and activists to address colonial injustices. While some have asked whether the global justice and anti-globalisation movement is anti-capitalist, it is also important to ask whether it is anti-colonial.

Similar questions could be posed regarding anti-racist and human rights campaigns, especially those that rely on international nongovernmental organizations (D. Lee 2011; McCormack 2011, 291).

When oppression originates in conservative or elite sectors, it is usually addressed by elements of the generic left, but the settler colonial underpinnings of the Canadian and American states, domesticated systems of capitalist dispossession, and the Indigenous-settler divide, which reinforces racism and racialization, are all consistently missing from these critiques (Choudry 2010, 98). In part, that is because the generic left draws on many of the master narratives of settlement and progress that are more commonly associated with overtly racist and conservative politics. David Austin (2010, 28) points out that although the political left and right may disagree on "official or conventional histories," it is "worth noting that ... White Left narratives do not fare much better than their more centrist and right-wing counterparts," as white leftists in Canada "generally relegate Indigenous, Black and other struggles to the margins of Canadian history, a reality of exclusion that is only compounded by the general marginalisation of Canada's generic Left." Contemporary leftist politics remain rife with nationalism, white supremacy, or material aspirationalism. In other words, because the left is purported to be the only political avenue for marginalized communities and because racialized and Indigenous communities in particular are frequently just as marginalized in leftist discourses as they are in the mainstream, there ends up being no popular path for Indigenous people to seek political redress.

With regard to the concept of institutions of privilege as defining the shifting topographies of power in the settler northern bloc, one of the common ways that all but the most radically positioned – the anarchic, or socialist, libertarian – leftist movements have sought to address Indigenous dispossession is by arguing for their inclusion or membership in a number of these institutions. For example, discourses of rights protection or full citizenship are commonly deployed by the generic left in reference to both racialized and migrant populations, as well as to Indigenous communities. These discourses inherently position the problem of settler colonialism as one of *not enough* state and juridical oversight. They are rooted in a call to *strengthen* rather than *weaken* institutions of privilege and to entrench settler colonial topographies of power (Grande 2013; A. Simpson 2014). The privileges that settlers expect to experience derive from a number of institutions requiring different kinds of performance – for example, whiteness or displays of frontier masculinity and violence – and these performances at the aggregate level inform everything from political and legal policies on difference to social discourses on the rights and responsibilities of citizenship (e.g., see Mackey 1998). These institutions are barred to Indigenous people as members of distinct nations and cultures, and accessing them requires individual acts of assimilation and accommodation, meaning that although some Indigenous bodies (or material presence) can be tolerated and even welcomed in settler colonial institutions, the privileges that settlers derive from these institutions are very much at the expense of Indigenous nationhood and sovereignty.

Perhaps as an extension of settler investment in the discourse of citizenship rights, many leftists have advocated appealing to or working through international bodies and frameworks (Uchida 2012). To be sure, much of the international Indigenous peoples' movement, which has resulted in the creation of spaces like the United Nations Permanent Forum on Indigenous Peoples Issues, has been driven largely or exclusively by Indigenous activists and advocates (Lightfoot 2016). The international sphere has also been of great interest to many non-Indigenous leftists looking for ways to blunt the creeping neoliberalism of the Canadian and American states. Yet their ambitions have not been particularly well received by the official state delegations of Canada and the United States or by the former white British settler colonies of Australia and New Zealand, which have explicitly opposed reformist calls for institutional rights and protections for Indigenous peoples. For years, both Canada and the United States refused to sign the United Nations Declaration on the Rights of Indigenous Peoples, adopted in 2007, even after expending great effort to water down key clauses in order to reduce the possible implications for their own countries. Although these settler states did eventually accede to international and domestic pressure and sign the declaration, approaches to Indigenous issues in Canada and the United States a decade after this historic event remained largely bound to recognition politics rather than to substantive change (Corntassel and Bryce 2012, 154–56; Coulthard 2014; Short 2005). The conduct of the provincial government of British Columbia under the ostensibly left New Democratic Party leadership of John Horgan drives this point home. In November 2019, "to cheers and applause ... on both sides of the house" (Little 2019), Horgan's government passed Bill 41, which purported to implement the full extent of the declaration in British Columbia – which would have been a monumental turning point in state-Indigenous relations if true. However, less than two months later, Horgan supported the use of federal paramilitary police to clear Wet'suwet'en and other Indigenous people off their traditional lands for refusing to allow fossil fuel pipeline construction through their territory without consent. The declaration and the law apparently had no bearing on this issue.

Citizenship, Rights, and Inclusion

Discourses of leftist or progressive recognition and inclusion are problematic not only because they may be misdirected or co-opted by state-centric or legalist discourses for use against Indigenous interests but also because they play into discourses of nationalism and whiteness that recruit newcomer populations into the settler colonial assemblage. Citizenship and membership in the institution of the state are basic but necessary goals of many newcomer people – for obvious reasons, including guarantees of civil rights and the right to remain – but as Harsha Walia (2010, 79) argues, discourses of citizenship are never neutral given that the selective denial of political participation and social protection associated with citizenship in the settler state has often been used as a tactic to discipline both migrant populations and racialized newcomers intending to stay. Immigrants who intend to stay and transition to settler status and recognition are held up in political and cultural discourses as proof that migrant populations whose members discipline themselves and assimilate into settler society can also receive the franchise and pursue the American Dream (or its Canadian or regional variants). This same discourse is then transferred to Indigenous people through an equivalency of minority status, and successful assimilation of newcomers to the settler colonial nation-state is weaponized against Indigenous people through favourable comparisons of the new settlers with those Indigenous people who continue to assert nationhood and land-based identities in direct opposition to the assimilatory system.

Meanwhile, Indian status – measured and managed in terms of blood quantum, band rolls, selective federal recognition, or treaty rights, all of which are used to limit the extent to which settler governments will recognize not only their own fiduciary and legal responsibilities, including their treaty obligations, but also the inherent and negotiated rights of Indigenous peoples – creates a similar system of denial and discipline. Walia (2010, 80) reminds us that citizenship, which grants one the right to participate in (or perhaps integrate into) wider civic life across the northern bloc of settler colonialism, "has, by and large, not been sufficient to lift immigrant women of colour and Indigenous women out of extreme poverty and dependency on dangerous and precarious labour in garment factories, domestic work, the sex trade and the general service sector." These institutions reject the racialized identities of some, along with the fundamental aspects of Indigeneity more generally, as they seek to exploit people as labour where possible while selectively accepting a variety of other positionalities and identities, whether in limited or full ways, meaning that they serve to generate a false hope that distracts both settler and exogenous subjectivities from the indefinite suspension of social justice and from the maintenance of liminal spaces of racialized disempowerment.

This project is accomplished in part by coercing those regarded as minorities to act like members of the dominating settler society, as can be witnessed in the construct of the model minority, discussed in Chapter 3, an undertaking that paradoxically increases the number of racialized bodies admitted into settler society while strengthening the institutions of whiteness. Tuck and Yang (2012, 18) explain this process clearly:

> The impossibility of fully becoming a white settler – in this case, white referring to an exceptionalized position with assumed rights to invulnerability and legal supremacy – as articulated by minority literature preoccupied with "glass ceilings" and "forever foreign" status and "myth of the model minority," offers a strong critique of the myth of the democratic nation-state. However, its logical endpoint, the attainment of equal legal and cultural entitlements, is actually an investment in settler colonialism. Indeed, even the ability to be a minority citizen in the settler nation means an option to become a brown settler. For many people of color, becoming a subordinate settler is an option even when becoming white is not.

Again, settler privilege is shaped by a topography of power in which some are lifted higher than others, and those heights may apply only in certain contexts as the terrain shifts around institutions of wealth, race, gender, and so on. The white-coded settler has access to more institutions of privilege than the racialized nonwhite settler, but both have access to some power and privilege in exchange for their participation in and upholding of these institutions. Therefore, both can and do contribute to settler colonization, although the capacity and extent of this contribution vary depending on their positioning in the topography and their membership in various institutions.

These levels of privilege – and "complicity" (Jafri 2012) – within the settler colonial assemblage are inevitably reflected in the ways that settler people pursue justice and equality. Crucially, and as but one example, heteronormativity and homonormativity are contesting aspects that shape the topography of power, but both can still be encompassed within this topography. This is to say that even though it is inarguable that homophobia exists and is a serious problem in Canada and the United States, it is also true that pinkwashed institutions and queer services that do not account for colonialism and Indigeneity among their communities can contribute to Indigenous dispossession (Greensmith 2016; Greensmith and Giwa 2013; Morgensen 2011). Only the most marginalized – like refugees and asylum seekers, although there are certainly others – do not have purchase in this shifting topography, and even then, they may aspire to the kinds of institutional membership that would increase their privileges in the settler colonial society, along with their complicity. The point here is again not to say *who* is a settler but to examine *how* settler colonialism recruits participants and creates biopower in order to demonstrate that inclusive, multicultural, and anti-racist politics, although liberatory in some senses, are not a priori *decolonizing* and may in fact act as new vectors for settler colonial domination. Insofar as many socialist calls for justice are framed through greater inclusion in the state and more equal distribution of resources, and given that these goals are laudable at face value and predictably attractive to marginalized or disenfranchised people and communities, the net outcome with regard to Indigenous peoples is a broader consensus on the need for and desirability of the state and a dismissal of arguments for return of land and resources and acceptance of Indigenous self-determination.

Settler Belonging and Solidarity

Generic left discourses are at times capable of successfully generating positive material impacts for marginalized communities. For many such communities, small shifts in racial power geometries have major impacts, whether in reducing racialized violence or in generating alternative supportive economies within and alongside the capitalist state (Gibson-Graham 2008; Massey 2009, 21–22). Further, as David Harvey (2000, 105) notes with respect to social and economic disruption resulting from shifts in the power of capital, although "instability" in the systems that we currently inhabit and identify with is inherently "disconcerting, sometimes destructive, and always difficult to cope with, it provides multiple opportunities for subversion and opposition on the part of the laborers." But who are the labourers in the wider context of the northern bloc, how does this subversion benefit them, and what is their relationship to settler colonialism and to the underlying issues of land and Indigenous sovereignty?

Complex changes over time in the racial and class divisions and hierarchies of the northern bloc have accompanied the growth, development, and social stratification of settler colonial societies. Overarching narratives of improvement and even class liberation and racial equality can obscure the histories and contemporary realities of settler colonialism. For example, the contemporary settler subject is often conceived of as racially white. Yet the complex debate over *who* is a settler colonizer, meaning which racial and ethnic communities count as part of settler society,[7] often results in critical race theorists and postcolonial theorists talking past each other (Veracini 2015, 44–48; see also Amadahy and Lawrence 2009; and Lawrence and Dua 2005). More to the point, the relationships between imperialism, settler colonialism, capitalism, racism, and state violence in the racial constructions of Canada and the United States have complex and entangled roots and have been surprisingly dynamic over time (Wolfe 2006). For an example of the complex ways that racial dispossession and settler colonialism can crosscut, consider that many communities widely considered to be comprised of settler people and collectives in the present have not been constructed or seen as white at previous times. These communities include the French (Austin 2010; R.J.F. Day 2005), Black United Empire Loyalists who settled in Nova Scotia and Jamaican Maroons who settled in Quebec (Austin 2010), Japanese settlers in Hawaii (Goodyear-Ka'ōpua 2011; Teves 2012), the Latino communities that either predated or followed American expansion (Gott 2007; Klor de Alva 1992), and many contemporary racialized economic migrants, some of whom may eventually stay and settle, attempting to gain entry to settler colonial institutions of power (Veracini 2015; Walia 2013).

All of these changes in the racial and cultural makeup of settler society are obviously a challenge to white supremacy and narratives of the ideal settler as someone with a homogeneously white, European, patriarchal background, and they are important and valuable on this ground alone. However, much like official citizenship, discussed above, the northern bloc's incorporation of all of these communities can be read as strengthening the settler colonial narrative, as it has positioned settler society as all-encompassing, while the widening of acceptable criteria to be accorded settler subjectivity is linked to the expansion of the biopolitical power that can be deployed by institutions of privilege and structures of governance. These changes in the collective makeup or membership of select institutions of privilege may seem traumatic or disruptive to settler people who perceive their own place in the settler colonial assemblage as changing – even though in reality it is the wider assemblage that is shifting to generate and accommodate new kinds of biopower – but what must be remembered is that, more often than not, the members of racialized and marginalized communities are forced to conform to the particular colonial norms of white settlers; it is almost never the other way around. In effect, the observable differences drawn between peoples along lines of race, gender, ability, age, and so on say less about the actual differences between these groups than about how settlers are expected to behave and what kinds of embodied social performance are acceptable or necessary for settler status. As a result, one way that settler colonialism advances and grows is by playing Indigenous peoples, exogenous Others, and less-privileged settlers off against each other. Positioned as disadvantaged groups in society, Indigenous peoples are portrayed as ethnic minorities competing for common streams of funding, assistance, and accommodation (Byrd 2011).

There is no doubt that among settler colonial elites – including elites in media, who wield great power over social discourse – this portrayal is a strategic move to divide and conquer "agonistic" Others (Featherstone 2008, 48–49), including on the political left and within marginalized communities. *Globe and Mail* newspaper columnist John Ibbitson, covering the contentious 2012 Assembly of First Nations elections in Canada, asserted that First Nations chiefs were facing "diminishing influence" because of the changing nature of Canadian demographics. Ibbitson (2012) argued that newer or more recently arrived Canadians – which seems to be a code for nonwhite, non-Anglo immigrants – did not feel empathy toward Indigenous peoples or care to pursue reconciliation and redress because they were not responsible for Indigenous dispossession. Harsh Zaran, a blogger and self-identified person of colour, responded directly, addressing several troubling points implicit in Ibbitson's argument. Notably, he refocused the conversation on the power wielded over both Indigenous peoples and exogenous Others by the – multicultural but still "whitestream" (Grande 2003) – Canadian state and its society:

> What [Ibbitson] is really hinting at is the fantastic job the Canadian state has done in "whitening" the idea of who is "Canadian," and how racialized folks are being coerced to "whiten" themselves to fit in. The forging of the citizenship contract is played out in the arena of "culture," which is supervised by the ideology of song-and-dance multiculturalism. This works to drive a strong wedge between possible decolonized alliances between indigenous peoples and racialized settlers. As racialized Canadians cultivate a stronger stake in the Canadian state, they are coerced to absorb and uphold the prejudices of white society. So, if the impatience on the part of racialized Canadians will arrive, it will be due to the completion of the white assimilation process. (Zaran 2012)

Zaran's intervention is particularly notable for what it reveals about the operation of colonial hierarchy based on race and minority status.

As Zaran identifies, those perceived by settlers to be exogenous Others are permitted access initially to the broadest spaces of settler society and subsequently to various institutions of privilege insofar as they performatively assimilate and can meet the criteria of settler desirability. Crucially, this assimilation involves rejecting solidarity with Indigenous peoples on common grounds of dispossession or experiences of colonization, which many immigrants from the global South have experienced through different colonial dynamics. In this way, exogenous Others are made responsible for their own belonging, the fundamental markers of assimilation being associated with complicit, colonial action. Exogenous Others become settlers through their performative pursuit of opportunity on Indigenous lands, which is mediated by the systems and structures of settler colonialism and informed by pervasive myths of settler exceptionalism but with the added complication of navigating an already constituted and shifting topography of power. The spatialities that exogenous Others must confront, pass through, and adapt to in becoming settler people or gaining space in settler societies are simultaneously colonized and racialized, and the tensions and pressures that they face serve to foreclose Indigenous affinity with these racialized communities.[8]

With regard to our earlier focus on how people are recruited into settler colonization, there are clearly groups who fall outside of the boundaries of settler colonial collectives. These groups are instructive both for reminding us that settler colonialism's totalizing claims have not been achieved and likely never will be and for revealing the dissonance that crosscutting currents of power create between situated settler states and globalizing capital. Celia Haig-Brown (2009) is correct that refugees present a complicating case given their lack of intent to stay and the extreme disempowerment that most refugees experience. Hawaiian political scientist Haunani-Kay Trask (2007) has commented that she does not hold the descendants of slaves responsible for the colonization of the Americas, as they had no choice about their transport to or dwelling on these lands, and she argues that their seeking rights and protections cannot be chalked up simply to attempts to bulwark their own society. Walia (2010, 2013) points out that some racialized and marginalized communities of migrant workers do not want to take advantage of Indigenous peoples and have pursued solidarity efforts with them, certainly an important consideration. Veracini (2010b, 17; 2015, 32–48) has stated that "migrants are not settlers," an argument that I agree with while also recognizing the often blurred lines between those who come and intend to stay (or settlers) and those who come and intend to stay only for a while (or migrants). However, even common experiences of deprivation, displacement, or disempowerment are not a guarantee of developing decolonizing relationships, as Walia (2010, 81) has described with respect to the 2010 anti-Olympics movement in Vancouver:

> In fact, there are many factors preventing this shared terrain of struggle from developing into genuine solidarity, especially the tangible role of immigrant and migrant workers in facilitating the removal and theft of Indigenous land and resources. As Indigenous activists called for the cancellation of the 2010 Olympic Games in BC under the banner of "No Olympics on stolen Native land," an increasing number of migrant workers were being employed in those same industries that were expediting the rate of sport tourism and mining on Native lands. Of course, migrant workers are not themselves responsible for the devastation of Indigenous lands but, as the Native Youth Movement has asked, how can one be a miner or a logger and still support Indigenous peoples' defence of the Earth?

The journey from exogenous Other to settler self is one that is not encompassed only by legal recognitions, political enfranchisement, or economic integration. Although all of these things are likely to signify the progress of becoming a settler, this process is a journey that involves movement in and through both the material landscape of settler colonial North America and the relational systems and structures of settler nations and communities. Moreover, despite mythistories to the contrary, this route is not open to everyone but only to those who can work in the interests of established settler people and institutions.

Anticipatory Geographies of the Settler Left

The larger point here is that, in the present, even purportedly inclusionary and egalitarian discourses on diversity and multiculturalism tend to feed back into established institutions of privilege and to strengthen state claims to authority over Indigenous peoples as minority populations. However, I posit here that we must consider another possibility. Settler colonialism in the northern bloc has historically found common cause with white supremacy and capitalism: these two sociocultural processes have combined to clear land, supply labour, and ensure that surplus value has ended up in the intended hands. The connection to whiteness and capitalism is also part of the link between settler colonialism and other colonial regimes and practices elsewhere. However, drawing from the failure of groups like Occupy to account for settler colonialism in their anti-capitalist visions and from the failure of the mainstream left to recognize the settler colonialism that persists in discourses of inclusion, multiculturalism, and diversity, I argue here that it is entirely possible that the settler colonial assemblage of the northern bloc could shift into a configuration that does not strictly require white supremacy and capitalism, just as it no longer requires the originary imperial hierarchy to ensure the survival of a settlement that has now become a society unto itself. Given that assemblages are not defined by their internal makeup but by their relationship with their environment, there are possible configurations of settler colonialism where other institutions replace whiteness and where settler sovereignty is invested in different political economies, without a change in the overall reliance on erasure, occupation, and bricolage to claim land and generate belonging. It is possible that racial discourses and political economies in North America could shift radically, such that one day we might see a socialist, diverse, egalitarian society that, although still founded on the basic terra nullius claim to land, distributes land and resources evenly and without racial hierarchy among settlers. More than anything else, being a settler is about finding belonging on the land through the structures, systems, and stories of settler colonialism, and this discourse of belonging is constantly negotiated and dynamic, as well as potentially all-encompassing.

We can ask, then, whether the increasing adoption of anti-colonial frameworks by social movements is a cause for hope. As discussed with respect to Occupy, the language of anti-colonialism and decolonization was present in the political discourse of the protest camps, and there were overt attempts to align Occupy with Indigenous movements – even though these attempts were of limited success (if any). To answer this question, we must first understand what an anti-colonial stance intends to oppose and what that implies for the spaces it creates or intends to produce. To begin, anti-colonialism is conceptually bound up with postcolonialism – the opposition to colonial power driven by the goal of moving past the structural impositions of colonial domination. The two are often used interchangeably; however, whereas postcolonialism has come under fire for failing to inform authentic Indigenous sovereignty and for obscuring the transition from one colonial formation to another, such as metropole to settler, anti-colonialism has not been subjected to nearly the same level of critique (Gilmartin and Berg 2007). The risks of leaving these concepts unpacked are significant. Social movement scholar Adam Lewis (2012, 231) defines colonialism as "based on power and oppression, and as long as social relations continue to be structured as such, there will be little justification for the 'post' in post-colonialism." This definition should caution us to consider whether or not anti-colonial activism actually challenges the social relations that fundamentally structure settler colonialism in North America. When used to inform strategies of social movement organizing, anti-colonialism is commonly constructed to leave certain kinds of power and oppressive social relations in place while rejecting and resisting others.

Consider, for example, settler activism motivated by an anti-colonial desire to prevent environmental destruction of lands important to Indigenous communities, which has been at the root of events such as the anti-clearcutting protests in Tla-o-qui-aht (Clayquot Sound) in 1993 (K. Shaw 2004), mentioned earlier in this chapter, and the longstanding anti-logging blockade at Grassy Narrows in northern Ontario (Willow 2011). In both of these examples, settler activists at times have displayed an anti-colonial naïveté, underestimating both the capacity and the complexity of Indigenous decision making and resistance practices. A prominent example from the United States is the struggles of the Makah Nation on the Pacific Coast to sustain and control its whaling practices. Whaling has always been a keystone of Makah cultures, spiritualities, governance structures, and economies. Makah activists found common cause with settler environmentalist groups in mutually opposing commercial whaling in the area. However, after commercial whaling was closed, the Makah and Nuu-chah-nulth, who continued to push for their rights to maintain traditional whaling practices, were immediately opposed by the settler anti-whaling movement, which had previously supported their legal and political arguments (Coté 2017; Kim 2015).

Tuck and Yang (2012, 18) assert that anti-colonialism, as opposed to decolonization, is often related to the ascendancy of an idealized postcolonial subject within colonial systems, arguing that this "anti-to-post-colonial project doesn't strive to undo colonialism but rather to remake it and subvert it." Anti-colonial actions may oppose the expansion or restructuring of colonial power without necessarily referencing, drawing on, or supporting the resurgence of Indigenous nationhood as such. Clear examples include the anti-colonial rationale for American independence from Britain, the late-nineteenth-century US response to European influence in the Caribbean, and the articulation and development of the Monroe Doctrine. There are pressing, contemporary reasons for considering the differences between anti-colonial and decolonizing action, including the popularity of emotive but immaterial apologies and territory acknowledgments among leftist and progressive political circles in North America (e.g., see M. Johnson 2011; Veracini 2011; Watts 2016; and Wood and Rossiter 2011). Conflicts between settler society and Indigenous people are increasingly seen as "bad for business" (Wood and Rossiter 2011, 409, 412), as demonstrated both by the cancellation of some fossil fuel pipelines due to Indigenous-led opposition (e.g., Enbridge Northern Gateway and Keystone XL) and by the bad political press received for forcing through others (e.g., Standing Rock, Kinder Morgan Trans Mountain, and Canadian Gas Link). To be sure, Indigenous activists and communities in resistance have forced even the mainstream in Canada and the United States to grapple with anti-colonial social discourses. The colonial 'past' of settler states must be reconciled – in the accounting sense of being made final – in order not only to demonstrate safety and security for investors but also to show that populations of potentially "agonistic" Others (Featherstone 2008, 48–49) have been disciplined.

Reconciliation on these terms is a process of box-ticking, which means engaging with Indigenous concerns enough to satisfy national discourses of guilt and responsibility rather than acknowledging Indigenous peoples' own articulations of how states and settler citizens should be responsible (Coulthard 2014). This approach is not true reconciliation, which would require the return of land and the reinvigoration of Indigenous governance structures as a minimum standard. Instead, it is a process for ending the conversation about colonialism. In the words of historical geographer Miranda Johnson (2011, 187),

> [This] peculiar form of nationhood ... is not dependent upon an actual shift in indigenous peoples' access to, or representation by, state power. Instead, what has happened through the affective phrasing of reconciliation is that the authority of the settler state has been cast away from the former imperial metropole and localized in terms of more indigenous claims of political belonging.

In other words, rather than acknowledging the fundamental usurpation of the land, Canada (and to a lesser degree, the United States) is cast as an aspiring postcolony that is moving toward a natural equilibrium with Indigenous peoples. Settlers and Indigenous people are cast as equally responsible for meeting in the anti-colonial middle, meaning that actual political and material restitution – essential for decolonization rather than anti-colonialism – is not on the table.

Raising awareness of power and domination in the present, a focus of much leftist activist work, is not often sufficient to dislodge settler people from their collective "dysconsciousness" (D.M. Johnson 2011, 110), even among those who would do the awareness raising (Tuck and Yang 2012, 19–22). By way of an illustrative example, I turn here to an instance of leftist activists commenting on their own frustrations with other activists. When I relocated to England in 2009, I was largely rendered a spectator to several large protests in Canada that followed closely afterward. I most clearly remember the 2010 protests against the G20 summit in Toronto, not far from where I grew up. It was with very mixed feelings that I watched the infamous video showing a crowd of protesters belting out the Canadian national anthem in full nationalist throes, only to be promptly charged by the police (Hui 2010). As much as I am an abolitionist and very much supportive of the anti-G20 protesters, I also did not find anything valorous in a mass expression of support for the very nation built by police unleashing far more violence on Indigenous communities across the country. At the time, I wondered whether I was the only one feeling such ambivalence and frustration – but I have learned that I definitely was not.

In early 2012, the Tumblr account #leftfail appeared.[9] The development of #leftfail was a direct result of the highly charged political environment in and around Toronto, beginning with the G20 protests in 2010 and the related political and police suppression of activists that led to the destruction of the Occupy Toronto camp in 2011, and it served as a way of venting frustrations with common problems facing radical activists, as well as a reaction to problematic tendencies in the activist communities at the time. Among many other images, the maintainers of the blog posted an image that bears description here (#leftfail 2012).[10] It shows a large group of protesters marching down an urban street. Almost all of the marchers are white-coded, and in the extreme foreground is a young white man wearing a knit cap and carrying an open, forward facing laptop – an odd choice during a protest march – and visible just behind him is another white activist with dreadlocks. Partially obscured signs from the next rank of protesters make reference to "'Genocide' on Native people" and to slogans being popularized by Occupy at the same time, including a reference to "The 99%" and another stating, "Natives Have Been Occupied Since Contact." However, there are no specific references to any Indigenous nations, no local Indigenous symbols, and no obvious Indigenous leaders in the protest march. The activists behind #leftfail added capitalized bold text to the top and bottom of this image:

> WE RECOGNIZE THE TRADITIONAL LANDS OCCUPIED
> WE JUST CAN'T NAME A SINGLE INDIGENOUS NATION

I admit that I both laughed and sighed with frustration upon seeing this post – for without even being at the protests, I knew exactly how the creator of the macro felt because I had seen and experienced this posturing many times before. Largely white settler activists have taken to the streets, ostensibly with support for Indigenous nations as part of their core ideology but without possessing even basic knowledge about Indigenous peoples in the present or having made any effort to acquire it, despite the widespread availability of resources produced by Indigenous people and communities. The frustration and absurdity expressed through this meme mirrors both the frustration evident in Tuck and Yang's (2012, 8–9) accounts of settler society "playing Indian" and the absurd difference between the solidarity asserted by leftists and their actual practices (see also Lagalisse 2011). These frustrations can intensify when settler people consider themselves radical enough to invoke words like "traditional lands" or "decolonization" as part of their struggles or when they assume that a land acknowledgment can stand in for actual relationship building (Watts 2016). The adoption of decolonization as a metaphor (and nothing else) is a sign that settler activists are engaging with Indigenous demands only just to the point that they must do so or only to the extent that the rhetoric of Indigenous liberation can be co-opted to serve their own goals and tactics.

Just as states' attempts to reconcile with Indigenous communities through box-ticked apologies are subsumed into and negated by official channels, activists' own attempts at reconciliation outside of these systems serve to "contain the unbearable searchlight of complicity, of having harmed others just by being one's self." For many activists, the "desire to reconcile" – meaning in this case to become a good settler ally – "is just as relentless as the desire to disappear the Native" in mainstream articulations of settler colonialism. Both constitute the "desire to not have to deal with this (Indian) problem anymore" (Tuck and Yang 2012, 9) and to be freed of personal complicity and its attendant discomforts. This desire is clearly evident in the reduction of all social ills, whether affecting settlers, Indigenous people, or exogenous Others, to a single, exploitative, exterior force such as capitalism. In this construction, defeating capitalism is synonymous with defeating the illegitimacy of settler people on the land. In reality, however, this is simply another exercise in settler colonial bricolage – an appropriation and use of Indigenous struggles against capitalist exploitation in order to build a new settler colonial narrative in which capitalist elites are a common enemy. That is precisely what occurred when members of Occupy plastered Sitting Bull's face across New York City and Internet message boards: the assumed purity of the Indigenous struggle, as exemplified by the calm leadership of Sitting Bull – who did eventually surrender to the United States government – was co-opted to self-assure Occupy protesters that their cause was just.

In the same way that early settlers imagined complex environments filled with Indigenous peoples and relational networks to be empty wilderness (or terra nullius), contemporary leftist settler people imagine multiple oppressions, whether colonial, racial, or class-based, to be flattened under singular impositions of power, whether imperial, whitestream, or elitist (Tuck and Yang 2012, 17–19). Rather than an untamed land requiring cultivation and civilization, which is the archetypical settler trope, leftist imagined geographies perceive contemporary spaces as filled with the wild and unchecked power of state and capital. It is this power, in turn, that needs to be dispersed so that personal and community advantage can be pursued. In this configuration, capitalism and the state are constructed as barriers to, rather than guarantors of, settler colonial opportunity. This view accords with Mitchell's (2012, 10) discussion of how the Occupy movements have identified and created "public space" through a perception of res nullius beneath private ownership. Radical movements that discount the validity of corporate claims to public space may attempt to construct spaces that straddle the public-private or public-corporate divide – like New York's Zuccotti Park – as empty, with all power geometries dispersed except for the social. This dispersal is targeted at those geometries of power created by the imbrication of concentrated capital and the capacity for state violence, but the oppression of colonization is expected to dissipate as well. Through the dynamics of struggle against these two oppressive structures, social justice movements appear to believe that they will be washed clean. By temporarily or partially sacrificing established privileges, settler leftists equate themselves with Indigenous peoples, whose very existence has been and remains under attack.

Ultimately, this imagined geography of perfectly dispersed power across empty, res nullius spaces betrays a longing for settler colonial transcendence. But this longing ignores the persistent issue of the land: so long as the land is under settler control, decolonization remains a fantasy. Contemporary leftist discourses rarely call for the explicit return of land, if for no reason other than the fact that the settler colonial imaginary cannot stretch this far.[11] Land is not seen as it is – that is, as related to Indigenous peoples and rightfully belonging to their political economies and diplomatic networks – but is seen as it could be in socialist fantasies of equal access and opportunity. For example, consider the American reading of the story of the French Revolution (1789–99) as both liberatory and a warning (Selbin 2010, 107–11). American discourses of liberty position the violence of the French Revolution, especially the executions during the Terror, as a sign that the revolution ultimately failed, having gone too far and become corrupted. In contrast, the American Revolution (1765–83) is portrayed as having stopped at precisely the correct moment, namely when the monarchy was overthrown but while individuals involved in the revolution remained free from the moral stain of bloody excess. Of course, this reading fails to account for the actual violence of this conflict, which is dismissed in hugely problematic normalizing and gendered terms as the birthing pains of a nation, just as the later violences of the War of 1812 (1812–15) and the American Civil War (1861–65) are disregarded, to say nothing of the myriad Indian Wars and the clearing of a continent. But the American genesis moment is narratively quarantined from such complications, allowing the French Revolution to appear impossibly complicated, messy, and violent by comparison. In this regard, the "land of liberty" – as Americans have considered their nation since the American Revolution (see A. Taylor 2010) – finds a limit in designating France to be a space where too much liberty exists, and in so doing, it justifies its own space as perfect.

Compare this historical discourse to Occupy Oakland's rejection of "Decolonize Oakland" as a moniker (Barker 2012; Ruiz-Lichter 2011; Tuck and Yang 2012, 24–26). Indigenous and Black participants in the Occupy protests came forth with concerns about the connotations of "Occupy" as a descriptor, and instead suggested "Decolonize Oakland" was more appropriate. After a contentious public discussion, the majority of participants rejected the suggestion, resulting in a major schism in the activist community. Occupy Oakland, although settler-dominated and focused on state and capital, was perceived as the perfect revolution in the same way that Americans view their own revolution as perfect only through bad-faith comparisons to the French Revolution and the Russian Revolution (1917–23) (Selbin 2010). Focusing on the comparatively radical character of Occupy Oakland with respect to previous movements co-opted by neoliberal and state power, but also prioritizing the need to unify and sustain the activist community in Oakland around Occupy, many members of Occupy Oakland dismissed Indigenous concerns over the use of the term "occupy" in the context of settler colonialism and displayed a distinct lack of interest in centring Indigenous peoples and their relations to the land. Indigenous resistance in this scenario would have gone too far, tipping the perfect revolution over into chaotic excess, so decolonization was rearticulated as something unfathomable and thus outside of consideration by activists, ultimately with the effect of creating a crisis of settler leadership with respect to decolonizing. Indeed, this case is illustrative of broader conclusions that have been drawn about the relationship between leftist activism and Indigenous concerns. Settler activists seem broadly unwilling to take direction from Indigenous peoples (Barker and Pickerill 2012, 1713; Kilibarda 2012, 28–30) or seem unable to self-organize to take concerted action on issues of clear concern to Indigenous communities (Lagalisse 2011). As a result, the settler left either tramples Indigenous concerns or cannot imagine acting on these concerns and so continues to search for a way to address class, racial, gendered, and other forms of inequality that traditionally concern the left but crosscut settler colonialism in complex ways. Because of this approach, leftist analyses frequently fall short of attending to the specificity of Indigenous displacement, racialization, and economic marginalization.

Settler people, no matter how motivated, well-intentioned, or educated, have difficulty grappling with settler colonialism; it is a slippery and mammoth task, and it is often simply too uncomfortable to be so unsettled and still work productively in that state (de Leeuw, Greenwood, and Lindsay 2013). That is part of the reason for the well-known, cyclical dynamic of activists repeatedly asking Indigenous peoples "What do we do?" without coming to the table prepared and with something to offer. Even critically engaged settlers often desire a straightforward set of steps that they can follow to exempt themselves from settler colonial complicity and to achieve or claim permanent ally status (Battell Lowman and Barker 2015, 115–16). In the absence of such a transparent process, and given the aversion to confronting one's own settler colonial relationships, the responsibility for identifying and confronting a settler's own colonialism is displaced onto Indigenous people. In this double move to innocence, critically engaged settlers continue to position themselves as those capable of making a difference without accepting risk or responsibility and without confronting the uncertainty, contingency, and open-ended processes of decolonization. Instead, the fundamental imbalance remains: the fate of Turtle Island continues to be determined by settler colonizers, and the narrative that accompanies this configuration of the topographies of power tells a story of liberal progressive settlers "listening to the subaltern" (Coronil 1994) and achieving enlightenment but retaining their unquestioned right to the land (de Leeuw, Greenwood, and Lindsay 2013; Grande 2013; Tuck and Yang 2012, 19–22). This is a particularly radical and pernicious vision of transcendence of the settler colonial form, one where the settler positionality is left behind through a particular act of socialist, revolutionary heroism. It is part of a larger set of leftist narratives whose portrayal of the settler struggle against oppression recentres 'us' as heroes while leaving the situation of Indigenous peoples and lands effectively unaltered. This manoeuvre primarily serves to reinforce the destruction and erasure of Indigeneity by subsuming Indigenous struggles into discourses that are anti-racist and anti-capitalist or environmentalist but persistently settler colonial.

Utopian Visions

There is a clear relationship between these leftist "moves to innocence" (Tuck and Yang 2012, 9–28), perhaps especially those that accompany actual radical opposition to state and capital or to systems of race and racism, and attempts to transcend the settler colonial form, thereby guaranteeing settler belonging. The imagined geographies of radical social movements include the possibility of a radical settler future "in which the Native (understanding that he is becoming extinct) hands over his land, his claim to the land, his very Indian-ness to the settler for safe-keeping" (14). Understanding that this is the case, we must be particularly critical of the just futures envisioned by leftist movements. Increasingly, leftist and progressive social movements in Canada and the United States find it difficult to articulate a vision for the world that is not essentially premised only on the absence of the violences and inequalities of state and capital (Haiven and Khasnabish 2014; Turbulence Collective 2010). Meanwhile, many political theories that prioritize investigating and articulating possible avenues through which subaltern peoples, social movements, and other radical agents of change can find spaces beyond the hegemony of state and capital rely on the same imaginary mobile, "rhizomatic" frontier (Young 2013) as settler colonial narratives of freedom and opportunity (Rifkin 2013). So we can expect to find in many visions of radically egalitarian futures a persistent settler colonialism that defines the limits of how settler people construct their version of a postcolonial future.

Here, I focus on one remarkably complete vision, generated by a longtime leftist critic of capitalism who is a geographer with deep understandings of North American power geometries. I refer to David Harvey's postcapitalist vision in the appendix to *Spaces of Hope* (2000, 257–81), which models a postcrisis utopia designed around radically democratic inclusion, decentralization of economies, freedom of movement, and the valuing of creative, scholarly, and familial labour. Developed prior to the massive and rapid expansion of northern bloc state security apparatuses post-9/11, Harvey's vision nevertheless predicts this increase in state surveillance and violence as a means of social control, as well as offering a remarkably accurate (although overly apocalyptic) prediction of the 2007–08 financial crash and associated regimes of austerity. Harvey's vision for the response of the people to these developments is a detailed and passionate attempt not only to demonstrate the possibility of imagining a postcapitalist future but also to articulate one possible, clear social progression by which this future could be reached. In this regard, his attempt is successful – and many aspects of his vision are inspiring and plausible. But if we read this future narrative attentive to settler colonial analyses, we see an example of the extent to which settler futurities and Indigenous erasure can inhere in radically different social configurations.

Harvey begins by defending utopian thinking, a position later echoed by sociologist Richard Day (2005).[12] Harvey (2000, 257) dismisses fears that utopian thought may lead to the construction of new hierarchies or to the reinforcement of existing ones as "all too fashionable." He makes a compelling argument that utopian thinking is needed in order to counter the hegemony of globalizing neoliberal capital, an argument with which I agree. Harvey then proceeds to sketch a utopian vision that, in his perception, is neither totalitarian nor disastrous but an escape from the tyranny of capital and the disaster of modernity. So how does Harvey's vision stand when subjected to settler colonial analysis?

First, notably absent is any mention at all of Indigenous peoples or Indigeneity. Rather, his vision is haunted by traditional socialist thinking, which subsumes all resistance movements into the materially deprived poor and, later, the disaffected masses. Harvey (2000, 262–63) attempts to recognize some disadvantaged peoples, such as his nod to women and feminism, but these peoples stand in as a representation of all dispossessed groups, and given that much of his vision is based on a radical reorganization of labour, Harvey actually *must* account for gender and racial divisions, which are used to create and maintain labouring underclasses. However, consistent with settler colonial drives that seek to eliminate and replace Indigenous labour with settlers – and their "chattel" workforces (Tuck and Yang 2012, 6) – Indigenous people and their unique land-based economic practices are not considered. Since Harvey's vision of a radically globalized-from-below world says very little about the specificity of place, the racialized and gendered dimensions of Indigenous displacement and erasure can be easily glossed over. Indigenous liberation is assumed to be coterminous with social democracy and with racial and gender equality of opportunity. This assumption parallels the homogenization of Indigenous peoples through catchall monikers such as "the 99%" – who are against the elites of finance capital and, when projected forward in time, become just 'us,' a multitude that, although radically equal, lacks any connection to a vital, lived Indigeneity. This is the sort of anticipatory geography that can shape contemporary actions, leading to the foreclosure of future possibilities as though this foreclosure were inevitable (B. Anderson 2010).

Second, Harvey's (2000, 258–63) utopia is achieved after passing through stages of extreme social repression, violence, and economic collapse. In addition to ignoring that many of the spatial configurations of this repression are already commonly deployed against Indigenous peoples – for example, the use of extensive systems of surveillance, criminalization and imprisonment, and segregation outside of cities (Crosby and Monaghan 2018; K.D. Smith 2009) – this oppressive phase is presented as exceptional or unusual in relation to earlier and later social contexts. In the context of settler colonialism, the founding violence that creates relative, situated advantage is disavowed (Veracini 2010b). This disavowal has seeped into Harvey's work. It not only glosses over the already existing forms of repression that help to render future injustices banal (Berg 2011; Flusty et al. 2008) but also ignores

Indigenous resistances to these structures of invasion, which should inform mass movements against them.

Third, Harvey (2000, 264) deals with social difference in his utopian vision by imagining a system that combines localized "hearths" – where home is attached to a spatial unit rather than a family unit – and nested scales of organization that maximize mobilities between "places where people who want to be different can express that want with the greatest freedom." From sexuality and preference to artistic expression, Harvey envisions all manner of difference to be accepted within these hearths, and if people cannot find the space that they need in one, they may relocate to another through a variety of processes. This mobility, however, denies the possibility of Indigenous sovereignties that, through relationships to place, promote understanding, respect, and cooperation with the "personality" of place (V. Deloria Jr. and Wildcat 2001, 145). Indigenous spatialities are flexible, and Indigenous traditions of treaty making and sharing place are well established, but they are not endlessly permissive. There are some nonnegotiable practices and protocols with respect to the land that must be observed. Indigenous knowledges and cultural practices often depend on the lived vitality of land-based practices informed by sacred histories (Watts 2013). These practices may relate to lands generally or to specific sacred sites (Basso 1996; V. Deloria Jr. 2003; Little Bear 2004), and although Indigenous communities have often dealt with difference and conflict by temporarily removing themselves to other parts of their territories, many maintain active and vital relationships with place over distance (Holm, Pearson, and Chavis 2003). None of these relationships are accounted for in Harvey's vision. His depiction of an almost restless mobility, the option of always finding a new collective to join in a new space, where one can finally be special if one cares to be industrious and forthright, seems to directly follow a settler colonial script of frontier escape and opportunity. Harvey does away with property without doing away with the settler colonial gaze; clear levelled ground in Harvey's utopia is ground free of capital and militarism but not necessarily of settler colonial power and narratives.

Postcapitalist settler colonial geographies like Harvey's, then, are not instances of productive and dynamic "convergence space," where different ways of knowing and being may cross-pollinate and evolve (Routledge 2003, 346), as they may at first appear to be. Rather, they are inherently spaces of collision where Indigenous and radical settler trajectories against or away from domination by state and capital unexpectedly push against each other. Settler imaginary geographies need not be capitalist or even internally homogenizing in order to be colonial; they need only erase the "militant particularism" (Harvey 2000, 55–56) that allows for Indigenous sovereignties. By implication, no social movement, no matter how radical, can be decolonizing if it does not start with an implicit focus on restoring and defending Indigenous connections to people and places, even – or perhaps, especially – at the expense of settler anticipatory geographies.

Transfer and Transcendence on a Postcapitalist Turtle Island

The settler colonial transfer of land in the northern bloc of settler colonialism has been facilitated by the might of the state and the leverage of capital. Transfer and transcendence, key impositions of the settler colonial assemblage, would likely appear to be very different processes in a postcapitalist space. Consider that discourses that identify and reject the coercive violence of state and capital but do not confront settler colonization assume a paradoxical position: systematized or institutionalized violence is rejected, but settler colonialism is exempted because it cannot be identified as or with a specific system or institution. Try as we might to identify elements around us that generate oppression, settlers remain unable to perceive the settler colonial assemblage, which is both foundational and hegemonic; we miss the forest because we are surrounded by trees.

Settler leftists attempt to reconcile this paradox through settler moves to innocence and moves to comfort. The former, described by Tuck and Yang, are responses to the juxtaposition of settler colonial imperatives against the ideals, such as human rights and social justice, that motivate leftist politics. Tuck and Yang (2012, 9–28) identify six different "moves to innocence":

- Settler nativism, where settler people pretend to have meaningful indigenous heritage, connections, or belonging to place
- Settler adoption fantasies, where tribal adoption is a legitimizing (but meaningless) fantasy
- Colonial equivocation, where repression of some kind of settler difference or imposition of exogenous status is equated with settler colonial dispossession, legitimizing minoritarian positions within settler society
- Free your mind and the rest will follow, where settler people focus on decolonizing the mind to the exclusion of material and political organizing
- A(s)t(e)risk peoples, where Indigenous peoples are conceptually and legally collapsed into various other at risk and asterisk, or underrepresented, groups
- Reoccupation and urban homesteading, where the anti-capital claiming of space by settler peoples is equated with decolonization, obscuring colonial dispossession behind capitalist exploitation.

Moves to comfort are similar, except that they do not necessarily involve an attempt to rationalize one's exemption from settler colonial critique. Rather, moves to comfort can at times dwell in settler colonial guilt as part of a strategy to centre the performative discomfort of the settler while also decentring the larger challenges issued by decolonial discourse and practice. As Emma Battell Lowman and I have described, this is a frequent occurrence in social movement organizing, where empathy, trust, and relationship building are crucial to the work of a group, which also opens up the possibility of abusing or co-opting the emotional resources of that group in order to make "moves to comfort" (Battell Lowman and Barker 2015, 99–104).

Settler moves to innocence and comfort are attempts to deal with the incommensurability of settler spaces and Indigenous lands without actually addressing the issue. Make no mistake: this incommensurability is not just theoretical but is enacted as genocide, segregation, dehumanization, and enslavement of Indigenous peoples in order to secure the settler colonial land base. Being confronted with this incommensurability is less problematic for conservative or right-wing political ideologies, which retreat quickly and easily into their own comfortable narratives of conquest and Manifest Destiny. Leftist movements, however, are deeply unsettled by the realization that they cannot support both settler socialist or egalitarian political economies of the kind that I have described and Indigenous sovereignties simultaneously:

> An ethic of incommensurability, which guides moves that unsettle innocence, stands in contrast to aims of reconciliation, which motivate settler moves to innocence. Reconciliation is about rescuing settler normalcy, about rescuing a settler future. Reconciliation is concerned with questions of what will decolonization look like? What will happen after abolition? What will be the consequences of decolonization for the settler? Incommensurability acknowledges that these questions need not, and perhaps cannot, be answered in order for decolonization to exist as a framework. (Tuck and Yang 2012, 35)

Transcendence, by extension, is the final reconciling of this incommensurability.

Since transfer occurs incompletely and unevenly, some kinds of transfer build off of others. For example, "multicultural transfer" – in which "the divide between indigenous and exogenous alterities is unilaterally erased and indigenous people are discursively transferred into a different category (e.g., the 'multicultural' nation)" (Veracini 2010b, 43) – would be unacceptable to many leftists, yet this transfer is actually supported in practice through many generic and radical discourses. That happens in part because of the perception that multicultural forms of recognition must be a priori better than more obviously violent and destructive forms of colonialism given that they are more progressive – a circular logic that refers back to assumptions about civilization and progress inherited from the earliest moments of colonization. As a result, moves to innocence and comfort can be seen as attempts to bridge earlier forms of transfer, now deemed too barbaric, and forms more applicable to the current constitution of settler society. In this context, the colonial difference can be clearly seen to comprise not just the difference between terra nullius and the already occupied reality of the northern bloc of settler colonialism but also the difference between the embodied experience of being a settler in the contemporary sense and the promises of how life could or should be in some fairer, more just future.

More Than Good Intentions

Even when pursued with the best of intentions, non-Indigenous efforts to create decolonizing social change may not succeed as hoped or intended (de Leeuw, Greenwood, and Lindsay 2013) because of the pervasiveness of settler colonialism, as evidenced by the ways that even self-aware, self-critical settler people can unwittingly act in the interests of settler colonization. For those with the best intentions, investing time, energy, and resources in progressive, positive social change may ultimately do more harm than good – and at best will be incomplete – if we do not also do the uncomfortable and always unfinished work of critically engaging with our own settler colonial complicity (390–92).

Reflexive removals, the flinch in response to the discomfort that comes with being confronted with our own settler colonial complicity, are common on the settler left. These removals, in the broadest sense, must be seen as consistent with settler colonial collectives that remove themselves from a fallen or decadent society as part of a return to purity. Leftist activists in North America position their spaces as more legitimate than spaces of state and capital with respect to Indigenous peoples rather than less, although this legitimacy relies on a number of problematic assumptions and oversimplifications. It seems that in order for settler people to engage in effective solidarity activism with Indigenous peoples, and to actually become part of decolonizing processes, settlers must actively identify and develop ways to deal with the discomfort that accompanies attending to the relationships and responsibilities that settler colonial narratives suggest we should abandon. We also must figure out how to attend to these relationships and responsibilities without following the well-worn but ultimately futile paths of anti-capitalist revolution (at least when positioned as panacea) and multicultural assimilation. This endeavour will unavoidably involve a great deal of failure. It is to failure – to that which exists beyond hope – that I now turn.

5

The Efficacy of Failure: Advancing Struggles in Support of Indigenous Resurgence

How do I talk about my activism if not in terms of failure? How do I remember my attempts to be a good ally if not through the lens of futility? From the time I set foot on my academic and intellectual journey, which has routed me through Indigenous politics and governance and back around to my own people's colonial past and present, I have failed and failed again. It does not feel good to remember or to talk about these failures, including the Indigenous Solidarity group that splintered under the weight of settler egos, including my own; the friends and companions I lost when my own internal anxieties blinded me to the mistakes that I was making in our collective anti-racism work, which marginalized Indigenous women in the group; my ill-considered and half-baked attempt to link an Indigenous struggle to research funding in England without speaking to the community first, which cost me even more friends and huge embarrassment; the time when I assumed that I knew enough about an Indigenous community to speak up on an issue and got it wrong, very publicly; times when I have trusted the wrong people or promoted the work of people who turned out to be Pretendians – those who falsely claim to have Indigenous ancestry – or, worse, proved to be abusers or abuse apologists. All of these failures started with the passionate belief that what I was doing was right and would make a difference.

Remembering how many times I have been inspired, determined, and motivated to make change immediately summons the results of those moments, almost uniformly associated with feelings of pain, shame, guilt, frustration, and self-loathing. I have spent a lot of time over the years trying to justify – to others and to myself – why I have done what I have. I have tried so many times to convince others and myself that my intentions were enough to override the ineffectiveness and harm of my actions. What arrogance. Now, I finally know my failures too well to ignore them. They make me weaker, not stronger, but perhaps they also expose how much of my perceived personal power is actually part of my participation in collective settler privilege. Regardless, I have made some kind of odd friendship with my failures. We are, at least, colleagues.

Uncertain Edges

The intent of the previous chapter was not to malign social movement activists in the northern settler bloc, many of whom are struggling to do good and better work, but to establish that settler colonial and decolonizing analysis is necessary in order to effectively confront Indigenous dispossession, displacement, and elimination. At the level of social movements, however, failures around decolonization are much more numerous and significant than successes. Nonetheless, there are individuals and groups involved in the political left in Canada and the United States of America who are working to prioritize and pursue decolonizing relationships with Indigenous peoples and communities. And some on the political left still hold the potential to act as allies. Adam Lewis (2012) has asserted particular interpretations of anarchism that are profoundly anti-colonial and decolonizing, and Harsha Walia (2010, 81) has noted that some "migrant justice groups like No One [I]s Illegal have prioritised solidarity with Indigenous struggles and acknowledged that demands of migrant communities will be short-lived if gained at the expense of Indigenous self-determination." There undoubtedly remains a greater potential for decolonizing relationships among settlers on the left than on the right if for no other reason than that leftist activists – especially those working from the resistant traditions of communities of colour – are less attached to some or all of the institutions of privilege that generate uneven topographies of power and provide disproportionate benefits to those most invested in the highest levels of the settler colonial topography of power.

However, it is not enough to decolonize by changing relationships between peoples and structures or forms of governance (Lewis 2012, 235); it is necessary to change relationships between peoples in place and between peoples and places. The settler colonialism revealed in various aspects of the settler left is an example of "deep colonizing" (Veracini 2011), and it is not easily confronted. Geographer Jenny Pickerill and I have argued that settler activists must confront this deep colonizing by critically examining their own positionality and actions through a lens of Indigenous sovereignty and relationships to place. The "true challenge" of doing so for those who "would be allies is to find their own new way of looking at – and being in – place that compl[e]ments but does not replicate what Indigenous peoples are attempting to do. Replication of relations, as with appropriation of voice, is an unwelcome and unneeded imposition" (Barker and Pickerill 2012, 1719; see also Barker and Pickerill 2019). Concentrating on complementarities foregrounds Indigenous understandings of place and recentres settler responsibility across difference as a responsibility to places rather than to paternalistic attempts at solidarity[1] or to assumed aid through political-economic contestation. Taking on this responsibility, however, is not as simple as it may seem both because, at this point, relatively few settler people in Canada or the United States support Indigenous concerns in principle or in action – consider for example the online comments on any article that even mentions Indigenous people, which are overwhelmingly hostile toward Indigeneity – and because social movements, as demonstrated, have largely failed to effectively challenge settler colonialism even when actively confronting other forms of oppressive power. So where do settlers seeking to participate in decolonizing work go? Where is the space from which that struggle might be engaged? Identifying the cracks and contradictions in settler colonialism is critically important because, in doing so, we can find the uncertain edges of this seemingly hegemonic world – the spaces and the opportunities where we can effect change.

I employ the term "uncertain edges" because of the important fact that it is not clear where the settler colonial assemblage ends. This is the case in part because other methods of hierarchical, oppressive, expansive spatial production overlap and interpenetrate settler colonialism due to the constant internal shifting of elements within the assemblage. It is also the case because Indigenous peoples have survived as *peoples* and are contesting colonialisms and (re)asserting their Indigeneity across Turtle Island, specifically their unique relationships with land and place. This persistence indicates that even within the settler states of the northern bloc, Indigenous sovereignties have not been completely extinguished, nor has the land been irrevocably transformed and transferred. The settler colonial project is ongoing and is not (yet) total; it only portrays itself as such. And since it is not total, there are spaces that do not conform to settler colonial structures – spaces that exist between settler colonialism and Indigeneity. These are the uncertain edges where colonial logic does not overwhelmingly structure social space. By finding, engaging, and working to expand these spaces, we can develop new conceptual and practical possibilities for decolonial action.

Decolonization and Resurgence

Two interrelated terms, which are sometimes used interchangeably and have significant overlaps but which also have salient differences, merit clarification here: decolonization and resurgence. Indigenous resurgence, the reassertion of Indigenous nationhood and cultures of place, is a process and end in itself. Decolonization, an evolving concept that refers to the broad process of reasserting and revitalizing Indigenous nationhood, regenerating Indigenous cultures, languages, and political economies, and deconstructing or displacing invasive, colonial structures, systems, and stories, is a desired outcome of Indigenous resurgence and also an important focus for non-Indigenous people seeking to act in solidarity with Indigenous communities. The reassertion of Indigeneity is part of the concept of Indigenous resurgence as it is increasingly articulated by Indigenous scholars like Audra Simpson (2014), Leanne Simpson (2011, 2017), Glen Coulthard (2014), and others (Daigle 2019; Dhillon 2018; Elliott 2018; Starblanket 2017).[2] The connection is perhaps best demonstrated by Audra Simpson's *Mohawk Interruptus: Political Life across the Borders of Settler States* (2014), which links together Mohawk sovereignty and nationhood as continuing and self-evident manifestations in a politics of refusal that rejects the need to participate in and to identify with settler nationalities and citizenships or, perhaps most importantly, with state borders and security regimes. Mohawk understandings of their sovereignty as self-evident is by extension a refusal to acquiesce to settler colonial governmentality expressed through particular spatial regimes. Indigenous presence on the land as part of dynamic networks of being stands in clear opposition to the hegemony of settler colonial spaces of opportunity and advantage. Likewise, Indigenous presence as "being Indigenous" is an oppositional act that not only disrupts settler colonial mentalities predicated on terra nullius and tropes of civilization versus savagery (Alfred and Corntassel 2005) but also reveals the tenuous nature of the sovereign claims of Canada and the United States (Asch 2014; Dunbar-Ortiz 2014). So the more that Indigenous resurgence is embodied and asserted on the land, the more settler colonialism must, by definition, be disrupted and cede both material and conceptual territory. Settlement must be unsettled. More than that, decolonization writ large must by necessity disrupt wider systems of capitalism (Coulthard 2014) and border imperialism (Walia 2013, 247–76), along with the institutions of incarceration and social control, such as prisons and migrant detention centres, that are connected to these systems (Gill et al. 2018). Thus the dismantling of settler colonial structures, systems, and stories implies a much larger project, one that is always led by and in support of both Indigenous resurgence and the end to systems founded on racial and economic oppression and on dispossession and exploitation of the land.

The assertion of Indigeneity in settler colonial space changes the spatialities of settler colonialism, often in unpredictable, powerful, and affective ways. It implies the assertion of the political orders, social systems, cultural processes, and so on that both evidence and support vibrant, sustainable Indigenous ways of being. This resurgence means asserting an Indigenous-centric network of relations directly within and against the settler colonial topography of power. Indigenous resistance directly confronts and confounds both the spaces of settler colonialism and the colonial mentalities of settler people, striking at the core of settler colonial spatialities. For this reason, before examining the spatialities of settler solidarity activists, it is important to understand some of the history and context of Indigenous land-based activism.

Land-Based Resurgence and Indigenous Sovereignty

During most of the twentieth century, Indigenous activists fought for the collective survival of their peoples and recognition of their basic existence. Much of this effort was intended to be self-determined, but given the political context of the northern bloc, including its high-profile civil rights struggles, Indigenous activism was largely perceived by outside commentators and historians as having been subsumed into popular discourses of rights and inclusion (V. Deloria Jr. 1970). However, Indigenous assertions of nationality and difference persisted, exemplified by the occupation of the town of Wounded Knee on the Pine Ridge Reservation in South Dakota in 1973, during which the town was declared a sovereign state, and by the clashes between the Mohawks of Kanesatake and the Canadian government during the Oka Crisis of 1990, during which a few relatively small and isolated Mohawk communities proved themselves beyond the capacity of the state to impose discipline through violence (York and Pindera 1991). Both Canada and the United States adopted less assimilationist policies in response to these Indigenous claims to land and title – and more than that, to sovereignty.

In Canada, the discourse was reframed through a kind of postcolonial responsibility, which resulted in the adoption of nation-to-nation self-government agreements for some First Nations (A. Simpson 2014) whereas tribal sovereignty and the plenary power that ambiguously attaches it to the sovereignty of the United States continued to confound and preoccupy American legal discourses (Bruyneel 2007; Olund 2002). These two different political constructs – the attempt to include Canada's First Nations in the body politic of the federation based on recognition and the attempt to situate Native Americans within, yet off to one side of, the state system based on the idea of "domestic dependent nations" (V. Deloria Jr. and Lytle 1984, ch. 2) – had the same effect of extending limited recognition of Indigenous claims to land while refusing to respond to them seriously (Coulthard 2014). The systems in which the discourses of self-governance and tribal sovereignty are conceptually grounded equally deny the possibility of achieving either goal beyond the settler state.

Currently, Indigenous nations in the northern settler bloc are in a period of post-treaty resistance. Whereas some First Nations bands have signed modern treaties – tantamount to land surrender agreements – such as the Nisga'a and Tsawwassen First Nations (*Nisga'a Final Agreement* 1999; *Tsawwassen First Nation Final Agreement* 2007), others have pulled out of treaty negotiations and consultation processes with governments and resource extraction corporations. A prime example is the Gitxsan and Wet'suwet'en, who in 2012 withdrew support from their respective treaty negotiators for having made deals related to the Enbridge Northern Gateway fossil fuel pipeline project and together physically blockaded the Gitxsan treaty office (Stueck and Bailey 2012). These actions came in the context of wider resistance from groups such as the Unist'ot'en, a clan of the Wet'suwet'en, whose "soft camp" has become a crucial focus of Indigenous land-based activism in northern British Columbia (Barker and Ross 2017, 205). Although British Columbia's claim to land is ambiguous and has given rise to a very obvious set of related conflicts, none of these incidents are isolated. Similar dynamics, for example, are occurring in the American Southwest, where the Diné (Navajo) have opposed the theft of water and the destruction of their sacred spaces (Chee 2011), and in California, where the Winnemem Wintu have declared war on the American state as part of their reclamation of sacred river spaces (Fimrite 2012).

The processes of post-treaty resistance are articulated in the works of Indigenous scholars who have developed the concept of resurgence beyond contestation for the purpose of gaining political power or social support. As Songhees land manager and activist Cheryl Bryce and Cherokee political scientist Jeff Corntassel (2012, 153) assert,

> When approaches to indigenous cultural revitalization and self-determination are discussed solely in terms of strategies, rights, and theories, they overlook the everyday practices of resurgence and decolonization. Indigenous resurgence is about reconnecting with homelands, cultural practices, and communities, and is centered on reclaiming, restoring, and regenerating homeland relationships. Another dimension centers upon decolonization, which transforms indigenous struggles for freedom from performance to everyday local practice. This entails moving away from the performativity of a rights discourse geared toward state affirmation and approval toward a daily existence conditioned by place-based cultural practices.

This refusal to chase rights and recognition is necessarily unsettling to settler people because, rather than seeking approval, Indigenous resurgence movements violate settler colonial expectations of appropriate use and ownership. In this sense, Indigenous resurgence is creatively transgressive since it disrupts settler colonial orders not simply to interfere with the operation of colonial power but also to generate the very basis of Indigenous sovereignty and futurity.

Indigenous sharing of territory as in treaties and other arrangements between Indigenous nations (e.g., see L. Simpson 2008) definitely violates settler colonial ideas of discrete property and territorial sovereignty, and in this regard, it is both a necessary refusal of colonial divisions into bands, tribes, and First Nations and a necessary assertion of Indigenous internationalism and diplomacy. In this same vein, Indigenous refusal to prioritize or centralize settler colonial territorial boundaries often brings Indigenous people into conflicts with rigid, state-bound ideas of jurisdiction and authority. With regard to Audra Simpson's (2014) discussion of enacting Mohawk sovereignty across colonial borders, it would be fair to say that Indigenous resurgence is defined by transversality rather than jurisdictional claiming of territory. This transversality is threatening to the settler colonial order, as political scientist Nezvat Soguk (2011) has argued, because "Indigenous transversality" – movements across Turtle Island through different territories and irrespective of colonial cartography – holds the potential for radically different ways of conceiving of belonging in and related to place. Soguk reminds us that all across Turtle Island, where many Indigenous societies have been dismissed by settler scholars because of their "nomadism," the land cycles and patterns, "ancient, ongoing, and organic," have guided political and economic activities (46). The movement that has accompanied these cycles and patterns is not "free wandering" but an enactment of community in movement (46). Soguk further describes how assertions of Indigeneity based on these transversal precepts undermine systems of state power, the extractive power of capital, and the discourse of rights-based equality by which individuals are separated from movements for resurgence. Leanne Simpson (2011), in her powerful and personal approach to Anishinaabe resurgence through rebuilding sacred and material relationships to the land, demonstrates how the renewal of connections to the land strengthens attachments to community and culture because the practices represent such a unique, singularly Anishinaabe, worldview. In this regard, Indigenous resurgence is doubly powerful: land-based practices of culture, spirituality, political ecology, and resource management build internal bonds of community even as they disrupt the threads that knit together settler colonial topographies of power. Indigenous resurgence picks away at the uncertain edges of settler colonial space.

Decolonization and Solidarity Politics

Decolonization remains less well articulated, particularly the relationships of settlers pursuing decolonization with Indigenous communities in resurgence.[3] There are comparatively few cases to draw from that have featured settler communities working in effective solidarity with Indigenous communities in Canada and the United States, although there are some useful examples. In 2009, settlers and Kanaka Maoli (Native Hawaiians) participated together in a Hawaiian ceremony on the lawns of the Iolani Palace, a provocative direct action designed to simultaneously unsettle the claim of the state of Hawaii to sovereignty and renew Kanaka Maoli relationships to a sacred place. This act, which Hawaiian political scientist Noelani Goodyear-Ka'ōpua (2011, 132) identifies as an instance of "anarcha-indigenism," was an effective moment of cooperation in a larger movement for Native Hawaiian independence.

Perhaps more representative of settler solidarity efforts is geographer Soren Larsen's (2003) study of the resettlement of Ootsa Lake in the interior of British Columbia during the early twentieth century. Despite the colonial usurpation of land and the deterritorialization of Indigenous nations that had been affecting the Pacific Northwest for decades, in rural areas like Ootsa Lake, Indigenous communities still held great advantages over many settlement communities. They had stable and diverse food security, were adept at the use of technologies specifically suited to their homelands and the wildly varying seasonal conditions, and were often called on to support their new settler neighbours. In exchange, settler people often ignored or altered the dictates of the colonial government, based in Victoria on the southwest coast of the province. Taking advantage of the complicating factor of distance, settlers often collaborated with the Cheslatta, who were their friends and, in many cases, also their relatives, as there was a significant amount of intermarriage between the settler and Indigenous communities. Larsen demonstrates that intimate, familial ties between Indigenous and settler communities helped to undermine – but not disperse – colonial power, especially in rural areas. Some of the ties mapped by Larsen continue to have an enduring influence a century later.[4]

As much as these crosscultural spaces challenged tropes of frontier segregation (Larsen 2003, 93–94), they were predicated in part on the effective absence of colonial authority emanating from the regional capital (94–95) and were rendered moot when concentrated capital investment resulted in the relocation of both the settler and the Indigenous communities in the 1950s (88n4). Further, in a study of collaborative efforts between settler environmentalists and Indigenous communities around Anahim Lake, also in the BC interior, Larsen (2008, 180) demonstrates the difficulty of maintaining "frame alignment" between settler and Indigenous activists in the absence of an "external threat," resulting in fragmentation of spatial discourses such that "the community and its ... agenda cease to exist in the mind of the residents." In Larsen's study, the external threat is the potential for large-scale corporate logging, which brought environmentalists, Indigenous communities, and local supporters into a shared conversation about the need to develop an alternative way to regulate the forestry industry that was environmentally sustainable, respected Indigenous rights and title, and economically supported communities around the region. However, once the imminence of the threat was removed, this shared conversation broke down, in no small part because of the insistence by the settler communities that their property and prosperity be given priority in governance decisions.

A similar situation played out on a national scale across Canada during the winter of 2012–13, when the Indigenous protest movement Idle No More was at its peak. This movement effectively brought many settler and non-Indigenous people into public direct-action protests that centralized Indigenous leadership, ceremony, and rights. The round-dance flash mob, as an embodied form of open protest, was especially effective in this regard. However, by 2014 Idle No More had lost momentum, in part because of the capricious affinity politics of those settler Canadians mobilized by resentment toward Stephen Harper, the divisive Conservative prime minister of Canada from 2006–15 (Barker 2015, 56–57). The course of the anti-Harper discourse was altered by settler people hesitating to support the more direct assertions of sovereignty, such as roadblocks, and by a shift in the media's attention away from the Idle No More protests in order to cover a number of political scandals that rocked the prime minister, including the exposure of corrupt senators whom he had appointed and the sideshow distraction of the endorsement of Harper and his policies by the dangerously elitist Rob Ford, dubbed the "crack-smoking Mayor of Toronto" in popular media after he was filmed engaging in the act. However, the success of temporary assertions of Indigeneity in spaces of state and capital such as those undertaken by the Idle No More movement has demonstrated the potential for solidarity in the pursuit of decolonization.

The Trouble with Settlers Redux: Decolonizing Settler 'Allies'

Indigenous resurgence provides a powerful, impossible to ignore counterfactual refutation of settler perceptions of erasure and fantasies of naturalization and settler indigenization. However, awareness of settler colonization and Indigenous resistance is not enough. We must make sense somehow of a recurrent and irrefutable fact: settler decolonization efforts have been fraught with failure. It is not my intention here to cast aspersions, nor to rehash the earlier critique of leftist movements. Instead, I intend to implicate myself directly in this study through my embodied, unsettling, and ultimately failure-ridden attempts to act as an activist in solidarity with Indigenous peoples.

I Was Not Surprised

It was reading ethnologist Lisa Stevenson's article "The Psychic Life of Biopolitics: Survival, Cooperation, and Inuit Community" (2012) that brought me around to the conclusion that I needed to write here in a deliberately (and for me, uncomfortably) personal voice. Stevenson's study is a scathing indictment of the power and practice of biopolitics by well-meaning settler Canadians in Inuit communities of the Far North. From tuberculosis epidemics to suicides, these communities have often measured the impacts of colonization in a grim ledger sheet of Inuit deaths. Stevenson argues that suicide hotlines comprise a "strategic exemplar of a particular form of sociability" (602). But it was her comment on the reactions of suicide hotline workers to Inuit suicides that brought home a sudden and familiar discomfort. No one is surprised by Inuit suicides, she says, and "the absence of surprise is significant" (603). Indigenous suicide, Stevenson argues, "is at once prohibited and awaited" by settler society. She describes suicide "as a counterfactual" occurrence that "evokes ambivalence. Future suicides are imagined and the thoughts then suppressed. Suicide, too awful to think about, is a possibility that is articulated and then denied" (603). This discussion of a struggle that in failure brings not defeat but ambivalence provides a useful parallel to my own activism and attempts to build decolonizing alliances.

I think of the times – and there are more than a few – when I have been accused of being colonial or acting like a colonizer. The accusations came from both Indigenous and settler people. When I look back, I see that, more often than not, they were correct. I try to think of my emotions when these accusations arose, and I can remember feeling many things: angry, resentful, aggrieved, ashamed, humiliated, and probably as a result of all of these responses, speechless. However, I was rarely *surprised.* Sometimes, I was shocked by the context or by the (perceived) hostility of my accuser. But my surprise was tempered by the fact that the event had happened over and over in my mind before that moment. Waiting to pick up my teaching partner, Chaw-win-is, for our frequent forty-five-minute commute to and from the Saanich Adult Education Centre,[5] I would triumphantly picture myself being *right* in our conversations only to admit as she approached that I had these fantasies only because I was usually wrong – which Chaw-win-is never had a problem explaining to me. And I did learn, but I was never surprised about being wrong, about failing to understand.

Chaw-win-is, however, called me colonial without pulling punches; in fact, she had frequently done so, going back to our time as students together. She often did so forcefully and never without cause. I learned a great deal from her and from the (many) other times that Indigenous people whom I attempted to approach in friendship and alliance pointed out my colonizing acts. In my essay "From Adversaries to Allies: Forging Respectful Alliances between Indigenous and Settler Peoples" (2010), I argue that it is necessary for settler people to engage in radical experimentation.[6] I posit that a necessary reason for this method of engagement is that settler people need to risk – and practise – being wrong in order to avoid being immobilized by a fear of failure. Perhaps ironically, however, I have never stopped fearing failure, even as I have come to expect it. Given the concerns raised by Stevenson, this observation has prompted me to reconsider *failure* in the context of what settler solidarity activists might consider *success*.

Like Stevenson's (2012) suicide hotline workers – or even the 'heroic' bureaucrats, doctors, and nurses she describes flocking north earlier in the twentieth century, who lamented but were unfazed by Inuit deaths – I was saddened but not surprised by these accusations of colonial complicity or action. I was not surprised by any of my failures to decolonize my relationships with Indigenous people or groups because I expected those efforts to fail. In most cases, I expected that I would, in my ignorance and despite my preoccupation with behaving respectfully, overstep the acceptable boundaries of my settler positionality. This expectation allowed me to apologize – mea culpa! – and in so doing to claim for myself the comfortable settler colonial position of being the one who apologizes (M. Johnson 2011; Veracini 2011). I imagine the hotline workers and tuberculosis nurses glumly shaking their heads over another failed project and lamenting their inability to do more or better, before moving on to the next project in the form of a near-death patient or suicidal youth. I was often quick to claim for myself the position of apologizer. I intended for my assumption of this role to be a means of making amends in a productive way, but it actually had the effect of reminding everyone of my power in social spaces by dint of my membership in some fundamental institutions of privilege: racial, gendered, economic, nationalistic, and otherwise. I engaged in deep-colonizing behaviour, reinscribing my position and power by recognizing it over and over again.

At other times, my response was to dehumanize and derationalize my accuser, whether by transferring responsibility for their own anger back onto the Indigenous people who confronted me or by dismissing the critiques of other settlers as their own failings to grasp the nuance of my position or actions. I would assert – if only in my mind – that those who confronted me were angry because of my whiteness or my privilege rather than because of my actions. Upset by my positionality, they had failed to see *me* as an *individual* – or so I thought. I wished that they could just see that I was trying to help! And I knew a thing or two about colonization, so I could help strategically, right? They were just too *emotional* to see it because of the effects of all that colonization, colonization from which I benefited directly and indirectly in all areas of my life. The lack of connection between cause and effect is a clear example of behaviour rooted in "dysconsciousness" (D.M. Johnson 2011, 110), but a side effect of a lack of critical mind is the inability to know how uncritical that mind is. So I was alternately baffled by and resigned to these responses. I could not understand the responses, but I expected them.

Uneasy Activism and the Uncertain Edges of Settler Colonialism

I have always had a difficult relationship to activism and the concept of being an activist. Scholars of activism, such as Chris Bobel (2007) and Paul Chatterton (2006), have taught me that this difficulty is not uncommon. I also know that some of my insecurities and perceptions are a result of my coming of age in the world of globalizing power and anti-globalization protests at the turn of the millennia. I began to formulate my political awareness in the late 1990s in the wake of the implementation of the North American Free Trade Agreement between Mexico, Canada, and the United States in 1994 and the conclusion of the five-year Royal Commission on Aboriginal Peoples in Canada in 1996 and right before the Battle of Seattle in 1999 and, on its heels, 9/11. Still immature but feeling ready to become active and engaged, I rarely made my way to protests or marches. I was not attracted to rugged individualist positions, but I did come to identify as an anarchist, with perhaps unavoidable fantasies of victory over power through civil disobedience. But I never found my analogue to the iconic barricades of the French Revolution or the communal chaos of Seattle. I never clashed with police or was arrested. I never occupied a squat. In a strange way, the fact that my involvement in radical politics came about through Indigenous politics directed me away from these types of activism.

I remember hearing in my teen years about the Royal Commission on Aboriginal Peoples – primarily about its roots in the Oka Crisis of 1990 and its cost but little about its content. It was only years later that I would learn that the commission had directed a lot of grassroots mobilization in Indigenous communities into long, bureaucratic processes of research, gathering evidence, hearing testimony, and preparing reports. By the time everyone had finished trying to figure out the implications of the commission's final report (RCAP 1996) and its twenty-year agenda for implementing its recommended changes, it had become clear that the government had no plans to implement its recommendations. This much I did understand, as by that time I was interning in the office of my local member of Parliament, who was a member of the Liberal majority, and Indigenous peoples' concerns were simply never on the agenda. But even as I was starting to think more deeply about Indigenous politics, the wider Canadian discourse was shifting: a nation that had been captivated by the images of armed standoffs seemed to have grown blasé about Indigenous protests and political contention in the new millennium, distracted by the spectacle of summit protests, by the emerging War on Terror, and by a normalized and even promoted image of the unruly Native warrior in need of discipline (D.M. Johnson 2011). The local politics of Indigenous peoples that motivated standoffs at places like Grassy Narrows in northern Ontario were treated as 'law and order' nuisances by the settler community (Willow 2011).[7] That the state could not physically prevent these Indigenous resistances was beside the point: their defeat seemed inevitable, despite having persisted for decades, if not centuries.

At the same time, a generation of Indigenous scholars was inspiring new radicalism in the academy. Leanne Simpson (2008, 15) lists "John Mohawk, Sakej Youngblood Henderson, Vine Deloria, Jr., Leroy Little Bear, Winona LaDuke, Linda Tuhiwai Smith, Taiaiake Alfred, Haunani-Kay Trask, [and] Trish Monture" as "Indigenous scholars and activists who nurtured" today's generation of radical, Indigenous scholars. I have read the work of all of these incredibly important scholars, and between 2001 and 2009, my formative years in both academia and activism, I was fortunate to meet and learn directly from several. As the anti-globalization movement changed into the alter-globalization movement of movements, I was busy trying to understand the individual and social legacy of settler colonialism in Canada. I tried and failed to keep one foot in a current of global activism through mass physical contention and the other in a current that consistently carried me away from all that and toward introspection.

In 2006, when the Ontario Provincial Police violently moved in on the Six Nations reclamation site near the town of Caledonia (McCarthy 2016), I was in Arizona presenting a paper in the American Indian Studies section of the Western Social Sciences Association annual conference. Caledonia is a place that I know well; it is a short drive from my family home, relatives have lived there, and I frequently drove through the town on the way to university classes taught by Mohawk healer and educator Jan Longboat on the Six Nations of the Grand River Reserve. Friends and former classmates were involved in the reclamation and were at risk of harm. I heard the play-by-play of the police invasion on the Internet through CKRZ radio, a Six Nations station in Ohsweken.[8] A colleague and I delayed the session that he was scheduled to chair that afternoon in order to alert anyone who may not have heard. But I needed to do something more: my understanding of what an activist does, my feelings of activist inferiority, and my nascent understanding of settler responsibility drove me to look for a greater opportunity – in retrospect, a dead giveaway that I should have known better – to help or, rather, to take responsibility. By the time I was back in my apartment in Victoria, British Columbia, I was riled up, ready to fly to Ontario, my long-time home, and take care of my perceived responsibilities. But my Indigenous classmates and teachers at the University of Victoria told me not to. They asked me what I intended to do there. Years after the fact, I have to admit that I was not sure then and still do not know what, if anything, I could have done.

Suffice it to say that I have never lived up to my own ideal of what an activist should be or do. In part, that is because the ideal is a silly, heroic one – no different, in all likelihood, from the ideal of heroic nurses and bureaucrats conquering the tuberculosis epidemics of the Far North on a mercy mission to the Inuit. Such an ideal is but a new colonial frontier for settlers harbouring fantasies about the opportunities to be found in an unruly space that is waiting for occupation by the willing and righteous in the conflicted currents of protest and activism. This is how creative settler colonizers' fantasies can be – or more accurately, *my* settler colonial fantasies. My imagined clear levelled ground was one where Indigenous presence was neutralized as a threat not because of elimination but because Indigenous people liked me. In this fantasy, 'they' no longer saw me as a colonizer because of my credibility as an activist. But this narrative was pure settler colonial bricolage. It was based on a few Indigenous individuals standing in for a heroic but lost Indigenous sovereignty, their approval being the necessary factor for my transcendence of the settler colonial formation and achievement of self-indigenization.

In my own personal "moves to innocence" (Tuck and Yang 2012, 9–28), I was trying to render myself exceptional with respect to the rest of settler society through my own settler colonial mythistories. This was my localized and powerful variant of "the colonizer who refuses" (Memmi 1965, 63–88) and an adaptation of the "peacemaker myth" (Regan 2010, ch. 3). Albert Memmi argues that colonizers who refuse to accept colonization deny not only the validity of the colonial enterprise but also their own culpability and responsibility. Theirs is a rhetorical move to distance themselves from the undeniably negative effects of invasion and its structures and to claim a moral superiority while holding on to material privileges. Rather than the colonizer who accepts or the colonizer who refuses, both of which are still colonial positions, I was to be the colonizer who changes sides. Crucially, however, this narrative centred *my* agency, as the recognition was to come after the fact of my choosing to try to decolonize – a project that I expected would fail, meaning that I expected to not actually achieve any change and still be exempted from guilt. The difference between my position and that of the colonizer who refuses was a matter of degrees; I was trying to prove that I could refuse *more* or *harder* or *better* than any other settler person, without my refusal ever having to be measured by results. Of course, my expectation of how Indigenous friends and colleagues would perceive my actions and how they actually did and responded to them have been worlds apart.

It is important to remember that these interactions did not involve a distanced, amorphous postcolonial construct but real people who were and are important to me. Through friendships and shared spaces of learning, work, and struggle, they learned exactly how to speak to me in order to compel my attention, and what I was told were stories of my own colonialism. These conversations had more impact on my understanding of the world around me and on my place in it as a settler Canadian in a settler colonial world than any book learning, and they were so effective and transformative particularly because they happened on one of the uncertain edges of settler colonial space. These spaces generally exist in the tensions around personal relationships between people and communities that do not neatly fit into the expected subjectivities of the settler identity but instead arise across blurred boundaries and through complex webs of relationality. This is to say that the radical experimentation that I set out to undertake was an experiment in my own abilities both to identify – or to accept others' identification of – and to compensate for my internalized settler colonial ideologies and narratives, and in so doing, I relied on Indigenous friends and colleagues who cared for me enough to tell me when an experiment was failing, something that I had little ability to judge on my own. Without failing in these experiments, I could not have learned how to do otherwise. I had to fail, again and again, in order to learn how to succeed – something that I have yet to achieve.

The Efficacy of Failure: Decolonization, One Error at a Time

What to make of all this failure? I am certainly not extraordinary when it comes to activism, and I have seen similar patterns of experience in friends and associates. I think that the sorts of failures that I describe here are fairly typical of many settler people who seek to act as allies to Indigenous people and communities. Returning to Stevenson's (2012) discussion of how failure can lead to ambivalence, I suggest that this outcome is something to be avoided not because it is failure but because it is *safe.* Similarly, failures that lead to unsettling but do not build the possibilities revealed in the moment of being unsettled into a larger decolonial movement are best understood not as failures for the individuals in question but as victories for settler colonial systems – that is, as instances of their success in recapturing and disciplining the resistance of unruly communities. Well-intentioned but ultimately self-referential, these approaches to solidarity activism fail to bridge the difference between settler and Indigenous interests. And herein lies the problem. It is impossible to build this bridge as long as settler interests are related to investments in, or one's capacity to invest in, settler colonial institutions of privilege. Insofar as settler people remain embedded in settler colonial spaces, and to the extent that these colonialisms and their attendant spatial constructions can shape-shift, settler people can perhaps only ever fail in attempts at decolonial solidarity. But are these grounds for pessimism?

Failure is a recurrent theme in social movement literature but is often approached or considered only indirectly. Social movement theorists who discuss failure often examine the reasons why a particular movement did not achieve its stated goals or did not prevent a particular action or event from occurring. Studies have demonstrated that social movements fail because of an inability to control messaging (Culp 2013), mixed messages from leadership over tactics (Barker 2015), competing submovement interests fracturing lines of solidarity in particular power contexts (Leitner, Sheppard, and Sziarto 2008), disagreements over who legitimately holds authority and knowledge (Pickerill 2009), the high cost of government surveillance and the carceral threat to radical activists (Starr 2006), and any number of other situation-specific practical and material concerns. However, these failures are very different from the systematic failures of settler activists. Coming perhaps closer to the nature of the situation is some of the literature that addresses the participation of white individuals in anti-racism activism and education (Byrne 2015; McGuinness 2000; McLean 2013; W.S. Shaw 2006). These studies make clear that white activists often do not appreciate the degree to which their whiteness, as a performative social process frequently linked to the accumulation of social privilege in the form of political and economic mobility, is inherently disruptive to spaces created and claimed by communities of colour. In their inability to stop performing whiteness, these activists act as a vector for the power of white supremacy to invade anti-racist spaces. Settler people, as Emma Battell Lowman and I have discussed in the Canadian context

(Battell Lowman and Barker 2015), often similarly act as sources of settler colonial erasure, displacement, and violence as they seek an escape from unsettlement and a return to comfort. This impact can and does occur in spaces of solidarity or where Indigenous communities are asserting their sovereignty, particularly when a sort of settler colonial "fragility," to borrow from race educator Robin DiAngelo's (2011, 2018) concept of "white fragility," moves settlers to hijack a solidarity group meeting, a political protest, or a conference presentation with an expression of settler guilt and hurt feelings or to impose their particular vision for Indigenous liberation, both of which are examples of the kinds of action that recentre the settler and displace Indigenous people and authority.

As much of the literature on whiteness makes clear, one of the primary contributions that white solidarity activists can make to the struggles of racialized communities is to respect boundaries by not violating the spaces that these communities construct for themselves. Another contribution is to directly confront white supremacy in primarily whitestream communities and contexts. These same recommendations could be made with respect to settler activists, who likewise should not invade Indigenous spaces and should work to dismantle settler colonialism. Yet these admonitions are easier to assert than to envision in practice. As I have shown, the mutability of settler colonial spaces, the social normalization of practices rooted in identifying and seizing spatial opportunity and advantage, and the endlessly open system of recruitment into the material and narrative trajectory of settler colonialism mean that even activists educated by and experienced in working with Indigenous communities can wind up replicating settler colonial relations.

So what is the path forward for settler people who want to engage in the transformative struggle of decolonization? How can settler people contribute to Indigenous resurgence and the establishment of respectful relationships between Indigenous people, settlers, and exogenous Others on Turtle Island if the mere presence of settlers is necessarily colonial, other than by simply going away?[9] Although we must accept that decolonization will necessarily involve some (re)moving of settler populations, the belief that a mass exodus is the solution to settler colonialism actually defers the responsibility for decolonization to some future, more practically prepared, and frankly mythical settler polity. It is another flight to a metaphorical frontier, another move to elsewhere and otherwise that leaves the here and now unchanged. We seem to be stuck in a paradox: settler people cannot escape their responsibilities for decolonization if they leave, nor can they succeed as agents of decolonization if they remain on Indigenous lands. Settlers seem destined to fail to decolonize either way.

For a useful aid in thinking through the issue of settler solidarity failure, I turn to the work of queer theorist Jack Halberstam, particularly *The Queer Art of Failure* (2011). This work of "low theory," which is intended to "locate all the in-between spaces that save us from being snared by the hooks of hegemony," fundamentally rejects the norms and standards of mainstream acceptance by which "success" is judged for queer communities (2). Noting that success under these terms means accepting a permanent subject position under regimes that are heteropatriarchal, cisnormative, racist, classist, and otherwise violent and conservative, Halberstam demands that we think through whether failure might not be a better option. As Halberstam provocatively asks, "What comes after hope?" (1) – a question that has some obvious resonance with the similarly "low theory" (2) of settler colonial spatiality and territorialization that I have outlined here. Whether through racist narratives of progress, multicultural Aboriginalism, or inclusion based on recognition, the standards by which Indigenous peoples are judged as successful within settler colonial society are likewise nearly impossible to achieve and similarly convey dubious benefits for those who succeed. But more pertinent to this discussion of the failures of settler solidarity activism are the standards by which settler people in Canada and the United States are judged to be successful settler subjects. Here, too, the "hooks of hegemony" entreat settlers to seek success by accumulating privilege and by investing sovereignty in as many overlapping institutions as possible – buying property in the suburbs, performing whiteness through consumption and display, conspicuously displaying nationalism by belting out the anthem at a sporting event just before a military flyover, and so on. The most powerful, such as the political-economic norms of capitalism, the cultural performances of heteropatriarchy, and the racial divisions of white supremacy, have become almost ubiquitous; it is now nearly impossible to imagine any social life without these parameters. Settler people are subsumed into and largely defined and subjectivized by these institutions, and so Halberstam's question becomes even more pertinent. If a successful flight to the "rhizomatic West" simply mobilizes a frontier space of exception, as settler colonial literature scholar Alex Young (2013) has argued, thus restarting the entire settler colonial project again in a new time and place, whereas a successful commitment to being in place means reinscribing existing settler colonialism and more deeply entrenching the settler colonial topography of power, we are bound to fail to escape settler colonialism. We cannot hope to simply escape or remove ourselves from these structures, so we must search for something beyond or after such a hope: the failure of the entire enterprise and ourselves along with it.

Halberstam (2011) entreats activists, artists, and everyday people to intentionally fail in part to defy the expectations of hegemonic power structures. "Legibility," he reminds us, "is a condition of manipulation" (10, citing Scott 1999, 183). Working within any system opens us up to control through systemic standards that serve aggregations of power. Being embedded in structures and systems of power comes with certain performative expectations that are reinforced through social and cultural coding in the form of stories and narratives and that are enforced through a variety of surveillance and disciplinary apparatuses, from the deployment of police and the use of violence to the denial of employment and the threat of economic deprivation. Halberstam does not suggest, however, that people seeking change should not participate at all in these systems and structures. That would be impossible given the omnipresent and hegemonic nature of the neoliberalism that they inscribe and their similarity to the pervasive settler colonial spaces that I have articulated here.

Instead, Halberstam argues that we must use our positions in these systems and stories to become illegible – that is, to queer the processes of production and consumption around us that rely on our physical, mental, and emotional labour. This approach means at times accepting complicity with dominating power as an inevitable part of struggle, and settler people seeking to act in solidarity with Indigenous people and communities must not hide these complicities and complications. Doing so simply obscures the workings of manipulation within these systems. Legibility within the system is not affected by denials of complicity, but legibility to other subaltern or resistant agents is. Instead, Halberstam suggests that complicity is something to be explored, its depths plumbed for new insights into the functioning of hegemonic power. There is an inspiration on the other side of hope in Halberstam's (2011, 23) argument that "to inhabit the bleak territory of failure we sometimes have to write and acknowledge dark histories, histories within which the subject collaborates with rather than always opposes oppressive regimes and dominant ideology."

Beyond recognizing and exploring our complicity, and in order to avoid being legible within systems of power, we must frequently seek to do the wrong thing – that is, to do those things that seem to our settler colonial sensibilities to be utter failings of our social projects. We must seek to centralize the ongoing power of Indigenous sovereignty and self-determination in our political and social lives because Indigeneity is the antithesis of settler colonialism. We must recognize settler people not as a singular and growing group of those who are like 'us' but as a diverse and far from unified group, even as we search for new ways of thinking about ourselves and our socio-political bonds. We must openly, publicly, and likely with great discomfort question the narratives and myths of nationalism, liberalism, multiculturalism, progress, and prosperity attached to Canada and the United States, even if it means failing to uphold peace with friends and family and failing to participate in polite society. We must fail to be good employees who stay silent when the colonialism and racism of workplaces are casually asserted, even if doing so means failing to keep the workplace productive. There is no singular way to pursue any of these failures. Rather, we must look for new and creative ways to fail "as a way of refusing to acquiesce to dominant logics of power and discipline and as a form of critique" (Halberstam 2011, 88). This critique must be more than a simple rejection, as rejection alone is an inherently conservative move that "slips easily into racism, sexism, and deep homophobia" (91). Rather, these critiques can serve as the first step in imagining something different or beyond the spaces imposed by dominating logics of power. This is not a politics of resentment or grievance but something different: a politics that accepts responsibility for our own inabilities to escape dominant settler colonial norms, and resolves to *fail better,* because "there is something powerful in being wrong, in losing, in failing" and because "all our failures combined might just be enough, if we practice them well, to bring down the winner" (120).

Of course, "the winner" is conceptualized differently under settler colonialism than under the neoliberal systems that Halberstam describes. Just as we must be wary of anti-capitalist or anti-racist approaches that still turn on the success of individuals to transcend both their conditions of oppression and their enduring complicity, we must be wary of equating neoliberalism to settler colonialism or queerness to decolonization. There is certainly a resonance between queering and decolonizing, as Sarah Hunt and Cindy Holmes (2015) explore in their meditation on the way that decolonization impacts their personal lives and domestic spaces as two queer women, the former Indigenous and the latter settler. They articulate queering as a process that can run parallel to decolonization, both of which they regard as "active, interconnected, critical, and everyday practices ... As a verb, queer is a deconstructive practice focused on challenging normative knowledges, identities, behaviors, and spaces thereby unsettling power relations and taken-for-granted assumptions" (155). However, they also note that Indigeneity is often ignored within queer discourses. Colonialism is not frequently recognized as a process of dispossession and social control relevant to contemporary queer activists and scholars, and decolonization has been articulated through a particular focus on land and place that queer theory has at times lacked. Hunt and Holmes go on to explore their own efforts to bring queering and decolonizing into alignment, and I strongly encourage engaging directly with their text. But I diverge here to undertake a more sustained examination of how failure as a concept can, and must be, altered specifically to address settler colonialism across Turtle Island.

Bad Settlers

Halberstam (2011, 2) argues that failure is a particularly appropriate project for queer communities in resistance because "queers fail well." I would argue that it is dangerous to make a similar assumption about settler people. In fact, settlers fail very poorly: the failure of an endeavour in one location usually simply results in the impetus to seek out another location – a new space of opportunity to occupy. The perception of and drive toward new frontiers creates a relentless forward momentum through the narrative structure of settlement, success, and supersession. If settler people consider themselves special by dint of occupying a particularly "special locale" (Veracini 2010b, 55), then the failure of a settler colonial enterprise is the failure of the place itself to be special, not necessarily the failure of the settler polity to make that place special. Settler collectives, as "strategic decenterers,"[10] are by definition excellent at focusing attention on the failings, losses, shortcoming, or mistakes of others as a way not only to buttress their own identities and attachments to institutions of privilege but also to generate spaces of opportunity and advantage relative to perceived Others. As a result, exogenous Others and Indigenous peoples are both used as foils for articulating a settler sense of belonging that never actually relies on evaluating settler collectives directly (Veracini 2015). Thus, in order for settler failure to be a concept (or practice) worth engaging, we must first remember that because individual failures are too easy to decentre and rearticulate as new opportunities for success and transcendence of the settler colonial form, failure needs to be positioned in such a way as to be undeniable to settler people. We must articulate failure as the irrecoverable collapse of the entire settler enterprise. Failure has to be considered as the wilful act of being bad at being settler colonizers, to the extent that this multitude of failures brings down "the winner" – the successful settler colonizers who benefit so much from the exploitation of Indigenous lands and from the deaths of Indigenous peoples.

This approach to failure runs parallel to the way that some Indigenous artists and activists have conceptualized resistance through the failure to be a "good Indian." In the poem "Bad Indians," Osage activist, artist, and comedian Ryan Red Corn (2011) riffs on the settler colonial belief that the "only good Indian is a dead Indian" with the line "they used to say the only good Indians were dead Indians / I must be no good at being Indian / 'cuz I feel alive and kicking." In this context, being a "bad Indian" is taken to mean a living, complex, defiant Indigenous person, one who is actively seeking to live and act as an Indigenous person belonging to an Indigenous community, to connect with culture and ancestry, and to refuse the expectations of the settlers' killing gaze. Conversely, failure as a settler must be understood as a kind of ending, as a foreclosure of privilege due to an inability to find or create a space of advantage, as the halting of social processes of occupation, erasure, and bricolage and the breakdown of the spatial structures and divisions built through these processes. It must also be rooted in the expected failure of all settler politics, even radical and liberatory traditions of anarchism and socialism, and in a failure to envision and strive toward a secure settler futurity. These failures entail certain kinds of fear that must be faced, if not overcome, in order to fail effectively. These are the fears of a return to rootlessness or exile, to a 'wilderness' that is absent 'civilization' in the form of wealth and privilege and beyond the geographical imaginary of the settlement. Decolonization, insofar as it implies that some of these very failures are necessary for the success of Indigenous resurgence, is supported by the failure of the settler colonial project in this way – by the failure of the biopolitical settler polity and the power that it wields over Indigenous lands and lives.

There is also a notable difference with respect to applying failure to settler colonialism in that certain tactics that Halberstam describes for pursuing failure do not map neatly onto settler colonial failure. For example, Halberstam (2011, 69–82) attends closely to articulating forgetting as a form of failure. However, forgetting is frequently a necessary part of settler colonial transfer, as I have discussed in reference to a number of national myths, legal decisions, and claims to property. Settler collectives must forget their encounters with living Indigenous peoples in order to uphold the fantasy of terra nullius and must forget their own violent betrayals of Indigenous trust in order to maintain their mythic histories as peacemakers or heroic pioneers. The kind of forgetting that would queer settler colonial space would be forgetting what it means to settle – that is, how settler colonial logics function – and this forgetting would require a rearticulation and reassertion of these disavowed memories and histories. Even then, we should question whether forgetting settler colonialism is a good thing since such an absence of memory opens up the possibility of resurgent settler colonization arising in the future.

Halberstam also considers the role of the body in contesting hegemonic forces. This focus is of particular use given the necessarily embodied nature of settler colonization, reflected in my own portrayal of a settler colonial assemblage that needs embodied acts of settlement and thus recruits settlers through aspirational narratives and anticipatory geographies, while disciplining them through extreme feelings of fear and guilt or through fantasies of transcendence. The body is the interface between the mind and the world; embodied experiences colour how we know, learn, and identify. Halberstam (2011, 103) notes that for queer communities, the body is often seen as a site of social failure insofar as queer bodies often fail to provide a stable reference point for identity – or identification – within existing gender norms. Obviously, these same (patriarchal) gender norms also overlap with settler colonial norms, such as the masculine ideal of the pioneer husband and the feminine domesticity of the civilized settler wife contrasted with the wild and overly sexualized Indigenous woman. So queer bodies that fail to meet or achieve gender norms also queer settler colonial spaces in significant ways. However, just as neoliberalism has adapted to absorb many, yet hardly all, of these gendered challenges within the hegemonic system of capitalist reproduction, so too can settler colonial relationships survive beyond challenges to gender norms (see Greensmith 2016, 2018; and Morgensen 2011).

The point, however, is not to dismiss embodied gender as a site of challenge but to call for widespread settler support for nonbinary people, transgender activists, sex workers, and their advocates, for the many other groups whose members do not meet the polarized standards of heteronormative sinfulness versus virtue, and for all other radical challengers of hegemony across Turtle Island, regardless of which binary they fail to embody. Further, this challenge has to be made in explicit relation to settler colonialism. Obviously, not everyone can or should embody the binary failures or refusals of gender and heterosexuality, but by enthusiastically accepting nonbinary embodiments as normal and expected, we are effectively centring the diversity of bodily experience and expression contra the "hooks of hegemony" and its power (Halberstam 2011, 2). It is necessarily up to settlers to fail to normalize not only the connections between the patriarchal gender binary and the settler colonial binary that juxtaposes civilization and savagery but also the white supremacist racial binary of white versus not white that justifies these divisions. Further, settler people need to extend this failure to embody settler colonialism in a self-conscious way in relationships to the land (Hunt and Holmes 2015). Here, we find another embodied binary in the culture-nature divide that positions humans as separate from the natural environment, a perception that is being challenged in many academic disciplines but one that nonetheless has great influence on how settler societies function in North America.

This divide raises a more fundamental question. Beyond performances of masculinity and whiteness, which reinforce the triangular relationships of settler colonial subjectivities, how are settler colonial relationships to the land embodied and performed? More appropriately, how might we fail to embody and perform these norms of settler colonialism's place relationships? To this point, I have focused on answering the first question. As to the second, drawing from understandings of how settler institutions of privilege can shift their relative levels of power and advantage without destabilizing larger settler colonial spaces, as well as from the failures of Occupy participants and other radical activists to escape these spaces through the occupation of contentious anti-capitalist "convergence space" (Routledge 2003), I advocate here for a focused turning toward Indigenous systems of governance, law, and treaty making. When we act consciously with respect to (and for) Indigenous governance, rather than without or beyond Indigeneity, which entails ignoring Indigenous laws, sovereignty, customs, and rituals, we demonstrate that the body of the settler can fail to act as a vector for settler colonialism, even if only momentarily. In that moment, we help to renormalize the existence and vitality of Indigenous governance systems on the land. Our bodies stop representing and materially asserting settler colonialism only when they contribute to and dwell with or alongside spaces of Indigeneity that represent the ultimate failure of the collective settler colonial project. I return to this idea in Chapter 6, where I consider the affective politics of settler solidarity with Indigenous resurgence and decolonization movements.

We should be careful here not to confuse the failure to be a 'good settler' with the settler colonial narratives around the failure of the settler colony. For example, the fear of settlers 'going native' is a longstanding narrative of (settler) colonial failure (Huhndorf 2001; Kupperman 2007), but settlers aspiring to or claiming indigeneity for themselves is a settler colonial success rather than a failure when it happens on the grounds of established settler colonial topographies of power. Conversely, there is a clear narrative in settler colonial literary traditions that the death of settlers and the potential "extinction" of the settler society – the failure of the settler project – makes settlers and Indigenous peoples somehow equivalent (Dailey 2018). That is, the very possibility of imagining a postsettler future is used to justify refusals to decolonize in the present, as settler and Native are positioned as equally ephemeral concepts in need of protection rather than juxtaposed subjectivities locked in a relationship of domination. Of course, neither historically or in the present has this rigid binary – settler or Indigenous, life or death, dominating or dominated – reflected the messy embodied reality of relationships between Indigenous and settler communities. There are many instances of Indigenous communities choosing to absorb, adopt, assimilate, or otherwise incorporate non-Indigenous people. Many of these instances involve everyday processes of adoption and community building (D. Lee 2015; K.J. White 2018). Others, such as the historical failure of the Roanoke colony (Kupperman 1977, 2007), have become closely entangled with the settler fear of the wilderness beyond the frontier. Assimilation into Indigenous communities, insofar as they are often perceived to be part of nature in the settler imagination, is positioned as the same as disappearing into the woods, never to return, and being presumed dead. Thus in white, rural society (O'Connell 2010) and in resource extraction communities such as the Alberta tar sands (Preston 2013), masculine frontier virtues are reinforced by the proximity to these feared spaces. It should be remembered that these spaces are socially constructed through narratives and jurisdictional definitions such as territories, wildlife preserves, and national parks.

Likewise, we should be wary of back to the land movements of any type that do not centralize Indigenous governance structures, uses of lands, permissions, and protocols. Here, I do not simply refer to the survivalist rhetoric of groups like the Bundy Ranch supporters – who, it should be noted, were eventually ousted from their 'sovereign' federal building in the heart of Malheur National Wildlife Refuge in Oregon. Cliven Bundy and his supporters bear more than passing resemblance to many deep-green environmental movements that have been notoriously entangled with white supremacy and anti-Indigenous racism specifically, and too many others rely on romanticized narratives of Indians at one with nature to justify their occupations of lands that settler colonial states and polities have historically denied to Indigenous people (Aldred 2000; Barker and Pickerill 2012; McLean 2013; Pulido and De Lara 2018; Sturgeon 1999). For socialists and social justice advocates, 'back' to the land rhetoric should immediately raise the question, "Whose land and who is going back?" Instead notions of the commons and collective property are often invoked to dodge the colonial question, much as Occupy's hopeful assertion of an anticapitalist res nullius added to the settler erasure of Lenape jurisdiction and presence. These narratives can be flexible enough to incorporate settlers who are withdrawing from many institutions of privilege or who are intentionally, whether for economic reasons or because of deeply held cultural and political values, distancing themselves from spaces of obvious, embodied settler colonial performance. This is not an appropriate way for settler people seeking to work in solidarity with Indigenous peoples to be 'bad settlers.'

Similarly, the settler fear of being made to go away is deeply seated and often motivates the most extreme and reactionary tendencies of settler peoples when confronted by resurgent Indigeneity embodied by real, living Indigenous people. In my work with Emma Battell Lowman, we discuss a number of extreme reactions by settler people confronted with their own settler colonialism or by public assertions of Indigeneity in a variety of circumstances (Battell Lowman and Barker 2015, 99–105). Many of these reactions hinge on a resistance to feeling shame or guilt simply for being on Indigenous lands. This resistance is related to the tendency, even among engaged activist settler peoples, to ask rather inauthentically, "What do *they* want?" (Barker 2009) – meaning, of course, what do Indigenous people want me to do other than not be here? Profound settler fear and reluctance are attached to this perceived but unimaginable option of not being here (Battell Lowman and Barker 2015, 92–95). When settler collectives have been forcibly repelled from Indigenous spaces, in response of course to the fact that settlement is an ongoing invasion and inherently violent, these events are remembered by settler colonial societies as massacres. Stories of atrocities, including made-up or wildly exaggerated stories, are woven into the fabric of settler colonial societies; remember that the settling of the American West was famously said to be necessitated by the Lakota's defeat of George Armstrong Custer and the 7th Cavalry in 1876. Given that Custer's death was both a synecdoche for the deaths of all of his men and especially grievable in light of the regard for him as an exemplar of settler masculinity and virtue, it was used as an excuse to violate the sovereignty of the Lakota and many other nations in a classic move to organize settler biopower along with the deployment of state violence (Morgensen 2011). It is only recently that this story has been remembered differently, this time as a moment of infamy for Americans and as an act that precipitated a full-on war that ultimately resulted in the clearing of vast swaths of the Plains for settlement through military force, followed by the violence that settlers would inflict in the coming years through forced relocation, massacres, sexual assaults, and systematic starvation.[11] This reality, not the trope of heroic homesteaders, is the history of the Wild West that settler people are slowly learning and accepting. Even this changed remembrance, however, is not necessarily indicative of productive settler colonial failure but has been thoroughly repackaged to support the fear-induced drive of American settlers to pursue pre-emptive self-defence.

The narratives of settler colonialism can withstand acknowledgment of the violences of settlement, especially when embodied through a politics of official apologies (Corntassel and Holder 2008). Such apologies historicize the violence of settlement and also lead individual people to seek reconciliation with Indigenous peoples by participating in ceremonial acts of national and state apology and responsibility without altering their own lives. Similarly, popular culture can recognize Indigenous oppressions and satirically skewer white privilege with respect to racialized Indigenous peoples, as has been done successfully on television programs, without necessarily challenging settler colonialism. For example, the American situation comedy *Parks and Recreation* (2009–15) made frequent reference across seven seasons to the massacres of the fictional Wamapoke tribe, which were foundational to settlement of the fictional town of Pawnee, Indiana. These references included an episode featuring a map of the town indicating where the massacres had occurred. The map featured a number of small, coloured dots that, rather than indicating massacre sites, as one might expect, were revealed to be the only spaces where an atrocity had not taken place. Similarly, in an episode titled "Homer vs. Dignity" (2000), the popular animated series *The Simpsons* (1989–present) featured a Native American float in the Springfield Thanksgiving Parade that was given special attention by the commentators, Kent and Leeza, as they narrated the event for a television broadcast:

> *Kent:* "Here's a float saluting the Native Americans, who taught us how to celebrate Thanksgiving."
>
> *Leeza:* "Interesting side note on this float: The papier-mâché is composed entirely of broken treaties."
>
> *Kent:* [laughs good-naturedly] "They're good sports."

Settler people can revel in these kinds of satire and can support narratives that inspire feelings of national guilt when this guilt is also somehow inevitable (Macoun and Strakosch 2013, 436–38). This self-conscious behaviour is a pop culture reflection of the same dynamics that lead municipal governments and similar bodies to acknowledge Indigenous territory and then engage in behaviour such as gentrification and the active displacement of Indigenous communities without any sense of irony (Watts 2016). The resistance of Indigenous peoples is subsumed in these overdone narratives through which settlers revel in telling other settlers how powerful settlers were or are.

Finally, and importantly, the stories of actual failures of settler colonies due to Indigenous-led resistance movements are often read and represented in settler colonial societies in ways that de-emphasize resurgent Indigeneity. Rather than regarding these historical events as instances of a settler polity being expelled, settler Canadians and Americans frequently recast them in terms of a more palatable narrative. For example, the Algerian resistance to and overthrow of French rule is often presented both through the lens of nationalism (Veracini 2013, 317–18) and through a classical metropole-colony dichotomy akin to that of the American Revolutionary War (1775–83) (Selbin 2010), which in turn is set against the overarching narrative of the Cold War (1947–91). As a parallel example, consider the ways that the deployment of Indigeneity in the fight against South African apartheid is likewise obscured in the creation of a more simplistic binary of Black versus white that homogenizes the complex actors in the Black South African communities and justifies the ongoing entanglement between settler colonialism and white supremacy in the country through a liberal narrative of rights-based equality (Lester 2005; Nagy 2012). This narrative has taken great purchase in settler colonial nations like Canada and the United States, and there is likely a form of Eve Tuck and K. Wayne Yang's (2012, 9–28) "moves to innocence" at play here, one in which *those* settler colonizers were bad – because they were relics of empire and openly racist – whereas *we*, contemporary American and Canadian settlers, are good because we are concerned with and aware of these global struggles for liberty.

If failure must do more than reinforce settler colonial binaries by other means, how do we figure out how to fail properly at being settler colonizers? I propose that we must look at what settlers' fears of 'going native' (Huhndorf 2001; Kupperman 2007) or of being forced to leave their settled lands tell us about individual settler motivations. It is not, as some might expect, death or deprivation or loss of community that settlers fear. Death and the special meaning and import of the dead settler body are things on which settler colonial claims to land can hinge, whether in cemeteries, memorials, or other settler colonial "deathscapes" (see Barker 2018). Instead, I argue that the ultimate failure of the settler colonial endeavour is for the settler body to remain even as the settler world disappears – to be cast into the 'wilderness,' to be outside of 'civilization,' to be adrift with no land to call one's own, a frequent fate to which settlers have condemned others in the process of displacing them. This outcome is the failure that settler colonial structures, systems, and stories most strongly resist and resent. It is the horror that settler people cannot bear to contemplate.

The task of translating decolonization into real, actionable goals requires a reinterpretation that takes into account the motivation for many settler colonial "moves to innocence" (Tuck and Gaztambide-Fernández 2013, 86n4; Tuck and Yang 2012, 9–28) – that is, the powerful pull of settler futurity, understood as the deeply felt need to establish a secure future for settler people, one where they do not have to move or have to acquiesce to the unbearable sovereignty of Indigenous nations. The concern with settler futurity is required in order to provide ballast for the existential fears that settler society will fail and that settler peoples will be uprooted and permanently unsettled. Many of the narratives discussed here are linked to different ways of projecting settler belonging into the future irrespective of both the current configuration of settler colonial topographies of power and Indigenous nationhood. The survivalist fantasies of back to the land movements, like the economization of small house advocates across North America (Veracini 2015, 77–79), are an attempt to imagine a radically different political ecology but not necessarily a decolonized one.[12] To decolonize, settler people must learn to give up on assurances, or even possibilities, that they can remain on the land and also remain anything like they are now – individually or collectively.

In part, the suspension of settler futurity thinking, which so frequently infiltrates and derails settler attempts to build relationships with Indigenous people and communities, is achieved through embracing an ethic of failure. But this ethic of productive personal failure must be pursued amid larger movements of Indigenous resurgence and nationhood that achieve a variety of successes. I have previously advocated that settler people need to figure out how to work in solidarity with Indigenous movements through an ethic of radical experimentation. However, experimentation implies failure, or at the very least its real possibility, and frequently many failures on the way to repeatable success. A method that centralizes failure can be applied ethically only if the failures do not negatively or disproportionately impact Indigenous resurgence movements. Our experimentations must therefore follow the lead of and add to Indigenous resurgence movements by design and in such a way as to ensure that the failure of our solidarity efforts will not be the deciding factor in the larger efforts of Indigenous communities. Settler people must build capacity and continue to take the lead from Indigenous communities alongside the other well-proven pillars of solidarity work. More than that, settler solidarity work must recognize that we can fail safely – that is, without doing harm to Indigenous people and resurgence – only if neither our comfort nor our futures dictate our definitions of failure and success to begin with.

Insofar as part of being a 'bad settler' requires recognizing and participating in Indigenous governance structures, there must be a corresponding decentring of settler governance structures. Likewise, the centralization of Indigenous resurgence in decolonization implicitly marginalizes the importance of settler solidarity activists. The fact that decolonization must be driven largely by Indigenous activists, scholars, elders, and community members should be axiomatic. The ironic lesson of this book is that after all of these words and chapters about settler colonialism and the settler people of Canada and the United States, I want other settler people to understand that *we really don't matter*. To clarify, I mean that part of learning to suspend settler futurity is to learn that settlers do not matter to the ultimate success of Indigenous resurgence movements because Indigenous resurgence movements do not and never have needed external salvation. Indigenous communities hold the knowledge necessary to survive and thrive as peoples based on their traditional ways of knowing and being, and they already have centuries of experience resisting settlement and colonization – which settler people cannot likewise claim. The struggle against settler colonialism, in order to be personally transformative, must be without end and thus without the finality of success. This understanding implies that we cannot be motivated by the hope of achieving success or victory in any final form. The only end that we can concentrate on is the one where we, ultimately, fail our way into transformation. As Halberstam (2011, 88) eloquently states, "The queer art of failure turns on the impossible, the improbable, the unlikely, and the unremarkable. It quietly loses, and in losing[,] it imagines other goals for life, for love, for art, and for being." When we fail so utterly as a settler collective as to be forced to imagine goals other than maintaining settler futurity –which we can further sabotage by failing to adhere to and replicate the discursive and material processes by which settler colonial systems and structures grow and replicate – our sovereignty crumbles, and we are left to negotiate another way of belonging on this land.

This failure of the settler project must be based on our personal, intentional failures to live up to the settler colonial ideal, similar to the process that Halberstam describes with respect to queer communities. It will inevitably also be based on our individual failures to effectively support Indigenous resurgence movements, which are better considered as losses rather than failures. To understand how we can invest our sovereignty differently, we must make attempts, however ultimately hesitant or wrong-headed they may be, to build new communal relationships, to accept responsibility as a *minimum* standard, and to seek out and attend to relationships rooted in accountability. Then we must be held to account, and importantly hold each other to account again and again, until settler colonialism is permanently unsettled.

Toward Settler Decolonization and Indigenous Resurgence

Scholarship taught me to understand the premises of settler colonialism and Indigenous resurgence, but it was my activist experiences that led me to perceive the impact of deep colonizing on my own settler identity. However, the question of how to address my continued entanglements with settler colonial power has been harder to address. I can intend to be decolonizing and even strive to decolonize, but I remain settler colonial because I cannot extract myself from the institutions of privilege and flows of power that settler colonialism has and does situate around me. I cannot *refuse* my way out of settler colonial space (as Albert Memmi well knew).

But there is a thought experiment here worth pursuing: all settler people and any individual settler are connected through their common perception of being the people who settle. Sociologist Richard Day (2000) regards this shared perception as rooted in the endlessly open system of identifying self and Other, and Lorenzo Veracini (2010b) talks about the settler colonial need to empty first indigenous Others and later exogenous Others from the triangular set of relationships that settler colonialism institutes. Therefore, in this expanding but flattening spatiality, settler people relate to each other above all else through their location in and benefit from settler colonial spaces. These are spaces that they make through their presence as settlers on the land and that are exposed through assertions of Indigenous sovereignty. These spaces are the foundational referent of settler identity, the condition that must be accepted for membership in the settler collective.

If settler society is colonial, so too am I colonial, and any individual act of resistance does not necessarily disrupt the topographies of power in the northern bloc. Geographer James D. Sidaway's (2000, 265) observations with respect to the academy – another institution of power and privilege in which I am complicit – also apply to settler colonialism, as both constitute "a 'value/power/knowledge' system [that] allows and even thrives on ... periodic disciplinary revolution, innovation accompanied by devalorisation of earlier works, and theoretical breaks." In this sense, a personal refusal of one's settler colonial positionality is part of a strategic manoeuvre – whether evident in American suburbs or in radical movements – to always claim that the preceding settlers were the colonizers, whereas we are different. But the same is true in reverse: if I am decolonizing, then in some small way, so too is settler society. If some settlers choose to attempt to "become decolonizing" (Battell Lowman and Barker 2015, 110–23), then larger settler society is also unwillingly, contestedly, perhaps minutely, and maybe even futilely pushed toward becoming decolonizing. Self and Other in the settler colonial collective must be viewed through the framework of "nondiscrete nonbinary dualism" (Waters 2004)[13] and thus understood as inextricably linked by their positionings in settler institutions and by assertions of colonial sovereignty. I may have to accept my own colonial nature, but settler society must also deal with my decolonizing trajectory.

6

Affinity and Alliance: Breaking the Boundaries of Settler Colonial Space

In May 2013, I was in the right place at the right time. I had travelled from England to attend a week-long event hosted at the University of Victoria. Because of this trip, I had the good fortune of being able to participate in an incredible grassroots initiative driven by the local Coast Salish communities of W̱SÁNEĆ (Saanich) and Lekwungen (Songhees): the reclamation of PKOLS. In this context, PKOLS refers to a mountain, just north of Victoria, named Mount Douglas after James Douglas, the first governor of the Colony of Vancouver Island and the man who signed the Douglas Treaties (1850–54) with the Coast Salish peoples – the first of which was, in fact, signed at the top of the mountain that came to bear his name. Of course, long before Douglas, the mountain already had a name, and that name, PKOLS, is a powerful signifier of a spiritual, historical, and cultural connection between people and their lands.[1]

At the urging of local leadership, a broad coalition was organized to march in numbers up the paved pathway to the top of the mountain. Accompanied by Coast Salish and other Indigenous drummers and singers, the group carried a large cedar sign carved by renowned W̱SÁNEĆ artist Charles Elliot. The proceedings opened with a re-enactment of the signing of the first Douglas Treaty from the perspective of the Coast Salish peoples, who had agreed to share lands with the settlers but never to cede their claims to territory or governance, as they had signed the treaty in part to avoid bloodshed and violence. After an explanation in both English and SENĆOŦEN (the W̱SÁNEĆ language) of the significance of the place, the beautiful sign that visibly restored the sacred name of the mountain was affixed to a previously prepared concrete pad at the summit. The police arrived, observed warily, and then departed; there was no threat of violence, and it was clear that everyone was taken by a powerful, positive collective mood.

That day did not change the world. But it changed a part of it. It changed many of us who were there, who joined together as a community, if only for a moment. It continues to do so across time and space.[2]

Individual Decisions, Collective Actions

It is not enough to say that we must decolonize relationships without plans for material actions. The colonial assemblage does not care about awareness. It is certainly not enough to declare, "Physician, heal thyself!" Many settler people are content as they are, and no wonder; the topography of power may be uneven, but institutionalized privilege of all kinds discourages settler decolonization or even recognition of the problems caused by the present settler disposition, along with recognition of the possibilities for settlers to be disposed otherwise. And all the while, aspirational anticipatory geographies of settler colonialism draw more people ever deeper into complicity with this genocidal assemblage. However, opportunities for change do exist.

When we shift the locus of settler colonial power away from governments, corporations, or even persistent systems of social hierarchy and labour and toward the biopower generated by settler people living ordinary lives, both individually and en masse, it becomes possible to think strategically about how we can direct our embodied efforts to generate social change and decolonization. Indigenous resurgence movements have established the importance of biopower in very clear terms: no change can come solely from individual actions and choice, but none can come without them either. Consider the way that Anishinaabe scholar Leanne Simpson thinks through the thorny issue of the extent to which tradition should dictate behaviours and choices in the present and the way that she connects her own individual decision-making process both to the collected wisdom of generations and to the considered needs of other Indigenous folks affected by these social conventions. This is only one of many examples, and common to all of them are individual decisions and actions that are not rooted in individualism but are demonstrations that "decolonization and regeneration will emanate from transformations achieved by direct-guided experience in small, personal, groups and one-on-one mentoring towards a new path" (L. Simpson 2011, 60–61). This is a call to engage not as atomized individuals but as communities in struggle, where engagement comes in the form of intensely affective personal relationships with those close to us – materially and/or emotionally – that support and drive forward co-learning, experimentation, and iterative action. Such relationships are the current basis of Indigenous resurgence and decolonization movements, and we must centralize them in our own organizing as settler people. All of us – settler, Indigenous, and migrant and diasporic peoples of all backgrounds – can and do encounter spaces and moments where we are faced with the choice either to confront our own internalized settler colonialism or to retrench and remain complicit. Having strong interpersonal relationships, whether between settler and Indigenous people and communities across the colonial difference or in mutual support of settler decolonization within our own communities, can positively shape the choices that we perceive and the decisions that we make.

None of this work is quick or easy, not even with group support. Jeff Corntassel and Cheryl Bryce (2012, 157), in their critical reflections on the work done near Victoria to clear Scotch broom and other invasive species from traditional Lekwungen fields used for cultivating *kwetlal*, or "*camas*, a starchy bulb that has been a staple food and trade item for indigenous peoples in the region for generations," demonstrate that a certain scale of longitudinal thinking is required. Regardless of calculations concerning how much more space needs to be cleared of invasive plants or how many more people need to be involved to roll back settler colonial incursion into Indigenous territories, Bryce, who is Lekwungen, situates her individual acts of resistance as simultaneously insufficient, necessary, and educational (159–61). Any settler decolonization movement must adopt a similar approach of thinking about settler colonization as the common opponent that settlers share with Indigenous peoples and about settlers themselves as individual actors in a collective struggle.

There is a resonance here with the efficacy of failure: efforts recognized from the start as insufficient can be seen as failures on their own, but collectively, they move Indigenous communities in resistance closer to successful resurgences of Indigenous nationhood, and they move settler communities toward meaningful decolonization. So it is worth returning to and thinking through queer theorist Jack Halberstam's (2011, 1) original question: "What comes after hope?" If we admit that decolonization is possible and also assert that the best way for settler people to contribute to the decolonization of Turtle Island is to be 'bad settlers,' how might settler people go about frustrating the goals of settler colonialism in order to transform themselves and their societies while also avoiding the settler colonial "hooks of hegemony" (2)? In this final chapter, I draw from the constructions of settler colonial spaces and the efficacy of failure developed throughout this book to argue for the need not only to change place-based relationships, especially between settler people and Indigenous people, but also to permit settler-Indigenous relationships to affect settler people's relationships to lands and places. These changes in relationships, I argue, cannot be simply intellectualized and subsumed into existing rights discourses or state-driven processes of recognition and reform but must be slowly developed through three separate and distinct stages: first, the affective, unsettling engagement of settler people with the evidence of settler colonial harm and complicity and with the fact and future of resurgent Indigeneity; second, the self-organization of settler communities around particular affinities or common interests and the extension of these affinity practices in order to mutually support the efforts of Indigenous communities; and third, alliance building between Indigenous and settler people based on clear, local visions for resurgent Indigeneity and settlers "co-becoming" different people (Bawaka Country et al. 2016).

Affective Politics, Personal Responsibility, and Lines of Accountability

I will never forget the feeling of being a part of the march and the crowd reclaiming PKOLS, especially as drummers and singers played an honour song while the sign proclaiming the ancient and deeply rooted name of PKOLS was bolted in place. In that moment, I was overcome with indescribable waves of emotion, and years after the fact, I still cannot articulate those feelings exactly. I felt simultaneously proud and ashamed, guilty and motivated, included and alone. More than anything else, I was energized: my pulse literally raced, and I barely slept that night despite a long, exhausting day. The next morning, I returned to the University of Victoria to find that everyone else who had attended was in a similar state. Some had stayed up all night – talking, exploring, dreaming, planning, and strategizing. We all seemed to have a contagious light in our eyes. We were literally in a new world where everything impossible was made possible.

This is a memory of a time when I was deeply affected, moved in a way that defies categorization as emotion or through intellectualization. Affect has been important to my explanations of why settler people often express antipathy toward assertions of Indigeneity. Here, I turn to the other side of affective geography, when a state of affective unsettlement is generated through personal connections and relationships that generate emotional responses that trouble settler colonial narratives and expectations. These affective responses, when generated in the context of strong, supportive relationships, can be the impulse that moves settler people toward further decolonizing efforts and actions. The change of state ignited by such affective interruptions, experiences, and relationships can potentially instigate the change from occupying an imagined geography with settlers at the centre to moving into and through geographies that centre Indigeneity and send the assumed normality of settlement to the margins.

This affective resistance is premised on the understanding that social relationships – the foundations of the spaces that people build and occupy (Massey 2009, 16–17) – are a crucial site of struggle. As we seek to make fundamental social change, our emotional attachments are inevitably challenged or implicated in our struggles. Social movement studies tell us that, regardless of the form or function of oppression, resistance builds and spreads not just when people are convinced that there is a problem but also when people *feel* personally implicated in the search for a change or solution – excepting "moves to innocence," of course (Tuck and Yang 2012, 9–28). Critical social movement scholar Stevphen Shukaitis (2009, 143) frames this as a dynamic process, linking affective relationships to effective tactics of resistance:

> One can ultimately never separate questions of the effectiveness of political organizing from concerns about its affectiveness. They are inherently and inevitably intertwined. The social relations we create every day prefigure the world to come, not just in a metaphorical sense, but also quite literally: they truly are the emergence of that other world embodied in the constant motion and interaction of bodies.

Affective relationships involving settler people, whether between settlers and Indigenous communities or between privileged settler elites and racialized, marginalized communities, always and inescapably involve uneven geometries of power and privilege. Settler peoples even engage with each other on "uncommon ground" (Chatterton 2006). This concept, developed by Paul Chatterton, reminds us that all actors in social contestation, whether protesters, labourers, bystanders, agents of the state, or people in other positionalities, find themselves engaged together because of a common entanglement or concern yet carry with them very different thoughts, feelings, responsibilities, ambitions, and identities. These differences matter to how we engage in resistance and to what effect (and affect), such that the common activist tactics of argument, awareness raising, and public shaming may not actually promote change but serve to alienate "activists" from "ordinary people" (Chatterton and Pickerill 2010, 483).

That settler people have thoughts, feelings, and opinions on colonization and Indigenous peoples must be remembered – not because we should be wary of bruising their sensibilities but because it means that we cannot rationalize, research, or study people into decolonization. These emotional and affective structures are almost by definition coloured by privilege, racism, classism, and Othering, but that does not negate their resiliency or their powerful positioning in settler identities. Settler identities cannot be both dismissed and engaged at the same time; no matter how racist or warped, affective positions must be taken seriously, which is to say, compassionately but also critically. Consider Eva Mackey's (2016) extensive study on the reactions of Canadian and American settlers in southern Ontario and upstate New York when faced with Indigenous-led struggles to gain and protect some sort of land base, whether as a reserve or through title. Whereas some of the settler community in Ontario spread untruths and hostility, saying that Indigenous people did not take care of the land, and fantasized terrible harms for the settler population in the area if a reserve was created, some settler Americans in the New York area supported the attempts by the Onondaga to gain title to their land because these settlers had a deep desire to see – and be part of – justice being done. In both cases, settlers were convinced to act one way or the other not based on a rationalist, materialist argument but based on narratives that tapped into deep-seated emotional impulses, whether an impulse to defend one's space against perceived Others or an impulse to act on the structures of feeling that form around concepts like justice, thus bringing compassion, and even personal pride, to the centre of political organizing.

Considering affective desires compassionately but also critically is not about letting people off the hook for colonialism and racism. Rather, it is about understanding what affective space others occupy and finding ways to communicate with them in a way that will penetrate that space and unsettle individuals enough to make moving beyond that space possible, if not inevitable. The point is not to find a way to erase the differences between people before we engage with them but to find ways to engage and relate irrespective of our unique positionalities and individual differences. Further, settler people must be conscious of the shifting spatialities around them. As geographer Helga Leitner and colleagues (2008, 167–69) discuss, contained and "safe" environments – in the case of their research, buses – lend themselves to far different affective connections than do environments permeated with power, like New York City, a node of interconnecting structures and networks of power. Given that power relationships are constantly shifting, affective engagements have to be pursued in an open-ended way, without a preconceived script or conclusion, and indeed, without a definition of success. Affective engagements must be experienced and lived, as well as rigorously interrogated both through personal education and research and through collective social discussion and debate. These pursuits cannot be purely intellectualized or confined to academic study; they must be shared. Almost every affective engagement is an opportunity for co-learning, and settler perspectives, no matter how informed, will likely always need to be affectively unsettled since there is no pure activist form and no pure decolonizing settler form and since actions and beliefs that are correct in one context may be insufficient or harmful in another. Pursuing this kind of affective engagement is difficult. In some senses, spontaneity is required, and the right moment to create an affective impact can be encouraged but never assumed or willed into existence. Given that the social circulation of affect has been likened to a contagion, it can be impossible to tell who will be susceptible and who will be immune to affective impacts. The right moment may never come.

But there are all sorts of situations that lead to affective engagement, including colonial and oppressive ones (Clough 2012). Affective engagement can present itself as an option in the midst of conflicts between settler people as much as during cooperative efforts. Within the academy, it is easy to think that through scholarly study and the purity of intellectual inquiry, settler people can come to understand decolonization, like a coming to enlightenment. But truly coming to grips with the impacts of privilege and one's own complicity is necessarily a much messier process. Geographer Sarah de Leeuw and colleagues (2013) have written extensively on the importance of staying engaged with circumstances that make settler people uncomfortable, as unsettlement is necessarily a discomforting process. Affective unsettlement is so uncomfortable because it amounts to a change of state, albeit partial and incomplete, as one moves from the hegemonic topographies of settler colonialism to the very different spaces of resurgent Indigeneity. This drastic shift in the way that settler people phenomenologically experience place will almost inevitably involve resistance and avoidance, retrenchment and moves to innocence (Larsen and Johnson 2012b). However, echoing the conclusions of de Leeuw and colleagues, geographers Soren Larsen and Jay Johnson (Delaware and Cherokee) (2012a, 5) note that just because a process is painful or difficult does not mean that it is not also incredibly powerful; like a "metamorphosis," social transformation "is neither entirely nor primarily a euphoric, blissful experience. It is just as equally if not more so characterized by discomfort, pain, angst, failure, disappointment, and readjustment, all of which can be thought of as expressions of ecstatic encounter."

To be clear, these ecstatic encounters must be pursued in order for decolonization to be possible, but they are not likely to be pleasant or easy, and there is an ongoing need for social support against retrenchment given that, both materially and psychologically, decolonization can be painful and difficult in the face of the privilege and security offered by settler colonialism. Moreover, social support for and through decolonization is required in order to figure out how a given settler collective specific to place or community can scale up affective engagements from the level of the personal – something that is known to be difficult (Pile 2010) but necessary in order to build effective, sustainable decolonizing relationships.[3] Of course, the temptation exists to avoid engaging *as* settler people *with* other settler people in favour of pursuing affective engagements primarily or only with Indigenous communities and individuals. This avoidance is a move to innocence that raises problematic notions of responsibility (Noxolo, Raghuram, and Madge 2012), one that potentially falls into my own trap of trying to refuse my way out of settler colonialism by seeking the approval of Indigenous friends and community members. Settler people must be aware that interactions with Indigenous communities and people, although they are one way to pursue such affective moments, may not be welcome and that the refusal of relationship must be respected as the bare minimum of any decolonization effort (A. Simpson 2014). Such interactions may also involve kinds of engagements that are very different from what settler people expect. As professor of education Celia Haig-Brown (2010) cautions, honest attempts to learn are often wrapped up in appropriating action. This appropriation is part of the subtle construction of settler colonial bricolage. Indigenous peoples' perspectives and concerns are and will continue to be paramount in any discussion of decolonization, but the hard work to be undertaken by the decolonizing settler self and society *is not an Indigenous responsibility*.[4]

Engagements with Indigenous people are crucial as long as these are invited and respectfully structured. Mining for community experience or solutions is intensely problematic, as is reifying Indigenous people as 'wise Indians' dispensing knowledge. Given both the wide possibility for Indigenous-settler relationships to break down in emotionally charged, affective contexts and the ethical demand not to download the emotional labour of settler decolonization onto Indigenous friends and colleagues, settler people must prioritize affective engagements with other settler people wherever possible. Such efforts and engagements can be painful and traumatic, so it is important to remember that there must be "space for emotion in the spaces of activism" (G. Brown and Pickerill 2009).

In reflecting on her participation with Idle No More, settler scholar and activist Stephanie Irlbacher-Fox (2012) came to the realization that one of the important aspects of the protest space itself is that it provides "a place to land relationally" and "creates a stronger rationale for unsettling established systems." She argues that occupying these protest spaces fundamentally reworks relationships, as "knowing and being with Indigenous peoples, even if it is just to be welcomed to stand alongside [them] at marches and rallies, or to join the drum dance circle, creates a tangible bond." I agree with these reflections, which certainly mirror my own experiences working in and struggling through Indigenous-led spaces as a participant both in institutions and in grassroots activism. But we must also have spaces where we go to do the dirtier work of struggling with parts of our identities that we would rather deny and disavow without distracting from the core struggle of Indigenous resurgence.

Decolonization and Affective Relationships

The unsettlement described above is an affective response to moments of encountering or being forced to engage with Indigeneity in settler colonial spaces as Indigenous people seek to reclaim the centre of political lifeways on Turtle Island, which exiles settler aspirations and desires to the margins, an inversion of the foundational core-periphery binary. This centring of Indigeneity can be self-consciously pursued by settlers through participation in Indigenous protocols of governance. Participating in resurgent Indigenous systems of law, politics, treaty making, and social relationships – and importantly, doing so from the position of an outsider while respecting Indigenous traditions of consent and hospitality – can be more than a symbolic act. For an example, I turn to a personal story of participating in a welcoming protocol on Haudenosaunee lands.

In 2007, Emma Battell Lowman and I attended the Mohawk Nation Conference, hosted by Six Nations Polytechnic, located on the Six Nations of the Grand River Reserve in southern Ontario. We had been invited by one of the organizers, Kawennakon Bonnie Whitlow, Mohawk educator, language teacher, and activist. This conference, unlike many that I have attended, started in a field on the edge of the reserve territory. About a dozen people, gathered in three small clusters, were in the clearing when we arrived. We were met by several local Mohawks participating in the conference who explained that we needed to start with a ceremony in order to ask permission to enter the home of the Six Nations community. These folks turned our attention to a small group of people standing to one side by a fire pit, where a small amount of kindling was laid out but not yet burning. They, our hosts explained, were kin who had also come from abroad: they had travelled from the Mohawk communities of Akwesasne and Kanesetake to the east. They too needed to ask permission to enter but would lead the ceremony. We were directed to stand off to one side of their group, and as the sun slowly rose, we were joined by another white settler Canadian and by a few Indigenous people from different nations, including Cree and Anishinaabe folks.

Without any fanfare, the visiting Mohawk contingent suddenly set to work on the fire and quickly had it burning brightly. Then they dragged evergreen boughs, just trimmed and still damp, and raised and lowered them above the fire, setting the needles smouldering and choking the fire of air. Big billows of dark smoke rose above the trees surrounding the clearing. We watched this happen, silently, and we waited.

After some time, we heard drums as the host contingent approached. On foot, about two dozen people, from children to elders, entered the clearing from the road, playing water drums and singing. Soon, an elder stepped forward to explain what was happening. Traditionally, Haudenosaunee villages were built inside a palisade, and around the palisade was a clearing – all trees and brush having been removed for some distance. When visitors wished to enter a village, they would step into the clearing and light a fire to show themselves and then wait for the village to respond. They had to be visible, present, and patient. That was what we were doing. And we were welcomed. Shortly afterward, we were back in our car, and with children and young folk running ahead of the convoy or balanced on side boards, we drove to Six Nations Polytechnic, knowing that something special had occurred, although we were not quite sure what. Our participation in this protocol was a deep learning experience for us, and much that occurred was outside our ability to perceive or understand. In this way, our experience that day was imperfect and partial but nonetheless important and productive, and it serves as an example of one way that an ethic of failure helped us to learn experientially what was expected of us as visitors on Haudenosaunee territory. Our failure to fully grasp the contents of the ritual set us on a cautious footing and encouraged us to go slowly in seeking relationships, to look for opportunities to contribute when they arose, and to step back when we sensed that conversations were again moving beyond us.[5]

In retrospect, I see that this was an important affective encounter for us. We felt unsettled, not because of fear or trepidation or pain but simply because we were disoriented and very aware of the gravity of our embodied actions, even though we lacked the ability to explain what we were experiencing. However, as the conference progressed, the initial feeling of unsettlement gave way to a productive energy as we learned from and with members of the Mohawk and Haudenosaunee nations in an educational setting informed by and rooted in Haudenosaunee principles. We were unsettled by exposure and, I think, by openness to Indigenous sovereignty, cultural norms and protocols, and knowledge and expertise, of which we had some intellectual understanding but had not experienced in this immersive and expert context. By dwelling in this unsettled state intentionally and together, we opened up the possibility of making new connections, both intellectually through paradigm shifts and personally through interpersonal affinities, which I return to below.

Thinking through the argument that I have already made – that settler people must begin to create spaces for unsettling, affective encounters between each other – how can we pursue effects similar to those generated by participation in the protocols described above? I do not have a systemic answer, but on an interpersonal level, I believe that we must start by generating frameworks within our existing relationships for the kinds of transformative change that we want. Just as the protocols of engagement around Mohawk space were clearly set in treaties and traditions, we need to begin identifying and building on particularly important and valuable practices that we observe being deployed by other settler people to good effect and then try to implement versions of these practices among our own communities.

Two of the settler people who have had an affective impact on my life are Paulette Regan, author of the groundbreaking *Unsettling the Settler Within: Indian Residential Schools, Truth Telling, and Reconciliation in Canada* (2010), and my long-time collaborator and writing partner, Emma

Battell Lowman. Both are historians, or at least keen students of history and its power in the present. Paulette was one of my earliest mentors in the study of settler colonialism and the first person I ever knew to use the term "settler" self-referentially. In addition to her research, she has experience working with the Gitxsan and Wet'suwet'en folks in the interior of British Columbia to pursue reconciliation with the church that administered the local residential school. In her work, Regan (2010, 13) seeks to "unsettle" settler people – to shake up and disturb our sense of self and to underscore the "dysconsciousness" (D.M. Johnson 2011, 110) at work in settler colonial space – partially by sharing her own unsettling experiences confronting the pervasiveness of contemporary colonialism and the challenge of pursuing reconciliation in this context (Regan 2010, 190–91). Paulette became my mentor and friend as I went through my own unsettling engagements with colonialism during my graduate studies and beyond. I still turn to her for compassionate but critical assessments of my work. Emma, meanwhile, seeks connections in all things, exemplified by her development of the concept of "always in relationship" – a core feature of our co-authored book *Settler: Identity and Colonialism in 21st Century Canada* (Battell Lowman and Barker 2015, 116–20) – as a way of understanding how settler people are always already implicated in both settler colonialism and Indigenous resistance. Assuming that everyone she encounters is already in relationship to herself and her work in some way, she approaches discussions of settler colonialism with other settler people through a lens of critical compassion and has brought this same lens to her work on the need to rethink and reconnect with, on a personal level, overlooked settler peoples, such as twentieth-century missionaries, whose lives may reveal a great deal about powerful, layered settler colonial histories and narratives (Battell Lowman 2011). She has been my partner in all of the intellectual endeavours that have made this work possible, but more than that, she has also willingly gone through the emotional, affective, and relational turbulence that has inevitably resulted from attempts to embody and enact our understandings. Our work has now carried us around the world – physically and virtually – and into contact with a vibrant and growing network of folks striving to understand, resist, and dismantle settler colonialism.

Taken together, these two scholars generate – in both their writing and their practice and methods – a kind of "low theory" (Halberstam 2011, 2) or "weak theory" that relies on "re-reading to uncover or excavate the possible" (Gibson-Graham 2008, 619–20). In this context, what is being reread is settler belonging, with the violent colonizing acts of settlement being revealed for what they are rather than being viewed through the triumphal nationalist tropes that usually surround them. At the same time, both Paulette and Emma reveal the incredible possibilities for settler people to be otherwise. Both have been crucial to my own struggles to think, see, and be other than a settler colonizer who refuses, and both have held space with me during emotional moments of rejection, depression, confusion, frustration, and anger. It is not an exaggeration to say that without these strong relationships, I would not be able to work through my own affective responses to being exposed to the truths of settler colonization on Turtle Island and that my intellectual projects would be at best curtailed and at worst harmful.

Unsettling and Compassion

Drawing from my experiences learning from Paulette and Emma, I believe it is important to further discuss the use and importance of unsettling and compassion in relationships between decolonizing settlers. Unsettling forces settler people to resituate themselves as the spatial orientation of being a settler suddenly shifts. During this process, the disavowal of Indigeneity at the core of settler colonialism, which underpins so many of the social, political, cultural, and economic institutions of Canadian and American life, is displaced by resurgent Indigenous nationhood, and the entire core-periphery polarization of colonial spatial thought is inverted. Unsettling is not itself a decolonizing turn; rather, it is the world turned right-side in, to riff on Lorenzo Veracini's (2012, 345) idea of settler colonialism turning the world "inside out." It is a forced change in perspective that situates settler people in a sort of double vision: unsettled from familiar settler colonial spaces, the settler subject can either proceed toward the source of the unsettlement or pursue a course back toward a settled state.[6] Absent the physical and conceptual insulations of settler colonial space and participation with a like-minded settler colonial collective, settlers are revealed in their most basic form: as usurpers and synthetic mimics (Tuck and Yang 2012, 8–9).

Affective relationships are an emergent property of "the ontological relation of bodies coming together and increasing their capacity to act through interconnection" (Clough 2012, 1669). They can be deeply personal and intimate, especially when they result from a relatively small number of people coming together, when they are already strengthened by affective bonds of some type, or when they are sustained over long periods. Unsettling can also be quite risky in the sense that the most effective forms of unsettling are made possible through strong, pre-existing affective bonds, like those with friends and family. As implied by Irlbacher-Fox's (2012) observation regarding the role of relations in "unsettling established systems," we are more likely to justify sacrifices and struggles pursued in the interests of those we care about, those we are intimately connected with, and those who are responsible for our personal and emotional well-being. However, in addition to being unsettling, these relationships can also be empowering and inspiring. As geographer Nathan Clough (2012, 1671) discusses with respect to the importance of considering emotion in activism, "the emotional states of activists are important for movement growth and recruitment of new members, for the capacity of movements to sustain collective orientation and action, and for the ability of groups to carry out oppositional actions. In this manner, emotion is always connected to affect, to the ability of a movement to organize [itself] and become powerful." Settler people must get emotional about decolonization in their own lives, and both space and time for emotional connection, consideration, and recovery must be a part of our collective decolonizing efforts, whether we situate them as activism or not.

Alongside unsettlement, compassion is an important concept, yet it has not been much explored in the context of settler decolonization. As an affective engagement, it is in some sense the opposite of Lisa Stevenson's (2012, 598) concept of "a-nonymous care," where settler people impose standards of care on Indigenous people not as individuals but as indigenous Others, a problem for settler society that needs solving. This care is a method of control and says more about the dominance asserted by settlers over Indigenous peoples under settler colonialism than it does about actual attempts by settler people to care for the well-being of others. Consider how concerned Canadians became over the corruption of band governments, particularly how it was disadvantaging First Nations peoples, as soon as Chief Theresa Spence of the isolated community of Attiwapiskat, near James Bay, began a hunger strike to protest state-induced poverty conditions in her community. This same concern for the welfare of distant Indigenous peoples drove a patriarchal critique of Spence's appearance and weight in contrast to images of malnourished Indigenous children (A. Simpson 2016). This concern was ultimately disembodied and abstract because it was never intended to make an impact in any way other than to derail Spence's critique.

By contrast, compassion is personal rather than categorical: it is care in action for specific people that takes into account the particular things that happen to them and that they do, while recognizing the connections between their reality and one's own. These connections comprise the relational spaces that either unite or divide across and through difference. Compassion is also about taking steps to address discomfort, even if doing so means having conversations that spread and share this discomfort before it can be dissipated. Compassion drives us to act in ways that we might not otherwise consider, and in this regard, it can be made productively transgressive and disruptive; although not inherently subversive, compassion can motivate people to act contrary to the larger settler colonial assemblage despite all the coercion to conform. Compassion can be constructed as a basis for Chatterton's (2006, 277) concept of a morality of common ground – that is, as "a social and spatial practice ... based upon non-essentialist and relational understandings of the self, openness and connection, hybridity, negotiation, and a global and more ecological sense of place."[7] The etymology of the term "compassion" is important here, as it comes from the Latin *com,* meaning "together," and *pati,* meaning "to suffer," with *pati* being the direct root of the word "passion," which itself often references suffering but also endurance. Enduring, in space and as oneself while cognizant of the complexity of forces at work on everyone to produce conformity to power, is simply being. Compassion is not just sharing pain but also sharing being. It is not simply co-occupation – *passively* being together in space – but is *actively* being together in place.

Compassion thus constructed does not imply a condescension because it can and must be positive; sharing passion regarding the happenings and victories that excite others means being excited not about the events (as with anonymous involvement) or about one's own benefits or costs (as with self-interested involvement) but because the happenings and victories matter to them specifically. In this way, compassion is interest and involvement in exchange for nothing, as it is motivated only by the fact that one must be authentically who one is in and through the relationship. Compassion can be a bridge that lets us stand together on "uncommon ground" (Chatterton 2006). Larsen and Johnson (2012b, 639) situate compassion as "a kind of clarity based on the insight that to make sense of being-in-the-world, to find one's proper place in it, requires helping others to do the same." And in this sense – as seen with settler people who are prompted by their awareness of settler colonialism and by their struggles with the settler identity to offer compassion to another struggling settler person – it is a powerful and potentially transformative affective connection.

Affect, Indigeneity, and Settler Responsibility

The decolonization of settler colonial space, meaning the elimination of space structured by coloniality of any kind, ultimately implies decolonization of the places that settler peoples occupy, which is necessary for the restoration and regeneration of Indigenous sovereignties and nations. Indigenous scholars, leaders, and community members have repeatedly invited settler people into conversations on decolonization, as exemplified in Anishinaabe scholar and poet Leanne Simpson's (2012) engagement with Occupy Toronto over concerns that the radical protest camp was replicating settler colonial racism, but there are almost innumerable other examples. With this invitation, however, comes an implicit responsibility that leads us away from the cosy idea of responsibility that inheres in self-aggrandizing declarations of allyship embodied in self-serving land acknowledgments (Watts 2016) and in attempts to "free" our minds without progressing to action (Tuck and Yang 2012, 19–22).

This cosy responsibility is one whereby settler people imagine that they can create a fair society through top-down reforms without fundamentally altering the underlying geometries of power that have been created through settler colonization. Settler people commonly attempt to address glaring inequality between Indigenous and settler communities through nongovernmental organizations whose focus on capitalist or corporate greed results in Indigenous peoples being "reduced to a token sidebar in policy statements and declarations, a tragic case study, or otherwise rendered invisible or marginal in narratives designed to appeal to liberal audiences" (Choudry 2010, 98). Even radical challenges to neoliberal orders are often organized around Canadian nationalisms that leave unaddressed the fundamental appropriation of Indigenous lands as the basis of any political economy – capitalist, socialist, or otherwise.

Contrast these positions with those of Regan (2010, 183–89) or writer and activist Harsha Walia (2013, 251–72), both of whom call for alliance building between Indigenous peoples and settler and other non-Indigenous peoples premised on the necessity of restitution before respectful relationships can be established. Restitution is very far from a cosy concept when we consider the historical and contemporary facts of settler colonial dispossession: in their entirety, Canada and the United States of America, as political entities, practised cultures, and material societies, comprise an imposed topography of power that is suspended between settler individuals and collectives, that is enacted through relationships to and in place, and that overwhelms Indigenous networks of being with the goal of destroying and consuming them. In fact, restitution raises the most unsettling question of all: what and how much are settler people willing to give up in order to be welcomed on the land? Thus far, the answer has been that we are prepared to relinquish very little. Settler people might give occasional money, time, and effort to improving relationships within the context of the settler nation-state, but they refuse to accept the possibility of Indigenous authority over place, and when pushed to go beyond what is comfortable from their positionality within the settler colonial assemblage, they withdraw even these small concessions. In recent years, it has become frankly common to observe settler people coming out of the woodwork to declare that they are withdrawing their support from Indigenous struggles because of Indigenous activists' militancy, their refusal to moderate their tone and expectations, or most especially, their refusal to stop using labels like "settler," "colonizer," and "white." The disavowal of Indigenous authority, which stands as a counterfactual refutation of settler naturalization, reinscribes settler colonization through the settler's acceptance of the role of the powerful person who must give gifts to legitimate the settler's rejected colonial position and privilege. If settler peoples wish to avoid this dynamic, which traps them in a cycle of violence due to their own arrogant refusal to take Indigenous peoples' lead on their own land, they must pursue relationships that "are contested, complicated and productively unsettling" (Noxolo, Raghuram, and Madge 2012, 425). They must accept a positionality that is as far from the norm of being in control and in authority as possible.

From Affect to Affinity

Both unsettling and compassion occur on uncommon ground and help to create a space for dialogue there. As Chatterton (2006, 265) asserts, "defensiveness or moral indignation can be swapped for dialogue," even in tense circumstances, when dialogue is positioned in a space of two people coming together in common cause across difference. The uncertain edges of settler colonialism are everywhere: they exist between settler people whose relationships to each other and to place generate the power of settler colonialism and, by extension, other imbricated systems of power and oppression, including our own oppression. As geographer David Featherstone (2008, 37) has demonstrated, relational dynamics coproduce both antagonisms and solidarity, and solidarity itself is "dynamic, contested and networked." Orienting settler society toward decolonization does not involve a monolithic clash between colonizing and decolonizing forces. It is the repeated, conscious decision to be differently with people and place, every day, without end. And although no settler person can be made to interact differently with people or place generally, we can insist on different standards in our personal relationships and work to spread these standards to others through our networks of solidarity and mutual aid.

The motivation for pursuing these differently conceived relationships must come from affect, but it must be sustained by understanding the affinities between many settler struggles and Indigenous resurgence once we have made the structures, systems, and stories of settler colonialism visible and therefore the focus of further intervention. Settler people must come to understand the way that their own lives are actually limited and controlled by a variety of settler colonial elites, who manipulate settler collectives to produce and apply a variety of biopower effects (Morgensen 2011). Settler colonization is not good for any of us – not for Indigenous peoples targeted for erasure, not for exploited and alienated exogenous Others, not for settler peoples constrained within the role of genocidal tyrant, and not for the land itself or any of those beings with which we share the land that are constantly commodified, consumed, contaminated, or controlled by settler hierarchies and extractive economies (Veracini 2015, 91–94). And if it is not good for us, then our failures in the service of being 'bad settlers' can make us actually good to each other. Of course, this understanding runs completely counter to the anticipatory geographies of settler colonialism, which provide the carrot of settler benefits alongside the stick of narratives of chaos and destruction if the 'uncivilized' should triumph over the settler project. That is why decolonization must follow from unsettling moments that pierce the hegemony of established narratives and allow for consideration of other ways of being together.

Affective relationships to and in place are necessary for the development of affinity-based politics. Sociologist Richard Day (2005, 193–97) has developed the concept of affinity and affinity groups with respect to the "newest social movements," clearly taking inspiration from Indigenous struggles in his arguments. Affinity also has a long history of theory and practice among non-Indigenous peoples, such as the affinity groups among Spanish anarchists and International Brigades during the Spanish Civil War (1936–39) (Dupuis-Déri 2010). Affinity groups have likewise been a feature of many radical protests since the late twentieth century, from the protests of the late 1990s in opposition to globalization and the World Trade Organization to the Occupy movements and similar protest camps of the 2010s (R.J.F. Day 2004; Murray 2014). Affinity begins with the discovery of common ground. Following the affective experiences that begin the process of bridging difference on uncommon ground, affinity is a return to engagements across difference but from a changed or changing positionality; affinity implies relationship but also sustained effort.

Larsen and Johnson (2012b) discuss affinity politics as potentially growing out of common phenomenological experiences of being in place. More specifically in the context of decolonizing relationships between Indigenous and settler peoples, being in place must be an experience founded on respect for Indigenous understandings of the personality of place, even (or especially) if the full details of these relationships remain obscured to the would-be settler participants (Barker and Pickerill 2012). Affinity is the point at which decolonizing settlers must choose to "give up activism" (Chatterton 2006), which is to say, stop thinking about or approaching Indigenous issues as something that should be specially acted upon in addition to one's daily struggles and instead understand that decolonization must become the daily struggle. Affinity is the recognition of already existing intimate and fundamental interconnections, both negative ones arising from the colonizer-colonized binaries and positive ones arising from the sharing of place or common history, which can be beneficial when done properly and respectfully. Regardless, there are connections between settlers and Indigenous peoples that, despite implicating each differently, demand recognition of ongoing relationships (Battell Lowman and Barker 2015, 116–20).

Relational Protocols

These affinity politics imply that settler people already perceive the ongoing power and strength of Indigenous communities in resistance and resurgence. Affinity also requires settler people to centre the Indigenous political, legal, and social systems – such as treaty-making protocols but also many other practices of making law and governance – by which newcomers are accounted for on the land. It bears repeating that Indigenous peoples, even when decimated by disease and demographically overwhelmed, have never been powerless. Hybridity and flexibility are two aspects of Indigenous knowledge and practice that have manifested as adaptive strategies for dealing with outsiders (C. Andersen 2014, 27–41). Indigenous ways of knowing produce bodies of knowledge that are constantly in flux. The personal and experiential nature of Indigenous knowledge production, combined with the holistic rejection of anomalies, results in social systems that must be able to incorporate new and unexpected elements.[8] The Hopi, for example, are deeply rooted in their sacred homeland, but also ritualistically send groups out to travel through the world, whose members then return with knowledge and changed perspectives that must be incorporated into the social collective (Jojola 2004, 90–93). The Hopi world, then, is always expanding and changing through the incorporation of new or revised place knowledge. The Hopi ontological imperative is to change in step with this emergent knowledge while remaining rooted in tradition; the result has been a sustainable relationship to place that is among the most stable and enduring.

Flexibility and contingency in Indigenous place-based practices extend to ways of being with other people, as diplomacy, adoption, trade, and similar interchanges are well-developed practices in most Indigenous societies. That was how the Haudenosaunee longhouse could be extended to include the Tuscarora and European collectives (Hill 2017, 111; Wallace 1994). That was also how Indigenous communities in the Pacific maritime fur trade of the nineteenth century were quickly able to assess foreign traders and make shrewd decisions about what and when to trade, despite European and American military might (Clayton 1999). Indigenous peoples have also appropriated various European conventions to their own ends, as with the Warrior Flag – more properly, the Unity Flag, a symbol of peace (Doxtater 2010, 98) – which is commonly seen at protests involving Indigenous communities. A flag is generally "a European construct and for it to be displayed so prominently amongst Indigenous peoples is extraordinary" (105). However, the point here is that these flexible and adaptive strategies are not simply a response to colonization; rather, they are fundamental to Indigeneity on Turtle Island.

FIGURE 10 Flag carried during the multinational Beyond NoDAPL March in Washington, DC, December 2016. This flag is often associated with Mohawk warriors and has become widely adopted by Indigenous resurgence movements. | *Original photo:* Wikimedia Commons user Rob87438, used under Creative Commons Attribution-Share Alike 4.0 International license

Indigenous peoples have always had protocols for relating to newcomers and integrating them conceptually into Indigenous worldviews (e.g., see Asch 2014; Borrows 2002; Treaty 7 Tribal Council et al. 1996; and Turner 2006). Indigenous peoples treated early Euro-American newcomers, both sojourners and settlers, as different but not incomprehensible. They "sought to incorporate these new people into their own systems ... [which] necessarily involved trying to figure out the nature of the others" (Kupperman 2000, 1). Such crosscultural protocols have often been embodied in treaties. Crucially, these treaties are living documents describing a relationship rather than static political agreements. Teme-Augama Anishnabai political scientist Dale Turner (2006, 26) articulates the Indigenous treaty position as "the political stance that the treaties represent not only binding political agreements but also sacred agreements, and that to violate them is morally reprehensible." Treaties such as the Haudenosaunee Two Row Wampum Treaty were designed to integrate newcomers into Indigenous networks.[9] The beaded belt representing this treaty is the material symbol for a political relationship premised on coexistence and mutual noninterference, but it would be wrong to suggest that these treaties call for segregation or noninteraction. It must also be understood that the relational values of peace, respect, and friendship form the core of these treaties (Hill 2017, 85–6; Turner 2006, 48). They represent not just a political arrangement but also a statement of relationship and alliance with the entire networks of place occupied and relied upon by Indigenous nations. It is difficult to conceptualize settler people existing on the land as something other than settler colonizers and as actually honouring treaties like the Two Row Wampum (Barker 2015, 51–54). In fact, given present conditions, it is almost impossible. We still need to collectively learn how to be in place *differently* and *together* (Larsen and Johnson 2012a). Decolonization, like colonization, is a social process.

If it is recognized that settler people and Indigenous people are already in relationship and that these relationships are often heavily shaped by uneven geometries of settler colonial power that result in settler colonial spaces being built around and through the act of relating, then the real goal of affinity is to reconfigure ways of relating rather than founding them anew. This is inherently a *prefigurative* act (R.J.F. Day 2005, 24–45). That is to say, pursuing relationships differently in the shared spaces of Turtle Island is a form of direct action against settler colonialism that prefigures whatever broad social and societal changes are being more widely envisioned. Geographer Jamie Heckert (2010, 404), writing on relating differently in the context of sexuality, explains the transformative possibilities in this type of direct action:

> [Relating differently means] *meeting* another – listening bodily, with empathy, to what is currently alive in them, as opposed to responding to one's own thoughts of who another is, one's image of another ... Relationship, in this sense, sidesteps and undermines a moral economy of person-hood and "the subtle ruse of power" (Butler, 1990: vii) on which it depends, for there is neither truth of the self nor judgement ... Relating as equals serves as a gentle form of direct action – engaging directly with others to address oppressions rather than through representation, elected or imagined.

As prefigurative relationships take hold, other relationships become implicated through the personal networks that every individual brings into affinity spaces. Spaces of affinity thus shift as the relationships in them change, progress, and are contested.

Because these spaces of affinity are neither structurally bounded, where one type of relationship is insisted on and imposed, nor spatially bounded, where relationships are contained by jurisdictions or juridical institutions, they are always uncertain spaces. This uncertainty contributes to the anticolonial character of these spaces: as uncertain edges of settler colonial space, they may appear as "mutinous eruptions" (G. Brown 2007) or even remain invisible to those not engaging with them, but they are always shifting and impossible to permanently discipline or control. They constitute, in some senses, what I call the unimaginable geographies of settler colonialism – in this case, a space with all the characteristics of a frontier, including the possibility of opportunity, but without any capacity for advantage as a settler colonizer would understand it. The settler gaze cannot clear and level ground that is co-constituted and remains pre-occupied by Indigenous sovereignties. Settler colonial sovereignty cannot exile Indigenous peoples to spaces of exception since doing so would necessitate settlers' permanent acceptance of colonizer status and thus foreclose their transcendence and naturalization.

It should be remembered, however, that the label "affinity" is borrowed; it is applied to many spatial arrangements that are not necessarily decolonizing. Affinity is a widely used term in anarchistic organizing in the "newest social movements" (R.J.F. Day 2004, 2005). As environmental geographer Jenny Pickerill and I have argued, the prefigurative, affinity-based spaces of anarchism do not necessarily correspond to the needs and desires of Indigenous peoples (Barker and Pickerill 2012). The nature of the affinity matters: rather than a singular affective moment, what is needed is constant affective engagement in order to ensure continuous reflection on individual differences (or uncommon ground) as part of the search for affinity (or common ground).

Toward Possible Alliances

Settler social engagements are the sites where settler colonial power is produced and where relationships, spaces, and power are constantly shifting. The lesson to take from this fluctuation is that alliances must always change. Affinity must always be reconstructed, and affective engagement must constantly be pursued without assumptions that we know or can define the terrain of struggle. As Halberstam (2011) argues, we must reject mastery as part of our efforts to fail more effectively. Individual settler activists and scholars should never become so arrogant as to consider themselves sufficiently decolonial if they truly support and pursue collective transformative change through decolonizing struggle. I do not claim to be decolonial; I am a member of actively colonizing settler polities, and I will remain a colonizer as long as we all do. However, whether settler individuals or groups are actually decolonizing – or even whether decolonization is achievable for any individual or group – it is vitally important that settlers come to perceive decolonization as *realistically possible*. Whether it is complete and permanent or partial and temporary is beside the point; what is important is the intrusion of unimagined geographies into the settler colonial geographical imagination. Even perceiving the possibility of Indigenous-settler coexistence is disruptive to the settler colonial identity, creating the conceptual possibility of becoming other than a colonizer. This creates the space for *critical hope* – the idea that there is something to strive toward beyond not feeling guilty or making moves to innocence.[10]

Just as affinity is based on constantly renewed affective engagements, so must settler-Indigenous alliances for decolonization be based on constantly renewed spaces of affinity. This is a return to activism, perhaps, but pursued differently. It is an embodied, active, directed commitment to pursuing decolonizing relationships through expanding, dynamic, and growing communities of affinity. This undertaking must inevitably manifest both as social transformation in the form of self-directed decolonization of relationships in and between settler and Indigenous communities and as strategic resistance in the form of contention against the imposition of relational norms and privileged spatial configurations. Given that relationships constantly shift across the terrain of common and uncommon ground, alliance entails the development of protocols and practices that both encourage and ensure the respectful creation of decolonizing relational spaces. These protocols can serve to mirror Indigenous "rituals of renewal" at the core of Indigenous political, social, and cultural practices (Little Bear 2004) because they not only assert ideas of ways to coexist but also demonstrate patterns of trust, obligation, responsibility, and reciprocity over time.

As a statement about respectful relationships rather than segregation, the Two Row Wampum Treaty illustrates that the agreement of respectful noninterference and coexistence is not about lines drawn on maps or juridical definitions decided by courts; it is, in fact, a relational agreement between peoples that, like affinity, is open-ended and shifting. The constant is the spirit – the foundational assumptions being made, especially about the importance of relationships – in which parties to the treaty approach it, each other, and importantly, themselves, and it is on this ground that settler governments have consistently failed in not upholding both the honour of the Crown and the principles of fairness and liberty that should have underpinned authentic treaty relationships. Further, treaties like the Two Row Wampum are as much enduring reminders as they are formalizations of positive, decolonizing relationships; they cannot be established without some evidence that both parties can fulfil the agreement, and therefore treaties constitute an enduring call to accountability, a call to do what we said we would and could do. Given the historical and present-day failure on the part of settlers to uphold treaties – a failure entirely due to a lack of willingness rather than a lack of ability – settler people trying to decolonize relationships should not expect Indigenous peoples to be willing to formally recognize positive relationships with settler people until these relationships have been active for some time. Alliance building requires a commitment to working as an ally in the absence of being perceived as such; being called an ally should be a recognition of specific work and efforts, not a promotion, reward, or shield. Being an ally carries no special cachet but is simply something that one does (Battell Lowman and Barker 2015, 116).

The development and practice of protocols are also vitally important, and they can be difficult to learn and understand. The protocol for entering Mohawk spaces by entering the clearing and waiting to be welcomed, in the example above, is part of a larger complex of protocols developed to deal with newcomers seeking entrance to Haudenosaunee Confederacy territory (B.E. Johansen and Mann 2000, 315–17). Likewise, our march up PKOLS in Coast Salish territory seemed a riotous and joyous mass action, but it was deeply framed by the words and wisdom of elders, language keepers, and those who knew the true history of the place. The re-enactment of the original signing of the first Douglas Treaty was itself an enactment of ritualized coming-together, reminding the participants – both Indigenous and settler – of their agreed upon responsibilities in that place. Rituals demonstrate the importance of ceremony not just as a personal spiritual practice but also as a method for pursuing particular kinds of place relationships, co-becomings, and ontological discoveries. Ceremony is related to protocol in that particular practices and behaviours are conducted publicly to ensure that diverse and dynamic communities are able to come together to exercise and witness effective governance.[11] Protocols – specific, shared rituals for governing good behaviour – are a sign of consent to particular kinds of relationships. They also involve demonstration of sufficient knowledge, respect, and comprehension to justify allied relationships. Protocols and their deep meanings in Indigenous contexts can be especially important with regard to the tricky issue of settler people and Indigenous territory.

Clearly missing from this consideration, however, is the need for new relational protocols and agreements between Indigenous peoples and would-be settler allies. As Corntassel and Bryce (2012) suggest for Indigenous nations, it is more important to pursue traditional interconnections and to revitalize trade and political relationships between Indigenous nations than to appeal to state or international bodies for protection (see also Corntassel 2008). The same is true for settler peoples. Rather than constantly appealing to Indigenous people for guidance, for acceptance, and for authenticity on the land, settler people must collaborate with each other in undertaking the hard work of formalizing the decolonization of their relationships with one another. This collaboration involves not only the creation of new relationships but also the effort to develop existing relationships differently; it is important to recognize that, just as there are noncapitalist economic practices that are hidden by the overwhelming pre-eminence of neoliberalism (Gibson-Graham 2008), there are potentially decolonizing relationships spread throughout the northern bloc that are obscured by settler colonial power. Settler communities would do well to examine the diversities among their own constituents and own histories in order to find the ways that racism, classism, patriarchy, and the other imposed norms of settler colonial society affect their members in different ways. They may also find in these examinations important points of resistance and strategies for coping with settler colonial resistance as the lived experiences of diverse settler community members become woven together through the common experiences of unsettlement and compassion for each other. As one example, the Mennonite Church of Canada (MCC) has engaged in serious self-reflective practice around the concept of reconciliation, noting that while their institution did not participate in the residential school system, many Mennonite families did adopt Indigenous children out of their communities, including as part of the Sixties Scoop ("Mennonites Have Yet ..." 2015). The MCC has participated in and supported events and projects pursued by the Centre for Truth and Reconciliation since its inception, supported Bill-262 which was introduced by MP Romeo Saganash (Cree) and which called on the federal government to implement the Declaration on the Rights of Indigenous Peoples (Bergen 2019), and have held community events and released publications designed to bolster attempts to support Indigenous communities in the present and future.[12]

For Indigenous-settler alliances to be of any benefit to Indigenous peoples, settler peoples must have something to offer other than apology, postcolonial responsibility, and anonymous care. Settler communities must understand and articulate not just what they are *against* but also and especially what they are *for*, what they will *do*, and how they will replace colonial power with something else. Protocols need to be developed over time to recognize powerful articulations of decolonizing relationships if decolonizing spatialities are to be insulated from colonial pressures; this task must not be undertaken *for* Indigenous peoples but *for* and *by* settler peoples, who otherwise cannot effectively unsettle enough to pursue decolonizing futures. As well, reflective of the dynamics of affect and affinity, settler people must be flexible with regard to these protocols and alliances since Indigenous peoples may well not accept the proposed alliances, which is not a failure on their part. As discussed previously, Indigenous communities throughout Turtle Island have a long history of alliance building and relating across difference. If settler people fail to connect with these traditions, it is a sign of a deep colonial imbalance in need of redress, regardless of any pretence to good intentions.

Restitution and the Creation of Shared Spaces

The role of settler people in Indigenous movements to reclaim land, revitalize Indigenous knowledge and traditions, and reassert Indigenous nationhood is often indirect, and we must remain aware of Standing Rock Sioux scholar Vine Deloria Jr.'s (1988) famous demand for a cultural hands-off policy. In this regard, we must consider spaces of separation and spaces where we may come together across the colonial difference in horizontal, careful, and respectful ways. For a way of thinking through this issue, let us return to the organization of Haudenosaunee villages specifically in relation to meeting newcomers or travellers. Traditionally, as Mohawk historian Susan Hill (2017, 35) has described, Haudenosaunee villages were divided between field and forest – the agricultural area inside the village and the wooded areas for hunting, lumbering, and similar activities beyond it. These two spaces were separated by a clearing, a field around the village site, that was neither within it or beyond it, and it was at the edge of the clearing that these rituals of greeting were performed. This ritual is rooted in a particular tradition of spaces, and although the version that I participated in occurred in a clearing that was very different from the traditional space, the ceremony did not lose any of its power. Similarly, settler people need to contribute to the creation of clearings – that is, spaces where Indigenous peoples can embody Indigenous spatialities without settler colonial interference and where Indigenous belonging is centred – and settlers must ask for permission to enter these spaces and to participate. This is an example of the turning toward Indigenous sovereignty that I advocate. There is a similarity here to media and social justice scholar Max Haiven and anthropologist and activist Alex Khasnabish's (2014) analysis of how contemporary scholar activists can effectively support social justice movements. Among the most valuable tactics that they identify is "making space," which is using the resources and networks accessible to academics to generate places where relationships between various (at times agonistic) folks across the spectrum of social justice movements can be worked out. Making space means supporting people to be able to do this important work by prefiguring spaces to be accessible, establishing standards around abusive language or actions during these interactions, and simply ensuring that people can financially participate, whether by paying for their transport, providing them with daycare, or offering them food and refreshments. In a decolonial context, this undertaking implies creating spaces that are not only free of the influence of state and capital but also emptied as much as possible of the institutions of privilege and, often, of settler bodies and presence. Allowing for such spaces is not about segregation or division but about firmly placing settler people into spaces with Indigenous people by virtue of their shared situated, oppositional stance to colonization. All the same, settler people must remember that these remain spaces where the "common sense" rules of the settler colonial world (Rifkin 2013, 2014) do not apply; settler people cannot assume their belonging, and in response to articulations of "ethnographic refusal" (A. Simpson 2007), they must be willing to remove themselves when Indigenous communities request or require it. Clearings may be spaces where encounter is possible, but it must be remembered that no matter whose labour helped to generate the clearing, the centring of the Haudenosaunee village – that is, Indigenous lifeways – is meant to ensure that the balance of power in the clearing remains in Indigenous hands.

Likewise, restitution in and through these spaces must both materially restore land to Indigenous peoples and interrupt narratives of settler colonial belonging. Without restitution, Indigenous peoples cannot be expected to extend place-sharing practices (again) to settler peoples. Restitution in this sense is both exceedingly easy and deceptively complex; simply put, restitution means returning the land to Indigenous control and sincerely committing to the revitalization of place-based political economies and ecologies. These tasks are incredibly complicated; restitution is the re-establishment of balance in place. As discussed previously, the shifting nature of place and the fluid and layered geometries of power that permeate settler nations like Canada and the United States mean that this pursuit must be constantly enacted. Settler people would be wise, then, to engage with the complex concept of balance in Indigenous philosophy and governance.[13] Changing relationships with Indigenous peoples requires the consistent demonstration of efforts to change spatialities and to pursue rebalancing over time and despite adversity. Realizing these goals requires time to find appropriate practices, to implement them properly, to fully internalize them, and to build trust that the efforts toward decolonization are legitimate[14] and sustainable and that they will be ongoing. As well, understandings of restitution and balance in decolonizing contexts reveal something very uncomfortable to many settler peoples: Indigenous peoples are under no obligation to share space. The only obligation that Indigenous peoples and nations face is the obligation to themselves to figure out what to do with all of these settlers. If settler people choose to pursue decolonization, they may engage in cooperative efforts with Indigenous people to live on the land differently but legitimately. But it must be remembered that these efforts, even if cooperative, must happen according to Indigenous spatialities, legal traditions, and material needs.

The Other Side of Fear

This book has been intentionally wide-ranging. It has uncovered a number of important aspects of settler subjectivities, identities, and settler colonial spaces, and I have shown that settler people do not completely ignore or fail to see Indigenous sovereignties but are particularly effective at deconstructing Indigenous political ecologies and economies and at recontextualizing particular elements of Indigenous lifeworlds to settler colonial ends. These capabilities allow settler people to bridge settler colonial difference by forcibly changing the meaning of place over time through the implementation of settler colonial bricolage, whose dehistoricization renders it presumably normal and banal, contributing to settler peoples' mimetic character. That said, the production of settler colonial space is intended to be open-ended and highly flexible so that it can support the diverse settler relationships that obscure colonial responsibility. Thus there is the potential to turn settler people against settler colonization by stretching the definitions of "relationship" to include Indigeneity as a fundamental and irreducible element of place. This undertaking, however, implies massive reorganization of the spatial geometries that define or support most of the social, political, cultural, and economic institutions of privilege across North America. A decolonizing settler space would be unrecognizable to most settler people. It would also present peoples who are confronting growing crises of economic stratification, political corruption, and environmental degradation with new ways of organizing socially across difference.

Consequently, the next steps in both academic and activist decolonizing settler praxes are clear. The potentiality for settler decolonization may exist, but it is meaningless if not acted upon. Decolonization is pursued through changing relationships in and to place, and it must therefore be pursued collectively. Settler collectives have, almost exclusively, coalesced around settler colonization as an explicit goal. Can settler decolonization motivate similar mobilization against the pervasive geometries of power that support structures of invasion? Can small groups of settler people committed to living differently on and with the land contribute to rolling back the edges of settler colonial space to reveal potentially different ways of living in the clearing between colonial power and Indigenous resurgence?

The decolonizing relationships that build the unimaginable geographies of settler colonialism – the space that defies colonial oppression and supports the power of Indigenous resurgence – are messy and difficult to envision or describe. Even the attempt to articulate these spaces in some senses forecloses possibilities that could be vital to settler decolonization (Chatterton and Pickerill 2010; Turbulence Collective 2010). Simply put, settler people are not yet ready to envision or embody these different spaces. Settler people first need to start coming together around decolonizing concerns and ethics in order to understand the extent and possibility of their own interrelations before exploring how decolonization can be implemented together with Indigenous communities. Fully mapping the occupied terrain of settler colonial space will require a great deal of research and experimentation, certainly in the academy but even more so in the daily lives and collective activism of would-be settler allies. It will also require a reorientation of settler scholarship away from anti-colonial critiques of governments and markets and toward decolonization and challenges to the settler colonial dispossession of Indigenous peoples and lands as the basis of governmental, capitalist, and other kinds of power that can otherwise survive the demise of any particular settler social form. Settler scholars, if they wish to contribute to these new imagined geographies, must commit to learning about Indigeneity and Indigenous peoples and, even more importantly, to learning from Indigenous scholars, activists, practitioners, and knowledge keepers. Then they must commit to applying this knowledge to critical reflection on settler peoples and to action within settler colonial space.

Settler colonialism is not monolithic. Rather, it is the result of a multitude of forces, from the exceptional structural power imposed by elites to the banal, everyday lived dynamics of average settler people. The fact that settler people can conceivably decolonize is one implication of the difference between structure and dynamics; the fact that doing so is meaningful only if it is a collective act is another. How do settlers relate to each other and to place as decolonizing people? This question will require different answers across distinct places and times and in response to various oppressive, colonizing entities, whether they be capitalist, metropole colonial, or settler colonial, among others. It is a question that asks a great deal of settler people. It is a question that settler people must try to answer without ever being sure that there is an answer at all and despite knowing that settler people fear few things more than illegitimacy in place. It has been said that "freedom is the other side of fear" and that Indigenous peoples must seek liberation by confronting "fears head-on through spiritually grounded action; contention and direct movement at the source of our fears is the only way to break the chains that bind us to our colonial existences" (Alfred and Corntassel 2005, 613). Settler people do not have the spiritual traditions that ground this type of Indigenous resistance, so perhaps the first and most important goal for settler collectives engaged in decolonizing efforts is to articulate their own ethical grounding by answering the question "What are decolonizing settlers fighting for?" Somehow, settler people must come to accept their fear of never belonging, of always being in between spaces and in transition. Eventually, settler people must accept that if the disputes between Indigenous and settler peoples are to be truly resolved, we will have to unsettle ourselves and radically remake who we are. Only then can we contribute to restoring Indigenous nationhood and lifeways across Turtle Island.

Notes

Introduction

1 In specific contexts, I refer to North America or to the northern bloc of settler colonialism, but I frequently use the name Turtle Island to refer to Indigenous territories north of the Rio Grande, generally commensurate with the contemporary settler states of Canada and the United States of America. This name comes specifically from the Haudenosaunee tradition (Hill 2017; Watts 2013), which formed the basis of my education by Indigenous scholars, and is linked to the fact that I was born and raised in Haudenosaunee territory and lived a significant portion of my life there.

2 Emma Battell Lowman and I discuss this in much greater detail in our book *Settler: Identity and Colonialism in 21st Century Canada* (Battell Lowman and Barker 2015).

3 In much of my work, I capitalize "Settler" to refer to people who share a common settler identity (usually a national identity, like settler Canadian) and use "settler" to refer to conceptual settlers or settlements or to settler subjectivities created by complexes of colonial and imperial power. However, because the lines between identity and subjectivity are not always clear, I have defaulted to the use of the lower case throughout this book. For more on the rationale for capitalizing "Settler" as an identity and its use, see Battell Lowman and Barker (2015).

4 It should be noted here that although Daniel Clayton and Cole Harris, among others, have engaged with the colonization of Turtle Island through settlement as somehow different from other types of colonialism, they have not analytically disentangled settler colonialism from these other types.

5 This phrase is used in several places, perhaps earliest being in a widely published 1882 letter from Engels to Marxist theorist Karl Kautsky. See also Veracini's discussion of this distinction (2010a, 1–15).

6 Capitalist modernization has been portrayed as a historical inevitability, supportive of racist, white, conservative politics (Flannigan 2008), and also deployed critically to shine a light on the imbrication of urbanization and industrialization, globalizing capital, the settler colonization of Turtle Island, and metropolitan empire building in India (Bhambra 2007a, 2007b).

7 Throughout this book, I employ an orthography of "Indigenous" in reference to an identity as outlined here; "Indigeneity" in reference to the concept of a shared, embodied process of relating to traditional lands, sacred sites, and particular ecosystems through advanced cultural and political-economic systems; and "indigenous," "indigeneity," "indigenization," and "indigenized" in reference to a subjectivity or heritage aspired to by settlers. The lower case is also used for "indigenous Others," which does not refer to actual Indigenous people but to settler imaginaries of 'savage Indians.' These terms, of course, are contested, particularly within geography. For a current précis of these terminological debates, see Radcliffe (2017).

8 The colonial history of the northern bloc also has roots in Russian, Scottish, and various Scandinavian colonization projects; the invasion of Turtle Island has always been an international affair.

9 For a good explanation of social justice research and the role of scholar activists in struggling against oppressive systems and structures in the contemporary North American social landscape of austerity policies, rising right-wing nationalism, and ongoing racism and colonialism, see Haiven and Khasnabish (2014).

10 Resurgence is a very important concept that is discussed further in later chapters. For more on the concept, see especially Alfred and Corntassel (2005), Coulthard (2014), and L. Simpson (2017).

Chapter 1: Cores and Peripheries

1 Throughout this book, the terms "settling" and "settlement" are used to describe the material processes by which settler colonizers construct permanent dwellings, transform landscapes according to their purposes, and conceptually justify their attachments and claims to belonging in place. All of these undertakings, as discussed throughout this book, do not happen in isolation or benignly, and should be understood as inherently violent and dispossessive acts with respect to Indigenous peoples and their territories.

2 For further research on Indigenous travels to and through Britain, please see "Beyond the Spectacle," a research project based at the University of Kent and led by Professor of History David Stirrup: https://research.kent.ac.uk/beyondthespectacle/.

3 Kupperman (2000, 20) describes something similar, namely English colonization of the Americas as shaped by ambivalence and "double vision."

4 In addition to enslaved peoples and indentured servants, in both the settlement colonies and beyond, a great deal of this unfree labour was in the form of convicts. See generally Clare Anderson's *A Global History of Convicts and Penal Colonies* (2018). See also the Carceral Archipelago Project's website, Convict Voyages, for further resources on the role of transported convicts in empire building and colonization: http://convictvoyages.org.

5 Mackey (2016) does an excellent job of unpacking the contemporary relevance of terra nullius as a concept used to justify claims to property in the northern bloc.

6 This is a point that Canadian essayist John Ralston Saul correctly makes in *A Fair Country: Telling Truths about Canada* (2008) before inexplicably spinning this difference between North America and Europe into a fantasy of Canada-wide métissage or universal indigeneity that is an explicit attempt to deny settler colonialism.

7 My thanks to Emma Battell Lowman for pointing out that I had neglected to mention enslaved Indigenous people in earlier drafts, and for providing me with this source.

8 Agamben (1998) uses the term "bare life" to describe the condition of living in a space of exception. Excepted from all 'natural' rules of conduct, the person condemned to a space of exception may be alive but only that. Bare life is life without rights, protections, dignities, or sacredness in a social context and is therefore fundamentally dehumanizing. "Bare life" can be thought of as meaning that one has lost everything except the capacity to die.

9 I return to the concept of the frontier and the role that it plays in settler colonial imagined geographies in the next chapter.

10 However, there are grey areas; for example, Battell Lowman's (2011) study of the British-born missionary Stanley Higgs, who travelled to British Columbia in the early twentieth century, examines how he set out as a metropole colonizer with no intention to stay and became a settler Canadian through the process of his connection with Indigenous peoples and settler communities.

11 See the variety of types of transfer identified by Veracini (2010b, 33–50); see also the "moves to innocence" identified by Tuck and Yang (2012, 9–28).

12 Whereas Veracini (2010b, 26) uses the relational term "exogenous Others," Tuck and Yang (2012, 6n5) refer to "chattel slaves," focusing on political and economic dispossession as definitional to this subjective category, and Byrd (2011) uses the term "arrivants," referencing diasporic transit as key to understanding this category. All are somewhat similar attempts to describe the same group within the settler colonial imagination.

13 Veracini (2010b, 27–28) differentiates between "exogenous Others," seen as outside the settler subjectivity, and "abject Others," seen as irredeemably beneath the settler subject. Although this construction is worthy of further consideration, I construct exogenous Others as a more varied category here to avoid prescriptive analysis.

14 It should be noted that this process of emptying often involves attempts at physical and/or cultural genocide yet also exceeds both (Wolfe 2006).

15 Settler colonization has been a global practice for centuries (Cavanagh and Veracini 2017). The particularity of European-driven settler colonization, most notably the colonization of Turtle Island by means of this tactic, is exceptional from many earlier forms of colonization for its enduring genocidal violence, which is linked to the increased capacity of industrialized, militarized states to focus settler colonial violence.

16 It is worth noting that a mythistory has developed around Simcoe that attributes the ending of slavery in Canada to him. However, this account is fundamentally untrue and contributes to the erasure of histories of the enslavement of Black people in

Canada. On the history of Black enslavement and resistance in Canada, see Cooper (2007, esp. 66–106).

17 Although most common in the context discussed here, the focus on missing and murdered Indigenous women and girls (MMIWG) has been configured to include two-spirit people (MMIWGT) or to include trafficked Indigenous women (MMTIW). Other variations are also in current usage.

18 This specifically refers to the defeat of the *Forward* "despite overwhelming military superiority" by the Lamalcha in the Salish Sea, 1863, "the only tactical defeat ever inflicted by a tribal people on the Royal Navy" (Arnett 1999, 139). Arnett goes on to note that the "expectation of victory" was so great for British naval captains that "the British made every effort to deny their defeat" resulting in blatant lies being spread in the press.

Chapter 2: Spatialities of Settlement

1 It is worth noting that in more recent times Wilder's racism against both Indigenous and Black people has resulted in public criticism of both her and her works, including by the American Library Association (ALA) which made the decision in 2018 to drop her name from their children's literature award.

2 There were, of course, further restrictions even to this: property ownership was a frequent requirement, as was taking an oath, which precluded many religious communities including Jewish people and Quakers.

3 The Union of British Columbia Indian Chiefs has made a particularly accessible and relevant collection available: "Our Homes Are Bleeding" details the testimony, historical context, and impact of the 1913–16 Royal Commission on Indian Áffairs for the Province of British Columbia (ourhomesarebleeding.ubcic.bc.ca). Better known as the McKenna-McBride Commission (after the appointed commissioners), this process sought to evaluate Indigenous land use and resulted in the large-scale removal of highly valued land from Indigenous communities and the extension of authority to the federal and provincial governments to cut off land from Indian reserves without consultation or consent.

4 It should be noted that the American government happily encouraged both buying and speculating on land as a key means of raising funds. Following the American Revolution, Republicans fought to block any attempts by the state to raise funds through taxes, leaving the early United States nearly bankrupt. However, the government claimed title to huge areas occupied by Indigenous nations in areas previously barred by the Royal Proclamation, parcelled them off, and sold them. Mass property sales and speculations simultaneously provided a financial lifeline to the state and began the transfer of wealth from small property owners to elites, which came to mark much of American history.

5 In some cases, such as the nineteenth-century interactions among white settlers, current or former Black slaves, and Cherokee people in present-day Tennessee, it can be argued that even the balance of powers in a middle-ground arrangement can and does lead to the slow erosion of Indigenous cultures and national identities (Cumfer 2007), which leads us to seriously question the neutrality or desirability of middle-ground spaces.

6 Examples of such destruction or restriction include the James Bay Hydro Project, which displaced thousands of Cree in northern Quebec (Feit 1995), and the immersion of Mistaseni Rock, a boulder sacred to the Cree, which was dynamited and then sunk beneath an artificial lake in Saskatchewan (Indian Country Today 2014).

7 As Cole Harris (2004) notes, fur trade forts were not primarily intended as settlements and the companies involved were often largely uninterested in claiming land and property around the forts. But the very existence of the forts implied a need to begin mapping land and subduing perceived threats, both acts that precede and encourage mass settlement.

8 Veracini (2010b, 2015) has written extensively about Deadwood and the series has been a crucial and accessible example in other studies of settler colonialism (Georgi-Findlay 2018; Young 2013).

9 It is worth noting that Destination BC, a Crown corporation promoting tourism in British Columbia, uses the tagline "Super, Natural British Columbia."

10 Although still designated a dominion of the British Empire at the time, Canada was increasingly acting as an independent political entity, especially with respect to "Indian policy" and other domestic matters.

11 For more on the interesting case of James Teit, who not only served settler agendas but also helped several communities to record linguistic and cultural practices in order to aid in language and cultural revitalization and was an active supporter of Indigenous rights efforts in the early twentieth century, see Wickwire (1994, 1998, 2019) and H. Robinson and Wickwire (1989).

12 The fact that settler colonizers spread disease is undeniable. There is also a great deal of documented historical evidence to suggest that various political leaders, military officers, and other powerful settler colonial agents at times tried to encourage the spread of disease through tactics such as distributing smallpox-contaminated blankets that had been used by previous victims of the virus and leaving ill but not fully symptomatic individuals in Indigenous villages or territories (see broadly Daschuk 2013; Swanky 2012; and Wright 1992, 74, 103–4). Whether or not these techniques were effective – a subject of ongoing debate – is beside the point. The focus should be on what the material and archival evidence confirms, which is that settlers in positions of leadership have always been willing to encourage the widespread deaths of Indigenous peoples by disease in order to gain access to land, and that the widespread belief that Indigenous people 'died out' from disease assuages settler colonial guilt.

13 It is an enduring example of the resiliency of settler denial that Cole Harris, an articulate and groundbreaking analyst of the construction of colonial space in Canada and an enormous influence on this project, includes an introduction and a final chapter in his seminal work *Making Native Space: Colonialism, Resistance, and Reserves in British Columbia* (2002) that deeply retrench colonial mentalities based on a personal, familial connection to a colonized space, namely his family ranch in British Columbia, and the author's repeatedly stated desire for a "final solution" that will settle the question of land title and secure the future of the Canadian state and nation (xxix, 293). This juxtaposition is so stark that it has received an enormous amount of scholarly attention (C. Harris, Fiske, and Gibson 2003) without resolution.

14 For example, see John Ralston Saul's *A Fair Country* (2008) and my and Emma Battell Lowman's critique of *A Fair Country* as part of a liberalist settler colonial narrative (Battell Lowman and Barker 2015). Further, see Darryl Leroux's (2018) extended critique of Quebecois claims to indigeneity through heritage.

15 For a more explicit treatment of the concept of primitive accumulation in settler colonial spaces, see Coulthard (2014). This concept may also be understood as accumulation by dispossession (Harvey 2000), but in this case, the product of this dispossession is immediately routed into settler colonial place making, as described here, and is deserving of separate treatment.

16 This should not detract, however, from subtle acts of resistance on the part of Indigenous artists and artisans. For example, as historian Paige Raibmon (2000) demonstrates with respect to Kwakwaka'wakw dancers who performed for settler colonial spectators at the Chicago World Fair in 1893, Indigenous artists and performers often weave subtle messages of resistance into their art that is frequently invisible to the settler gaze.

17 Again, it is necessary to underscore the extent to which the lands encountered by settlers and imperial agents were not 'natural' but heavily curated, groomed, stewarded, and monitored by Indigenous people.

Chapter 3: Remaking People and Places

1 Indeed, political theorist Kevin Bruyneel (2007) has directly argued that similar forms of Indigenous resistance and resurgence are effective in both states, pointing to the similarity of settler formations across these jurisdictions.

2 For an extended consideration of how the purported benefits of membership in the settler collective are not necessarily accrued by all settler Canadians, see Battell Lowman and Barker (2015, 84–89).

3 It is possible for racialized subjects to find some level of belonging in settler colonial space, but this positionality must always take into account the vicious realities of white supremacy in settler Canada and the United States. I am not qualified to comment on the experience of settler colonialism from Black perspectives, but I encourage readers to seek out further discussion of this experience by Black, Indigenous, and other scholars of colour, starting with Amadahy and Lawrence (2009). For an examination of the intersections between Blackness and settler colonialism, with an excellent summary of the tensions between Afro-pessimism and settler colonial critique, see I. Day (2015), and for an examination of nineteenth-century and contemporary uses of anti-Blackness and settler colonialism, see Leroy (2016). On interrogating the differences between Indigenous and migrant conceptions of home and belonging, see Coleman (2016); on contemporary solidarity between racialized migrants and Indigenous people in Canada, see Walia (2013); and on parallels and tensions between Idle No More and Black Lives Matter, see L.B. Simpson, Walcott, and Coulthard (2018). For an excellent co-reading of Blackness Studies and Native Studies, and analysis for how this should change perspectives on both, see King (2019). Also to be considered is the significant community of Black Indigenous folks, including those of mixed heritage and those descended from Black adoptees into Indigenous societies before the rise of the settler northern bloc. I also encourage

readers to look beyond the academy – to spaces like social media or activist spaces of convergence – where there are already ongoing, intense, and productive dialogues between Black communities, other non-Indigenous communities of colour, and Indigenous peoples about their common opposition to white supremacy and settler colonialism.

4 One of the few places where Iyko Day and I disagree is in the way that she juxtaposes the United States with Canada, the latter of which she regards as a less racially polarized and less imperialistic state, a position that I think downplays the imperialism and racism of the Canadian state (Barker 2009). I believe that Day's general argument about American racial dynamics can be extended northward with little adjustment.

5 Of course, none of the Five Civilized Tribes actually assimilated into British or American societies and cultures. Adaptations based on the uptake of material and cultural practices in the context of colonialism do not imply that these Indigenous societies were becoming Euro-American or settler any more than settler colonial bricolage implies an indigenization process. Rather, we must remember that cultures change and that customs, fashions, and material practices flow between many cultures. All five nations resisted colonization through a variety of measures, including both warfare, such as the Seminole Wars (1816–58), and legal and diplomatic means, such as the famous case of *Cherokee Nation v. Georgia* (1831), which resulted not only in the legal distinction that individual states did not have jurisdiction over tribal lands or governments but also in the assertion by the US Supreme Court that the Cherokee comprised a "dependent nation," the legal root of state paternalism. The elements of cultural hybridity on display by all five nations may have been especially well received by settler colonial peoples characterized by mimetic qualities (Byrd 2011, 2014; Veracini 2010b, 14), and the uses of strategic mimesis in anticolonial struggles warrant further research.

6 Fracking is a particular concern for many Indigenous communities and has been explicitly articulated as a settler colonial process (see N.A. Brown 2014, 9–12; Hallenbeck 2015, 351–53; Huseman and Short 2012; Moore, von der Porten, and Castleden 2017; Preston 2013; and Willow 2014).

7 My thanks to Richard Day for the idea of using a semiotic square to interrogate this process, which is similar to the semiotic square that he uses to guide his exploration of Canadian multiculturalism (R.J.F. Day 2000), a method that has since been productively taken up by Veracini (2015).

8 The intersections of settler colonialism with planetary urbanism and other urban studies promise to be a fruitful area of future analysis (e.g., see Dorries et al. 2019; and Porter and Yiftachel 2019).

9 To be clear, urban spaces function as spaces of diversity in the settler imagination, but they need not necessarily be diverse for this narrative to be believed, and suburban and rural spaces are often less white and Euro-American than they are portrayed as being.

10 Although the association of whiteness with settler colonialism has been well established, it should be noted that for many the defining ability of a settler polity to reproduce itself implies biological reproduction and thus the centring of cisheterosexual relationships. This perspective does not abrogate the possibility of queer

settler colonialism (see Greensmith 2016; Greensmith and Giwa 2013; and Morgensen 2011), but it does position noncisgendered and nonheterosexual folks as problems for settler colonial society to manage.

11 This idea of Indigenous people as belonging to the past is not just a problem of popular perception. Rather, this particular imposition of temporal barriers to define difference and subjectivity, especially based on the assumption that modernity and tradition are incommensurate, has long been a feature of many academic endeavours, especially in the field of anthropology. On the ways that anthropologists have used temporality to Other many peoples, including Indigenous peoples of Turtle Island, see anthropologist Johannes Fabian (2002).

12 Much of this discourse has occurred in blogs and through grassroots anti-gentrification organizing rather than in scholarly journals. For one example, see Hunt (2011).

13 This phrase is a reference to the title of historian Jean Barman's essay "Race, Greed and Something More: The Erasure of Urban Indigenous Space in Early Twentieth-Century British Columbia" (2010), in which she demonstrates that early urban settlement in Victoria and Vancouver was shaped not only by perceptions of race and divisions of wealth but also by tensions that arose when settler colonial ideas of authority and ownership came into conflict with Coast Salish resistance to and subversion of colonial power.

14 My thanks to Emma Battell Lowman for pointing out the extreme irony in this context that coyotes made a comeback in suburbs across the continent in the late 2010s.

15 Although this phrase has been used by many scholars and activists, I was first introduced to it and its usefulness by Mi'kmaw (Mi'kmaq Nation) activist, educator, and warrior Sakej Ward.

16 It must be noted that these spaces were intentionally whitened: for example, the GI Bill which was intended to help WWII veterans receive a mortgage and buy property was largely restricted to white veterans (Woods 2013).

Chapter 4: Revolutionary Aspirations?

1 For a very good overview of protest camps as an activist tactic, see Feigenbaum, McCurdy, and Frenzel (2013), and G. Brown and Feigenbaum (2017).

2 This disparity, of course, is a common problem in much social movement organizing; for example, the summit hoppers of the late 1990s and early 2000s carried similar racial and class privileges.

3 The creators of the original poster – non-Indigenous activists Ernesto Yerena, Sandra Castro, and Orlando Arenas, based in Phoenix, Arizona – have not generally engaged in the arguments about the imagery. However, a supporter of theirs did make a statement in a blog post on the website Dignidad Rebelde on October 4, 2011 (Cervantes 2011). This post, despite recognizing some of Keene's critiques, also called her approach "abrupt and unresearched" and her tone "self-righteous," a clear example of tone policing, which is a tactic frequently used to silence activists, especially women of colour.

4 Although many of the online conversations around this issue in blogs and on social media have since been deleted, several have been maintained. For an example of the proposal to "colonize Wall Street," see Occupy Forum (2013).

5 I go into greater detail regarding settler colonialism in the imagery and governance processes of Occupy Wall Street in "Already Occupied: Indigenous Peoples, Settler Colonialism, and the Occupy Movements in North America" in *Social Movement Studies* (2012).
6 David Austin (2010, 28) uses the term "generic Left" in reference only to the Canadian context; I use it throughout this section to refer to mainstream leftist political parties and movements of the settler northern bloc.
7 Many racial and ethnic communities do count as part of settler society. I argue that the members of any community that is not explicitly barred from political enfranchisement and that seeks belonging in the established nations of Canada and the United States can be considered settlers, regardless of their particular positionalities with respect to race, class, gender, and other exclusionary hierarchies.
8 For more on multiculturalism and assimilation in the Canadian context, see R.J.F. Day (2000).
9 Though no longer maintained, the Tumblr can still be found online at https://leftfail.tumblr.com.
10 Unfortunately, like many macros produced for quick diffusion through online activist communities, the image is of very low quality and cannot be reproduced here.
11 Following the Shut Down Canada protests in opposition to the raid on the Unist'ot'en Camp by the Royal Canadian Mounted Police in January 2020, it was an exciting development that the slogan "Land Back" (or "#LandBack" online) began to spread widely, both in and beyond Indigenous activist communities. It currently occupies a central position in the reclamation of land adjacent to the Six Nations of the Grand River Reserve, which the Haudenosaunee community have named 1492 Land Back Lane.
12 Day, however, explicitly engages with Indigeneity and discusses the relevance of the Two Row Wampum Treaty to anarchist utopian visions. His engagement is more successful and nuanced but – crucially – less certain and clear, as well as more contingent and process-based.

Chapter 5: The Efficacy of Failure

1 I am grateful to Emma Battell Lowman for pointing out to me here the parallel to the Christian positioning of missionary service as benevolent sacrifice, which obscures the role of the missionary in colonization.
2 My original understanding of the formulation of Indigenous resurgence comes from Alfred and Corntassel (2005). However, resurgence as both a concept and a practice has been developed much further in the past fifteen years by the wider community of scholars discussed here.
3 The articulation of settler roles in decolonizing efforts has advanced considerably during the development of this book. For further reading in this area, see L. Davis, Denis, and Sinclair (2017), Mackey (2016), Dotson's (2018) consideration of Black feminist theory in conjunction with decolonization, and Steinman's (2020, 558) attempt to develop an "affirmative model for settlers to interrupt the routine institutional reproduction of settler colonial understandings."
4 Recently, the Cheslatta Carrier Nation has engaged in an important act of resurgence in the context of severe crisis. Despite being removed from their traditional

lakeshore home by the state in 1952, Cheslatta elders were moved back to the lake by their community members in the spring of 2020 to protect them from infection with COVID-19 (Soren Larsen, personal communication with author, July 2020).

5 I would like to thank Chaw-win-is, Nuu-chah-nulth warrior, mother, teacher, and friend, for her critical support and for her permission to share this story.

6 This essay appears in the volume *Alliances: Re/Envisioning Indigenous-Non-Indigenous Relationships* (2010), edited by Lynne Davis. This volume grew out of the 2007 conference "Re-Envisioning Indigenous-Non-Indigenous Relationships," held at Trent University. This conference was a formative moment in the development of my activist praxis, and the essay is a good representation of my thinking on these issues at that time.

7 By contrast, witness American states' appeals to the federal government to limit the economic benefits of tribal casinos, which are located on reservation land in part to avoid state regulations and taxes. These appeals often employ the rhetoric of state rights and the economic inequality of states with respect to tribes in order to force tribal submission to state legislatures (Corntassel and Witmer 2011, 18–19, 25).

8 CKRZ radio, "The Voice of the Grand," is run by the Southern Onkwehon:we Nishnabec Indigenous Communications Society and is accessible online at ckrzfm.com.

9 The Truth and Reconciliation Commission of Canada's (2015) final report on the impacts of the Indian residential school system rejected narrow definitions of "reconciliation" in favour of a broad definition that seems coterminous with concepts like decolonization. This rejection is important to note because it indicates that the question of Indigenous resurgence and respectful relationships is being asked in a variety of ways and through multiple institutional frameworks.

10 My sincere thanks to Lorenzo Veracini for this term and concept. Personal communication with author, May 9, 2015.

11 And, of course, settlers continue to negate the legacies of Indigenous sacrifice and loss in resistance to settler colonialism by appropriating the names and identities of leaders like Geronimo and whole nations such as the Apache to provide labels for imperialist military interventions and advanced military hardware (Bruyneel 2016).

12 To be clear, this is not a critique of the efficacy of "tiny house" building as a tactic for spatial assertions of sovereignty – quite the opposite. As environmental journalist Janice Cantieri (2018, 11) reports, "the Tiny House Warriors project was founded by Indigenous environmental and women's rights activist Kanahus Manuel of the Secwépemc and Ktunaxa Nations" and has successfully built multiple small independent dwellings across traditional Secwépemc territory, including in the path of proposed oil and gas pipelines. By contrast, settler people deploying this tactic without clear intent to do so in relationship to Indigenous people and nations are recklessly engaging in a powerful act of individually claiming land that is consistent with settler colonial systems, structures, and stories.

13 For application of the concept of "nondiscrete nonbinary dualism" to identity in the context of settler colonialism, see Battell Lowman and Barker (2015, 13–19).

Chapter 6: Affinity and Alliance

1 A few scholarly engagements have emerged that address the Reclaim, Rename, Reoccupy campaign to reassert the traditional name of PKOLS. PKOLS is one of

the examples that historians Amanda Murphyao and Kelly Black (2015) examine in their consideration of naming, territory making, and settler colonialism. Geographer Reuben Rose-Redwood (2016) takes a more critical perspective, noting that although Indigenous communities have been energized by the event, it has largely been ignored by settler colonial governments and institutions. However, it is likely that the effects of this event cannot accurately be measured. The affective impact continues to motivate many people, including myself, years later.

2 Because of its enduring affective impact, I frequently discuss this event in my teaching. In order to convey some of its feeling, I show the video posted by Social Coast (2013), a settler activist support group that helped with the action, including contributing the bus that took elders, drummers, and disabled folks up the mountain.

3 For example, see Larsen's (2008) examination of Indigenous and settler communities near Anahim Lake in the BC interior whose members were able to come together and bridge their different relationships to the environment; however, this affinity remained powerful only when resonance was generated by an external environmental threat. In the absence of this threat, the communities were unable to find the impetus to develop a common "place frame" (172).

4 This is not to say that Indigenous peoples and other dispossessed and racialized communities are not capable of pursuing decolonization without settler assistance – only that it is unjust to expect them to do so.

5 Versions of this story also appear in Battell Lowman and Barker (2015) and in Barker and Battell Lowman (2016).

6 Regan has written the most comprehensive discussion of unsettling developed to date. Her work in *Unsettling the Settler Within: Indian Residential Schools, Truth Telling, and Reconciliation in Canada* (2010) is invaluable and far more nuanced than I can justly express here; it should be read widely. An earlier version in the form of Regan's doctoral dissertation is freely available from eTheses Canada Online.

7 Chatterton (2006, 270) refers to "compassion" in the same essay as an emotional state that can divide self-identified "activists" from "non-activists." My construction of compassion here is partly influenced by the need to address this concern.

8 There are many excellent resources on Indigenous thought, several of which I have cited in this book. I recommend V. Deloria, Jr. (2003), Waters (2004), and Wilson (2008). For an introductory exploration of Indigenous thought applied by settler and non-Indigenous researchers, see Battell Lowman and Barker (2010).

9 Treaties and relationships were developed not only with respect to European newcomers but also between different Indigenous peoples both before and after Euro-American colonization.

10 Critical hope is a concept that I first encountered in conversation with Paulette Regan and Emma Battell Lowman. Fellow activist scholars had recently declared "fuck hope" as a rejection of status quo politics that suspend change in time by projecting it into the future, thus creating a paralyzing acceptance of present oppressions lest activists risk losing potential future gains. Regan and Battell Lowman's articulation positions hope as necessary to surviving demoralizing efforts to struggle against hegemonic settler colonialism, which cedes very little. Such hope can be justified only by a critical appraisal of collective struggles that are ongoing but have not yet borne fruit. Critical hope is the hope that if we continue to struggle, we will

eventually see change. It does not mean that we should wait for change to come but instead that we should continue in struggle until it does.

11 Traditional examples of this use of ceremony include the Haudenosaunee Condolence Ritual as outlined by Hill (2017) and the Thanksgiving Address as described by Swamp (2010).

12 Much of this work was driven forward by Steve Heinrichs, former Director of Indigenous Relations for the MCC. His speaking and writing features prominently in the MCC's online archive (see: https://www.mennonitechurch.ca/indigenous) and he was a prominent organizer and participant in "the Pilgrimage for Indigenous Rights (PfIR), a 600-kilometre march from Kitchener, Ont., to Ottawa, to engage churches in conversations around UNDRIP" (Klassen-Wiebe 2017). I was privileged to be in Kitchener at that time and participated in the opening ceremonies, and can attest to the enormous affective power of the event for a wide community of settler people (as well as the many Indigenous participants).

13 Although the literature on Indigenous peoples' concepts of balance is extensive, it is not often engaged with due to its marginalization in Native studies programs (L.T. Smith 1999) or because it is regarded as unscientific (V. Deloria Jr. 2003). Crucially, balance in Indigenous thought does not imply a static situation but dynamic and shifting action.

14 Here, "legitimate" means "worthwhile" rather than "sincere" or "honest." Settlers have often spoken sincerely about their respect for Indigenous peoples and cultures even as they have aggressively colonized.

References

Adams, H. 1989. *Prison of Grass: Canada from a Native Point of View*. Saskatoon, SK: Fifth House.

Agamben, G. 1998. *Homo Sacer: Sovereign Power and Bare Life*. Stanford, CA: Stanford University Press.

Aldred, L. 2000. "Plastic Shamans and Astroturf Sun Dances: New Age Commercialization of Native American Spirituality." *American Indian Quarterly* 24 (3): 329–52. https://doi.org/10.1353/aiq.2000.0001. Medline:17086676

Alfred, T. 2009. *First Nation Perspectives on Political Identity*. Ottawa: Assembly of First Nations.

Alfred, T., and J. Corntassel. 2005. "Being Indigenous: Resurgences against Contemporary Colonialism." *Government and Opposition* 40 (4): 597–614. https://doi.org/10.1111/j.1477-7053.2005.00166.x.

Alper, D.K. 1996. "The Idea of Cascadia: Emergent Transborder Regionalisms in the Pacific Northwest-Western Canada." *Journal of Borderlands Studies* 11 (2): 1–22.

Amadahy, Z., and B. Lawrence. 2009. "Indigenous Peoples and Black People in Canada: Settlers or Allies?" In *Breaching the Colonial Contract: Anti-Colonialism in the US and Canada*, ed. A. Kempf, 105–36. New York: Springer.

Andersen, C. 2014. *"Métis": Race, Recognition, and the Struggle for Indigenous Peoplehood*. Vancouver: UBC Press.

Anderson, B. 2010. "Preemption, Precaution, Preparedness: Anticipatory Action and Future Geographies." *Progress in Human Geography* 34 (6): 777–98. https://doi.org/10.1080/08865655.1996.9695488

Anderson, B., and C. McFarlane. 2011. "Assemblage and Geography." *Area* 43 (2): 124–27.

Anderson, C., ed. 2018. *A Global History of Convicts and Penal Colonies*. London: Bloomsbury Press.

Arnett, C. 1999. *Terror of the Coast: Land Alienation and Colonial War on Vancouver Island and the Gulf Islands, 1849–1863.* Vancouver: Talonbooks.

Asch, M. 2014. *On Being Here to Stay: Treaties and Aboriginal Rights in Canada.* Toronto: University of Toronto Press.

Ault, C.R., Jr. 2014. "The Ghost Forests of Cascadia: How Valuing Geological Inquiry Puts Practice into Place." *Journal of Geoscience Education* 62 (2): 158–65. https://doi.org/10.5408/12-389.1

Austin, D. 2010. "Narratives of Power: Historical Mythologies in Contemporary Quebec and Canada." *Race and Class* 52 (1): 19–32. https://doi.org/10.1177/0306396810371759

Baldwin, A. 2011. "Whiteness and Futurity: Towards a Research Agenda." *Progress in Human Geography* 36 (2): 172–87. https://doi.org/10.1177/0309132511414603

Baloy, N.J. 2016. "Spectacles and Spectres: Settler Colonial Spaces in Vancouver." *Settler Colonial Studies* 6 (3): 209–34. https://doi.org/10.1080/2201473X.2015.1018101

Banivanua Mar, T. 2010. "Carving Wilderness: Queensland's National Parks and the Unsettling of Emptied Lands, 1890–1910." In *Making Settler Colonial Space: Perspectives on Race, Place and Identity,* ed. T. Banivanua Mar and P. Edmonds, 73–93. New York: Palgrave Macmillan.

Banivanua Mar, T., and P. Edmonds, eds. 2010. *Making Settler Colonial Space: Perspectives on Race, Place and Identity.* New York: Palgrave Macmillan.

Barclay, F., C. Chopin, and M. Evans. 2018. "Introduction: Settler Colonialism and French Algeria." *Settler Colonial Studies* 8 (2): 115–30. https://doi.org/10.1080/2201473X.2016.1273862

Barker, A.J. 2009. "The Contemporary Reality of Canadian Imperialism." *American Indian Quarterly* 33 (3): 325–51. https://doi.org/10.1353/aiq.0.0054

–. 2010. "From Adversaries to Allies: Forging Respectful Alliances between Indigenous and Settler Peoples." In *Alliances: Re/Envisioning Indigenous–Non-Indigenous Relationships,* ed. L. Davis, 316–33. Toronto: University of Toronto Press.

–. 2012. "Already Occupied: Indigenous Peoples, Settler Colonialism and the Occupy Movements in North America." *Social Movement Studies* 11 (3–4): 327–34. https://doi.org/10.1080/14742837.2012.708922

–. 2013. "(Re-)Ordering the New World: Settler Colonialism, Space and Identity." PhD diss., University of Leicester.

–. 2015. "'A Direct Act of Resurgence, a Direct Act of Sovereignty': Reflections on Idle No More, Indigenous Activism, and Canadian Settler Colonialism." *Globalizations* 12 (1): 43–65. https://doi.org/10.1080/14747731.2014.971531

–. 2018. "Deathscapes of Settler Colonialism: The Necro-Settlement of Stoney Creek, Ontario, Canada." *Annals of the American Association of Geographers* 108 (4): 1134–49. https://doi.org/10.1080/24694452.2017.1406327

Barker, A.J., and E. Battell Lowman. 2016. "The Spaces of Dangerous Freedom: Disrupting Settler Colonialism." In *The Limits of Settler Colonial Reconciliation,* ed. S. Maddison, T. Clarke, and R. de Costa, 195–212. Singapore: Springer.

–. 2019. "Incarceration, Reserves, and Indigenous Deprivation and Death in 20th Century Canada." In *Corps en peines: Manipulations et usages des corps dans la pratique pénale depuis le Moyen Âge,* ed. M. Charageat, M. Soula, and B. Ribémont, 351–81. Paris: Classiques Garnier.

Barker, A.J., and J. Pickerill. 2012. "Radicalizing Relationships to and through Shared Geographies: Why Anarchists Need to Understand Indigenous Connections to Land and Place." *Antipode* 44 (5): 1705–25. https://doi.org/10.1111/j.1467-8330.2012.01031.x

–. 2019. "Doings with the Land and Sea: Decolonising Geographies, Indigeneity, and Enacting Place-Agency." *Progress in Human Geography* 44 (4): 640–62. https://doi.org/10.1177/0309132519839863

Barker, A.J., and R.M. Ross. 2017. "Reoccupation and Resurgence: Indigenous Protest Camps in Canada." In *Protest Camps in International Context: Spaces, Infrastructures and Media of Resistance*, ed. G. Brown and A. Feigenbaum, 199–220. Bristol, UK: Policy.

Barman, J. 2010. "Race, Greed and Something More: The Erasure of Urban Indigenous Space in Early Twentieth-Century British Columbia." In *Making Settler Colonial Space: Perspectives on Race, Place and Identity*, ed. T. Banivanua Mar and P. Edmonds, 155–75. New York: Palgrave Macmillan.

Barnett, C. 2008. "Political Affects in Public Space: Normative Blind-Spots in Non-Representational Ontologies." *Transactions of the Institute of British Geographers* 33 (2): 186–200. https://doi.org/10.1111/j.1475-5661.2008.00298.x

Barr, J. 2012. "The Red Continent and the Cant of the Coastline." *William and Mary Quarterly* 69 (3): 521–26. https://doi.org/10.5309/willmaryquar.69.3.0521

Barta, T. 2014. "'A Fierce and Irresistible Cavalry': Pastoralists, Homesteaders and Hunters on the American Plains Frontier." In *Genocide on Settler Frontiers: When Hunter-Gatherers and Commercial Stock Farmers Clash*, ed. M. Adhikari, 232–58. Oxford: Berdhahn.

Basso, K.H. 1996. *Wisdom Sits in Places: Landscape and Language among the Western Apache*. Albuquerque: University of New Mexico Press.

Battell Lowman, E. 2011. "'My Name Is Stanley': Twentieth-Century Missionary Stories and the Complexity of Colonial Encounters." *BC Studies* (169): 81–99.

–. 2014. "Indigenous Methodologies, Missionary Lives." PhD diss., University of Warwick.

–. 2017. "Mamook Komtax Chinuk Pipa/Learning to Write Chinook Jargon: Indigenous Peoples and Literacy Strategies in the South Central Interior of British Columbia in the Late Nineteenth Century." *Historical Studies in Education/Revue d'histoire de l'éducation* 29 (1): 77–98. https://doi.org/10.32316/hse/rhe.v29i1.4496

Battell Lowman, E., and A.J. Barker. 2010. "Indigenizing Approaches to Research." *The Sociological Imagination*, October 28. https://researchprofiles.herts.ac.uk/portal/en/journals/the-sociological-imagination(8c62e1d7-6899-4863-9d23-02638116123e).html.

–. 2015. *Settler: Identity and Colonialism in 21st Century Canada*. Halifax: Fernwood.

Bawaka Country, S. Wright, S. Suchet-Pearson, K. Lloyd, L. Burarrwanga, R. Ganambarr, M. Ganambarr-Stubbs, B. Ganambarr, D. Maymuru, and J. Sweeney. 2016. "Co-Becoming Bawaka: Towards a Relational Understanding of Place/Space." *Progress in Human Geography* 40 (4): 455–75. https://doi.org/10.1177/0309132515589437

Belcourt, B.R. 2018. "Meditations on Reserve Life, Biosociality, and the Taste of Non-Sovereignty." *Settler Colonial Studies* 8 (1): 1–15. https://doi.org/10.1080/2201473X.2017.1279830

Bell, D.S. 2005. "Dissolving Distance: Technology, Space, and Empire in British Political Thought, 1770–1900." *Journal of Modern History* 77 (3): 523–62. https://doi.org/10.1086/497716

Benn, C. 1998. *The Iroquois in the War of 1812*. Toronto: University of Toronto Press.

Berg, L.D. 2011. "Banal Naming, Neoliberalism, and Landscapes of Dispossession." *ACME: An International Journal for Critical Geographies* 10 (1): 13–22.

Bergen, R. 2019. "Mennonites Advocate for Bill-262." *Canadian Mennonite* 23 (8). https://canadianmennonite.org/c262-rally.

Bhambra, G.K. 2007a. "Multiple Modernities or Global Interconnections: Understanding the Global Post the Colonial." In *Varieties of World-Making: Beyond Globalization*, ed. N. Karagiannis and P. Wagner, 59–73. Liverpool, UK: Liverpool University Press.

–. 2007b. *Rethinking Modernity: Postcolonialism and the Sociological Imagination*. Basingstoke, UK: Palgrave Macmillan.

Bhandar, B. 2016. "Possession, Occupation and Registration: Recombinant Ownership in the Settler Colony." *Settler Colonial Studies* 6 (2): 119–32. https://doi.org/10.1080/2201473X.2015.1024366

Black, C. 2014. *Rise to Greatness: The History of Canada from the Vikings to the Present*. Toronto: McClelland and Stewart.

Black, K. 2015. "Localizing Settler Colonialism." Paper presented at the Canadian Historical Association Annual Conference, Ottawa, June 1.

Blanchard, W.H. 1996. *Neocolonialism American Style, 1960–2000*. London: Greenwood.

Blaney, F., and S. Grey. 2017. "'Empowerment, Revolution and Real Change': An interview with Fay Blaney." In *Making Space for Indigenous Feminism*, ed. J. Green, 234–52. Winnipeg: Fernwood.

Bobel, C. 2007. "'I'm not an activist, though I've done a lot of it': Doing Activism, Being Activist and the 'Perfect Standard' in a Contemporary Movement." *Social Movement Studies* 6 (6): 147–59. https://doi.org/10.1080/14742830701497277

Bonds, A., and J. Inwood. 2016. "Beyond White Privilege: Geographies of White Supremacy and Settler Colonialism." *Progress in Human Geography* 40 (6): 715–33. https://doi.org/10.1177/0309132515613166

Borrows, J. 2002. *Recovering Canada: The Resurgence of Indigenous Law*. Toronto: University of Toronto Press.

Braun, B. 2002. "Colonialism's Afterlife: Vision and Visuality on the Northwest Coast." *Cultural Geographies* 9 (2): 202–47. https://doi.org/10.1191/1474474002eu243oa

Bray, M. 2013. *Translating Anarchy: The Anarchism of Occupy Wall Street*. Winchester, UK: Zero Books.

Brody, H. 1981. *Maps and Dreams: Indians and the British Columbia Frontier*. London: Jill Norman and Hobhouse.

Brown, G. 2007. "Mutinous Eruptions: Autonomous Spaces of Radical Queer Activism." *Environment and Planning A* 39 (11): 2685–98. https://doi.org/10.1068/a38385

Brown, G., and A. Feigenbaum, eds. 2017. *Protest Camps in International Context: Spaces, Infrastructures and Media of Resistance*. Bristol, UK: Policy.

Brown, G., and J. Pickerill. 2009. "Space for Emotion in the Spaces of Activism." *Emotion, Space and Society* 2 (1): 24–35. https://doi.org/10.1016/j.emospa.2009.03.004

Brown, N.A. 2014. "The Logic of Settler Accumulation in a Landscape of Perpetual Vanishing." *Settler Colonial Studies* 4 (1): 1–26. https://doi.org/10.1080/2201473X.2013.784236

Bruyneel, K. 2007. *The Third Space of Sovereignty: The Postcolonial Politics of U.S.-Indigenous Relations*. Minneapolis: University of Minnesota Press.

–. 2016. "Codename Geronimo: Settler Memory and the Production of American Statism." *Settler Colonial Studies* 6 (4): 349–64. https://doi.org/10.1080/2201473X.2015.1090528

Butler, J. 1990. *Gender Trouble: Feminism and the Subversion of Identity*. New York: Routledge.

Butlin, R.A. 2009. *Geographies of Empire: European Empires and Colonies c. 1880–1960*. Cambridge, UK: Cambridge University Press.

Byrd, J.A. 2011. *The Transit of Empire: Indigenous Critiques of Colonialism*. Minneapolis: University of Minnesota Press.

–. 2014. "Follow the Typical Signs: Settler Sovereignty and Its Discontents." *Settler Colonial Studies* 4 (2): 151–54. https://doi.org/10.1080/2201473X.2013.846388

Byrne, B. 2015. "Rethinking Intersectionality and Whiteness at the Borders of Citizenship." *Sociological Research Online* 20 (3): 1–12. https://doi.org/10.5153/sro.3790

Cameron, D.J. 2010. "An Agent of Change: William Drewry and Land Surveying in British Columbia, 1887–1929." *BC Studies* (167): 7–46. https://doi.org/10.14288/bcs.v0i167.1064

Campbell, E.R.A. 2011. "A Critique of the Occupy Movement from a Black Occupier." *Black Scholar* 41 (4): 42–51. https://doi.org/10.5816/blackscholar.41.4.0042

Cantieri, J. 2018. "Tribes Build a Traditional Watch House to Stop Kinder Morgan Pipeline Expansion: And since the Fall, Tiny House Warriors Have Been Putting Homes in the Path of the Pipeline." *BC Studies* (198): 7–12. https://doi.org/10.14288/bcs.v0i198.190708

Carolan, M.S. 2009. "'I do therefore there is': Enlivening Socio-Environmental Theory." *Environmental Politics* 18 (1): 1–17. https://doi.org/10.1080/09644010802622748

Cavanagh, E. 2009. "Fur Trade Colonialism: Traders and Cree at Hudson Bay, 1713–67." *Australasian Canadian Studies* 27 (1): 85–94.

–. 2011. "Review Essay: Discussing Settler Colonialism's Spatial Cultures." *Settler Colonial Studies* 1 (1): 154–67. https://doi.org/10.1080/2201473X.2011.10648805

Cavanagh, E., and L. Veracini, eds. 2017. *The Routledge Handbook of the History of Settler Colonialism*. London: Routledge.

CBC Radio. 2016. "Artist Reclaims Toronto Streets Using Ojibway Language." *Unreserved*, May 13. https://www.cbc.ca/radio/unreserved/resisting-reclaiming-and-reconnecting-to-culture-1.3577136/artist-reclaims-toronto-streets-using-ojibway-language-1.3581118.

Centennial of the Province of Upper Canada, 1792–1892. 1893. Toronto: Arbuthnot and Adamson.

Cervantes, M. 2011. "Decolonize the 99%." Dignidade Rebelde blog, 4 October. https://dignidadrebelde.com/?p=7094.

Chatterton, P. 2006. "'Give up Activism' and Change the World in Unknown Ways: Or, Learning to Walk with Others on Uncommon Ground." *Antipode* 38 (2): 259–81. https://doi.org/10.1111/j.1467-8330.2006.00579.x

Chatterton, P., and J. Pickerill. 2010. "In, Against and Beyond Capitalism: The Messy Spaces, Practices and Identities of Everyday Activism in the UK." *Transactions of the Institute of British Geographers* 35 (4): 475–90.

Chee, C.R. 2011. "Protesters Arrested after Blocking Road to Snowbowl." *Navajo Times*, August 9. http://www.navajotimes.com/news/2011/0811/080911arrested.php.

Choudry, A. 2010. "What's Left? Canada's 'Global Justice' Movement and Colonial Amnesia." *Race and Class* 52 (1): 97–102. https://doi.org/10.1177/0306396810371769

Clayton, D.W. 1999. *Islands of Truth: The Imperial Fashioning of Vancouver Island.* Vancouver: UBC Press.

Clough, N.L. 2012. "Emotion at the Center of Radical Politics: On the Affective Structures of Rebellion and Control." *Antipode* 44 (5): 1667–86. https://doi.org/10.1111/j.1467-8330.2012.01035.x

Coleman, D. 2016. "Indigenous Place and Diaspora Space: Of Literalism and Abstraction." *Settler Colonial Studies* 6 (1): 61–76. https://doi.org/10.1080/2201473X.2014.1000913

Commager, H. 1927. "England and Oregon Treaty of 1846." *Oregon Historical Quarterly* 28 (1): 18–38.

Connell, R. 2007. *Southern Theory: The Global Dynamics of Knowledge in Social Science.* Sydney: Allen and Unwin.

Connolly, W.E. 2005. "The Evangelical-Capitalist Resonance Machine." *Political Theory* 33 (6): 869–86. https://doi.org/10.1177/0090591705280376

–. 2006. "Experience and Experiment." *Daedalus* 135 (3): 67–75.

Coombes, A.E. 2006. "Introduction: Memory and History in Settler Colonialism." In *Rethinking Settler Colonialism: History and Memory in Australia, Canada, Aotearoa New Zealand and South Africa*, ed. A.E. Coombes, 1–12. Manchester, UK: Manchester University Press.

Cooper, A. 2007. *The Hanging of Angélique: The Untold Story of Canadian Slavery and the Burning of Old Montréal.* Athens: University of Georgia Press.

Corntassel, J. 2008. "Toward Sustainable Self-Determination: Rethinking the Contemporary Indigenous-Rights Discourse." *Alternatives: Global, Local, Political* 33 (1): 105–32. https://doi.org/10.1177/030437540803300106

Corntassel, J., and C. Bryce. 2012. "Practicing Sustainable Self-Determination: Indigenous Approaches to Cultural Restoration and Revitalization." *Brown Journal of World Affairs* 18 (2): 151–62.

Corntassel, J., and C. Holder. 2008. "Who's Sorry Now? Government Apologies, Truth Commissions, and Indigenous Self-Determination in Australia, Canada, Guatemala, and Peru." *Human Rights Review* 9 (4): 465–89. https://doi.org/10.1007/s12142-008-0065-3

Corntassel, J., and R.C. Witmer. 2011. *Forced Federalism: Contemporary Challenges to Indigenous Nationhood.* Norman, OK: University of Oklahoma Press.

Coronil, F. 1994. "Listening to the Subaltern: The Poetics of Neocolonial States." *Poetics Today* 15 (4): 643–58. https://doi.org/10.2307/1773104

Correia, D. 2013. "F**k Jared Diamond." *Capitalism Nature Socialism* 24 (4): 1–6. https://doi.org/10.1080/10455752.2013.846490

Coté, C. 2017. *Spirits of Our Whaling Ancestors: Revitalizing Makah and Nuu-chah-nulth Traditions*. Seattle: University of Washington Press.

Coulthard, G. 2014. *Red Skin, White Masks: Rejecting the Colonial Politics of Recognition*. Minneapolis: University of Minnesota Press.

Counter Cartographics Collective, C. Dalton, and L. Mason-Deese. 2012. "Counter (Mapping) Actions: Mapping as Militant Research." *ACME: An International Journal for Critical Geographies* 11 (3): 439–66.

Cox, S. 2018. *Breaching the Peace: The Site C Dam and a Valley's Stand against Big Hydro*. Vancouver: On Point.

Cronon, W. 1996. "The Trouble with Wilderness: Or, Getting Back to the Wrong Nature." *Environmental History* 1 (1): 7–28. https://doi.org/10.2307/3985059

Cronon, W., and R. White. 1985. "Indians, Colonists, and the Environment." In *Major Problems in American Colonial History*, ed. K.O. Kupperman, 27–37. Toronto: D.C. Heath and Co.

Crosby, A. 1978. "Colonization as a 'Swarming.'" In *Major Problems in American Colonial History*, ed. K.O. Kupperman, 18–27. Toronto: D.C. Heath and Co.

Crosby, A., and J. Monaghan. 2016. "Settler Colonialism and the Policing of Idle No More." *Social Justice* 43 (2): 37–57.

–. 2018. *Policing Indigenous Movements: Dissent and the Security State*. Halifax: Fernwood.

Cruikshank, J. 2005. *Do Glaciers Listen? Local Knowledge, Colonial Encounters, and Social Imagination*. Vancouver: UBC Press.

Culhane, D. 2003. "Their Spirits Live within Us: Aboriginal Women in Downtown Eastside Vancouver Emerging into Visibility." *American Indian Quarterly* 27 (3): 593–606. https://doi.org/10.1353/aiq.2004.0073

Culp, A.C. 2013. "Dispute or Disrupt? Desire and Violence in Protests against the Iraq War." *Affinities: A Journal of Radical Theory, Culture, and Action* 6 (1): 16–47.

Cultural Survival. 2019. "President's Day under Trump: Dishonoring Native People." *Cultural Survival*, February 18. https://www.culturalsurvival.org/news/presidents-day-under-trump-dishonoring-native-peoples.

Cumfer, C. 2007. *Separate Peoples, One Land: The Minds of Cherokees, Blacks, and Whites on the Tennessee Frontier*. Chapel Hill: University of North Carolina Press.

Daigle, M. 2019. "Tracing the Terrain of Indigenous Food Sovereignties." *Journal of Peasant Studies* 46 (2): 297–315. https://doi.org/10.1080/03066150.2017.1324423

Dailey, H. 2018. "The Deaths of Settler Colonialism: Extinction as a Metaphor of Decolonization in Contemporary Settler Literature." *Settler Colonial Studies* 8 (1): 30–46. https://doi.org/10.1080/2201473X.2016.1238160

D'Arcus, B. 2010. "The Urban Geography of Red Power: The American Indian Movement in Minneapolis–Saint Paul, 1968–70." *Urban Studies* 47 (6): 1241–55. https://doi.org/10.1177/0042098009360231

Daschuk, J. 2013. *Clearing the Plains: Disease, Politics of Starvation, and Loss of Aboriginal Life*. Regina, SK: University of Regina Press.

Davis, L., ed. 2010. *Alliances: Re/Envisioning Indigenous–Non-Indigenous Relationships*. Toronto: University of Toronto Press.

Davis, L., J. Denis, and R. Sinclair, eds. 2017. "Pathways of Settler Decolonization." Special issue, *Settler Colonial Studies* 7 (4).

Davis, M. 2007. *In Praise of Barbarians: Essays against Empire*. Chicago: Haymarket Books.

Day, I. 2015. "Being or Nothingness: Indigeneity, Antiblackness, and Settler Colonial Critique." *Critical Ethnic Studies* 1 (2): 102–21. https://doi.org/10.5749/jcritethnstud.1.2.0102

–. 2016. *Alien Capital: Asian Racialization and the Logic of Settler Colonial Capitalism*. Durham, NC: Duke University Press.

Day, R.J.F. 2000. *Multiculturalism and the History of Canadian Diversity*. Toronto: University of Toronto Press.

–. 2004. "From Hegemony to Affinity: The Political Logic of the Newest Social Movements." *Cultural Studies* 18 (5): 716–48. https://doi.org/10.1080/0950238042000260360

–. 2005. *Gramsci Is Dead: Anarchist Currents in the Newest Social Movements*. Toronto: Between the Lines.

Dean, A. 2010. "Space, Temporality, History: Encountering Hauntings in Vancouver's Downtown Eastside." In *The West and Beyond: New Perspectives on an Imagined Region*, ed. A. Finkel, S. Carter, and P. Fortna, 113–32. Edmonton: AU Press.

–. 2015. *Remembering Vancouver's Disappeared Women: Settler Colonialism and the Difficulty of Inheritance*. Toronto: University of Toronto Press.

Deerinwater, J. 2016. "Weeding Out the Allies from the White Saviors at Standing Rock." *Autostraddle*, October 6. https://www.autostraddle.com/weeding-out-the-allies-from-the-white-saviors-at-standing-rock-354112/.

Delâge, D., and J.-P. Warren. 2017. *Le Piège de la liberté: Les peuples autochtones dans l'engrenage des régimes coloniaux*. Montreal: Boreal.

de Leeuw, S., M. Greenwood, and N. Lindsay. 2013. "Troubling Good Intentions." *Settler Colonial Studies* 3 (3–4): 381–94. https://doi.org/10.1080/2201473X.2013.810694

Deloria, P.J. 1999. *Playing Indian*. New Haven, CT: Yale University Press.

Deloria, V., Jr. 1970. *We Talk, You Listen: New Tribes, New Turf*. New York: Macmillan.

–. 1985. *Behind the Trail of Broken Treaties: An Indian Declaration of Independence*. Austin: University of Texas Press.

–. 1988. *Custer Died for Your Sins: An Indian Manifesto*. 2nd ed. Norman: University of Oklahoma Press.

–. 2003. *God Is Red: A Native View of Religion*. 30th Anniversary ed. Golden, CO: Fulcrum.

Deloria, V., Jr., and C.M. Lytle. 1984. *The Nations Within: The Past and Future of American Indian Sovereignty*. New York: Pantheon Books.

Deloria, V., Jr., and D. Wildcat. 2001. *Power and Place: Indian Education in America*. Golden, CO: Fulcrum.

DeVerteuil, G., and K. Wilson. 2010. "Reconciling Indigenous Need with the Urban Welfare State? Evidence of Culturally-Appropriate Services and Spaces for Aboriginals in Winnipeg, Canada." *Geoforum* 41 (3): 498–507. https://doi.org/10.1016/j.geoforum.2010.01.004

Dhamoon, R. 2015. "A Feminist Approach to Decolonizing Anti-Racism: Rethinking Transnationalism, Intersectionality, and Settler Colonialism." *Feral Feminisms* (4): 20–37.

Dhillon, J. 2017. *Prairie Rising: Indigenous Youth, Decolonization, and the Politics of Intervention*. Toronto: University of Toronto Press.

–. 2018. "Introduction: Indigenous Resurgence, Decolonization, and Movements for Environmental Justice." *Environment and Society* 9 (1): 1–5. https://doi.org/10.3167/ares.2018.090101

Diamond, J. 1997. *Guns, Germs, and Steel: The Fates of Human Societies*. New York: W.W. Norton.

DiAngelo, R. 2011. "White Fragility." *International Journal of Critical Pedagogy* 3 (3): 54–70.

–. 2018. *White Fragility: Why It's So Hard for White People to Talk about Racism*. Boston: Beacon.

Dittmer, J. 2010. *Popular Culture, Geopolitics, and Identity*. Toronto: Rowman and Littlefield.

–. 2014. "Geopolitical Assemblages and Complexity." *Progress in Human Geography* 38 (3): 385–401. https://doi.org/10.1177/0309132513501405

Dokshin, F.A. 2016. "Whose Backyard and What's at Issue? Spatial and Ideological Dynamics of Local Opposition to Fracking in New York State, 2010 to 2013." *American Sociological Review* 81 (5): 921–48. https://doi.org/10.1177/0003122416663929

Dorries, H., R. Henry, D. Hugill, T. McCreary, and J. Tomiak, eds. 2019. *Settler City Limits: Indigenous Resurgence and Colonial Violence in the Urban Prairie West*. Winnipeg: University of Manitoba Press.

Dotson, K. 2018. "On the Way to Decolonization in a Settler Colony: Re-Introducing Black Feminist Identity Politics." *AlterNative* 14 (3): 190–99. https://doi.org/10.1177/1177180118783301

Doxtater (Horn-Miller), K. 2010. "From Paintings to Power: The Meaning of the Warrior Flag Twenty Years after Oka." *Socialist Studies* 6 (1): 96–124. https://doi.org/10.18740/S4QW23

Driver, F. 2000. *Geography Militant: Cultures of Exploration and Empire*. Malden, MA: Wiley.

Dunbar-Ortiz, R. 2014. *An Indigenous Peoples' History of the United States*. Boston: Beacon.

Dunkley, C.M. 2004. "Risky Geographies: Teens, Gender, and Rural Landscape in North America." *Gender, Place and Culture* 11 (4): 559–79. https://doi.org/10.1080/0966369042000307004

Dupuis-Déri, F. 2010. "Anarchism and the Politics of Affinity Groups." *Anarchist Studies* 18 (1): 40–61.

Eberts, M. 2017. "Being an Indigenous Woman Is a 'High-Risk Lifestyle.'" In *Making Space for Indigenous Feminism*, ed. J. Green, 69–102. Winnipeg: Fernwood.

Edmonds, P. 2010. *Urbanizing Frontiers: Indigenous Peoples and Settlers in 19th-Century Pacific Rim Cities.* Vancouver: UBC Press.

Elkins, C., and S. Pedersen. 2005. *Settler Colonialism in the Twentieth Century: Projects, Practices, Legacies.* London: Routledge.

Elliott, M. 2018. "Indigenous Resurgence: The Drive for Renewed Engagement and Reciprocity in the Turn Away from the State." *Canadian Journal of Political Science* 51 (1): 61–81. https://doi.org/10.1017/S0008423917001032

Estes, N. 2019. *Our History Is the Future: Standing Rock versus the Dakota Access Pipeline, and the Long Tradition of Indigenous Resistance.* London: Verso.

Eyford, R. 2016. *White Settler Reserve: New Iceland and the Colonization of the Canadian West.* Vancouver: UBC Press.

Fabian, J. 2002. *Time and the Other: How Anthropology Makes Its Object.* New York: Columbia University Press.

Fanon, F. 1963. *The Wretched of the Earth.* New York: Grove.

–. 1967. *Black Skin, White Masks.* New York: Grove.

Farley, M., N. Matthews, S. Deer, G. Lopez, C. Stark, and E. Hudon. 2011. *Garden of Truth: The Prostitution and Trafficking of Native Women in Minnesota.* St. Paul: Minnesota Indian Women's Sexual Assault Coalition.

Featherstone, D. 2005. "Atlantic Networks, Antagonisms and the Formation of Subaltern Political Identities." *Social and Cultural Geography* 6 (3): 387–404. https://doi.org/10.1080/14649360500111311

–. 2008. *Resistance, Space and Political Identities: The Making of Counter-Global Networks.* Malden, MA: Wiley-Blackwell.

Feigenbaum, A, F. Frenzel, and P. McCurdy. 2014. *Protest Camps.* London: Zed Books.

Feigenbaum, A., P. McCurdy, and F. Frenzel. 2013. "Towards a Method for Studying Affect in (Micro)Politics: The Campfire Chats Project and the Occupy Movement." *Parallax* 19 (2): 21–37. https://doi.org/10.1080/13534645.2013.778493

Feit, H.A. 1995. "Hunting and the Quest for Power: The James Bay Cree and Whitemen in the 20th Century." In *Native Peoples: The Canadian Experience,* ed. R.B. Morrison and C.R. Wilson, 115–45. Toronto: McClelland and Stewart.

Ferguson, J. 2004. "Power Topographies." In *A Companion to the Anthropology of Politics,* ed. D. Nugent and J. Vincent, 383–99. Oxford: Blackwell.

Ferguson, J., and A. Gupta. 2002. "Spatializing States: Toward an Ethnography of Neoliberal Governmentality." *American Ethnologist* 29 (4): 981–1002. https://doi.org/10.1525/ae.2002.29.4.981

Fimrite, P. 2012. "Winnemem Wintu Tribe Stages War Dance as Protest." *San Francisco Chronicle,* May 26. http://www.sfgate.com/news/article/Winnemem-Wintu-tribe-stages-war-dance-as-protest-3588954.php.

Fisher, R. 1977. *Contact and Conflict: Indian-European Relations in British Columbia, 1774–1890.* Reprint, Vancouver: UBC Press, 1992.

Fixico, D.L. 1986. *Termination and Relocation: Federal Indian Policy, 1945–1960.* Albuquerque: University of New Mexico Press.

Flanagan, T. 2008. *First Nations? Second Thoughts.* Montreal and Kingston: McGill-Queen's University Press.

Flusty, S., J. Dittmer, E. Gilbert, and M. Kuus. 2008. "Interventions in Banal Neo-imperialism." *Political Geography* 27 (6): 617–29. https://doi.org/10.1016/j.polgeo.2008.06.003

Fowler, T. 1832. *The Journal of a Tour through British America to the Falls of Niagara.* Aberdeen: Lewis Smith.

Frank, G.J. 2000. "'That's My Dinner on Display': A First Nations Reflection on Museum Culture." *BC Studies* (125–26): 163–78. https://doi.org/10.14288/bcs.v0i125/6.1531

Freeman, V. 2010. "'Toronto Has No History!': Indigeneity, Settler Colonialism and Historical Memory in Canada's Largest City." PhD diss., University of Toronto.

French, L., and M. Manzanárez. 2004. *NAFTA and Neocolonialism: Comparative Criminal, Human, and Social Justice.* Lanham, MD: University Press of America.

Frenzel, F., A. Feigenbaum, and P. McCurdy. 2014. "Protest Camps: An Emerging Field of Social Movement Research." *Sociological Review* 62 (3): 457–74. https://doi.org/10.1111/1467-954X.12111

Frideres, J.S., M.A. Kalbach, and W.E. Kalbach. 2004. "Government Policy and the Spatial Redistribution of Canada's Aboriginal Peoples." In *Population Mobility and Indigenous Peoples in Australasia and North America*, ed. J. Taylor and M. Bell, 95–117. London: Routledge.

Frost, L. 2001. "The History of American Cities and Suburbs: An Outsider's View." *Journal of Urban History* 27 (3): 362–76. https://doi.org/10.1177/009614420102700307

Fujikane, C., and J.Y. Okamura. 2008. *Asian Settler Colonialism: From Local Governance to the Habits of Everyday Life in Hawai'i.* Honolulu: University of Hawai'i Press.

Galeano, E. 1997. *Open Veins of Latin America: Five Centuries of the Pillage of a Continent.* 25th Anniversary ed. New York: Monthly Review.

Gallay, A. 2003. *The Indian Slave Trade: The Rise of the English Empire in the American South, 1670–1717.* New Haven, CT: Yale University Press.

Garroutte, E.M. 2003. *Real Indians: Identity and the Survival of Native Americans.* Los Angeles: University of California Press.

Gaudry, A., and D. Leroux. 2017. "White Settler Revisionism and Making Métis Everywhere: The Evocation of Métissage in Quebec and Nova Scotia." *Critical Ethnic Studies* 3 (1): 116–42. https://doi.org/10.5749/jcritethnstud.3.1.0116

Georgi-Findlay, B. 2018. "'Stand It Like a Man': The Performance of Masculinities in Deadwood." In *Contemporary Masculinities in the UK and the US: Between Bodies and Systems*, ed. S. Horlacher and K. Floyd, 121–30. Singapore: Springer.

Gibson-Graham, J.K., 2008. "Diverse Economies: Performative Practices for 'Other Worlds.'" *Progress in Human Geography* 32 (5): 613–32. https://doi.org/10.1177/0309132508090821

Gill, N., D. Conlon, D. Moran, and A. Burridge. 2018. "Carceral Circuitry: New Directions in Carceral Geography." *Progress in Human Geography* 42 (2): 183–204. https://doi.org/10.1177/0309132516671823

Gilmartin, M., and L.D. Berg. 2007. "Locating Postcolonialism." *Area* 39 (1): 120–24.

Goodyear-Ka'ōpua, N. 2011. "Kuleana Lahui: Collective Responsibility for Hawaiian Nationhood in Activists' Praxis." *Affinities* 5 (1): 130–63.

Gott, R. 2007. "Latin America as a White Settler Society." *Bulletin of Latin American Research* 26 (2): 269–89.

Graeber, D. 2013. "Occupy Wall Street Rediscovers the Radical Imagination." *Fieldsights*, February 14. https://culanth.org/fieldsights/occupy-wall-street-rediscovers-the-radical-imagination.

Grande, S. 2003. "Whitestream Feminism and the Colonialist Project: A Review of Contemporary Feminist Pedagogy and Praxis." *Educational Theory* 53 (3): 329–46. https://doi.org/10.1111/j.1741-5446.2003.00329.x

–. 2013. "Accumulation of the Primitive: The Limits of Liberalism and the Politics of Occupy Wall Street." *Settler Colonial Studies* 3 (3–4): 369–80. https://doi.org/10.1080/2201473X.2013.810704

Green, J. 2017. "Taking More Account of Indigenous Feminisms." In *Making Space for Indigenous Feminism*, ed. J. Green, 1–20. Winnipeg: Fernwood Press.

Greensmith, C. 2016. "The Management of Indigenous Difference in Toronto's Queer Service Sector." *Settler Colonial Studies* 6 (3): 252–64. https://doi.org/10.1080/2201473X.2015.1079182

–. 2018. "(Unsettling) White Queer Complicities: Toward a Practice of Decolonization in Queer Organizations." *Intersectionalities* 6 (1): 16–36.

Greensmith, C., and S. Giwa. 2013. "Challenging Settler Colonialism in Contemporary Queer Politics: Settler Homonationalism, Pride Toronto, and Two-Spirit Subjectivities." *American Indian Culture and Research Journal* 37 (2): 129–48. https://doi.org/10.17953/aicr.37.2.p4q2r84l12735117

Greer, A. 2018. *Property and Dispossession: Natives, Empires and Land in Early Modern North America*. Cambridge, UK: Cambridge University Press.

Gregory, D. 1994. *Geographical Imaginations*. Cambridge, MA: Blackwell.

Hager, B., dir. 2006. *From Bella Coola to Berlin*. Documentary. Edmonton: Bella Coola to Berlin Productions.

Haig-Brown, C. 2009. "Decolonizing Diaspora: Whose Traditional Land Are We On?" *Cultural and Pedagogical Inquiry* 1 (1): 4–21. https://doi.org/10.18733/C3H59V

–. 2010. "Indigenous Thought, Appropriation, and Non-Aboriginal People." *Canadian Journal of Education* 33 (4): 925–50.

Haiven, M., and A. Khasnabish. 2014. *The Radical Imagination: Social Movement Research in the Age of Austerity*. London: Zed Books.

Halberstam, J. 2011. *The Queer Art of Failure*. Durham, NC: Duke University Press.

Hall, R. 2013. "Diamond Mining in Canada's Northwest Territories: A Colonial Continuity." *Antipode* 45 (2): 376–93. https://doi.org/10.1111/j.1467-8330.2012.01012.x

Hallenbeck, J. 2015. "Returning to the Water to Enact a Treaty Relationship: The Two Row Wampum Renewal Campaign." *Settler Colonial Studies* 5 (4): 350–62. https://doi.org/10.1080/2201473X.2014.1000909

Hardt, M., and A. Negri. 2000. *Empire*. Cambridge, MA: Harvard University Press.

Harper, R. 2018. *Unsettling the West: Violence and State Building in the Ohio Valley*. Philadelphia: University of Pennsylvania Press.

Harris, C. 1997. *The Resettlement of British Columbia: Essays on Colonialism and Geographical Change*. Vancouver: UBC Press.

–. 2002. *Making Native Space: Colonialism, Resistance, and Reserves in British Columbia*. Vancouver: UBC Press.

–. 2004. "How Did Colonialism Dispossess? Comments from an Edge of Empire." *Annals of the Association of American Geographers* 94 (1): 165–82. https://doi.org/10.1111/j.1467-8306.2004.09401009.x

Harris, C., and D. Demeritt. 1997. "Farming and Rural Life." In C. Harris, *The Resettlement of British Columbia: Essays on Colonialism and Geographical Change*, 219–49. Vancouver: UBC Press.

Harris, C., J. Fiske, and G. Gibson. 2003. "Forum: Revisiting the Native Land Question." *BC Studies* (138–39): 137–63.

Harris, C., and R. Galois. 1997. "A Population Geography of British Columbia in 1881." In C. Harris, *The Resettlement of British Columbia: Essays on Colonialism and Geographical Change*, 137–60. Vancouver: UBC Press.

Harris, R., and R. Lewis. 2001. "The Geography of North American Cities and Suburbs, 1900–1950: A New Synthesis." *Journal of Urban History* 27 (3): 262–92. https://doi.org/10.1177/009614420102700302

Harvey, D. 2000. *Spaces of Hope*. Berkeley: University of California Press.

–. 2014. *Seventeen Contradictions and the End of Capitalism*. Oxford: Oxford University Press.

Hatter, L. 2012. "The Narcissism of Petty Differences? Thomas Jefferson, John Graves Simcoe and the Reformation of Empire in the Early United States and British–Canada." *American Review of Canadian Studies* 42 (2): 130–41. https://doi.org/10.1080/02722011.2012.679153

Heckert, J. 2010. "Relating Differently." *Sexualities* 13 (4): 403–11. https://doi.org/10.1177/1363460710370651

Henceforward, The. 2016. "Season 1, Episode 3: Creative Interventions and Interruptions." *The Henceforward*, July 8. http://www.thehenceforward.com/episodes/?tag=Ogimaa+Mikana+project.

Hill, S.M. 2017. *The Clay We Are Made Of: Haudenosuanee Land Tenure on the Grand River*. Winnipeg: University of Manitoba Press.

Hixson, W. 2013. *American Settler Colonialism: A History*. New York: Palgrave Macmillan.

Holloway, J. 2010. *Crack Capitalism*. London: Pluto.

Holm, T., J.D. Pearson, and B. Chavis. 2003. "Peoplehood: A Model for the Extension of Sovereignty in American Indian Studies." *Wicazo Sa Review* 18 (1): 7–24. https://doi.org/10.1353/wic.2003.0004

Holmes, C., S. Hunt, and A. Piedalue. 2015. "Violence, Colonialism and Space: Towards a Decolonizing Dialogue." *ACME: An International Journal for Critical Geographies* 14 (2): 539–70.

Hoogeveen, D. 2015. "Sub-Surface Property, Free-Entry Mineral Staking and Settler Colonialism in Canada." *Antipode* 47 (1): 121–38. https://doi.org/10.1111/anti.12095

Hoxie, F. 2008. "Retrieving the Red Continent: Settler Colonialism and the History of American Indians in the US." *Ethnic and Racial Studies* 31 (6): 1153–67. https://doi.org/10.1080/01419870701791294

Huhndorf, S.M. 2001. *Going Native: Indians in the American Cultural Imagination*. Ithaca, NY: Cornell University Press.

Hui, S. 2010. "Riot Police Charge G20 Protestors Singing O Canada in Toronto." *Georgia Straight*, June 27. https://www.straight.com/article-331250/vancouver/video-riot-police-charge-g20-protesters-singing-o-canada.

Hunt, S. 2011. "An Open Letter to My Local Hipsters." *Media Indigena*, September 20. https://mediaindigena.com/an-open-letter-to-my-local-hipsters/.

–. 2014. "Ontologies of Indigeneity: The Politics of Embodying a Concept." *Cultural Geographies* 21 (1): 27–32. https://doi.org/10.1177/1474474013500226

Hunt, S., and C. Holmes. 2015. "Everyday Decolonization: Living a Decolonizing Queer Politics." *Journal of Lesbian Studies* 19 (2): 154–72. https://doi.org/10.1080/10894160.2015.970975

Huseman, J., and D. Short. 2012. "'A Slow Industrial Genocide': Tar Sands and the Indigenous Peoples of Northern Alberta." *International Journal of Human Rights* 16 (1): 216–37. https://doi.org/10.1080/13642987.2011.649593

Ibbitson, J. 2012. "Native Leaders Risk Missing Their Moment of Greatest Influence." *Globe and Mail*, July 16. https://www.theglobeandmail.com/news/politics/john-ibbitson-native-leaders-risk-missing-their-moment-of-greatest-influence/article4418458/.

Indian Country Today. 2014. "Remnants of Sacred Rock Destroyed in the 60s Discovered Underwater." *Indian Country Today*, August 27. https://newsmaven.io/indiancountrytoday/archive/remnants-of-sacred-rock-destroyed-in-the-60s-discovered-underwater-x-RAYbV8s0qGaPMga991Xw/.

Inwood, J., and A. Bonds. 2016. "Confronting White Supremacy and a Militaristic Pedagogy in the US Settler Colonial State." *Annals of the American Association of Geographers* 106 (3): 521–29. https://doi.org/10.1080/24694452.2016.1145510

Ireland, P.R. 2012. "Irish Protestant Migration and Politics in the USA, Canada, and Australia: A Debated Legacy." *Irish Studies Review* 20 (3): 263–81. https://doi.org/10.1080/09670882.2012.695613

Irlbacher-Fox, S. 2012. "#IdleNoMore: Settler Responsibility for Relationship." *Decolonization: Indigeneity, Education and Society*, December 27. https://decolonization.wordpress.com/2012/12/27/idlenomore-settler-responsibility-for-relationship/.

Jacobs, M. 2012. "Assimilation through Incarceration: The Geographic Imposition of Canadian Law over Indigenous Peoples." PhD diss., Queen's University.

Jafri, B. 2012. "Privilege vs. Complicity: People of Colour and Settler Colonialism." *Equity Matters*, March 21. Ideas-idees.ca/blog/Privilege-vs-Complicity-People-Colour-and-Settler-Colonialism.

Johansen, B. 2012. "Canoe Journeys and Cultural Revival." *American Indian Culture and Research Journal* 36 (2): 131–42.

Johansen, B.E., and B.A. Mann, eds. 2000. *Encyclopaedia of the Haudenosaunee (Iroquois Confederacy)*. Westport, CT: Greenwood.

Johnson, D.M. 2011. "From the Tomahawk Chop to the Road Block: Discourses of Savagism in Whitestream Media." *American Indian Quarterly* 35 (1): 104–34. https://doi.org/10.1353/aiq.2011.0005

Johnson, M. 2011. "Reconciliation, Indigeneity, and Postcolonial Nationhood in Settler States." *Postcolonial Studies* 14 (2): 187–201. https://doi.org/10.1080/13688790.2011.563457

Jojola, T. 2004. "Notes on Identity, Time, Space, and Place." In *American Indian Thought*, ed. A. Waters, 87–96. Malden, MA: Blackwell.

Jones, J. 2014. "Compensatory Division in the Occupy Movement." *Rhetoric Review* 33 (2): 148–64. https://doi.org/10.1080/07350198.2014.884416

Jones, R. 2016. *Violent Borders: Refugees and the Right to Move*. London: Verso.

Karagiannis, N., and P. Wagner, eds. 2007. *Varieties of World-Making: Beyond Globalization*. Liverpool, UK: Liverpool University Press.

Kauanui, J.K. 2008. "Colonialism in Equality: Hawaiian Sovereignty and the Question of US Civil Rights." *South Atlantic Quarterly* 107 (4): 635–50. https://doi.org/10.1215/00382876-2008-010

Kazdin, C., and D.L. Tu. 2016. "Cultures Clash at Standing Rock Protest Camp." *MEL Magazine*, November 30. https://melmagazine.com/en-us/story/cultures-clash-at-standing-rock-protest-camp.

Keene, A. 2011. "Representing the Native Presence in the 'Occupy Wall Street' Narrative." *Native Appropriations*, October 12. https://nativeappropriations.com/2011/10/representing-the-native-presence-in-the-occupy-wall-street-narrative.html.

Kelm, M.-E. 2012. *Colonizing Bodies: Aboriginal Health and Healing in British Columbia, 1900–50*. Vancouver: UBC Press.

Khasnabish, A. 2011. "Anarch@-Zapatismo: Anti-Capitalism, Anti-Power, and the Insurgent Imagination." *Affinities: A Journal of Radical Theory, Culture, and Action* 5 (1): 70–95.

–. 2013. *Zapatistas: Rebellion from the Grassroots to the Global*. London: Zed Books.

Kilibarda, K. 2012. "Lessons from #Occupy in Canada: Contesting Space, Settler Consciousness and Erasures within the 99%." *Journal of Critical Globalisation Studies* (5): 24–41.

Kim, C. 2015. "Makah Whaling and the Non-Ecological Indian." In *Dangerous Crossing: Race, Species and Nature in a Multicultural Age*, ed. C. Kim, 205–51. Cambridge, UK: Cambridge University Press.

King, T.L. 2019. *The Black Shoals: Offshore Formations of Black and Native Studies*. Durham, NC: Duke University Press.

Kino-nda-niimi Collective, ed. 2014. *The Winter We Danced: Voices from the Past, the Future, and the Idle No More Movement*. Winnipeg: Arbeiter Ring.

Klassen-Wiebe, N. 2017. "'For Christ's Sake, We Better Do Something about It': 'We Support Bill-262' Marchers of All Ages Declare their Solidarity." *Canadian Mennonite* 21 (19). https://canadianmennonite.org/stories/'-christ's-sake-we-better-do-something-about-it'.

Klor de Alva, J.J. 1992. "Colonialism and Postcolonialism as (Latin) American Mirages." *Colonial Latin American Review* 1 (1–2): 3–23. https://doi.org/10.1080/10609169208569787

Kuokkanen, R. 2017. "Politics of Gendered Violence in Indigenous Communities." In *Making Space for Indigenous Feminism*, ed. J. Green, 103–21. Winnipeg: Fernwood.

Kupperman, K.O. 1977. "American Perceptions of Treachery, 1583–1640: The Case of the American 'Savages.'" *Historical Journal* 20 (2): 263–87.

–. 1980. *Settling with the Indians: The Meeting of English and Indian Cultures in America, 1580–1640*. London: J.M. Dent and Sons.

–. 2000. *Indians and English: Facing Off in Early America*. Ithaca, NY: Cornell University Press.

–. 2007. *Roanoke: The Abandoned Colony*. Lanham, MD: Rowman and Littlefield.

Kymlicka, W. 2001. *Politics in the Vernacular: Nationalism, Multiculturalism and Citizenship*. Oxford: Oxford University Press.

LaDuke, W. 1994. "Traditional Ecological Knowledge and Environmental Futures." *Colorado Journal of International Environmental Law and Policy* 5 (1): 127–48.

–. 2002. *The Winona LaDuke Reader*. Stillwater, MN: Voyageur.

–. 2005. *Recovering the Sacred: The Power of Naming and Claiming*. Boston: South End.

Lagalisse, E.M. 2011. "'Marginalizing Magdalena': Intersections of Gender and the Secular in Anarchoindigenist Solidarity Activism." *Signs: Journal of Women in Culture and Society* 36 (3): 653–78.

Laidlaw, Z., and A. Lester, eds. 2015. *Indigenous Communities and Settler Colonialism: Land Holding, Loss and Survival in an Interconnected World*. Hampshire, UK: Palgrave Macmillan.

Larsen, S. 2003. "Collaboration Geographies: Native-White Partnerships during the Re-Settlement of Ootsa Lake, British Columbia, 1900–52." *BC Studies* (138–39): 87–114. https://doi.org/10.14288/bcs.v0i138/9.1672

–. 2008. "Place Making, Grassroots Organizing, and Rural Protest: A Case Study of Anahim Lake, British Columbia." *Journal of Rural Studies* 24 (2): 172–81. https://doi.org/10.1016/j.jrurstud.2007.12.004

Larsen, S., and J.T. Johnson. 2012a. "In between Worlds: Place, Experience, and Research in Indigenous Geography." *Journal of Cultural Geography* 29 (1): 1–13. https://doi.org/10.1080/08873631.2012.646887

–. 2012b. "Towards an Open Sense of Place: Phenomenology, Affinity, and the Question of Being." *Annals of the Association of American Geographers* 102 (3): 632–46. https://doi.org/10.1080/00045608.2011.600196

Lawrence, B. 2003. "Gender, Race, and the Regulation of Native Identity in Canada and the United States: An Overview." *Hypatia: A Journal of Feminist Philosophy* 18 (2): 3–31. https://doi.org/10.1111/j.1527-2001.2003.tb00799.x

Lawrence, B., and E. Dua. 2005. "Decolonizing Antiracism." *Social Justice* 32 (4): 120–43.

Lee, D. 2011. "Windigo Faces: Environmental Non-Governmental Organizations Serving Canadian Colonialism." *Canadian Journal of Native Studies* 31 (2): 133–53.

–. 2015. "Adoption Is (Not) a Dirty Word: Towards an Adoption-Centric Theory of Citizenship." *First Peoples Child and Family Review* 10 (1): 86–98.

Lee, E. 2002. "Enforcing the Borders: Chinese Exclusion along the U.S. Borders with Canada and Mexico, 1882–1924." *Journal of American History* 89 (1): 54–86. https://doi.org/10.2307/2700784

Lee, S.J. 1994. "Behind the Model-Minority Stereotype: Voices of High- and Low-Achieving Asian American Students." *Anthropology and Education Quarterly* 25 (4): 413–29.

#leftfail (blog). 2012. "We Recognize the Traditional Lands Occupied, We Just Can't Name a Single Indigenous Nation." January 3. https://leftfail.tumblr.com/post/15210432045/google-is-your-friend.

Leitner, H., E. Sheppard, and K.M. Sziarto. 2008. "The Spatialities of Contentious Politics." *Transactions of the Institute of British Geographers* 33 (2): 157–72.

Leroux, D. 2018. "'We've Been Here for 2,000 Years': White Settlers, Native American DNA and the Phenomenon of Indigenization." *Social Studies of Science* 48 (1): 80–100. https://doi.org/10.1177/0306312717751863

Leroy, J. 2016. "Black History in Occupied Territory: On the Entanglements of Slavery and Settler Colonialism." *Theory and Event* 19 (4): n.p.

Lester, A. 2005. *Imperial Networks: Creating Identities in Nineteenth-Century South Africa and Britain*. London: Routledge.

Lewis, A.G. 2012. "Ethics, Activism and the Anti-Colonial: Social Movement Research as Resistance." *Social Movement Studies* 11 (2): 227–40. https://doi.org/10.1080/14742837.2012.664903

Lightfoot, S. 2016. "Indigenous Mobilization and Activism in the UN System." In *Handbook of Indigenous Peoples' Rights*, ed. C. Lennox and D. Short, 253–67. New York: Routledge.

Lindquist, W.A. 2012. "Death and the Rise of the State: Criminal Courts, Indian Executions, and Early Pacific Northwest Governments." *American Review of Canadian Studies* 42 (2): 142–55. https://doi.org/10.1080/02722011.2012.679144

Little, S. 2019. "British Columbia Becomes 1st Canadian Province to Pass UN Indigenous Rights Declaration." *Global News*, November 26. https://globalnews.ca/news/6222331/british-columbia-passes-undrip/amp/.

Little Bear, L. 2004. "Land: The Blackfoot Source of Identity." Paper presented at the conference "Beyond Race and Citizenship: Indigeneity in the 21st Century," University of California, Berkeley, October 28–30.

Mackey, E. 1998. *House of Difference: Cultural Politics and National Identity in Canada*. London: Routledge.

–. 2016. *Unsettled Expectations: Uncertainty, Land and Settler Decolonization*. Halifax: Fernwood.

MacMillan, K. 2011. "Benign and Benevolent Conquest? The Ideology of Elizabethan Atlantic Expansion Revisited." *Early American Studies* 9 (1): 32–72.

Macoun, A., and E. Strakosch. 2013. "The Ethical Demands of Settler Colonial Theory." *Settler Colonial Studies* 3 (3–4): 426–43. https://doi.org/10.1080/2201473X.2013.810695

Maddison, S., T. Clark, and R. de Costa, eds. 2016. *The Limits of Settler Colonial Reconciliation*. Singapore: Springer.

Mandelker, B.S. 2000. "Indigenous People and Cultural Appropriation: Intellectual Property Problems and Solutions." *Canadian Intellectual Property Review* 16: 367–401.

Manuel, A., and R. Derrickson. 2015. *Unsettling Canada: A National Wake-up Call*. Toronto: Between the Lines Press.

Manuel, G., and M. Posluns. 1974. *The Fourth World: An Indian Reality*. New York: Free Press.

Maracle, L. 1996. *I Am Woman: A Native Perspective on Sociology and Feminism*. Vancouver: Press Gang.

Marsh, M. 1988. "Suburban Men and Masculine Domesticity, 1870–1915." *American Quarterly* 40 (2): 165–86. https://doi.org/10.2307/2713066

Marshall, D. 2018. *Claiming the Land: British Columbia and the Making of a New El Dorado*. Vancouver: Ronsdale.

Martin-Hill, D. 2004a. "Resistance, Determination and Perseverance of the Lubicon Cree Women." In *In the Way of Development: Indigenous Peoples, Life Projects and Globalization*, ed. M. Blaser, H.A. Feit, and G. McRae, 313–31. London: Zed Books.

–. 2004b. "Women in Indigenous Traditions." In *Women and Religious Traditions*, ed. L.M. Anderson and P. Dickey Young, 137–59. Oxford: Oxford University Press.

Massey, D. 2009. "Concepts of Space and Power in Theory and in Political Practice." *Documents D'anàlisi Geogràfica* (55): 15–26.

Matsui, K. 2005. "'White Man Has No Right to Take Any of It': Secwepemc Water-Rights Struggles in British Columbia." *Wicazo Sa Review* 20 (2): 75–101. https://doi.org/10.1353/wic.2005.0023

Matthews, H., M. Limb, and B. Percy-Smith. 1998. "Changing Worlds: The Microgeographies of Young Teenagers." *Tijdschrift voor Economische en Sociale Geografie* 89 (2): 193–202. https://doi.org/10.1111/1467-9663.00018

Mawani, R. 2009. *Colonial Proximities: Crossracial Encounters and Juridical Truths in British Columbia, 1871–1921*. Vancouver: UBC Press.

McCarthy, T. 2016. *In Divided Unity: Haudenosaunee Reclamation at Grand River*. Phoenix: University of Arizona Press.

McCormack, F. 2011. "Levels of Indigeneity: The Maori and Neoliberalism." *Journal of the Royal Anthropological Institute* 17: 281–300. https://doi.org/10.1111/j.1467-9655.2011.01680.x

McCoy, T. 2009. "Legal Ideology in the Aftermath of Rebellion: The Convicted First Nations Participants, 1885." *Social History* 42 (83): 175–201. https://doi.org/10.1353/his.0.0056

McGuinness, M. 2000. "Geography Matters? Whiteness and Contemporary Geography." *Area* 32 (2): 225–30. https://doi.org/10.1111/j.1475-4762.2000.tb00133.x

McKenna, S. 2011. "A Critical Analysis of North American Business Leaders' Neocolonial Discourse: Global Fears and Local Consequences." *Organization* 18 (3): 387–406. https://doi.org/10.1177/1350508411398728

McKittrick, K. 2011. "On Plantations, Prisons, and a Black Sense of Place." *Social and Cultural Geography* 12 (8): 947–63. https://doi.org/10.1080/14649365.2011.624280

McLean, S. 2013. "The Whiteness of Green: Racialization and Environmental Education." *Canadian Geographer* 57 (3): 354–62. https://doi.org/10.1111/cag.12025

Memmi, A. 1965. *The Colonizer and the Colonized*. Boston: Beacon.

Menchaca, M. 2001. *Recovering History, Constructing Race: The Indian, Black, and White Roots of Mexican Americans*. Austin: University of Texas Press.

"Mennonites Have Yet to Reckon with Their Role in 'Sixties Scoop.'" 2015. *Canadian Mennonite* 19 (18). https://canadianmennonite.org/stories/mennonites-have-yet-reckon-their-role-'sixties-scoop'.

Merrens, H.R., and G.D. Terry. 1986. "Dying in Paradise: Perception and Reality in Colonial South Carolina." In *Major Problems in American Colonial History*, ed. K.O. Kupperman, 330–37. Toronto: D.C. Heath and Co.

Merrifield, A. 1993. "The Struggle over Place: Redeveloping American Can in Southeast Baltimore." *Transactions of the Institute of British Geographers* 18 (1): 102–21. https://doi.org/10.2307/623071

–. 2003. "Dialectical Urbanism: Social Struggle in the Capitalist City." *Science and Society* 67 (4): 516–18. https://doi.org/10.2307/1556493

Meuwese, M. 2011. "The Dutch Connection: New Netherland, the Pequots, and the Puritans in Southern New England, 1620–1638." *Early American Studies* 9 (2): 295–323. https://doi.org/10.1353/eam.2011.0015

Mignolo, W.D. 2000. *Local Histories/Global Designs: Coloniality, Subaltern Knowledges, and Border Thinking*. Princeton, NJ: Princeton University Press.

Milkman, R., B. Barber, M.A. Bamyeh, W.J. Wilson, D. Williams, and D.B. Gould. 2012. "Understanding 'Occupy.'" *Contexts: Sociology for the Public*, May 19. https://contexts.org/articles/understanding-occupy/#milkman.

Mitchell, W.J.T. 2012. "Image, Space, Revolution: The Arts of Occupation." *Critical Inquiry* 39 (1): 8–32. https://doi.org/10.1086/668048

Monture, R. 2014. *Teionkwakhashion Tsi Niionkwariho:ten (We Share Our Matters): Two Centuries of Writing and Resistance at Six Nations of the Grand River*. Winnipeg: University of Manitoba Press.

Mooers, C. 2001. "The New Fetishism: Citizenship and Finance Capital." *Studies in Political Economy* 66 (1): 59–84. https://doi.org/10.1080/19187033.2001.11675211

Moore, M.L., S. von der Porten, and H. Castleden. 2017. "Consultation Is Not Consent: Hydraulic Fracturing and Water Governance on Indigenous Lands in Canada." *Wiley Interdisciplinary Reviews: Water* 4 (1): e1180. https://doi.org/10.1002/wat2.1180

Moreton-Robinson, A. 2015. *The White Possessive: Property, Power and Indigenous Sovereignty*. Minneapolis: University of Minnesota Press.

Morgensen, S.L. 2011. "The Biopolitics of Settler Colonialism: Right Here, Right Now." *Settler Colonial Studies* 1 (1): 52–76. https://doi.org/10.1080/2201473X.2011.10648801

Mosby, I. 2013. "Administering Colonial Science: Nutrition Research and Human Biomedical Experimentation in Aboriginal Communities and Residential Schools, 1942–1952." *Social History* 46 (1): 145–72.

Mott, C. 2016. "The Activist Polis: Topologies of Conflict in Indigenous Solidarity Activism." *Antipode* 48 (1): 193–211. https://doi.org/10.1111/anti.12167

Mudie, R. 1832. *The Emigrant's Pocket Companion: Containing, What Emigration Is, Who Should Be Emigrants, Where Emigrants Should Go; a Description of British North America, Especially the Canadas; and Full Instructions to Intending Emigrants*. London: James Cochrane and Co.

Mulroy, K. 2007. *The Seminole Freedmen: A History*. Norman: University of Oklahoma Press.

Murphyao, A., and K. Black. 2015. "Unsettling Settler Belonging: (Re)naming and Territory Making in the Pacific Northwest." *American Review of Canadian Studies* 45 (3): 315–31. https://doi.org/10.1080/02722011.2015.1063523

Murray, D. 2014. "Prefiguration or Actualization? Radical Democracy and Counter-Institution in the Occupy Movement." *Berkeley Journal of Sociology* 11: 1–12. https://doi.org/10.1177/0170840618759815

Nagy, R. 2012. "Truth, Reconciliation and Settler Denial: Specifying the Canada–South Africa Analogy." *Human Rights Review* 13 (3): 349–367. https://doi.org/10.1007/s12142-012-0224-4

Nash, C. 2003. "Cultural Geography: Anti-Racist Geographies." *Progress in Human Geography* 27 (5): 637–48. https://doi.org/10.1191/0309132503ph454pr

National Inquiry into Missing and Murdered Indigenous Women and Girls. 2019. *Reclaiming Power and Place: The Final Report of the National Inquiry into Missing and Murdered Indigenous Women and Girls.* https://www.mmiwg-ffada.ca/final-report/.

Nettleback, A., and R. Foster. 2012. "'As Fine a Body of Men': How the Canadian Mountie Brought Law and Order to the Memory of the Australian Frontier." *Journal of Australian Studies* 36 (2): 125–40. https://doi.org/10.1080/14443058.2012.671186

Nisga'a Final Agreement. 1999. https://www.nisgaanation.ca/sites/default/files/Nisga%27a%20Final%20Agreement%20-%20Effective%20Date.PDF.

Nitzan, J., and S. Bichler. 2009. *Capital as Power: A Study of Order and Creorder.* London: Routledge.

Noxolo, P., P. Raghuram, and C. Madge. 2012. "Unsettling Responsibility: Postcolonial Interventions." *Transactions of the Institute of British Geographers* 37 (3): 418–29. https://doi.org/10.2307/41678642

O'Bonsawin, C. 2010. "'No Olympics on Stolen Native Land': Contesting Olympic Narratives and Asserting Indigenous Rights within the Discourse of the 2010 Vancouver Games." *Sport in Society* 13 (1): 143–56. https://doi.org/10.1080/17430430903377987

–. 2012. "'There Will Be No Law that Will Come Against Us': An Important Episode of Indigenous Resistance and Activism in Olympic History." In *The Palgrave Handbook of Olympic Studies*, ed. H.J. Lenskyj and S. Wagg, 474–86. London: Palgrave Macmillan.

–. 2015. "From Black Power to Indigenous Activism: The Olympic Movement and the Marginalization of Oppressed Peoples (1968–2012)." *Journal of Sport History* 42 (2): 200–19.

Occupy Forum. 2013. "Let's *Colonize* Wall Street on #S17." September 13. http://occupywallst.org/forum/colonize-wall-street-s17/.

O'Connell, A. 2010. "An Exploration of Redneck Whiteness in Multicultural Canada." *Social Politics: International Studies in Gender, State and Society* 17 (4): 536–63. https://doi.org/10.1093/sp/jxq019

Olund, E.N. 2002. "From Savage Space to Governable Space: The Extension of United States Judicial Sovereignty over Indian Country in the Nineteenth Century." *Cultural Geographies* 9 (2): 129–57. https://doi.org/10.1191/1474474002eu240oa

Parenteau, B. 2012. "Reflections on the Great Land Rush: Snapshots from British North America." *Canadian Historical Review* 93 (2): 261–66. https://doi.org/10.1353/can.2012.0020

Parmenter, J. 2010. *The Edge of the Woods: Iroquoia, 1534–1701*. Reprint, East Lansing: Michigan State University Press, 2014.

Patel, S. 2016. "Complicating the 'Tale of Two Indians': Mapping 'South Asian' Complicity in White Settler Colonialism along the Axis of Caste and Anti-Blackness." *Theory and Event* 19 (4): n.p.

Perry, A. 1995. "'Oh I'm Just Sick of the Faces of Men': Gender Imbalance, Race, Sexuality, and Sociability." *BC Studies* (105–6): 27–44. https://doi.org/10.14288/bcs.v0i105/106.969

Pestana, C.G. 1983. "The City upon a Hill under Siege: The Puritan Perception of the Quaker Threat to Massachusetts Bay, 1656–1661." *New England Quarterly* 56 (3): 323–53. https://doi.org/10.2307/365396

Pickerill, J. 2009. "Finding Common Ground? Spaces of Dialogue and the Negotiation of Indigenous Interests in Environmental Campaigns in Australia." *Geoforum* 40 (1): 66–79. https://doi.org/10.1016/j.geoforum.2008.06.009

Pickerill, J., and J. Krinsky. 2012. "Why Does Occupy Matter?" *Social Movement Studies* 11 (3–4): 279–87. https://doi.org/10.1080/14742837.2012.708923

Pile, S. 2010. "Emotions and Affect in Recent Human Geography." *Transactions of the Institute of British Geographers* 35 (1): 5–20. https://doi.org/10.1111/j.1475-5661.2009.00368.x

Pollard, J., C. McEwan, N. Laurie, and A. Stenning. 2009. "Economic Geography under Postcolonial Scrutiny." *Transactions of the Institute of British Geographers* 34 (2): 137–42. https://doi.org/10.1111/j.1475-5661.2009.00336.x

Porter, L., and O. Yiftachel. 2019. "Urbanizing Settler-Colonial Studies: Introduction to the Special Issue." *Settler Colonial Studies* 9 (2): 177–86. https://doi.org/10.1080/2201473X.2017.1409394

Preston, J. 2013. "Neoliberal Settler Colonialism, Canada and the Tar Sands." *Race and Class* 55 (2): 42–59. https://doi.org/10.1177/0306396813497877

–. 2017. "Racial Extractivism and White Settler Colonialism: An Examination of the Canadian Tar Sands Mega-Projects." *Cultural Studies* 31 (2–3): 353–75. https://doi.org/10.1080/09502386.2017.1303432

Pulido, L., and J. De Lara. 2018. "Reimagining 'Justice' in Environmental Justice: Radical Ecologies, Decolonial Thought, and the Black Radical Tradition." *Environment and Planning E: Nature and Space* 1 (1–2): 76–98. https://doi.org/10.1177/2514848618770363

Radcliffe, S. 2017. "Decolonising Geographical Knowledges." *Transactions of the Institute of British Geographers* 42 (3): 329–33. https://doi.org/10.1111/tran.12195

Raibmon, P. 2000. "Theatres of Contact: The Kwakwaka'wakw Meet Colonialism in British Columbia and at the Chicago World's Fair." *Canadian Historical Review* 81 (2): 157–90. https://doi.org/10.3138/CHR.81.2.157

Ramirez, R. 2012. "Henry Roe Cloud to Henry Cloud: Ho-Chunk Strategies and Colonialism." *Settler Colonial Studies* 2 (2): 117–37. https://doi.org/10.1080/2201473X.2012.10648845

Red Corn, R. 2011. "Bad Indians." YouTube, March 17. https://www.youtube.com/watch?v=3FUgDutdauQ&feature=youtu.be&ab_channel=the1491s.

Regan, P. 2010. *Unsettling the Settler Within: Indian Residential Schools, Truth Telling, and Reconciliation in Canada*. Vancouver: UBC Press.

Rifkin, M. 2009. "Indigenizing Agamben: Rethinking Sovereignty in Light of the 'Peculiar' Status of Native Peoples." *Cultural Critique* (73): 88–124. https://doi.org/10.1353/cul.0.0049

–. 2013. "Settler Common Sense." *Settler Colonial Studies* 3 (3–4): 322–40. https://doi.org/10.1080/2201473X.2013.810702

–. 2014. *Settler Common Sense: Queerness and Everyday Colonialism in the American Renaissance*. Minneapolis: University of Minnesota Press.

Robertson, S. 2016. "'Thinking of the Land in That Way': Indigenous Sovereignty and the Spatial Politics of Attentiveness at Skwelkwek'welt." *Social and Cultural Geography* 18 (2): 178–200. https://doi.org/10.1080/14649365.2016.1164230

Robinson, H., and W. Wickwire. 1989. *Write It on Your Heart: The Epic World of an Okanagan Storyteller*. Vancouver: Talonbooks.

Robinson, M. 2018. "Moving beyond White Fragility: Lessons from Standing Rock." *Foundation for Intentional Community*, March 12. https://www.ic.org/moving-beyond-white-fragility-lessons-from-standing-rock/.

Rose-Redwood, R. 2016. "'Reclaim, Rename, Reoccupy': Decolonizing Place and the Reclaiming of PKOLS." *ACME: An International Journal for Critical Geographies* 15 (1): 187–206.

Ross, K. 1988. *The Emergence of Social Space: Rimbaud and the Paris Commune*. Basingstoke, UK: Macmillan.

Roth, C. 2002. "Without Treaty, without Conquest: Indigenous Sovereignty in Post-*Delgamuukw* British Columbia." *Wicazo Sa Review* 17 (2): 143–65. https://doi.org/10.1353/wic.2002.0020

Routledge, P. 1996. "The Third Space as Critical Engagement." *Antipode* 28 (4): 399–419. https://doi.org/10.1111/j.1467-8330.1996.tb00533.x

–. 2003. "Convergence Space: Process Geographies of Grassroots Globalization Networks." *Transactions of the Institute of British Geographers* 28 (3): 333–49. https://doi.org/10.1111/1475-5661.00096

Rowe, A.C., and E. Tuck. 2017. "Settler Colonialism and Cultural Studies: Ongoing Settlement, Cultural Production, and Resistance." *Cultural Studies ↔ Critical Methodologies* 17 (1): 3–13. https://doi.org/10.1177/1532708616653693

Rowe, J.K., and M. Carroll. 2014. "Reform or Radicalism: Left Social Movements from the Battle of Seattle to Occupy Wall Street." *New Political Science* 36 (2): 149–71. https://doi.org/10.1080/07393148.2014.894683

Royal Commission on Aboriginal Peoples (RCAP). 1996. *Report of the Royal Commission on Aboriginal Peoples*. https://www.bac-lac.gc.ca/eng/discover/aboriginal-heritage/royal-commission-aboriginal-peoples/Pages/final-report.aspx.

Ruiz-Lichter, R. 2011. "Open Letter to the 'Occupy' Movement: The Decolonization Proposal." YouTube, December 7. https://www.youtube.com/watch?v=r_s3X0uW9Ec&ab_channel=Rebeccista.

Sakai, J. 1983. *Settlers: The Mythology of the White Proletariat from Mayflower to Modern*. Reprint, Oakland, CA: PM Press, 2014.

Saranillio, D.I. 2013. "Why Asian Settler Colonialism Matters: A Thought Piece on Critiques, Debates, and Indigenous Difference." *Settler Colonial Studies* 3 (3–4): 280–94. https://doi.org/10.1080/2201473X.2013.810697

Saul, J.R. 2008. *A Fair Country: Telling Truths about Canada*. Toronto: Penguin.

Scott, J.C. 1999. *Seeing Like a State: How Certain Schemes to Improve the Human Condition Have Failed*. New Haven, CT: Yale University Press.

Scowen, P. 2014. "Conrad Black's Unique Take on the History of Canada." *Globe and Mail*, May 12. https://www.theglobeandmail.com/arts/books-and-media/conrad-blacks-unique-take-on-the-history-of-canada/article21835560/.

Secwepemecul'ecw Assembly. 2017. "What Are Man Camps?" https://www.secwepemculecw.org/no-mans-camps.

Seigworth, G.J., and M. Gregg. 2010. "An Inventory of Shimmers." In *The Affect Theory Reader*, ed. M. Gregg and G.J. Seigworth, 1–27. Durham, NC: Duke University Press.

Selbin, E. 2010. *Revolution, Rebellion, Resistance: The Power of Story*. London: Zed Books.

Shaw, K. 2004. "The Global/Local Politics of the Great Bear Rainforest." *Environmental Politics* 13 (2): 373–92. https://doi.org/10.1080/0964401042000209621

Shaw, W.S. 2006. "Decolonizing Geographies of Whiteness." *Antipode* 38 (4): 851–69. https://doi.org/10.1111/j.1467-8330.2006.00479.x

Shobe, H., and G. Gibson. 2017. "Cascadia Rising: Soccer, Region, and Identity." *Soccer and Society* 18 (7): 953–71. https://doi.org/10.1080/14660970.2015.1067790

Short, D. 2005. "Reconciliation and the Problem of Internal Colonialism." *Journal of Intercultural Studies* 26 (3): 267–82. https://doi.org/10.1080/07256860500153534

Shukaitis, S. 2009. *Imaginal Machines: Autonomy and Self-Organization in the Revolutions of Everyday Life*. London: Autonomedia.

Sidaway, J.D. 2000. "Recontextualising Positionality: Geographical Research and Academic Fields of Power." *Antipode* 32 (3): 260–70. https://doi.org/10.1111/1467-8330.00134

–. 2003. "Sovereign Excesses? Portraying Postcolonial Sovereigntyscapes." *Political Geography* 22 (2): 157–78. https://doi.org/10.1016/S0962-6298(02)00082-3

Simonelli, J. 2014. "Home Rule and Natural Gas Development in New York: Civil Fracking Rights." *Journal of Political Ecology* 21 (1): 258–78. https://doi.org/10.2458/v21i1.21136

Simpson, A. 2007. "On Ethnographic Refusal: Indigeneity, 'Voice' and Colonial Citizenship." *Junctures: The Journal for Thematic Dialogue* (9): 67–80.

–. 2014. *Mohawk Interruptus: Political Life across the Borders of Settler States*. Durham, NC: Duke University Press.

–. 2016. "The State Is a Man: Theresa Spence, Loretta Saunders and the Gender of Settler Sovereignty." *Theory and Event* 19 (4): n.p.

Simpson, L. 2008. "Oshkimaadiziig, the New People." In *Lighting the Eighth Fire: The Liberation, Resurgence, and Protection of Indigenous Nations*, ed. L. Simpson, 13–22. Winnipeg: Arbeiter Ring.

–. 2011. *Dancing on Our Turtle's Back: Stories of Nishnaabeg Re-Creation, Resurgence, and a New Emergence*. Winnipeg: Arbeiter Ring.

–. 2012. "Indigenous Perspectives on Occupation, Occupy Toronto Talks." Paper presented at the Beit Zatoun cultural centre, Toronto, January 23. https://betasamosake1.rssing.com/chan-9086664/article5.html.

–. 2017. *As We Have Always Done: Indigenous Freedom through Radical Resistance.* Minneapolis: University of Minnesota Press.

Simpson, L.B., R. Walcott, and G. Coulthard. 2018. "Idle No More and Black Lives Matter: An Exchange." *Studies in Social Justice* 12 (1): 75–89. https://doi.org/10.26522/ssj.v12i1.1830

Smith, K.D. 2009. *Liberalism, Surveillance, and Resistance.* Edmonton: AU Press.

Smith, L.T. 1999. *Decolonizing Methodologies.* London: Zed Books.

Smith, N. 1996. *The New Urban Frontier: Gentrification and the Revanchist City.* London: Routledge.

Social Coast. 2013. "Reclaim PKOLS – May 22nd Action." YouTube, June 3. https://www.youtube.com/watch?v=Ib_O9vdxDQY&feature=youtu.be&ab_channel=SocialCoast.

Soguk, N. 2011. "Indigenous Transversality in Global Politics." *Affinities* 5 (1): 37–55.

Sommers, J., and N.K. Blomley. 2002. "The Worst Block in Vancouver." In *Stan Douglas: Every Building on 100 West Hastings*, ed. Reid Shier, 18–58. Vancouver: Contemporary Art Gallery/Arsenal Pulp.

Soto, L. 2008. "Migration as a Matter of Time: Perspectives from Mexican Immigrant Adolescent Girls in California's Napa Valley." PhD diss., University of California, Berkeley.

Squires, G.D., and C.E. Kubrin. 2005. "Privileged Places: Race, Uneven Development and the Geography of Opportunity in Urban America." *Urban Studies* 42 (1): 47–68. https://doi.org/10.1080/0042098042000309694

Stanley, G.F. 1949. "Gabriel Dumont's Account of the North West Rebellion, 1885." *Canadian Historical Review* 30 (3): 249–69. https://doi.org/10.3138/CHR-030-03-03

Starblanket, G. 2017. "Being Indigenous Feminists: Resurgences against Contemporary Patriarchy." In *Making Space for Indigenous Feminism*, ed. J. Green, 21–41. Winnipeg: Fernwood.

Starr, A. 2006. "'... (Excepting Barricades Erected to Prevent Us from Peacefully Assembling': So-Called 'Violence' in the Global North Alterglobalization Movement." *Social Movement Studies* 5 (1): 61–81. https://doi.org/10.1080/14742830600621233

Steinman, E. 2012. "Settler Colonial Power and the American Indian Sovereignty Movement: Forms of Domination, Strategies of Transformation." *American Journal of Sociology* 117 (4): 1073–130. https://doi.org/10.1086/662708. Medline:22594118

–. 2020. "Unsettling as Agency: Unsettling Settler Colonialism Where You Are." *Settler Colonial Studies* 10 (4): 558–75. https://doi.org/10.1080/2201473X.2020.1807877

Stevenson, L. 2012. "The Psychic Life of Biopolitics: Survival, Cooperation, and Inuit Community." *American Ethnologist* 39 (3): 592–613. https://doi.org/10.1111/j.1548-1425.2012.01383.x

Stewart-Harawira, M. 2005. *The New Imperial Order: Indigenous Responses to Globalization*. London: Zed Books.

Storey, K. 2017. "Donald Fraser, the *London Times,* and the Gold Rushes of British Columbia." *BC Studies* (193): 65–88.

Stueck, W., and I. Bailey. 2012. "Gitxsan Blockade Coming to an End as Forensic Audit Begins." *Globe and Mail,* June 11. http://www.theglobeandmail.com/news/british-columbia/gitxsan-blockade-coming-to-an-end-as-forensic-audit-begins/article4246337/.

Sturgeon, N. 1999. "Ecofeminist Appropriations and Transnational Environmentalisms." *Identities: Global Studies in Culture and Power* 6 (2–3): 255–79. https://doi.org/10.1080/1070289X.1999.9962645

Sugden, J. 1999. *Tecumseh: A Life*. New York: Holt.

Sugrue, T.J. 2014. *The Origins of the Urban Crisis: Race and Inequality in Postwar Detroit*. Updated ed. Princeton, NJ: Princeton University Press.

Swamp, J. 2010. "Kanikonriio: Power of a Good Mind." In *Alliances: Re/Envisioning Indigenous–Non-Indigenous Relationships*, ed. L. Davis, 15–24. Toronto: University of Toronto Press.

Swanky, T. 2012. *The True Story of Canada's "War" of Extermination on the Pacific*. Burnaby, BC: Dragon Heart Enterprises.

Taylor, A. 2010. *The Civil War of 1812: American Citizens, British Subjects, Irish Rebels, and Indian Allies*. New York: Vintage Books.

Taylor, H.L. 2011. "The Historic Roots of the Crisis in Housing Affordability: The Case of Buffalo, New York, 1920–1950." In *Fair and Affordable Housing in the US: Trends, Outcomes and Future Directions*, ed. R.M. Silverman and K.L. Patterson, 243–76. Boston: Leiden.

Teves, S.N. 2012. "We're All Hawaiians Now: Kanaka Maoli Performance and the Politics of Aloha." PhD diss., University of Michigan.

Thistle, J. 2011. "A Vast Inland Empire and the Last Great West: Remaking Society, Space and Environment in Early British Columbia." *Journal of Historical Geography* 37 (4): 418–28. https://doi.org/10.1016/j.jhg.2011.04.004

Thomas, D.H. 2001. *Skull Wars: Kennewick Man, Archaeology, and the Battle for Native American Identity*. New York: Basic Books.

Thrift, N. 2004. "Intensities of Feeling: Towards a Spatial Politics of Affect." *Geografiska Annaler: Series B, Human Geography* 86 (1): 57–78. https://doi.org/10.1111/j.0435-3684.2004.00154.x

Thrush, C. 2016. *Indigenous London: Native Travelers at the Heart of Empire*. New Haven, CT: Yale University Press.

Tieleman, B. 2015. "Which Right-Wing Strategist Inspired Harper's 'Old Stock'? Cracking the Coded Message within Tory Leader's Debate Comment." *The Tyee,* September 22. https://thetyee.ca/Opinion/2015/09/22/Strategist-Inspired-Old-Stock-Canadians/.

Trask, H.-K. 1991. "Natives and Anthropologists: The Colonial Struggle." *Contemporary Pacific* 3 (1): 159–67.

–. 1996. "Feminism and Indigenous Hawaiian Nationalism." *Signs* 21 (4): 906–16.

–. 1999. *From a Native Daughter: Colonialism and Sovereignty in Hawai'i*. Honolulu: University of Hawai'i Press.

–. 2007. "Settler Colonialism in Hawai'i." Paper presented at Fifth Galway Conference on Colonialism: Settler Colonialism, National University of Ireland, Galway, June 29.

Treaty 7 Tribal Council, W. Hildebrandt, S. Carter, and D. First Rider. 1996. *The True Spirit and Intent of Treaty 7*. Montreal and Kingston: McGill-Queen's University Press.

Truth and Reconciliation Commission of Canada. 2015. *Honouring the Truth, Reconciling for the Future: Summary of the Final Report of the Truth and Reconciliation Commission of Canada*. http://nctr.ca/reports.php.

Tsawwassen First Nation Final Agreement. 2007. https://www.aadnc-aandc.gc.ca/DAM/DAM-INTER-BC/STAGING/texte-text/tfnfa_1100100022707_eng.pdf.

Tuck, E., and R.A. Gaztambide-Fernández. 2013. "Curriculum, Replacement, and Settler Futurity." *Journal of Curriculum Theorizing* 29 (1): 72–89.

Tuck, E., M. McKenzie, and K. McCoy. 2014. "Land Education: Indigenous, Post-Colonial and Decolonizing Perspectives on Place and Environmental Education Research." *Environmental Education Research* 20 (1): 1–23. https://doi.org/10.1080/13504622.2013.877708

Tuck, E., and K.W. Yang. 2012. "Decolonization Is Not a Metaphor." *Decolonization: Indigeneity, Education and Society* 1 (1): 1–40.

Tucker, B., and R. Rose-Redwood. 2015. "Decolonizing the Map? Toponymic Politics and the Rescaling of the Salish Sea." *Canadian Geographer* 59 (2): 194–206. https://doi.org/10.1111/cag.12140

Tully, J. 1995. *Strange Multiplicity: Constitutionalism in an Age of Diversity*. Cambridge: Cambridge University Press.

–. 2000. "The Struggles of Indigenous Peoples for and of Freedom." In *Political Theory and the Rights of Indigenous Peoples*, ed. D. Ivison, P. Patton, and W. Sanders, 36–59. Cambridge, UK: Cambridge University Press.

Turbulence Collective. 2010. *What Would It Mean to Win?* Oakland, CA: PM Press.

Turner, D. 2006. *This Is Not a Peace Pipe: Towards a Critical Indigenous Philosophy*. Toronto: University of Toronto Press.

Uchida, Ayako. 2012. "Searching for Indigenous Alliances: International NGOs of the United States and Canada in the 1970s." *Japanese Journal of American Studies* (23): 209–30.

United States or Canada? Points for the Consideration of All Who Are Hesitating Whether to Direct Their Views to the United States of America or to the Canadas. 1833. London: George Mann and Thomas Griffiths.

Valentine, G., and J. McKendrick. 1997. "Children's Outdoor Play: Exploring Parental Concerns about Children's Safety and the Changing Nature of Childhood." *Geoforum* 28 (2): 219–35. https://doi.org/10.1016/S0016-7185(97)00010-9

Van Kirk, S. 1980. *Many Tender Ties: Women in Fur Trade Society, 1670–1870*. Norman: University of Oklahoma Press.

Van Rijn, K. 2006. "'Lo! The Poor Indian!' Colonial Responses to the 1862–63 Smallpox Epidemic in British Columbia and Vancouver Island." *Canadian Bulletin of Medical History* 23 (2): 541–60. Medline:17214129

Veracini, L. 2007. "Historylessness: Australia as a Settler Colonial Collective." *Postcolonial Studies* 10 (3): 271–85. https://doi.org/10.1080/13688790701488155

–. 2008. "Settler Collective, Founding Violence and Disavowal: The Settler Colonial Situation." *Journal of Intercultural Studies* 29 (4): 363–79. https://doi.org/10.1080/07256860802372246

–. 2010a. "The Imagined Geographies of Settler Colonialism." In *Making Settler Colonial Space: Perspectives on Race, Place and Identity*, ed. T. Banivanua Mar and P. Edmonds, 179–97. Hampshire, UK: Palgrave Macmillan.

–. 2010b. *Settler Colonialism: A Theoretical Overview*. New York: Palgrave Macmillan.

–. 2011. "Isopolitics, Deep Colonizing, Settler Colonialism." *Interventions* 13 (2): 171–89. https://doi.org/10.1080/1369801X.2011.573215

–. 2012. "Suburbia, Settler Colonialism and the World Turned Inside Out." *Housing, Theory and Society* 29 (4): 339–57. http://doi.org/10.1080/14036096.2011.638316

–. 2013. "'Settler Colonialism': Career of a Concept." *Journal of Imperial and Commonwealth History* 41 (2): 313–33. https://doi.org/10.1080/03086534.2013.768099

–. 2015. *The Settler Colonial Present*. New York: Palgrave Macmillan.

Vimalassery, M. 2013. "The Wealth of the Natives: Toward a Critique of Settler Colonial Political Economy." *Settler Colonial Studies* 3 (3–4): 295–310. https://doi.org/10.1080/2201473X.2013.810701

Vizenor, G., ed. 2008. *Survivance: Narratives of Native Presence*. Lincoln: University of Nebraska Press.

Voss, B. 2005. "From Casta to Californio: Social Identity and the Archaeology of Culture Contact." *American Anthropologist* 107 (3): 461–74. https://doi.org/10.1525/aa.2005.107.3.461

Vowel, C., and D. Leroux. 2016. "White Settler Antipathy and the Daniels Decision." *TOPIA: Canadian Journal of Cultural Studies* 36: 30–42. https://doi.org/10.3138/topia.36.30

Wagner, J.R. 2008. "Landscape Aesthetics, Water, and Settler Colonialism in the Okanagan Valley of British Columbia." *Journal of Ecological Anthropology* 12 (1): 22–38. https://doi.org/10.5038/2162-4593.12.1.2

Walia, H. 2010. "Transient Servitude: Migrant Labour in Canada and the Apartheid of Citizenship." *Race and Class* 52 (1): 71–84. https://doi.org/10.1177/0306396810371766

–. 2013. *Undoing Border Imperialism*. Oakland, CA: AK Press.

Walker, G. 2011. "Primitive Accumulation and the Formation of Difference: On Marx and Schmitt." *Rethinking Marxism* 23 (3): 384–404. https://doi.org/10.1080/08935696.2011.583016

Wallace, P. 1994. *White Roots of Peace: The Iroquois Book of Life*. Santa Fe, NM: Clear Light Books.

Waters, A. 2004. "Language Matters: Nondiscrete Nonbinary Dualism." In *American Indian Thought*, ed. A. Waters, 97–115. Malden, MA: Blackwell.

Watts, V. 2013. "Indigenous Place-Thought and Agency amongst Humans and Non-Humans (First Woman and Sky Woman Go on a European World Tour!)." *Decolonization: Indigeneity, Education and Society* 2 (1): 20–34.

–. 2016. "Smudge This: Assimilation, State-Favoured Communities and the Denial of Indigenous Spiritual Lives." *International Journal of Child, Youth and Family Studies* 7 (1): 148–70. https://doi.org/10.18357/ijcyfs.71201615676

Whaley, G.H. 2010. *Oregon and the Collapse of Illahee: US Empire and the Transformation of an Indigenous World, 1792–1859*. Chapel Hill: University of North Carolina Press.

White, K.J. 2018. "Adoption, Incorporation, and a Sense of Citizenship and Belonging in Indigenous Nations and Culture: A Haudenosaunee Perspective." *AlterNative* 14 (4): 333–42. https://doi.org/10.1177/1177180118808143

White, R. 2011. *The Middle Ground: Indians, Empires, and Republics in the Great Lakes Region, 1650–1815*. Cambridge: Cambridge University Press.

Wickwire, W. 1994. "To See Ourselves as the Other's Other: Nlaka'pamux Contact Narratives." *Canadian Historical Review* 75 (1): 1–20. https://doi.org/10.3138/CHR-075-01-01

–. 1998. "'We Shall Drink from the Stream and So Shall You': James A. Teit and Native Resistance in British Columbia, 1908–22." *Canadian Historical Review* 79 (2): 199–236.

–. 2019. *At the Bridge: James Teit and an Anthropology of Belonging*. Vancouver: UBC Press.

Wilhite, K. 2012. "Contested Terrain: The Suburbs as Region." *American Literature* 84 (3): 617–44. https://doi.org/10.1215/00029831-1664737

Willow, A.J. 2011. "Conceiving Kakipitatapitmok: The Political Landscape of Anishinaabe Anticlearcutting Activism." *American Anthropologist* 113 (2): 262–76. https://doi.org/10.1111/j.1548-1433.2011.01329.x

–. 2014. "The New Politics of Environmental Degradation: Un/Expected Landscapes of Disempowerment and Vulnerability." *Journal of Political Ecology* 21 (1): 237–57. https://doi.org/10.2458/v21i1.21135

Wilson, S. 2008. *Research Is Ceremony: Indigenous Research Methods*. Winnipeg: Fernwood.

Wolfe, P. 1999. *Settler Colonialism and the Transformation of Anthropology: The Politics and Poetics of an Ethnographic Event*. London: Cassell.

–. 2006. "Settler Colonialism and the Elimination of the Native." *Journal of Genocide Research* 8 (4): 387–409. https://doi.org/10.1080/14623520601056240

Wood, P.B., and D.A. Rossiter. 2011. "Unstable Properties: British Columbia, Aboriginal Title, and the 'New Relationship.'" *Canadian Geographer* 55 (4): 407–25. https://doi.org/10.1111/j.1541-0064.2011.00366.x

Woods, L.L. II. 2013. "Almost 'No Negro Veteran ... Could Get a Loan': African Americans, the GI Bill, and the NAACP Campaign against Residential Segregation, 1917–1960." *Journal of African American History* 98 (3): 392–417. https://doi.org/10.5323/jafriamerhist.98.3.0392

Wright, R. 1992. *Stolen Continents: The "New World" through Indian Eyes since 1492*. New York: Viking.

York, G., and L. Pindera. 1991. *People of the Pines: The Warriors and the Legacy of Oka*. Toronto: Little Brown.

Young, A.T. 2013. "Settler Sovereignty and the Rhizomatic West, or, The Significance of the Frontier in Postwestern Studies." *Western American Literature* 48 (1–2): 115–40. https://doi.org/10.1353/wal.2013.0037

–. 2015. "The Settler Unchained: Constituent Power and Settler Violence." *Social Text* 33 (3): 1–18. https://doi.org/10.1215/01642472-3125680

Zajko, M., and D. Béland. 2008. "Space and Protest Policing at International Summits." *Environment and Planning D: Society and Space* 26 (4): 719–35. https://doi.org/10.1068/d0707

Zaran, H. 2012. "Why Racialized Canadians Need to Pay Attention to the AFN National Chief Race." *It Is a Harsh World*, July 16. Accessed August 16, 2012. http://itisaharshworld.wordpress.com/2012/07/16/why-racialized-canadians-need-to-pay-attention-to-the-afn-national-chief-race.

Index